KU-444-638

The Marketing Series is one of the most
comprehensive collections of textbooks in marketing
and sales available from the UK today.

Published by Butterworth-Heinemann on behalf of the
Chartered Institute of Marketing, the series has been
specifically designed, developed and progressively
updated over a number of years to support students
studying for the Institute's certificate and diploma
qualifications. The scope of the subjects covered by
the series, however, means that it is of equal value to
anyone studying other further or higher business
and/or marketing related qualifications.

ON BEHALF OF
THE CHARTERED
INSTITUTE OF MARKETING

THE
MARKETING SERIES

Formed in 1911, the Chartered Institute of Marketing
is now the largest professional marketing management
body in Europe with over 21,000 members and 20,000
students located worldwide. Its primary objectives are
focused on the development of awareness and
understanding of marketing throughout UK industry
and commerce and in the raising of standards of
professionalism in the education, training and practice
of this key business discipline.

International Marketing

Stanley J. Paliwoda BA, MSC, PHD, MBIM, MCINST.M

Butterworth-Heinemann Ltd
Linacre House, Jordan Hill, Oxford OX2 8DP

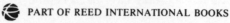 PART OF REED INTERNATIONAL BOOKS

OXFORD   LONDON   BOSTON
MUNICH   NEW DELHI   SINGAPORE   SYDNEY
TOKYO   TORONTO   WELLINGTON

First published 1986
Reprinted 1988, 1989, 1990, 1991

© Stanley J. Paliwoda 1986

All rights reserved. No part of this publication may be reproduced in any material form (including photocopying or storing
in any medium by electronic means and whether or not tran-
siently or incidentally to some other use of this publication)
without the written permission of the copyright holder except in
accordance with the provisions of the Copyright, Designs and
Patents Act 1988 or under the terms of a licence issued by the
Copyright Licensing Agency Ltd, 90 Tottenham Court Road,
London, England W1P 9HE. Applications for the copyright
holder's written permission to reproduce any part of this publication should be addressed to the publishers.

British Library Cataloguing in Publication Data
Paliwoda, Stanley J.
International Marketing
1. Export marketing—Great Britain
I. Title
658.8'48'0941   HF1009.7.G7

ISBN 0 7506 0315 1

Printed and bound in Great Britain by
Redwood Press Limited, Melksham, Wiltshire

Some books are lies from end to end,
And some great lies were never penn'd;
Even ministers, they have been kenn'd,
In holy rapture
A rousing lie at time to vend,
And nail it wi' Scripture

Robert Burns, *Death and Dr Hornbrook*

CONTENTS

PREFACE

The cover design incorporates the new map design of the German historian, Arno Peters. The difference between the new Peters map and the Mercator map which was the one which we learned at school, is that the Peters map is accurate in its proportions, whilst the long-established Mercator map has always shown an unrealistically enlarged Europe as the centre of the world. The challenge then is for those of us, born in Europe, whether we are capable of accepting this new reality of a world where we have less importance than before.

In the same way, the parallel appears appropriate in that in writing this text, it is a challenge posed by the author to write of the world as it is. It is to be hoped that this text does so, composing a picture which will help explain tomorrow as well as describe today.

Without a doubt, international marketing is suddenly coming of age. The increasing expansionism of the EEC and of its indigenous industries have helped demolish both actual as well as psychological frontiers to business. Global product standardisation has helped but industrial co-operation is becoming the keynote of business in the 1980s. Market sharing and sharing of the high costs and risks of research and development is becoming much more common between companies which only a few years ago would have regarded each other as arch-rivals. Industrial co-operation has arisen because the means of achieving this have been developed. This has meant a move away from joint ventures based on an equity relationship to one that is based on a contractual agreement. It means too that knowledge, including marketing skills, is becoming an increasingly saleable asset. As individual markets merge into regional markets, a new atmosphere is created and the terms of doing business change. This book addresses this new environment. The first half of the book examines the theory and techniques whilst the second half places them into several different contexts representing different but important global trading areas.

The intention here has been to move away from the purely narrow perspective of the large multinational company and examine equally the needs of the small company when faced with an export decision. In this present work, an attempt has been made to bridge this gap between small exporters and multinationals. Whereas foreign trade examines exchange flows between nations, here we concern ourselves with, at the lowest level, the smallest of these units, the small company. Britain as an island has always been dependent upon foreign trade for the import of food and raw materials, but with a declining manufacturing sector, the need for new exports of goods or services to pay for these necessary imports becomes an increasingly urgent quest. A growing trade has been taking place in services, traditionally in freight and insurance, but more recently in tourism and ancillary services, as well as computer software, sale of licences, know-how agreements, etc. These changes are important and are described in the pages which follow.

Overall, it is hoped that this text is sufficiently practical in nature as to play some role towards the shaping of future international marketers. Commissioned for the Chartered Institute of Marketing Diploma, this should nevertheless prove useful for an ever increasing number of under-graduate and postgraduate courses on international marketing, both in depth of coverage and perspective. There will also be something here for the experienced practitioner to agree or disagree with. Above all, it offers opportunity to challenge traditional established working practices in the light of changes taking place elsewhere, may even awaken the way in which international marketing is taught. For Chartered Institute of Marketing readers, one note of caution – the section on political risk exceeds the requirements of the Chartered Institute of Marketing.

I thank the Chartered Institute of Marketing and Heinemann Professional Publishing Ltd for paying me the compliment of commissioning this book which I have enjoyed writing. I trust that their confidence will be rewarded. To Dr Owen Adikibi special thanks are due for reading, revising, and updating the section on Nigeria. To the individual reader, I crave your indulgence for present errors and omissions but welcome your correspond-ence as to suggested improvements. My very best wishes to you whether studying or practising the art of international marketing.

Stanley J. Paliwoda
University of Manchester Institute
of Science and Technology

1. THE IMPORTANCE OF INTERNATIONAL MARKETING

The first difficulty is always in defining what is meant by 'international marketing'. Too often, attention is devoted only to those activities conducted between companies which constitute in their aggregated total a foreign trade balance for individual countries. Yet here we are studying trade between nations. We are studying instead the principal actors, the companies at home and abroad who are the buyers and sellers. We examine the variables which they deal with both theoretically and in the context of certain geographic regions so as to arrive at an understanding of international marketing as a dynamic force.

The Greeks and Romans were active in international trading thousands of years before the term 'marketing' entered the language. Indeed, international marketing is seen as a relatively new adjunct even of marketing itself. Even so the meaning of the word 'marketing' has come to be devalued during the relatively short post-war period that it has been with us. It has come increasingly to be used, quite wrongly, as a synonym for 'selling' rather than as a term to describe a management process which in the words of the Chartered Institute of Marketing

seeks to identify, anticipate and satisfy customer requirements profitably.

Or, according to the American Marketing Association

Marketing is the process of planning and executing the conception, pricing, promotion and distribution of ideas, goods and services to create exchanges that satisfy individual and organisational objectives.

Either or both of these definitions will serve our purpose as there is much in common between them.

World markets changed considerably even between Roman times and the great age of discovery which was the period of Renaissance in fifteenth-century Europe. The Renaissance, a comparatively short period in history, was significant in changing how we saw the world. This period witnessed scientific advances in astronomy, in architecture and in art as a result of a better understanding of anatomy, the discovery of new continents with new and rich resources in minerals, strange new fruit and vegetables, spices, and raw materials. The discovery of America, of tobacco, and of the potato were the results of expeditionary travels to a new and uncharted world that had just been discovered. No period in history experienced such massive change yet the nineteenth century witnessed in many ways a similar upheaval in the arrival of first, the

1

Industrial Revolution and later, the Agrarian Revolution. Both of these started in Britain and spread quickly worldwide, changing the face of cities as the population started to move towards industry and create conurbations; and of the countryside also, where the parcelling of narrow strips of land ended and new ideas emerged. This was taking place amongst a society which was quite different to that of today, in that the major European countries were then colonial powers of some dominance.

Britain did then indeed rule the world and her merchant navy was indeed sizeable, with well established trading links with all the countries of the world. The passing of the Victorian era and the advent of the two World Wars redrew the world map and many individual country boundaries on each occasion. Political boundaries were recast and colonialism, at least that wielded by the major European powers, was on the wane. In the period of peace which we have known since the Second World War, world markets have changed even further, not because of boundary changes but because of internal market changes taking place simultaneously worldwide.

Competition has changed, it is no longer possible for former colonial powers to offer aid as before to their former dependencies that is in some way 'tied' to only certain goods. In the search for trade, other countries have willingly stepped in with offers of loans and credits which were not as restrictive as those then offered by the European colonial powers. This has been one of the major changes to world trade, together with the new forms of financing which have emerged postwar including the World Bank, IMF, Bank for International Settlements and Eurodollar Market.

Meanwhile, other newer, industrial, countries were now aggressively establishing themselves on the international scene, and it was also seen to be politically important for them to develop trade, and, through trade, a relationship and understanding with the developing countries which also enhanced their own power and prestige. At the same time, the international trading companies of colonial times such as Britain's East India company or Hudson Bay Company were no longer recognisable as regional trading companies but now were to be seen in a new light as 'multinationals'.

The multinational phenomenon of the twentieth century trades more within itself and its subsidiaries and affiliates than between nations. With more than a quarter of world trade taking place between multinationals, the multinationals have created in effect their own internal markets. This internalisation theory is one explanation of the growth of the multinational (Reference 1). The multinational corporation escapes an internationally-agreed definition, being referred to as an international corporation by some, as a transnational by the United Nations, and a multinational enterprise or 'megacorp' by yet others. While it is impossible to agree a definition, the multinational may be said to meet two important criteria, with the stress being laid particularly on the second:

(a) Foreign Direct Investments either in manufacturing or service industries in more than two countries.

(b) Corporate planning which employs a worldwide perspective and impartially allocates resources such as management, other personnel, company-specific technology, business expertise and funds on a global basis.

The working definition offered here states that:

A multinational enterprise is a corporation which owns (in whole or in part) controls and manages income-generating assets in more than one country. In so doing, it engages in international production, sales and distribution of goods and services across national boundaries financed by foreign direct investment (Reference 2).

The multinationals have been active in dismantling psychological as well as geographical frontiers. An increasing number of truly global brands such as Pepsi-Cola or Coca-Cola underline this point. Language may change with the country concerned, there may be quite different environmental conditions of use but still the bottle, the logo and all that is normally associated with it, including product formulation, will remain intact and instantly recognisable worldwide. For others, such as IBM who produce and sell what are essentially industrial products worldwide, this requires a different form of co-ordination, integrating multinational sourcing of components and division of labour. With IBM's degree of integration, 'foreignness' is a relatively meaningless capacity as the company needs to know as much about its operations in say, Britain, and its market situation there as it does of its home base, the US. With business becoming more international in a search for capacity, new competitive pressures are created which result in a greater dynamism. Technological change; societal change; increasing protectionism internationally (despite the existence of the General Agreement on Trade and Tariffs), and creeping nationalism on a regional, as opposed to national, scale in purchasing, as practised by the EEC, are only a few of the challenges posed to business corporations seeking to do business in the global arena today.

The Dilemma of the multinational – A force for good or evil?

The case for the multinational is as strong as that against it (Reference 3).

It fiddles with its accounts. It avoids or evades its taxes. It rigs its intra-company transfer prices. It is run by foreigners, from decision centres thousands of miles away. It imports foreign labour practices. It overpays. It underpays. It competes unfairly with local firms. It is in cahoots with local firms. It exports jobs from rich countries. It is an instrument of rich countries' imperialism. The technologies it brings to the third world are old fashioned. No, they are too modern. It meddles. It bribes. Nobody can control it. It wrecks balances of payments. It overturns economic policies. It plays off governments against each other to get the biggest investment incentives. Won't it please come and invest? Let it bloody well go home.

Source: 'Business Brief', *The Economist*

Reasons for the nation state to be involved

The UK share of world trade has decreased from around 25 per cent at the end of the last century to 9 per cent today. Nevertheless, the UK still earns a greater, although declining, percentage of its GDP from exports than any other of the major industrial countries: 30.3 in 1977; 28.8 in 1978; 28.5 in 1979; 27.9 in 1980; 27.3 in 1981 and 26.9 in 1982. The need to import at the same time raw materials plus half her food needs, underlines Britain's dependency on foreign trade. The accompanying table shows that if we focus particularly on the export sector we find that exports, indexed over 1980 levels, have been stagnating in volume but increasing in value overall. Britain is showing level pegging in manufactures in terms of exports and imports for 1983, but had a deficit in manufactures for the first time ever in 1984. It is too early yet to talk of trends but this may prove to be indicative. Inflation is down but over the last two years imports have edged ahead of exports both in total and in unit value. More will be said of this in Chapter 11. However, it is worth bearing this point in mind when reading later of the product trade cycle and how the product life cycle theory may be applied to explain international trade.

Table 1.1
US external trade indices. (1980=100)

	Total exports		Total imports	
	Volume	*Value*	*Volume*	*Value*
1979	98.3	88.9	104.7	87.3
1980	100.0	100.0	100.0	100.0
1981	98.6	107.4	99.2	109.4
1982	101.6	116.6	100.1	116.8
1983	102.6	126.6	107.9	127.7
1984	110.7	136.9	117.3	139.3

Source Adapted from the CSO, *Monthly Bulletin of Statistics*, various issues.

Changing nature of exporting and foreign investment

The early 1960s saw a movement away from raw material investment projects which were mainly the preserve of British and American firms, to investment in manufacturing and trade within Europe. The demise of the Bretton Woods Agreement in 1972, which stabilised post-war convertible currencies, created an attraction for foreign investors to move into the US and take advantage of a weak dollar. Two massive oil price rises in 1974 created petrodollar accounts in the West which immediately made possible large-scale construction and industrial projects in the new oil-rich countries of the Middle East, Nigeria and South America. These, in turn often required the creation of an international consortium. Furthermore, a more accommodating political climate termed 'Détente' and an easing of East-

West tension created its own trade momentum in the mid-1970s and the arrival of East-West contractual joint ventures. At its height there were more than 1,200 agreements and the UN Economic Commission for Europe estimated approximately 749 such industrial co-operation joint ventures still in force between Western multinationals and East European state enterprises in 1983 (966, if Yugoslavia is included). Each of these market opportunities presented a particular response of its own. As for the state of the less developed countries, their share of world domestic product and of exports has been declining since the 1970s. Higher interest rates and fewer intergovernmental credits – few governments having convertible currency reserves of their own – have caused a return to what is popularly but wrongly termed 'barter' and is more accurately to be termed 'countertrade', which has a number of important variants as will be seen in later chapters.

The question of extra-territoriality and of supranational legislation

Government everywhere has generally failed to keep pace with the demands of the business world. A fine example of this is that multinational corporations are incorporated under articles of association in a particular sovereign state (most commonly Britain after the US) or federal state in the case of the US (most commonly Delaware). There is no international body as yet equipped to standardise international articles of association for multinational corporations. There is no such thing either as international law, only the application of domestic law to international disputes. For joint ventures which are increasing worldwide, the question of legal jurisdiction and of arbitration in the event of a dispute is very important. Very often a neutral third country may be chosen but whereas neutrality reassures us on impartiality of judgement, there is as yet no national code or constitution sufficiently comprehensive to easily embrace the problems of international trading.

Increasingly the EEC is projecting itself as a legislator on regulations for trading within its boundaries, but although the EEC accounts for the home base of very many large multinationals (British, German, French and Italian) this does not solve a global problem of accountability and control. Meanwhile, the US is increasingly acting in the eyes of its NATO allies as *ultra-vires* or 'beyond legal power' in its desire to control not only US multinational corporations at home but their subsidiaries and technology licensees abroad.

For example, at the time when the Soviet gas pipeline was being constructed to bring Soviet gas into Western Europe, diplomatic difficulties arose over the American ban on General Electric rotor blade technology in the British export of turbines for the pipeline. Attempts were made by the US Administration to influence the British firm of John Brown to stop the shipment or else face reprisals against its subsidiaries in the US. At the same time, the British Government took the line of threatening reprisals directly at the British company if it did not proceed with the export order immediately. The company found itself placed between two Governments in dispute. In this particular case, the US Government backed down. Other examples of US extra-territoriality exist, such as the Foreign Corrupt Practices Act which affects even foreign multinationals with a US base and proscribes bribery and corruption (which is difficult to define anyway) by any part of the company anywhere in the world, not in relative terms as to customs or practices regarded as normal in the country concerned, but in terms of US commercial practice. Yet another is related to the continual watch which the US maintains over sophisticated computer technology exports to the Soviet Union and Eastern Europe. Early 1984 saw some press comment in Britain as to how the Reagan Administration was requesting British-based American companies to seek US licences when selling advanced American computers to customers in the UK. This was brought to light by a circular from IBM (UK) to thirty leasing companies. While the British Government is seeking to settle this protracted and embarrassing conflict, the US Administration uses the opportunity to reinforce its policy on technology sales.

Since then, there has been an even greater and more concerted outcry over the ability of two dozen states in the US to levy a tax on businesses based there according to a 'unitary' method (Reference 4). In addition to revealing worldwide accounts, the unitary system artificially apportions a share of a company's overall profits to a state, based on the size of the company's sales, property and payroll there compared with the same elements around the US or worldwide. This 'profit' which is typically larger than what a company claims to have earned, is then taxed at the normal corporate rate.

Table 1.2
Top six US states by number of foreign manufacturing investments

	1983	1982	1981	1980	1979	1978
New York	36	36	39	23	50	38
North Carolina	25	12	27	36	25	13
California	19	19	34	30	50	44
Texas	18	14	24	20	31	15
Massachusetts	13	7	30	7	13	12
New Jersey	13	21	9	18	17	14

Source New York State Department of Commerce, 1985

California presently collects two-thirds of the revenue by this tax. California's right to levy this tax was, however, upheld in a US Supreme Court decision in June 1983. Meanwhile British, French, German and Japanese companies are actively lobbying for the repeal of this tax law using industry representation and government to back their case. Their only leverage is in being able to hold back an intended investment or actively discourage others from entering the 'unitary tax' states. To date, New York repealed unitary tax in 1983 and Florida in November 1984.

President Reagan announced in January 1986 that his administration will pursue federal legislation to limit states' ability to tax multinational corporations on profits earned outside the US. He expressed the hope that the states would base their corporate taxes only on income earned within the United States. This is the 'water's edge' approach to taxation.

Six states currently use unitary taxation but US legislation could affect 26 other states that tax dividends received by US based multinationals from foreign subsidiaries and affiliates. The price of agreement required soon for renewal of the US-UK Double Taxation Agreement is greater financial reporting to the Internal Revenue Service which will then pass this on to the State auditors.

From the point of view of a foreign company looking at the US irrespective of what may subsequently happen (and total repeal or amendment seems unlikely) there is a very great danger that this example may be copied in the developing trading nations who must also be interested in the question of corporate accountability. It is said that the measure was designed to end tax evasion by transfer pricing but it will only exacerbate it, if only towards the US which is unlikely then to make a complaint. Unitary tax looks only at the size of a company's operation in a state, not its profits, and this is sure to create an opportunity for some. It is important to note, however, that the state of Delaware in which most US multinationals are incorporated, does not feature on this list of states imposing unitary taxation.

Table 1.3
US methods of taxing corporate income

States which tax worldwide corporate income by unitary method (brackets indicate States which previously supported unitary taxation)	States which use unitary method to tax US income (but could extend tax to worldwide operations)
Alaska	Arizona
California (and Colorado)	Illinois
Idaho	Kansas
(Indiana)	Kentucky
(Massachusetts*)	Maine
Montana	Minnesota
New Hampshire	Mississippi
North Dakota	Nebraska
(South Dakota)	New Mexico
(Oregon)	North Carolina
(Utah)	West Virginia

*Applying only to US companies' worldwide operations

A need for international marketing

A National Economic Development Office (NEDO) report of 1979 (Reference 5) concluded that the poor state of UK export activity could be related to three factors, which we will deal with in greater detail in ensuing chapters:

1. Turning to exporting when domestic demand is low, so it becomes a marginal activity and merits low investment
2. Insufficient attention to non-price competition (e.g. new product development, delivery, after-sales service, etc.)
3. Companies spreading their exporting effort across all markets rather than concentrating on the key growth markets.

These changes were echoed also in a European-wide survey of suppliers, conducted by Swedish, Italian, French, German and British buyers (Reference 6). This survey pointed to the reasons for a poor UK trade performance relative to all the other countries surveyed as being because of:

1. Low productivity
2. Uncompetitive prices
3. Poor product design
4. Poor marketing

The meaning of international marketing

International marketing concerns itself with the application of marketing operations across national frontiers. Whereas international marketing refers to marketing abroad, comparative marketing refers to purely domestic marketing comparing one system alongside another (Reference 7). Within Eastern Europe, where marketing is recognised only as something necessary for trade with the West, international marketing is practised only by the State Foreign Trade Enterprises (FTEs, see Chapter 11) and researched by the Institute of Foreign Trade, whereas comparative marketing is a subject for study by an Institute of Domestic Trade which literally compares their own internal marketing and distribution channels with those of a different country.

Implementing the four Ps of marketing – product, place, promotion and price – involves interactions with variables which will be different for the domestic and international markets (see Table 1.3). In domestic marketing one is familiar with the extent of political risk, the extent of government power in curbing cheap imports, with the quality of human and natural resources, and with the ramifications of legislation on such areas as safety, hygiene, employment, ownership of capital, etc. International marketing, on the other hand, involves dealing with societies where politics, beliefs and values may be very different from those in the home market and legislation in other countries may have important ramifications for international marketing – there may, for example, be legislation requiring the employment of a majority of local nationals, or majority equity ownership of joint ventures by local nationals, etc.

In this context it is useful to consider alternative views on the marketing function. Some see marketing as somewhere between an art and a science; others view marketing as having two facets: technical and social. The

Table 1.4
Domestic versus international planning

Domestic Planning	International Planning
1. Single language and nationality	1. Multilingual/multinational/multi-cultural factors
2. Relatively homogeneous market	2. Fragmented and diverse markets
3. Data available, usually accurate and easily collected	3. Data collection a formidable task requiring significantly higher budgets and personnel allocation
4. Political factors relatively unimportant	4. Political factors frequently vital
5. Relative freedom from government interference	5. Involvement in national economic plans – governments influence business decisions
6. Individual corporation has little effect on environment	6. 'Gravitational' distortion by large companies
7. Chauvinism helps	7. Chauvinism hinders
8. Relatively stable business environment	8. Multiple environments, many of which are highly unstable (but may be highly profitable)
9. Uniform financial climate	9. Variety of financial climates ranging from overconservative to wildly inflationary
10. Single currency	10. Currencies differing in stability and real value
11. Business 'rules of the game' mature and understood	11. Rules diverse, changeable and unclear
12. Management generally accustomed to sharing responsibilities and using financial controls	12. Management frequently autonomous and unfamiliar with budgets and controls

Source William W. Cain, 'International Planning: Mission Impossible?', *Columbia Journal of World Business* (July–August 1970), p. 58

technical facet or the 'science' consists of the application of principles, rules or knowledge relating to the non-human elements of marketing. It is these concepts and generalisations which are held to have a universality transcending national boundaries and cultural differences.

On the technical level, we are dealing with universals without regard to time and space. We are dealing with concepts which have applications across natural boundaries and language barriers such as economies of scale, distribution channels, etc. On the social level we deal with interactions among individuals acting in role positions in the various systems involved in the distribution of goods and services. This facet emphasises the human element, the individual acting under the full range of influences both economic and non-economic which affiliation with the social institutions of his society imposes upon him. As a social process, marketing in two nations may differ quite markedly. While the roles in which individuals interact may be identical, their expectations and behaviour patterns in two societies may be quite different.

As an organisation, companies with international operations may exhibit one of three behavioural profiles (Reference 8):

- ethnocentric (or monocentric) whereby the identity of the foreign subsidiary is strongly identified with the parent company. The products of the foreign subsidiary may benefit from being closely identified with the image of the parent company – for example, Levi's or Wrangler jeans which have a strong American image; or Rolls-Royce or double-decker buses which have a strong British image; or Scotch whisky. This association with a national image can, however, be a disadvantage when incidents occur which cause ill-feeling towards the country of the parent company – for example, the overseas offices of British Airways have suffered in times of anti-British feeling.
- polycentric is a 'half-way house' – the firm may have a few international subsidiaries but be well integrated and operate on a decentralised basis.
- geocentric is a cosmopolitan outlook which applies only to those truly multinational corporations who have to choose between investments in perhaps South America or Australia or Britain and have to take a group view as to what is the optimal strategy for the future of the parent group. Investment decisions like raw material sourcing, product sourcing, personnel deployment, regional and functional reporting systems, all require integration and close co-ordination if a large company is to respond to competitive challenge.

Strategy and structure are closely interrelated and, as we shall see in Chapter 4 on market-entry strategies, there is a variety of alternative structures for large multinationals. Organisation may be along functional, product, geographic or matrix organisation lines; these are dealt with in detail in Chapter 10.

Reasons for the company to go abroad

1. The product trade cycle

The market for the product may be in decline at home but may still have potential for growth abroad. This theory of a product trade cycle in international trade is similar to a biological life cycle and was developed at Harvard Business School by Professors Wells and Vernon (Reference 9) but although offered first as an explanation for American multinational behaviour, the theory has never succeeded in offering more than a partial explanation. In its essence, it identified four stages

1. US export strength
2. Foreign production starts
3. Foreign production becomes competitive in US export markets
4. Import competition begins

In the first phase, cost is secondary. The product sells on its own features. Foreigners purchase from the US during this phase of production. As a result of this 'demonstration effect', product familiarity abroad increases and foreign production starts. In the next phase, as the early foreign manufacturers become larger and more experienced, their costs should fall. According to the 'experience curve' theory a doubling of production should produce cost savings of about one-third. The foreign manufacturers begin to reap the advantages of scale economies previously available only to US manufacturers.

Finally, the foreign manufacturer reaches mass production based on his home and export markets but now his lower labour rates (relative to the US) and newer plant may enable him to produce at lower cost than an American manufacturer. The cost savings may be sufficient to enable him to pay ocean freight and American duty and still compete with American producers on their own market. For the American producer in this situation the only strategy is exit and future sourcing from abroad. This points to the phenomenon of 'runaway industry' where multinationals manufacturing products which are mature and therefore more price-sensitive, may continually move their bases of production around the world in a never-ending search for lower operational costs.

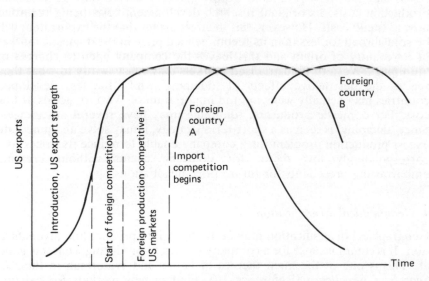

Figure 1.1 The product life cycle for international trade

In support of his theory Wells cited ratios of the value of 1962–3 exports over the value of 1952–3 exports and categorised goods in a table from left to right into *necessity*, *discretionary*, and *luxury*. Over time there was a movement from the right column to the left with products like televisions now becoming a necessity, not discretionary nor a luxury as before. The compilation of such a table today would depend on factors like per capita disposable income, tastes, and environmental factors such as climate which may make air conditioners a necessity rather than a luxury, etc.

2. Competition

Competition may be less intense abroad than at home. This area has been the subject of study for many international economists but suffice it to say that there may be significant differences in factor costs between the home country and other countries. Other countries may, for example, have cheaper raw material or labour costs, or they may have gained 'experience curve' cost advantages, so that it becomes advantageous to operate abroad. Also, the market structure of other countries may reveal advantages like centralised buying, perhaps state-buying, where market access may be assured in return for guarantees on investment, employment, etc.

3. Excess capacity utilisation

This concept is drawn also from economies, whereupon a given manufactured item which has been on sale in the domestic market for sufficiently long to have recouped its original research and development costs, may find new profitable export markets, costed only at its actual production costs; its original research development costs being regarded now as 'sunk' costs. However, this in effect means that the export item will be sold abroad for less than its recommended price in the domestic market of its country of origin and this leaves the company open to charges of 'dumping'. Western industrialised markets may react swiftly to what they see as the destructive effects of 'dumping' whilst the less developed countries may actually welcome the importation of Western goods at low cost. For domestic producers, 'dumping' may have several advantages. Since 'dumping' is seen as a short-term strategy, it may solve an immediate excess production problem for a company unable to reduce its prices to a correspondingly low figure for domestic clients without creating embarrassing precedents for future price negotiations.

4. Geographical diversification

Geographical diversification may be preferable to product-line diversification. It is commonsense for a company to stick to producing what it is good at. This is one of the main themes of Peters and Waterman in their *In Search of Excellence* (Reference 10). Finding new markets for existing products or modified products does not expose the company to the attendant risks of expanding the product range simultaneously with foreign market entry. In terms of corporate strategy, it makes sense to focus on the strengths of the company and not to depart too greatly from these strengths whether in product innovation, adaptation or service. Recent US corporate case histories which have seen companies such as Gulf and Western moving away from the conglomerate pattern to specialisation in their mainstream business activity have emphasised this point. Elsewhere, rival companies seem to be uniting together in sharing research and development on parts, components, subassemblies and product range extension as will be seen in Chapter 4.

5. Potential of population and purchasing power

Where there is a need, and willingness to find, plus an ability to pay for, a solution to that need, a market will be created. Assessing market potential requires data. Not all countries produce data with the frequency or detail of the Central Statistical Office. Very often, and particularly with developing countries, there will be significantly large gaps between the publications of national economic data. Even when data exists it may be of questionable value, it may be collected for different reasons on a quite different statistical base and therefore may not be directly comparable to the exporter's known domestic situation. For this reason, more is said in Chapter 3 of the techniques of foreign country selection where economic indicators are poor or non-existent.

The internationalisation process

Although now being disputed, the theory advanced here is that for small firms, internationalisation is the consequence of a series of incremental decisions. 'A gradual process occurring in stages' rather than large spectacular investments was how Johanson and Wiedersheim-Paul (1975) (Reference 11) viewed the internationalisation process, in research conducted amongst four Swedish firms. They found also that some expansion immediately outside the domestic market but within the immediate region preceded internationalisation and therefore maintained that it was reasonable to assume that the same held true for many firms from other countries with small domestic markets. By expanding first out of the nation state into the immediate neighbouring markets of Scandinavia, reduced perceived risk and the uncertainty of exporting.

What was interesting to note from their research was that the nature of pre-export activity influences the likelihood of a firm becoming an exporter. The firm will have a natural preference for operations in the nearby geographic areas. Again, the question of regional expansion is affected by the personal perception, individual characteristics and experience of the decision maker. Within the context of the firm, this involvement in international marketing could be viewed as an innovation. In the final analysis, finally, it would move ahead with much rational analysis or deliberate planning.

Stages in internationalisation

Another sequential or 'stages' model evolved from research undertaken in North America by Bilkey and Tesar (Reference 12) amongst Wisconsin exporters. They then offered the following patterns of behaviour or stages:

1. Management is not interested and would not even fill an unsolicited order.
2. Management is willing to fill solicited orders but makes no effort to explore the feasibility of active exporting.
3. Management actively explores the feasibility of exporting.
4. The firm exports experimentally to some psychologically close country.

5. The firm is an experienced exporter to that country.
6. Management explores the feasibility of exporting to additional countries, psychologically more distant.

This model was subsequently refined by Cavusgil and Nevin who went on to identify yet further characteristics, finding that the internal company factors explaining export marketing behaviour fell into four groups:

- expectations of management, as a result of the impact of exports on growth;
- level of commitment;
- differential advantages to the firm;
- managerial aspirations, often related to security.

This incremental model identified three stages of internationalisation:

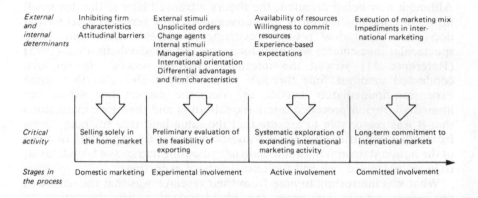

External and internal determinants	Inhibiting firm characteristics Attitudinal barriers	External stimuli Unsolicited orders Change agents Internal stimuli Managerial aspirations International orientation Differential advantages and firm characteristics	Availability of resources Willingness to commit resources Experience-based expectations	Execution of marketing mix Impediments in international marketing
Critical activity	Selling solely in the home market	Preliminary evaluation of the feasibility of exporting	Systematic exploration of expanding international marketing activity	Long-term commitment to international markets
Stages in the process	Domestic marketing	Experimental involvement	Active involvement	Committed involvement

Figure 1.2 A model of the incremental internationalisation process of the firm

1. Stimuli for experimental international involvement. Non-exporters need stimuli to enter exporting. Cavusgil and Nevin identified external and internal stimuli. External stimuli often take the form of unsolicited orders from buyers or distributors abroad or domestic export agents. Banks, trade associations, and middlemen also serve as change agents. External stimuli clearly exceed the number of internal stimuli received. In eight separate studies, external stimuli (Cavusgil, 1976) accounted for 54–84 per cent of all stimuli. Firms which start exporting as a result of external inquiries exemplify a passive approach in international marketing, with an involvement which was fortuituous, marginal and intermittent, with short-run profits being likely to be the motivating force, rather than clearly formulated long-term objectives.

2. Active international involvement. This involves a systematic exploration of marketing opportunities imposing demands upon the resources of the firm – physical, financial, and managerial which will test the willingness of management to allocate these resources. Smaller firms face an obvious disadvantage in not being able to commit resources, financial incentives do not immediately change matters. Another major determinant of active involvement in international marketing is management's experience-based expectations of the attractiveness of exporting for the firm.

3. Committed international involvement. The firm moves into the position of committed participants in international marketing. Now managers are constantly making choices in the allocation of resources between foreign and domestic markets.

Taken all in all, the internationalisation approach does not appear to be a sequence of deliberate planned steps beginning with a clearly defined problem and proceeding through a rational analysis of behavioural alternatives. Personal characteristics of the decision makers; lack of information; perception of risk and presence of uncertainty seem to be especially valuable in understanding a firm's involvement in international marketing.

References

1. Rugman, Alan, *New Theories of the Multinational Enterprise*, Croom Helm, 1982.
2. Adapted from Hood, Neil and Young, Stephen, *The Economics of Multinational Enterprise*, Longmans, 1979, p. 3.
3. 'Business Brief', *Economist*, 24 January 1976, p. 68.
4. *Financial Times*, 4 February 1984 'How Unitary taxes hit the multinationals', *Business Week*, 16 January 1984, pp. 30–34.
5. Connell, David, 'The UK's Performance in Export Markets: some evidence from international trade data', NEDO, 1979.
6. Turnbull, P. W. and Valla, J. P., *Strategies for International Industrial Marketing*, Croom Helm, 1986.
7. Bartels, Robert, 'Are Domestic and International Marketing Dissimilar?' *Journal of Marketing*, Vol. 32, July 1968, pp. 56–61.
8. Perlemutter, H. V., 'Some Management Problems on Spaceship Earth: the megafirm in the Global Industrial Estate', *Academy of Management Proceedings*, New York, August 1969.
9. Wells, L. T. (Jr), 'A product life cycle for international trade?', *Journal of Marketing*, vol. 32 (July 1968), pp. 1–6.
10. Peters, T. J. and Waterman, R. H., *In Search of Excellence*, Harper and Row, 1982.
11. Johanson, J. and Wiedersheim-Paul, F., 'The Internationalisation of the Firm: Four Swedish Cases', *Journal of Management Studies*, 12(3), October 1975, pp. 305–22.
12. Bilkey, W. J. and Tesar, George, 'The export behaviour of smaller sized Wisconsin manufacturing firms', *Journal of International Business Studies*, Spring 1977, pp. 93–98.
13. Cavusgil, S. Tarner and Nevin, John R., 'Conceptualisations of the Initial Involvement in International Marketing', in Charles W. Lams and Patrick M. Dunne (eds) *Theoretical Developments in Marketing*, American Marketing Association Theory Conference, Phoenix, April 1980.

2. MARKET INFRASTRUCTURE

In attempting to analyse the component parts of the international marketer's environment and the variables influencing his decision-making process, we have first to consider the question of exactly what constitutes a market.

Individual purchasing power is often used as a measure of comparison, taking perhaps an approximation of Gross National Product per capita as a worldwide indicator of personal disposable income. As an approximate measure of wealth per head of a population, this statistic is quite misleading in that it is only an arithmetic average (mean) giving no indication whatsoever of the median or of the mode, only of a 'smoothed' approximation for a national population. However, even this does not yield true personal disposable income since, in the case of the Comecon countries, for example, both wages and prices are politically set and only 'black market' prices reflect near market forces of demand and supply. The nation may therefore be earning income but may choose not to let its people spend it directing it instead towards other applications, e.g. defence. This has important ramifications for marketing. From an examination of per capita GNP in India it would be impossible to identify a market for luxury goods or what, if anything, and why, companies should seek to advertise and sell their wares there. More will be said of this later in relation to international market research and to international advertising. The fact remains, though, that there is a small but sizeable market for luxury goods in India. We must therefore adopt a means of foreign market appraisal which identifies important sub-markets, and avoids the problems of aggregating large populations en masse.

Affluence does not necessarily bring even a basic level of literacy. Certain of the poorer less-developed countries such as Egypt or India have long had a managerial and professional elite, whereas others which have perhaps only recently discovered new-found wealth, often through oil funds, have had to import advisers and create afresh this infrastructure for themselves. Nigeria and many of the Middle-Eastern countries illustrate conditions where less than ten years ago there was little schooling and yet now universities exist. Again, affluence and the desire for status enhancement by-passes the need for market research and the identification of market demand for services such as international airports which are very plentiful in the Middle East and are of a size out of proportion to their indigenous population but in keeping with their self-perceived status and wealth.

The social environment

As a result of the increasing global standardisation of goods and services international marketing is no longer an activity that is practised only in foreign parts. Some brand names have become universally recognised family brands, e.g. Kelloggs cornflakes, Coca-Cola, Ford Fiesta; and in some cases brand names have taken the place of the product class, e.g. Formica or Thermos.

This latter category is perhaps the least fortunate. It is so taken for granted that it is difficult to retain any individuality for the marque. Of global products overall, they are perhaps few in number but their number is increasing. All are accepted as being classless, stateless products, the accepted products of a consumer society and as such, consumers need only to be reminded of them.

The social environment determines the collective attitude to companies perceived as being 'pure British' or 'pure American' or ethnocentric in management, product line, or orientation. Products which capitalise on their home origins may fall from favour quickly whenever political climates change. In the past this has happened to American multi-nationals such as Coca-Cola and to a lesser degree British Airways who have had windows broken at their overseas sales offices in a backlash of anti-British feeling over a political problem of the day in which Britain may be involved. To some observers it is simply the law of colonial ingratitude. Nevertheless, it will be interesting to see whether in future the Soviets ever suffer a similar backlash with their Lada cars as a possible retaliation against their foreign policy in any part of the globe.

Generally it may be said that the product or service must be acceptable to the society for which it is intended. Here there are three levels at which the marketing mix operates as a possible agent of change:

1. *Folkways or conventions*, where social behaviour is learned and accepted, and followed habitually and is devoid of rational thought. If someone devises a better way of doing things, it may very well be adopted, otherwise things are very likely to stay as they are, and the status quo will remain. Calculators in Britain are very different today compared with ten years ago when they were relatively scarce and quite expensive; nowadays, they are used widely and often include additional features such as an alarm, a stopwatch, a musical instrument, etc. Persuading people to buy requires first selling them the product concept and making them aware, and then moving towards an understanding not only of what the product is about, but also of its advantages and benefits. Having arrived at this stage, it is relatively easy then to move to a trial stage. Electronic cash registers are everywhere to be found in Britain today not just because they are more dependable than their electric forerunners but because they also incorporate a stock control or sales tax function as well.

2. *Mores* is a Latin word for morals but these are the more strongly held, less easily assailable customs of the nation. A country may be composed of many nations, many peoples, many languages. It is unwise

to cause offence in the promotion of a product, particularly when it may offend against the religion of the people concerned. An example in recent years was the arrival in Britain of 'Jesus Jeans' which featured the rear view of a girl in torn denim shorts. This would have been entirely acceptable but for the slogan underneath: 'If you love me, you'll follow me'. This company had to face the wrath not only of indignant church organisations but of many who, although they did not attend church regularly, nevertheless felt outraged. Their sensibilities were shocked by this form of blatant commercialisation of the words of a man whom one half of the world regard as the son of God, and most others as a prophet. The moral here is that it is neither easy nor particularly wise to try to change the norms of a country; it is much easier and wiser perhaps, not to try.

3. *Laws* are the embodiment of the mores or the social norms of a country, but laws are always subject to review and pressure can be brought to bear by lobbying the legislature to make them aware of a given situation and to try and motivate them towards changing it. Laws are seldom more than a 'freeze frame' of society's views or wishes on a specific topic at a specific moment in time. In a dynamic world, the relevance of laws must be steadily monitored for effectiveness. Financial penalties stated in an Act on the Statute Book may quickly be eroded by inflation; new technological developments such as video cassette recorders and personal computers arouse arguments over the question of copyright designed for written text; social trends such as a rise in illegitimate births create problems over the inheritance of property on the death of a parent; social change motivates pressure for that which was previously taboo, e.g. Sunday opening of shops etc. In other respects from being anachronistic, the law may exhibit certain curious anomalies. For example, in England it is possible for video cassette shops to be raided by police and to be served summons for pornographic video material that is approved for nationwide general release in the cinemas.

Increasingly, the interpretation of national laws has a great bearing on the activities of the international marketer. Polaroid started proceedings against Kodak when the Kodak instant film camera was launched in England. Although the argument is sufficiently complex for a whole battery of solicitors, barristers and technical experts to mull over for, it is thought, nine years, Kodak were permitted in the interim to manufacture and sell the camera in the UK. Although the decision will not have any direct bearing on its activities elsewhere, an English judgement will affect Kodak activities worldwide for better or for worse. Similarly a decision by the FDA in the US that a specific drug is found in certain circumstances to produce carcinogenic reactions will usually ensure a blanket ban in the UK as well, not because of jurisdiction, since the US has no jurisdiction over the UK but as a precaution for the public well-being. In the same way the British Committee on the Public Safety of Drugs and Medicines may produce a similar effect in the US.

Perhaps one of the great weaknesses of the age in which we live is that there is no international law for commercial disputes, only domestic law travelling imperfectly abroad. For example, in the creation of joint ventures with overseas partners, the terms of jurisdiction in the event of a breakdown have to be decided at the outset of the agreement. Very often a neutral country such as Switzerland proves useful, although its legal code such countries may later be found to lack and so industry-wide international agencies may then be asked to arbitrate in case of dispute. However, no nation state has yet enacted laws within its national legal code or constitution which will allow it to effectively deal with all international trade disputes. Consequently the decisions of industrial arbitration councils are always considered carefully in the event of a subsequent court hearing. In addition there is the International Chamber of Commerce in Paris. Yet the situation overall is unsatisfactory. Joint ventures which fail are allowed to lapse rather than be subject to divorce proceedings. Companies realise that once a venture fails it is probably too late for litigation, it being seen that litigation in the local national courts may produce only an unfavourable outcome anyway. Litigation then is only really for cases where large sums of money have been lost through what appears to be negligence.

In other respects, the law and practice relating to commerce and industry can lead to changes in the social fabric. Product distribution in developed markets provides an example of various channels of distribution existing alongside each other – direct selling, retailing, wholesaling, 'cash-and-carry', factory-direct, door-to-door selling, house party selling, etc. Mail-order and the 'house party' is American in origin but the concept has travelled well to other countries, including Japan. It is possible for a country nevertheless, to make a quantum leap from developmental to advanced forms of retailing as France did in the 1960s with the introduction of hypermarkets without first experiencing a growth in the US-style supermarket. Legal flexibility allowed this to happen in France but has constrained its development in the UK.

The cultural environment

Culture is an extrapolation of the past. It is learned behaviour rather than innate, a characteristic emphasised in the Oxford English Dictionary definition which defines culture as the:

Improvement or refinement of mind, tastes and manners; the condition of being thus trained and refined: the intellectual side of civilisation.

It is ironic therefore to consider how the Nazi general Hermann Goering was once quoted as saying, 'When I hear anyone talk of culture, I reach for my revolver'. Culture is popularly used as a loose term to embody what is in effect a syndrome, as when we refer to the whole set of social norms and responses which condition society's behaviour. More than that, we tend to measure other cultures by our own. A self-reference criteria always comes into play in the assessment of a foreign culture. When visiting foreign countries, a British salesman may find it unusual that the standard working day in Eastern Europe starts at 7.30–8.00 a.m., and continues without a lunch break until approximately 3.00 p.m. Unless conditioned for it, he may find it difficult to adjust to a working pattern so different from the normal British one, of one meeting in the morning and one in the afternoon. The same occurs with the length of the working week in the Middle East where Friday is not a working day. Again we could introduce, too, the further difficulty encountered with the multiplicity of local holidays worldwide. Local time differences are published and easily quantifiable; local resistance to change and innovation, the degree of psychological distance between developed and developing country is many times more difficult to quantify.

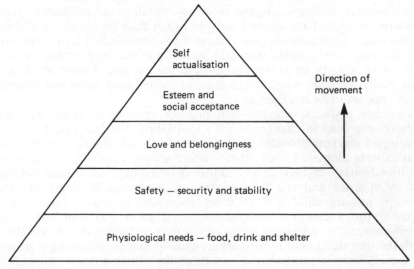

Figure 2.1 The Maslow hierarchy of needs

   Maslow's Hierarchy of Needs (Reference 1) suggesting a pyramid hierarchy of needs would imply that lower-order needs must first be satisfied before higher order needs can initiate or influence behaviour. As each important need is satisfied, the next most important need will come into play. It is interesting to see how many of our so-called global products, e.g. Kellogg's Cornflakes, Coca-Cola, Pepsi-Cola, are intrinsically American products with global acceptance and so global availability. Their corporate approach is definitely ethnocentric, but on this Hierarchy of Needs is it a physiological or a higher need – e.g. esteem and social acceptance – which they satisfy? In many less developed countries, including the Soviet Union, Coca-Cola and Pepsi are available at a premium. Other local products would suffice to quench the physiological need of thirst. Perhaps then there is more to these American products in terms of benefits brought to the consumer, of which some kudos, a taste perhaps of luxury, of merely being able to afford and have ready access to a Western product, are often motivations themselves in many countries. What people say they drink at home, what they in fact drink at home, and what they will drink in company, are subject to a number of peer-group influences. This is society at work. Freud (Reference 2) believed that the real motives guiding behaviour were shaped in early childhood, where need gratification was not always satisfied; this led to frustration, which led to the development of more subtle means of gratification. Frustration and denial of need gratification led to repression and feelings of guilt and shame with regard to that particular need.

The marketer's task is to try to understand the persona or personae, plural, in each country in which he is operating and this can only be achieved by an understanding of the culture or cultures prevailing.

Human motivation, according to Herzberg, (Reference 3) could be more readily understood when studied in terms of what he called 'hygiene' and 'motivator' factors. Firstly, there were those factors which did not in themselves create satisfaction but their very absence may well cause dissatisfaction. Our expectations of that particular product are such that although this may well be a first-time purchase, we expect it nevertheless to be equipped to a certain specification. Cars, for example, are supplied with wheels and an engine as standard, although a stereo radio, digital clock and air conditioning may be included as 'extras', depending upon the sophistication of the buyer market itself. These features are not motivators which are supplied as standard. Motivator factors were the second category according to Herzberg. These were the factors which did influence behaviour. To identify exactly what these factors were, would involve researching the specific situation concerned, but the potential rewards for so doing are great. When the Japanese first started shipping cars to Britain around 1972 they met with instant success because they contained as standard many features traditionally only found as 'extras' on other makes of car which would therefore involve extra payment.

Let us be sure then that we understand the meaning of culture and its importance by examining alternative definitions to the one cited earlier from the Oxford English Dictionary. It is worth noting how each of the following seems to highlight a slightly different aspect of which may be understood to mean culture.

Culture consists in patterned ways of thinking, feeling and reacting acquired and transmitted mainly by symbols, constituting the distinctive achievements of human groups, including their embodiments in artefacts; the essential core of culture consists of traditional (i.e. historically derived and selected) ideas and especially their attached values.
(C. Kluckhohn, 'The Study of Culture', in D. Lerner, H. D. Cesswell (eds.), *The Policy Sciences*, Stanford University Press, 1951)

The *Longman Dictionary of Contemporary English* defines 'culture' as:

1. Artistic and other activity of the mind and the works produced by this. 2. A state of high development in art and thought existing in a society and represented at various levels in its members. 3. The particular system of art, thought and customs of a society; the arts, customs, beliefs and all the other products of human thought made by a people at a particular time. 4. Development and

improvement of the mind or body by education or training. 5. The practice of raising animals and growing plants or crops. 6. The practice of growing bacteria for scientific use or use in medicine.

Chamber's 20th Century Dictionary (1983 edition) offers:

Cultivation: the state of being cultivated; refinement; the result of cultivation; a type of civilisation; a crop of experimentally grown bacteria or the like.

Webster's Third New International Dictionary states:*

1. The art or practice of cultivating; the manner or method of cultivating. 2. The act of developing by education, discipline, social experience: the training or refining of the moral and intellectual faculties. 3a. The cultivation or rearing of a particular product or crop or stock for supply. 3b. Steady endeavour of improvement of, or in, a special line. 3c. Professional or expert care and training. 4a. The state of being cultivated especially the enlightenment and excellence of taste acquired by intellectual and aesthetic training: the intellectual and artistic content of civilisation: refinement in manners, taste, thought. 4b. Acquaintance with and taste in fine arts, humanities, and broad aspects of science as distinguished from vocational, technical, or professional skill or knowledge. 5a. The total pattern of human behaviour and its products embodied in thought, speech, action and artifacts and dependent upon man's capacity for learning and transmitting knowledge to succeeding generations through the use of tools, language, and systems of abstract thought. 5b. The body of customary beliefs, social forms and material traits constituting a distinct complex of tradition of a racial, religious or social group. 5c. A complex of typical behaviour or standardised social characteristics peculiar to a specific group, occupation or profession, sex, age grade or social class. 5d. A recurring assemblage of artifacts that differentiates a group of archaeological sites. 6a. Cultivation of living material (as bacteria or tissues) in prepared nutrient media. 6b. Any inoculated nutrient medium whether or not it contains living organisms.

Matthew Arnold also had much to say on the issue of culture, viz:

Culture, the acquainting ourselves with the best that has been known and said in the world, and thus with the history of the human spirit.
                    (*Literature and Dogma*, Preface to the 1873 edition)

Not all countries are linguistically or culturally homogeneous but may, to take the example of India or Nigeria, comprise many proud peoples each with their own language or dialect but communicating at a national level only by means of the language of their former colonial master, usually English but sometimes French or German. This reduction of population demographics into homogeneous units has been termed by one management author (Reference 4) as 'clans', whereby members share a common set of values or objectives plus beliefs about how to co-ordinate efforts in order to reach common objectives. This is the beginning of marketing segmentation, which is discussed more fully in the next chapter.

Cultural sensitivity is important in international business. In this respect it is important for the manager to be as aware of the similarities as the

*By permission. From Webster's Third New International Dictionary © 1981 by Merriam-Webster Inc., publisher of the Merriam-Webster® Dictionaries.

dissimilarities between the foreign market and his own. When communication necessitates translation, a message is open to distortion by means of various idioms peculiar to that foreign language. A standardised global advertising campaign is therefore most vulnerable to this form of local market distortion, but differences will be found also (Reference 5) in other aspects of culture, e.g.:

- Material culture, e.g. attitudes towards acquisition of goods and services.
- Language (or languages plural which may run into hundreds if we consider India or Nigeria).
- Aesthetics, e.g. attitudes towards colour, brand names, design, music.
- Education, degree of national literacy, opportunities for university education.
- Mores – religion, beliefs and attitudes.
- Social organisation whether hierarchical or not; role of women in society; etc.
- Political life – period of time it has been a sovereign independent nation; characteristics of its political life, whether democratic, one party state; etc.

Attitudes may be expected to be different towards work and achievement; towards management; towards the concept of profit. Indeed the role of the consumer is clearly seen to be much more influential in the developed countries than the developing countries where some multinationals continue to sell products which have been banned or voluntarily removed from their home market in the West some years before. This may apply to drugs or to high tar cigarettes, for example. Lack of education, low levels of literacy, poor communication and low levels of general awareness together with political opposition prevent consumerism from becoming a popular movement in the developing countries.

Assessing the cultural environment

Many attempts have been made over the years to devise a means of testing for cultural significance across countries. The all-pervading effect of culture to be found in all aspects of life is reflected in the fact that Murdoch composed a list of 72 cultural 'universals'. These could be found in all societies and encompassed amongst them courtship, dancing, incest, taboos, and sexual restrictions, although not necessarily in that order. These cultural 'universals' were to be found in every society known to man. They composed the essential social infrastructure.

On a comparative basis, differences could be more easily spotlighted by identifying differences in attitudes to any of these 72 universals. Hall went further with his *Map of Culture* which listed 10 aspects of human activity which he referred to as Primary Message Systems. Some things such as different languages could be compensated for by translation and interpretation but not so with differences relating to the language of time; space;

Table 2.1
Cultural universals

Age grading	Food taboos	Music
Athletic sports	Funeral rites	Mythology
Bodily adornment	Games	Numerals
Calendar	Gestures	Obstetrics
Cleanliness training	Gift giving	Penal sanctions
Community organisation	Government	Personal names
Cooking	Greetings	Population policy
Cooperative labour	Hairstyles	Postnatal care
Cosmology	Hospitality	Pregnancy usages
Courtship	Housing hygiene	Property rights
Dancing	Incest taboos	Propitiation of
Decorative art	Inheritance rules	supernatural beings
Divination	Joking	Puberty customs
Division of labour	Kingroups	Religious rituals
Dream interpretation	Kinship nomenclature	Residence rules
Education	Language	Sexual restrictions
Eschatology	Law	Soul concepts
Ethics	Luck superstitions	Status differentiation
Ethnobotany	Magic	Surgery
Etiquette	Marriage	Tool making
Faith healing	Mealtimes	Trade
Family	Medicine	Visiting
Feasting	Modesty concerning	Weaning
Fire making	natural functions	Weather control
Folklore	Mourning	

Source George P. Murdock, 'The Common Denominator of Cultures', in *The Science of Man in the World Crises*, ed. Ralph Linton, Columbia University Press, 1945, p. 123–42.

things; friendship; and agreements. If, as a company, we were interested in attitudes to learning we could not only examine responses to each of these ten variables separately but cross-refer also, to check what kind of interaction was at work between play and association or play or subsistence. Eighteen possibilities would provide us with a more structured view of that particular culture. Looking then to each of his 10 Primary Message Systems, we have;

- Interaction, i.e. interaction with the environment through language or any of the five human senses.
- Association, i.e. grouping and structuring of society.
- Subsistence, i.e. feeding, working, making a living.
- Bisexuality, i.e. differentiation of roles along the lines of sex.
- Territoriality, i.e. possession, use and defence of space and territory.
- Temporality, i.e. use, allocation, and division of time.
- Learning, i.e. adoptive process of learning and instruction.
- Play, i.e. relaxation, leisure.
- Defence, i.e. protection to include medicine, welfare, and law.

- Exploitation, i.e. turning the environment to man's use through technology, construction and extraction of minerals.

An understanding of any civilisation could therefore be attained through a study of the interaction of any single one on the above list, with any other.

This attempt at using matrices to explain culture was developed further by Farmer and Richman who (Reference 6) expanded the number of variables examined to 77. As a firm moved abroad, factors which were previously held constant – e.g. labour law or contract law – became variable as the firm found itself working within an individual framework in each country in which it was represented. Such differences could have an important effect upon relative costs, influencing sourcing of inputs; forcing changes in production, marketing or financial processes; or by restricting price changes of outputs.

These variables could be identified as falling within four categories: economic; political-legal; sociological-cultural; and educational. Farmer and Richman define an environmental constraint as

some factor which prevents a firm from performing in a given way. The term 'constraint' implies some limitation of action, usually in the negative sense. . . . In one sense, every environmental factor is a constraint. One cannot have everything, and the limiting factors are the constraints referred to here.

Some of these variables have a direct effect as when there is a law relating to the employment of women or children. The second kind of impact which these variables have is in relation to the decisions and activities of managers. Managers are a product of their own culture, they argue, and their attitudes and perceptions are based on prior experience which, in turn, is in large part determined by the educational and sociological setting in which they have lived. The self-reference criteria, we mentioned earlier. These research findings help us to understand and to put parameters on culture, but culture still does not help us with an understanding of markets. Could one differentiate between markets as between cultures? To some extent, this question was answered by Barnhill and Lawson who developed (Reference 7) a theory of modern markets characterising markets as follows:

1. *Markets are purposive.* Exchange transactions are entered into and consummated primarily because participants to the exchange are seeking to achieve some purpose or self-interest. Exchanges are made to gain value, be that value in the form of personal, family or tribal sustenance; individual or corporate wealth; sales; market share; profits or some other purpose or desired conditions.

2. *Markets are allocative.* Markets are initiated by the desire of bodies to re-allocate their value, e.g. goods for other goods, goods for services, goods for money, etc. Markets provide means and stimulate activities that distribute goods, services, money, and other media of exchange.

3. *Markets are active.* While market potential and other latent conditions are ascribed to markets, interactive exchanges involving co-operation, competition, and conflict provide the overt characteristics of markets. These

overt characteristics are necessary for classifying, organising systematically, expressing quantitatively, and for predicting and controlling marketing.

4. *Markets involve operative activities or functions*. While an extensive list of functions characteristic of exchange transactions can be developed, four fundamental functions are production, finance, distribution, and promotion.

5. *Markets tend to function in the form of exchange flows* at various levels of complexity, e.g. dyads, processes, and systems. In a single dyadic transaction there is a two-way flow of value, typically manifested by the movement of goods, services, money or other items of value between the two participants. Except where ultimate consumption occurs, exchanges seldom are limited to a single dyadic transaction. The flows inherent in market transactions continue as an on-going process that, in total or in aggregate, take on the attributes of more complex systems.

6. *Markets are dynamic*. Markets reflect the dynamics and complexity of exchange transactions and the conditions surrounding those transactions. The source of these dynamics can be identified as: (a) environmental, i.e. those forces and conditions that influence market participants but are outside their control; (b) transactional, i.e. those influences resulting from the exchange between and/or among the participants or a mega-body to the transaction; and (c) participant, i.e. those influences emanating, from time to time, from the parties involved in exchange transactions. Each of these sources may have a direct or indirect dynamic influence on exchange transaction(s) or the market(s) functions.

7. *Markets are constrained or inhibited*. Markets are not free or unfettered. They are constrained or inhibited by various forces and influences – among them being the ecology; resources; socio-cultural conditions; technology; economy; competition; and political, governmental, legal, and participant influences.

A set of 10 inhibitors were then identified:

- ecology
- resources
- economy
- technology
- competition

- socio-cultural forces
- political influences
- legal influences
- governmental influences
- organisational influences.

These ten were then related to three stages of market activity – viz. entry, performance, and exit – in addition to four market functions – viz. production, finance, distribution, and promotion.

However, this still leaves one important part of culture: the meaning and identification of cultural signs. The notion that all the seemingly disparate products of society work together to create a cultural framework has given rise to a new area of research which business is turning to, and has been termed semiotics.

Semiotics (Reference 8), derived from the Greek word *semeion* or 'sign', is the art of identifying and deciphering cultural signs in advertising, fashion, music, literature, politics, mores, etc. and the hidden messages they emit. The study of semiotics was begun by the Swiss linguist

Ferdinand de Saussure and the American philosopher Charles S. Peirce about 80 years ago, and was heavily influenced by the work of French anthropologist, Claude Levi-Strauss. Semiotics is said to have come to prominence following the English translation of Roland Barthes' *Mythologies*. In essence, every positive trend will eventually give rise to a negative trend and so to take one example, the problems of inner-city living will create an interest in small-town and rural life. Pursuing this line of thought further, according to semiotics there can be no creativity in advertising as we are simply borrowing themes from our everyday experience, e.g. nostalgia and togetherness, and so we are not creating them. The semiotician (the practitioner of Semiotics) and the advertising executive differ in that the semiotician believes that one must relate to more than one cultural sign. It is indeed likely that in future years, more will be heard about semiotics in international business activity.

Economic environment

A macro-environment is created when trade and transactions take place across, rather than within, national frontiers; but it is important to note that there may well be greater economic environmental differences between different parts of the same country than between countries belonging to the same geographical region. Many countries exhibit this, e.g. Italy has great poverty in the south whilst Britain's most affluent sector of the population is in the south of England. There are large gaps between disposable incomes and prices in these areas and those elsewhere in the same country. This is a marketing problem, but these differences pose both problems and opportunities for foreign firms.

With regard to the economic environment, very often the constraints which are imposed upon foreign firms are in the form of tariff barriers or, increasingly 'non-tariff' or 'invisible' barriers such as health and safety standards, hygiene standards, etc. The rationale behind these measures is simply to stem the flow of imports into the country, and sometimes also to protect an infant indigenous industry from the pressures of overseas competition flooding into the home market.

General Agreement on Tariffs and Trade (GATT)

The General Agreement on Tariffs and Trade (GATT) has done much since its inception in 1948 to reduce tariff barriers but each of its negotiating 'rounds' has lasted an average of nine years which illustrates clearly the difficulties involved in freeing trade. The most recent, the Tokyo Round, was the most difficult because negotiations were already taking place in a changed world trading situation moving further into recession and towards protectionism. Examples of protectionism abound in the practices of industrial countries *vis-a-vis* the less developed nations of the world.

There are now 88 member countries of GATT which account for four-fifths of world trade. The basis of GATT is that trade should not be discriminatory and that preference should be given to the developing countries which account for two-thirds of the membership. Under the terms of GATT membership, nations agree to apply their most favourable or lowest tariff rate to fellow GATT signatories, but within GATT it is possible still to have preferential tariff rates. There is a basic GATT signatory tariff rate but also a preferential rate which the UK, for example, may wish to use to encourage trade with Commonwealth countries, particularly the less developed countries. Much Favoured Nation (MFN) status is the highest degree of preferential treatment that may be accorded to a fellow GATT signatory and is accorded on a bilateral basis. The Soviet Union failed a few years ago to receive MFN status when the Carter Administration was unable to get the measure through Congress, where it ran aground over criticism of human rights within the Soviet Union. Subsequently, the Reagan Administration withdrew MFN status from East European countries as a result of the imposition of martial law in Poland. MFN status may be seen then to have become a political means of rewarding or punishing countries.

The EEC, now accounting in itself for 44 per cent of world trade, is divided amongst its members. The EEC has its own famous surpluses of agricultural produce and so is unable to make concessions in the way of trade for developing countries which are crop dependent. The situation for both industrial and less developed countries has been exacerbated by the world trade recession, in which agriculture looks likely to tear down the structure of GATT itself. The GATT Council, meanwhile, appears impotent, lacking consensus amongst its members to take any firm action that cannot be easily circumvented. A blend of hostility and apathy combine to ensure that GATT continues to serve as no more than a workshop for ideas on trade liberalisation.

Table 2.2
Tariff on agricultural tractors

Country	Tariff on goods from EEC	Tariff of goods into EEC
India	60 per cent; plus import licence	zero
Turkey	55 per cent	zero
S. Africa	40 per cent (zero if without engine)	10.9 per cent
Poland	35 per cent	10.9 per cent
Brazil	30 per cent; plus import licence	zero
Argentina	30 per cent; Import licence subject to local manufacturers' agreement	10.9 per cent
Mexico	30 per cent; import licence	zero
Romania	30 per cent	zero
Spain	17.3 per cent; plus quota restriction on smaller vehicles	4.3 per cent
Yugoslavia	16 per cent	zero
Pakistan	15 per cent; Import licence	zero

Note EEC zero rate is under generalised system of preferences, subject to certain specifications. Turkey has zero-rating by special arrangement.
Source Massey Ferguson

Non-tariff barriers (NTB)

These are becoming increasingly more common. As GATT continues to fight for the reduction of tariffs worldwide, sovereign states apply their ingenuity to the creation of 'invisible tariffs'. These may take many forms but their ultimate aim is to exclude, or at least stem the flow of, foreign imports of any given good political sensitive item. NTBs may take the following forms:

1. Quotas and trade control. Once the quota is filled, the price mechanism is not allowed to operate.
2. Discriminatory governmental and private procurement policies, e.g. 'buying national'.
3. Restrictive customs procedures, reducing the number of ports of entry for any given good. Examples are given later.
4. Selective monetary controls and discriminatory exchange rate policies, e.g. the requirement for an advance deposit equal to the value of the imported goods.
5. Restrictive administrative and technical regulation.

'Buy national' policies

It is a common enough phenomenon to find companies pursuing an implicit or explicit 'buy national' policy. Governments do likewise as they have to consider the employment effects of sourcing. They also have to consider the national interest in the placing of any orders for defence equipment or for products resulting from a research programme that has been heavily funded by government finance. Local government authorities often also choose to exercise their political right to choose suppliers of equipment on such bases as these. What has changed is that some very large companies such as British Leyland are moving towards single sourcing of components. This makes open-tender contracts more lucrative and the loss of such contracts can have a serious impact on the firms involved. EEC regulations, which came into force in early 1981, are now being used to challenge the status quo and open up competitive bidding to outsiders.

Accusations still continue unabated of 'dirty' business regarding government grants to companies who buy national, etc. In 1982, Burroughs, for example, brought a court action against the Oxford Regional Health Authority which awarded a contract to ICL Computers Ltd for a pilot half million pound deal leading to an eventual 16 million pound deal. The British Government is then said to have stepped in and recommended ICL for the contract. Unsubstantiated evidence which had come the way of Burroughs had indicated that they had won the contract on both price and performance and that ICL had come last of the bidders for the contract. The fact was that ICL were now being awarded the contract. Burroughs then took the matter to the High Court and to the Appeal Court but lost their action on each occasion, the courts refusing to award an injunction to halt the contract as they believed that it would be impossible to police

Table 2.3

Tariff averages* on industrial products (excluding petroleum†) for ten developed markets before and after the implementation of the Tokyo Round agreements

Market	Simple average			Weighted average‡		
	Pre-Tokyo round	post-Tokyo round	Per cent reduced	Pre-Tokyo round	post-Tokyo round	Per cent reduced
United States	12.1	7.0	42	6.2	4.4	30
European Community	8.1	5.6	31	6.6	4.8	27
Japan**	10.2	6.0	41	5.2	2.6	49
Canada	12.4	7.2	42	12.7	7.9	38
Sweden	5.9	4.8	19	5.2	4.3	23
Norway	8.5	6.5	23	4.2	3.2	23
Switzerland	3.8	2.8	26	3.2	2.5	23
New Zealand	26.2	20.0	24	22.4	17.6	21
Austria	11.6	8.1	30	9.0	7.8	13
Finland	13.0	11.2	14	6.0	4.8	20
Total	10.6§	6.5§	38	7.2§	4.9§	33

*The comparability of tariff levels, and of their practical incidence, is affected by differences in methods of valuation for customs purposes. The tariff averages set out in the table cover duty-free items.
†Items CCN 2709 and 2710 are excluded.
‡Here the simple average on each tariff line is weighed by each market's MFN imports on that line. In due course the GATT Secretariat will no doubt calculate weighted averages on the basis of total world trade in each tariff item.
**After implementing the Kennedy Round agreement Japan reduced her tariffs unilaterally by 20 per cent across-the-board.
§Weighted by the trade of each country.
Source Euro-Asia Business Review, February 1985, p. 41.

'. . . as it would involve tracing the thought processes of the Authority's members, were they to meet again and confirm the ICL contract'.

Another similar case arose over the award of a 14 million pound contract by the Severn Trent Water Authority to ICL. This time it was over the heads of IBM who then sought in the High Court an order to require the Authority to review its decision, alleging that the Authority had violated its own rules and criteria. The Severn Trent Water Authority did decide to meet and review the decision but only ratified the contract that had already been awarded to ICL. Being a semi-autonomous body, it was also outside the EEC regulations on competitive bidding. Whilst accepting this, IBM, then left with no shots to fire, pointed out that it was a ratepayer in the Water Authority area and that it was protecting ratepayers' interests.

Trade classification

Approximately two-thirds of all world trade is now conducted under tariffs based on the Brussels Trade Nomenclature (exceptions are the USA, Canada and Japan). Although widespread in use there is a constant flow of new products and new materials constantly being introduced into manufacturing processes which bring with them new problems of classification.

Duties

Import duties include the following:

1. *Ad valorem*. This is a percentage of the value of the goods, calculated on the landed CIF cost at port of entry.
2. *Specific duty*. This is a specific amount of currency per weight, volume, length, or number of units of measurement. It is expressed in the currency of the importing country.
3. *Alternative duty*. Applicable rate is that which yields the higher amount of duty.
4. *Component or mixed duties*.
5. *Countervailing duties or variable import levies* are used to increase the price of imported goods to domestic levels.
6. *Temporary import surcharges*. Under GATT rules these must only be temporary. This device has been used in the past by Britain and by the US.
7. *Compensatory import taxes*. Manufacturers in VAT countries do not pay VAT on exports to non-VAT countries but all US manufacturers still pay and have no tax relief from the tax equivalent in the US.
8. Anti-dumping duties.

Dumping

Anti-dumping regulations are aimed at preventing the sale of products in one country at prices lower than those fixed in the country of origin. Dumping may be of three types:

1. *Sporadic* – where it makes better commercial sense to unload surplus abroad at advantageous prices rather than on the home market where discounts once offered would create a precedent for future behaviour.
2. *Predatory* – when foreign producers use low prices to weaken indigenous competition abroad. Accusations of hidden governmental subsidies have been levelled against Italian producers of refrigerators and washing machines. These subsidiaries support a low price structure and allow the company to buy market share abroad.
3. *Persistent* – the continued sales of products at prices lower than those of its country of origin. The case of Polish exports of electric golf-carts to the USA illustrates the difficulty in implementing these regulations. Firstly, Poland does not have golf courses nor need for electric golf-carts so there was no comparable domestic price which in any event would be distorted, because in a communist country all prices are politically set and need not bear any relation to their material or labour costs.

Generally, the most contentious imports for a nation to receive are steel, textiles and agricultural produce together with basic industrial chemicals such as ethylene or soda ash, which would also come under this close political scrutiny.

The US International Trade Commission imposed a 40 per cent duty on some EEC steel producers; whilst the EEC joined together to forestall imports of steel from Eastern Europe. At the same time, Britain, for example, reserves the right to impound any ship found to be discharging steel products within its territorial waters. Sanctions when applied are meant to be punitive, and it is interesting in this regard to note the role of the EEC which acts on behalf of all members of the community. The EEC imposed dumping duties of up to 33 per cent on Japanese makers of hydraulic excavators on models from 6 to 35 tonnes, following complaints from eighteen European manufacturers. Japan's market share in the UK excavator market has risen from negligible in the late 1970s to 40 per cent in 1984, during which time the British company Ruston Bucyrus left the market and Hymac and Priestman went into liquidation. The judgement delivered in March 1985 imposed 33 per cent on Kobelco-Kobe Steel; 27 per cent on Komatsu; 22 per cent on Mitsubishi Heavy Industries; 12 per cent on Hitachi and 3 per cent on Japan Steel Works.

With textiles the problem has been that the industrial countries have been successful in selling the machinery to the less developed countries who quickly start to produce lower cost textiles and in higher volumes than our indigenous textiles industry, and so in a very short space of time, direct competition ensues. When it became apparent that an industry response was required in Western Europe, to meet this damaging threat, a body known as CIRFS emerged. This body is known by its French initials but is in fact a European man-made fibre producers' association, and has acted to reduce West European capacity from 2.9 million tonnes in 1979/80 to a projected 2.4 million tonnes by 1984/5.

It may be alleged too, that dumping incorporates hidden subsidies from its home government, perhaps in manufacturing location, selective employment assistance, etc. As these subsidies reduce factor costs, they also reduce final price, hence the occurrence of dumping. Dumping only occurs, though, if the goods are sold at one price in the home market, and another in the foreign market. Whilst the EEC will institute anti-dumping measures on behalf of its member states, it will nevertheless 'dump' butter and other surplus dairy products in the Soviet Union because (a) agricultural prices have to be protected within the Community and (b) storage costs for butter and beef mountains and milk and wine lakes are high. To the Soviet Union, with its centralised inefficient agricultural system, it is a windfall. For the EEC it is a temporary respite. See Figure 2.2.

In textiles Britain has reduced its production capacity by 41 per cent; West Germany by 22 per cent; France by 40 per cent but Italy has in fact increased its production capacity by 8 per cent since its textiles production is located in the very poor south of the country. In 1985, US nylon, polyester, and acrylic were kept out of Europe, and particularly the UK, by a strong dollar. When the dollar was weak in 1980, US fibre flooded the UK and led to the closure of the ICI plant at Kilroot, Courtaulds at Carrickfergus, and DuPont at Maydown – all in Northern Ireland. When the dollar improves this threat can easily re-emerge.

The EEC concluded new agreements in 1982 with 25 leading Third

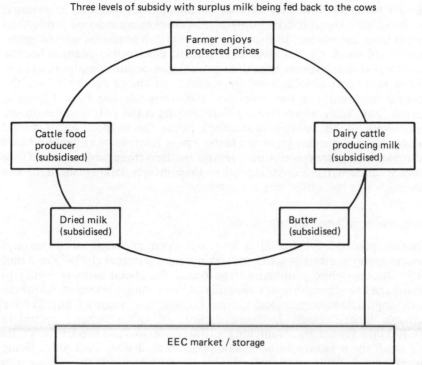

Three levels of subsidy with surplus milk being fed back to the cows

Figure 2.2 EEC milk: a model of EEC efficiency?

Note After a number of revolutions of this cycle, deposits begin to build up and surpluses accrue, which usually have to be off-loaded onto the world market at a loss.

World textile exporters. It took two years of negotiation to conclude the new Multi-fibre agreement, to stay in force until mid-1986. The only country not to have initialled an agreement with the EEC is Argentina, but there will now be unilateral controls on Argentinian exports. The British Textile Confederation was particularly concerned at exports from the Mediterranean countries in general and from Turkey in particular, and also China. In the case of three dominant suppliers – Hong Kong, South Korea, and Macao – the new regulations provide for a 7–8 per cent cut from 1982 levels on the import of T-shirts, jeans, and certain other clothing products. In a Commons statement the Minister for Trade, Mr Peter Rees, announced that for the UK, the annual rate of growth for the eight most sensitive textile and clothing products between 1983 and 1986 will be substantially below 1 per cent.

Agriculture is a contentious topic within the EEC as overproduction means that surpluses have either to be stored, destroyed, or exported by means of subsidies. GATT is facing pressure over this question but it is being argued that the disciplines of industrial trade cannot be applied to agriculture as the products and technology are different. While demands then are made for some new international committee or forum to examine the question, those countries enjoying surpluses in agricultural production benefit from the market disarray to exploit their commercial advantage on a unilateral basis. Organisation may lead to unpalatable changes for the developed countries with regard to prices, competition and perhaps the ending of export subsidies on agricultural produce. In the EEC, the farming community is too powerful and overprotected by a Common Agricultural Policy which ensures that farming is the only industry in the Community to be assured guaranteed prices for output. The US and Canada have important grain interests. These interests may well find that their own self-interest is not best served by 'free trade' and are therefore likely to abstain from anything other than merely talking about it, but preferably not too often, nor for too long.

Does anyone still practise 'free trade'?

Whether professing belief in a free and open exchange of goods and services many in effect practise something quite different. In 1983 and into 1985, Britain, while professing 'free trade', has been actively trying to discourage French exports of milk and has been using hygiene standards to block importation at the docks. The French, too, pursued an effective 'invisible tariff' against Japanese exports of video cassette recorders (VCRs) into France by channelling all Japanese-sourced exports of VCRs to a small town known to be ill-equipped to deal with the traffic. Being undermanned, this caused interminable delays which was the precise aim of the policy. This was effective in persuading the Japanese manufacturers into coming to a form of accommodation with the French.

In theory, neither France nor Britain, as members of the EEC, have the unilateral right to impose tariffs as these are decided now by the EEC Commission in Brussels. The system works in the following way. Each member state has an anti-dumping unit which collects information and sends it to Brussels, which then decides on official action for the Community as a whole. In some rather sensitive areas, such as steel, agreement is easily reached; in others, where one member may be benefiting at the expense perhaps of another, agreement on action is delayed. In practice, unilateral action continues to exist. Britain has a voluntary restraint agreement with the Japanese car manufacturers restricting them to 11 per cent of the market; France has a similar understanding whereby they revealed that their market research showed that the Japanese could not hope for more than 7 per cent of the French market! The case indeed of 'an iron hand in a velvet glove', but these are illustrations only of a much greater and more general *malaise*.

Moving to finance, another important facet of trade (discussed more fully in Chapter 7), twenty-six countries including the Western industrial-ised nations established in 1934 the regulatory framework of the Berne Union to try to prevent a disastrous 1930s-style price war taking place between rival government-backed export credit guarantees departments and their lines of credit. In theory, this meant that Hermes, the export-credit guarantee body in West Germany, could not offer lower terms than say the Export Credit Guarantee Department (ECGD) of Britain but they could match ECGD terms where these may be lower. Here was the danger. ECGD insists on British content in the lines of credit which they insure, Hermes and others are much less strict. Where the companies involved are also multinational, the bidding situation develops where one country is set against another for the prize of winning perhaps a large export order. Precedents once established cannot easily be forgotten. Nevertheless, the multinationals may exercise choice as regards which country should deal with which markets, and obviously will choose to base their business on the more accommodating countries.

To restore order to what was becoming a 'merry-go-round' with each Western partner bidding one against the other, the Western nations met in summit in 1977. As this was in breach of existing conventions, the meeting was therefore under the aegis of OECD, but due to the pressures of finding profitable trade in a recession, these meetings have been taking place rather regularly and as they have been successful in finding agreement between themselves over export finance, this grouping of the Western industrialised states has become known as the 'Consensus'. The Consensus sets minimum interest rates and maximum lengths of credit for a wide range of capital goods sold on officially supported credit terms of two years or more.

The framework of the 'Consensus' has now evolved to the degree where it was asked by the US to implement higher interest rate charges for the

Table 2.4
Consensus guidelines on the cost and duration of official credit

	Importing country (per cent)		
	Relatively Rich	intermediate	relatively Poor
Minimum payment by delivery	15	15	15
Minimum interest rates for credits between two and five years inclusive	7¾	7¼	7¼
Minimum interest rates for credits over five years	8	7¾	7½
Minimum credit period (years)	5–8½	8½	10
Minimum interest rates for credits between two and five years inclusive	7¾	7¼	7¼
Maximum credit period (years)*	5–8½	8½	10

*Only for very large projects will ECGD agree terms exceeding five years credit or if there is evidence that such terms are being offered by foreign competitors with official credit insurance of equivalent support other than through an aid programme.
Note Certain specific types of capital equipment, for example aircraft (including helicopters), nuclear power plant and ships will remain subject to special arrangements outside of the Consensus guidelines.
Source Bank of England, *Money for Exports*, London, 1979, p. 77.

Soviet Union and its East European allies as a political retaliation for the invasion of Afghanistan. Politics can never be far removed when trade is taking place across two ideologies.

In the same way as a company may be impelled forward to trade, so it is with nation states aware of the advantages accruing to their balance of payments and of the potential for gaining international goodwill, image, and prestige. The 1970s, which will be known as the period of East-West *détente*, revealed increasing opportunities for Western trade with the Eastern bloc while the atmosphere remained cool and relaxed. This created many joint ventures between partners in the East and West who were, on the face of it, ideologically polar opposites but in effect united in the aim of earning profits. Since then, relations have deteriorated. On the political level, it is no longer acceptable to deal with these states whilst, on the economic level, one must note that a few at least – such as Poland, Hungary, and Romania – are in sufficient financial difficulties to prevent any significant levels of trade taking place even if the will was there.

Article 80 of the Treaty of Rome is supposed to prohibit any measures in defiance of free trade within the EEC area. In the case of the US which ironically, earns less than 10 per cent of GDP from foreign trade, domestic legislation while national in character has always had international ramifications. The Foreign Corrupt Practices Act, for example, applies to companies with an American Stock Exchange listing; therefore many multinationals from different countries of origin will find themselves under the jurisdiction of this legislation which relates to acts of bribery and corruption abroad, in fact anywhere the company may operate. It can and does mean that a company will be pilloried for activities viewed as 'unseemly' from a home American viewpoint but which may be totally in keeping with the commercial life in the country concerned. Bribery and corruption, whilst emotive words in the West, may be meaningless to many local nationals of the less developed countries.

Yet another development which has arisen in the economic environment of the last 10 years has been increased government activity in enticing foreign investment into its boundaries by means of tax holidays, low-cost factory buildings, low-interest loans or grants, and employment subsidies. Governments are becoming more involved and, as they do, are demanding a say in the running of operations which are based within their jurisdiction. This has meant a sharp increase in the number of countries now seeking joint ventures with local partners rather than 100 per cent direct foreign investment. Whereas previously Japan was the only country actively pursuing the benefits of foreign equity and participation but with some degree of local control, there are now a number of developed countries eager for this form of investment.

References

1. Maslow, A. H., *Motivation and Personality*, Harper and Row, 1954, pp. 80–106.
2. Freud, Sigmund, *Interpretation of Dreams*, translated by A. Strachey, Allen and Unwin, 1955.

3. Herzberg, F., *Work and the Nature of Man*, William Collins, 1966.
4. Ouchi, William, *Theory Z – How American Business can Meet the Japanese Challenge*. Addison-Wesley, 1981.
5. Hall, Edward T., 'The Silent Language in Overseas Business', *Harvard Business Review*, May/June 1960, pp. 87–96.
6. Farmer, Richard N. and Richman, Barry M., *International Business – An Operational Theory*, Cederwood Press, Bloomington, Indiana, 1971.
7. Barnhill, J. A. and Lawson, W. M., 'Toward a Theory of Modern Markets', *European Journal of Marketing*, vol. 14 no. 1, pp. 50–60.
8. Whalen, B., 'Semiotics: An Art or Powerful Marketing Research Tool?', *Marketing News*, May 13 1983, pp. 8–9.
9. Thompson, Hugh, 'Caught in the Tender Trap', *Marketing*, 12 August 1982, pp. 27–8.

Recommended further reading

John H. Dunning (ed.), *Multinational Enterprises, Economic Structure and Inter-national Competitiveness*, Wiley, 1985.
John M. Stopford and Lewis Turner, *Britain and the Multinationals*, Wiley, 1986.

3. IDENTIFYING INTERNATIONAL MARKETING OPPORTUNITIES

Political risk appreciation

The section which follows exceeds the requirements of the Institute of Marketing Diploma syllabus. However it may lead to a better understanding of identifying market opportunities if this section is read rather than omitted.

Companies may often prefer to operate within their region or within their political and economic bloc. For British companies, the transition has been from the British Empire to the Commonwealth to the EEC. Now in the EEC there are many aspects of indeterminate political risk in dealing with our new partners if we consider, for example, the nationalisation polices of a socialist Mitterand government in France. Political boycotts of the Soviet oil pipeline by the United States created difficulties for Western countries determined to meet their obligations and the Western countries were thwarted by the American refusal to deliver any parts or supplies for this project. During the period of this boycott the British firm of John Brown Engineering were threatened by the US Administration if they did go ahead with their delivery of turbines to the Soviet Union, but threatened with repercussions equally by the British Government if they did not deliver.

Political risk may be obvious where a new government comes into power with fixed and unfavourable ideas of the role of foreign companies in the economy. Political risk may be latent, where, like a slowly burning fuse there is the danger of suddenly and unexpectedly losing one's assets in a possible action in expropriation or nationalisation. Political risk may also be partial in that it may refer particularly to certain sectors of industry and commerce and not others with regard to investment, local national pricing, local content laws, and taxation.

A 'Go-No-Go' study is very often made with regard to a market where the market will be accepted or rejected on the basis of a cursory examination of one or two characteristics, often made by a company employee visiting the foreign market for less than a week and not fully conversant with the local language or customers. It may be appropriate therefore to look at a few more realistic methods for assessing political risk.

Business Environment Risk Index (BERI)

Launched in 1972, the Business Environment Risk Index is the brainchild of Frederich Haner, Associate Professor at the College of Business and

Economics, University of Delaware, USA. BERI (Reference 1) has since expanded into country-specific forecasts and country risk forecasts for international lenders but its basic service is the Global Subscription Service. BERI's Global Subscription Service assesses 48 countries four times per year on 15 economic, political, and financial factors on a scale from 0 to 4. Zero indicates unacceptable conditions for investment in a country; one equates with poor conditions; two with acceptable or average conditions; three with above average conditions; and four with superior conditions. The key factors are individually weighted according to their assessed importance as with ingredients. Thus, if the panellists score a country's political stability at an average of 1.7, this is multiplied by the top weighting of 2.5 and becomes 4.2. Since the total weightings add up to 25, and the top of the rating scale is 4, 100 is the maximum points any one country can score.

At present more than 500 companies use the BERI service which also includes detailed in-depth reports on countries personally visited and assessed by its founder; each quarter 98 unpaid panellists sit down to assess up to 12 countries each.

There are two points worth mentioning here: firstly, BERI tries to get nationals of the country being examined as panel members as they tend generally to be more objective; secondly, to eliminate a bias within the panel the original panel of 34 has been increased to 98 by asking each panellist to find two other panellists. The panellists, however, remain anonymous and unpaid. More recently, the panel has been increased to 170 business, banking, and political specialists. The users of the service are seen to be varied. It may, for example, allow a company to determine more fairly how their managers around the world are performing other than on a profit and loss basis; for example, a manager may be able to hold sales even when the economy is on a downturn, or to evaluate expansion projects and new investment possibilities, to decide whether and where to conclude licensing and trade agreements.

It is also worth pointing out that not every country in the West has the same number of people reporting on it, so Haner has started a computer programme which tests each statistic and sends out an alarm if there are inadequate statistics for any country. Since major investment decisions require three or four months deliberation, panellists try to predict nine months or a year ahead. Panellists receive their sheet back every quarter and if they wish to change their assessment of any country they simply mark over the old ratings with a red pencil. Total points is a possible 100 but a country that rates 80 or more has a very advanced economy plus an environment favourable to foreign investors. A score of over 70 would also imply an advanced economy, but not so favourable an investment climate. The range between 55 and 70 embraces developing countries with investment potential, but also includes '. . . a few mature economies having mentalities not fully compatible with modern business'. The next level, 40 to 55, includes high risk countries which sometimes offer profits in relation to the risks. But even when potential earnings are in proportion to the risk, the quality of management 'has to be superior to realise potential'.

Table 3.1
Business Environment Risk Index

MAIL TO:
F. T. Haner
P. O. Box 4697
Newark, Del.
1971 USA.

	Political stability	Attitude – foreign investor & profits	Nationalisation	Monetary inflation	Balance of payments	Bureaucratic delays	Economic growth	Currency convertibilist	Enforceability of contracts	Labour cost/productivity	Professional services & contracts	Communications – tele mail, air, telex	Local mgt. & partners	Short-term credit	Long-term loans/venture capital	Negative Adjustment:* Worker Co-determination Impact on Profits
Rate up to 12 countries. Identify any 6 for weight	3	1½	1½	1½	1½	1	2½	2½	1½	2	½	1	1	2	2	
	1	2	3	4	5	6	7	8	9	10	11	12	13	14	15	0 1 2 3 4

AMERICAS: 9
1 Canada
2 Mexico
3 United States
4 Argentina
5 Brazil
6 Chile
7 Colombia
8 Peru
9 Venezuela

ASIA/AUSTRALASIA: 14   0 1 2 3 4
10 Australia
11 China (Taiwan)
12 Indonesia
13 Japan
14 Korea
15 Malaysia
16 Philippines
17 Singapore
18 India
19 Iran
20 Israel
21 Lebanon
22 Pakistan
23 Turkey

EUROPE/AFRICA: 20   0 1 2 3 4
24 Belgium
25 Denmark
26 France
27 Ireland
28 Italy
29 Germany (West)
30 Greece
31 Netherlands
32 Norway
33 Portugal
34 Spain
35 Sweden
36 Switzerland
37 United Kingdom
38 Kenya
39 Libya
40 Morocco
41 Nigeria
42 South Africa
43 Egypt

New Countries: 0 1 2 3 4
44 Equador
45 Saudi Arabia

Ratings: 0 – Unacceptable conditions
      1 – Poor conditions   3 – Above average conditions
      2 – Acceptable or average conditions   4 – Superior conditions

*Give a number on the 1–4 scale for your impression of worker co-determination's impact on profits from operations in the country being rated.

With a score below 40 it would take a very unusual situation to justify the commitment of capital. Generally, ratings do not change very much nor very quickly, although Chile and Venezuela have proved to be exceptions.

Despite the growing importance of Eastern Europe as a trading bloc BERI do not presently rate Poland nor any of the other East European countries and do not plan to do so in the future.

The Country Environmental Temperature Gradient

In a study ostensibly of the marketing middleman – the agent – in international business (Reference 2), two Canadian researchers, Litvak and Banting, prepared a classification system of country environmental factors on a temperature gradient whereby when the temperature was 'too hot' the agent would find himself pushed towards new institutional structures in order to survive. The variables which Litvak and Banting identified were: the nature of the product; concentration of customers; intensity of competition; resources of the middleman; market potential; degree of industrialisation; cultural, linguistic, and geographical distance; legislation; and degree of political stability.

It was found to be the case that agents will be used: the greater the degree of political volatility; the greater the degree of cultural, linguistic and geographic, distance; and the greater the degree of legislation relating to foreign investment.

Countries were defined as being 'hot' where the market was dynamic and the agent was forced to adapt to meet the needs of the market. A market was 'cold' where there was less competition, and the agent is allowed complete freedom of movement. The variables of classification as to whether a country is 'hot', 'moderate' or 'cold' are as follows: political stability; market opportunity; economic development and performance; cultural unity; legal barriers; physiographic barriers (obstacles created by the physical landscape); geo-cultural distance.

Table 3.2
Country environmental temperature gradient

Degree of environmental characteristics	*Hot country*	*Moderate country*	*Cold country*
Political stability	High	Medium	Low
Market opportunity	High	Medium	Low
Economic development and performance	High	Medium	Low
Cultural unity	High	Medium	Low
Legal barriers	Low	Medium	High
Physiographic barriers	Low	Medium	High
Geo-cultural barriers	Low	Medium	High

Source Litvak and Banting.

Taking an example of an agent in Canada, a score may emerge of five 'hot' and two 'moderate' variables which would place Canada as relatively 'hot'. An example of an agent in South Africa may reveal four 'cold' and three 'moderate' variables which would place South Africa as relatively 'cold'. It is emphasised, however, that all such ratings will of course change over time. The positioning on the gradient scale is approximate but finer calibration is possible with the introduction of further subjective weights. The gradient scale shows the susceptibility of agents to change, and also predicts how the institutional structure is most likely to evolve. A firm operating with heavily committed investments in a 'hot' country may be guided by this gradient to relinquish control if the environment becomes 'cooler'.

The gradient depends upon continual auditing. However, it does suggest the favourability of new markets and the ease with which their opportunities may be realised; the degree of control the foreign principal can exercise; and the degree of local control in the planning and development of operations in the foreign country.

This threefold classification (hot-moderate-cold) of countries using seven environmental factors on a hot-cold scale has since been further developed. Firstly, as a guide to long-range planning, it presents a method of allocating scarce resources selectively. Secondly, it specifies both the magnitude and type of foreign investment involvement depending upon the 'temperature' of a country. Thirdly, the conceptual framework neatly summarises the evolutionary process of emergence of a multinational enterprise from a single export house. Finally, the framework suggests how a large body of secondary data or environmental factors can be effectively utilised to undertake long-range planning.

The following shortcomings of the Litvak-Banting model were identified by Sheth and Lutz (Reference 3) before proceeding to describe their own multivariate model within the Litvak-Banting framework.

- No analytical framework is developed to transform values into the gradient of 'hotness'.
- The operational indicators from secondary data banks are not described.
- The threefold classification is judgmental and arbitrary rather than empirically derived.
- There is no weighting attached to the individual environmental factors.
- Market opportunity, being specific to an industry or product, is different from the other six variables. This factor requires primary data whereas the other six can utilise secondary sources of information.

The Sheth-Lutz model classifies countries on six factors and then investigates the market potential in those countries which appear to be most promising for foreign investment. To do this, Sheth and Lutz used three data sources related to 1961–2 which give profiles of 82 countries including China and the USSR, this left 80 countries which were then examined from the point of view of US corporate foreign investment. Fifteen variables were finally selected which related to the six environmen-

Table 3.3
The 'hot-cold' gradient from US viewpoint

Country	Value	Country	Value
USA	13.22	Venezuela	−0.40
UK	4.60	Panama	−0.41
W Germany	3.44	Costa Rica	−0.47
France	2.64	Turkey	−0.47
Netherlands	2.12	Bulgaria	−0.47
Canada	2.01	Ecuador	−0.52
Belgium	2.00	Libya	−0.60
Denmark	1.44	Bolivia	−0.61
Italy	1.32	Philippines	−0.64
Taiwan	1.16	Egypt	−0.72
Japan	1.13	Peru	−0.73
Sweden	1.13	Lebanon	−0.80
Poland	0.93	Haiti	−0.88
Switzerland	0.86	Guatemala	−0.93
Ireland	0.83	Liberia	−0.94
Argentina	0.81	Ceylon	−0.97
Australia	0.76	Albania	−0.99
Norway	0.73	Thailand	−1.00
Austria	0.73	Mongolia	−1.07
E Germany	0.72	Paraguay	−1.13
Mexico	0.58	N Korea	−1.16
Finland	0.47	Iran	−1.23
Brazil	0.46	Indonesia	−1.23
New Zealand	0.40	S Korea	−1.24
Czechoslovakia	0.33	Ethiopia	−1.25
Spain	0.23	Cambodia	−1.28
Colombia	0.22	Saudi Arabia	−1.31
Greece	0.16	Syria	−1.32
Hungary	0.05	S Africa	−1.33
Portugal	−0.00	S Vietnam	−1.37
Uruguay	−0.13	Jordan	−1.42
Yugoslavia	−0.16	Iraq	−1.44
Honduras	−0.16	Pakistan	−1.52
El Salvador	−0.17	Burma	−1.55
Chile	−0.18	Israel	−1.57
India	−0.19	N Vietnam	−1.62
Nicaragua	−0.23	Nepal	−1.68
Cuba	−0.26	Afghanistan	−1.86
Dominican Rep	−0.29	Laos	−1.89
Romania	−0.29	Yemen	−1.99

Source Sheth and Lutz.

tal factors. Political stability is indicated by governmental stability, freedom from group opposition and political incultivation. Cultural unity is represented by religious, racial, and linguistic homogeneity, each on a three-point scale. Economic development and performance is reflected by economic development on a four-point scale; and energy consumption in megawatt hours. Legal barriers are indicated by two indirect variables. The first is the level of imports and exports measured in millions of US dollars. It is argued that a greater degree of international trade will be present in a country characterised by fewer legal barriers, and vice versa. Similarly, the second variable is the level of tariff on imports as a percentage of the total value of imports. Again, the greater the number of legal barriers, the more likely it is to find a higher levy of tariffs, and vice versa. Physiographic barriers are also included, although indirectly, by the three models of transportation. It is assumed that the greater the physiographic barriers present in a country due to mountains, deserts, and rivers the less will be the density of air, road, and railroad transports. By simultaneously taking into account all the three major surface and aerial methods of transportation, we presume that substitution effects among them, if any, are included. Finally, geo-cultural distance is measured in two ways, both of which are related primarily to the distance of a country from the US – the first measure is an index of Westernisation on a six-point scale; the second is the air distance from the United States:

The multivariate method which follows, resembles factor analysis except that:

(a) In factor analysis, typically the interest is in the correlational structure among variables (R-type factor analysis) whereas in our model the interest is in the structure among countries (Q-type factor analysis).

(b) Typically factor analysis is performed as a correlation matrix. In our model we obtain the rank of the data matrix X through its cross-products matrix.

(c) The emphasis in factor analysis is on the overall parsimony of the data matrix. In our model, parsimony is directly related to the specific viewpoints the researcher is interested in. Accordingly, the rotational procedures may vary between the two methods.

The relative positive values of countries reflect the degree of 'hotness' and the relative negative values of countries reflect the degree of 'coldness' from the viewpoint of US corporate foreign investment.

Generally, advanced countries were found to have the highest 'hot' values. Although Canada and Mexico are closer in geographical proximity, other countries were found to be better candidates for investment purposes. Relative to other countries, Portugal was found to have a zero value from an investment viewpoint. The East European and other Communist countries in Latin America, Africa, and Asia do not systematically cluster together in the cold spectrum of the continuum. For example, Poland (rated 12), East Germany (rated 19), Czechoslovakia (rated 24), and Hungary (rated 28) have positive values. It is somewhat surprising to find that even the 'hottest' country, the UK, is considerably separated on the continuum from the US. This implies that overseas investment in general is more problematic than domestic investment.

Hansz and Goodnow (Reference 4) have further refined the Litvak-Banting model with stepwise multiple discriminant analysis. The 59 variables used in a cluster analysis of 100 'free-world' countries were gathered from published sources and expert opinion. The aim was to determine:

(a) how many unique groups of countries would best portray the 100 countries;
(b) in which group a country belonged;
(c) a statistical profile of the environmental characteristics of each group.

Variables were selected as which best predicted group membership: seven economic and market-opportunity variables, six political and legal variables, three cultural variables, and one physiographic variable. The discriminant model was tested to determine its ability to reproduce the original country groupings. 98 out of 100 countries were classified correctly by the 17-variable discriminant factors. This was a result, firstly, of the country groupings being statistically determined by a 59-variable hierarchical cluster analysis, and, secondly, the model being tested upon the same data that was used to construct it. Overall, the 17-variable discriminant model was found to fare far better than the traditional univariate method of GNP per capita.

Marketing research problems in foreign markets

Conducting market research in one's own country, one enjoys the benefit of a certain degree of familiarity with the nature of the society, its values

Table 3.4
Correlations of corporate behaviour with environmental indicators

Strategy	GNP per capita		Environmental index		
	Variation r^2	explained	Variation r^2	explained	% increase invariance explained
Ranking of countries by % of US Companies entering market	.63	40%	.75	56%	40%
Ranking of countries by % of US Companies going via direct channels given market entry*	.49	24%	.63	40%	67%

*Direct market entry channels include: wholly or partly-owned subsidiaries and branches, licensing agreements and direct export through overseas company owned channels or company sales forces overseas.

Source Hansz and Goodnow, *op. cit.*, p. 194.

Table 3.5
US firms using selected market entry strategies

Market entry strategy	Average 'hot' country	Average 'moderate' country	Average 'cold' country
	Percentage of firms using strategy		
Majority-owned plant	145	6.1	1.5
Combination (majority-owned plants + other strategies)	11.0	2.9	0.7
Export via company-owned overseas channels	19.2	29.9	32.5
Joint venture	3.0	2.2	0.7
Licensing agreement	7.6	4.2	3.5
Combination – Export via company-owned channels, joint venture, and/or licensee and/or less direct exporting	16.4	12.8	10.4
Export via overseas agents or distributors	24.2	35.6	43.4
Combination – Overseas Agents, distributors, indirect exports	0.9	0.7	0.4
Indirect export	2.9	5.3	6.4

Notes
1. Marketing subsidiaries were included as a form of direct export through company-owned overseas facilities.
2. These percentages represent the proportion of US firms employing a particular market entry strategy to a typical country in each respective cluster.
3. Preliminary analysis of the data indicates that the largest companies tend to exercise more control over market entry strategies in all markets than do smaller firms. In fact, respondents in Fortune's 'Top 250' were willing to establish some manufacturing facilities in the 'moderate' cluster whereas most of the remainder of the 750 firms would not. The additional resources of the top 250 firms make it possible for them to take more risks.
Source Hansz and Goodnow.

and laws. Foreign market research is like a great leap into the dark where many variables are unknown unless it is conducted by local nationals in the country concerned. The scope for error is vast, particularly so where a multinational may be enquiring about the local acceptability of a product, concept, service, or slogan currently in use in other parts of the world. 'Come alive with Pepsi' may be a familiar slogan in the English-speaking world but how would the English-speaking manager react upon hearing that his product slogan had been translated as in China (PRC): 'Pepsi reawakens your dead relatives'? Everywhere, careful checking and preparation is everything (Reference 5). Generally, the problems revolve around language, because language is a living thing. The world of commerce is constantly innovating products and language to communicate new product concepts. Information, or the lack of published market information, is a general problem with regard to the developing countries. To take but one example, the population of Nigeria is currently estimated to be between 80 and 120 million people. Curiously, product availability and general market demand conditions are often more easily assessed by personal visit than are national demographic characteristics through delays in the census, errors in the collection, or publication delays. Availability of products and current demand may be more easily gleaned, for example, where trade associations exist but there may also be governmental statistical publications, industry association publications, and outside research and consultancy reports.

Time is required for good market research and familiarity with the market and the product concerned. However, this may be a stated ideal and the pressures on executive time may force a decision to be made upon data which is often incomplete in many respects. One of the most serious problems for a multinational headquarters is the lack of a common statistical base amongst data collected by subsidiaries worldwide. Keegan in his book (Reference 5) illustrates how a confusing array of units of measurement for Pepsi – whether in can, bottle or glass; whether daily, weekly or number of times daily – points to the lack of any coherent standardisation of data within the Pepsico organisation as a whole. Complementarity between statistical bases is one of the single greatest problems of foreign market research. It is interesting to note how the OECD and EEC are making moves towards standardisation. Elsewhere, a consortium of international publishers have produced a Pan-European survey of readership habits and profiles (Reference 6).

Demographic, economic, and social statistics are often not comparable since they are compiled by different agencies for different purposes (Reference 7). To pursue a few of these distortions:

- *Degree of concentration of population.* Figures may be distorted because not all of the land mass is actually habitable, as for example with Japan or Switzerland. Urban concentration will therefore be greater than the national average mean which is smoothed and will inevitably include lakes and mountain ranges in the number per square kilometre.
- *The extent of car ownership.* This may be distorted, firstly, by leasing and, secondly, by the fact that in a country such as Britain, approximately 70 per cent of the car market is accounted for by company cars. Attempts to assess car ownership as against cars per household will yield quite different results, particularly if it is a study of usage.
- *Level of individual prosperity.* Beware again of per capita GNP and also of self-reference criteria that suggest that foreign market X will, with increasing personal incomes, display the same consumer wants and desires as your own domestic market. Firstly, there is the effect of culture. Secondly, there is the infrastructure to be considered – for example, whether there is adequate electricity power supply or simply, maintenance, and repair facilities.
- *Level of female emancipation.* The role of women in society differs

greatly between Europe and North America and, for example, the Middle East. The UK and India have had women as Prime Ministers, whilst in the Middle East women have still to walk cloaked totally in black, behind their husbands. Again educational opportunities, career opportunities, and equality of treatment between the sexes varies greatly between countries. In the extreme, 'the role of women is in the kitchen and the birthing-bed'.

- *Labour supply.* The shortage of labour and/or the cost of labour may not always be too apparent. West Germany in the early 1970s had to import labour but when industrial conditions changed and labour unions began to complain, this method was dropped in favour of contractual joint ventures in Eastern Europe whereby production was secured with none of the attendant problems of immigrant labour. More will be said of this later.
- *Level of industrialisation related to the infrastructure.* It is costly to transfer a general technology; it is simpler and less expensive to transfer industry-specific or product or process technology. Markets must be recognised as being at different economic stages of industrialisation, some actually industrialising, others remaining essentially raw-material supplying countries.
- *Level of retail integration.* This gives some indication as to available channels of distribution, discussed more fully later. Enormous variances exist – from long channels in Japan to short retail channels in France where the hypermarket concept. Note, too, that quantum leaps are possible in development and that France made a quantum leap in retailing, bypassing the supermarket stage directly to hypermarkets. Again, this was aided and abetted by a commercially favourable legal system.

Language creates difficulties particularly with regard to multicultural multilingual questionnaires. A researcher has to be quite certain that data gathered in English will be directly comparable with the same gathered in French data. This involves a great deal of testing and extends the time required for completion, the cost of final completion, and the credibility of the final effort to management.

Where data does not exist that is either timely or specific to the problem in hand, often primary data collection – i.e. fieldwork – has to be undertaken. The costs and time involved cannot be exaggerated.

Where data exists to some degree but there is difficulty in establishing fieldwork, then certain approximation measures have to be turned to and this we shall deal with shortly. There are other sources – the political and economic press of the country concerned; possibly, too, discussions with importers and end-users; and reports of either government departments or trade associations. The dynamism of the market place means that competitors can often find, quite quickly, a lucrative market in an altogether touristically undesirable market. This creates a pressure for competitors to follow into that market without the prior knowledge and information of the leader. A 'bandwagon' effect is created. Companies therefore find themselves in markets, not entirely of their own choosing, simply by following the market leader or other close rivals.

The environment for business we can model as we have already seen but thinking now along functional lines, marketing systems are more difficult to model quantitatively than finance or production systems and for eight reasons (Reference 8).

1. Non-linear relationship
2. Threshold effects
3. Time-lag effects
4. Multivariate relationships
5. Interaction effects
6. Constantly changing environment
7. Competitive responses
8. Measurement problems

These features are not unique to marketing but the frequency and complexity of these eight difficulties is highest in the marketing area.

Table 3.6
Matrix of corporate strategic choices

Products or services / Markets	Present products	Improvement of present products	New products from related technology		New products from unrelated technology
User markets present markets	Market Penetration Strategy (1)	Product Reformulation Strategy (3)	Obsolescence Strategy (5)	Strategy of Extension of Product Line (7)	Strategy of Horizontal Diversification (9)
New markets	Market Development Strategy (2)	Market Extension Strategy Through Product Reformulation (4)	Market Segmentation and Product Differentiation Strategy (6)	Strategy of Concentric Diversification (8)	Diversification Strategy of the Conglomerate Type (10)
Resource and/or intermediary markets				Vertical Integration Strategy (11)	

Sources I. Ansoff, *Corporate Strategy*, Penguin Books; S. C. Johnson and C. Jones, 'How to organise for new products', *Harvard Business Review*, May–June 1957.

Overseas market information analysis

This has to be undertaken by means first of an internal diagnosis of the firm, establishing strengths and weaknesses with regard to production; finance; human resources; and the current standing and client base of the firm. Against this, the opportunities and threats of the foreign market may be viewed with regard to legal; ethical; market; competition; and technology variables.

Information
↓
Analysis → Objectives of the company?
↓ ↗
Setting commercial targets

The basic objective simply stated is to identify opportunity which, if we relate to the Ansoff matrix (Reference 9), may arise in any one of 11 permutations from combining new or present markets with new, present, and improved products. See Table 3.6.

We need to measure (a) overall market size and (b) competitive market conditions. Given that many of the 146 countries with a population in excess of one million have very limited market data, particularly amongst the less developed countries. So, to undertake this market study and fulfil these information requirements, the following nine-point plan is proposed which systematically evaluates prospects and therefore helps make recommendations for definite action.

1. Background information

This is derived from published secondary sources of information and would include:

A. Rates of growth of the population, workforce, and GNP (but, as mentioned earlier, GNP has its limitations as a measure of anything)
B. Balance of payments
C. Composition of exports and imports
D. Consumer expenditures
E. Formation of fixed capital in construction and equipment.

2. Analysis of supply

A. *External competition* can be ascertained by analysing import statistics, via
   - *UN World Trade Annual*
   - *UN Commodity Indexes for the Standard Industrial Trade Classification*, 2 vols.
   - *OECD Trade by Commodities* (*Foreign Trade Statistics*, Series 'C', Paris, half-yearly).
B. *Import analyses* usually show:
   a Import flows over past five years, by major supplying countries, by quantity, and by value
   b Percentage growth of imports over the years studied.
C. *Apparent domestic consumption* may therefore be computed as
   Total Supply = (local production − exports) + imports.

3. Demand and end-use analysis

The aim is to study the various kinds of principal users of a product to discover where the growth points may be. The following need to be studied:

A. Economic sectors that use the product
B. Each sector's share of total consumption
C. Growth pattern of each of these sectors
D. Plans and forecasts of future growth for each major sector and the related sectors (future secondary demand).

4. Demand forecasts

It is best to concentrate on five- to ten-year prospects. The following points should be noted:

A. Examine long-term trends, remembering cyclical pattern associated with industrial development.
B. Examine substitutability of some goods!
C. Ignore short-term economic forecasts as current events can bias thinking.
D. Examine national plans.
E. Listen and interpret intelligently, e.g. ask a manufacturer about his competitors.

5. Information on prices

A. Extrapolation of unit prices over a five-year period may indicate the way in which prices are moving.
B. Field enquiries at home can yield manufacturer and fob prices.
C. Field enquiries in target country can yield cif prices and distribution costs.

6. Access to the market

Conditions of access to the market may be influenced by the following:

A. Customs tariffs
B. Import charges
C. Non-tariff barriers
D. Import regulations

7. Trading practices

A. Sizes and grade of goods most often in demand
B. Preferred types of packaging or product presentation
C. Most popular qualities/assortments of goods
D. Standardisation at national/international level
E. Usual channels of trade

F. Conditions of payment
G. Problems of transport
H. Insurance terms

8. Sales promotion

A. Target audience and theme of message
B. When, where, how should this sales message be delivered?
C. Media availability
D. Publications readership profile
E. Costs of advertising per prospective customer, by various media
F. Strengths and weaknesses of present and prospective customers
G. What marketing approaches have been effective there in the past?
H. Trade fairs – which groups attend them and what are the conditions for
   participating?

9. Documentation and useful addresses

- *British Business* Includes a weekly index of statistics, giving date of past
  or forthcoming publication dates.
- *International Directory of Published Market Research*, British Overseas
  Trade Board, London.
- *Trade Directories of the World*, Croner.
- *'SITPRO'* (Simplification of International Trade Procedures) London.
  (Technical documents and occasional market reports as well as a recent
  one on Nigeria.)
- British Standards Institution, 'Technical Help to Exporters' Service,
  Hemel Hempstead, Herts. HP2 4SQ.
  (Publish *Technical Export News* monthly plus international product
  surveys, technical translations, and international product standards.)
- Statistics and Market Intelligence Library, 1 Victoria Street, London.
  (Contains data on foreign markets only by market and by industry.)
- *McCarthy Index* has two services on offer: a subject index and a
  company index and will reproduce photocopies of newspaper articles on
  subjects in either index for a fee.
- *Extel Cards* summarise financial statistics.
- *Research Index* – a fortnightly publication acting as a guide to newspaper
  articles.
- *Business Periodicals Index* (W. H. Wilson) is American and therefore
  mainly American periodicals but is useful.
- *SCIMP* (Key word index) devised by the British Business Schools'
  Libraries. Scans and indexes the major British, European and American
  management journals.
- *Anbar Abstracts* – British series arranged by functional area of
  management which give a one paragraph abstract of articles from the
  publications which they have screened.

Market-selection decisions

It is a regrettable fact that the existing literature on the subject points to market selection as being an informal decision. Often it is the result of a competitive move; or a chance sighting of a product from that particular market; the result of a business conversation or a chamber of commerce seminar; or a market is chosen simply because the target market is a pleasant location, the people are 'nice' and the managing director's wife enjoys going there on holiday! Curiously, more attention appears to be paid to 'industry talk' than to the reports and publications produced by different trade and governmental bodies. This behaviour has been reported in the UK and in the US as well, although it must be remembered that since the US does not have the same degree of dependence on trade as we have in the UK, this only serves to make this finding more incomprehensible.

Market selection means that you choose the markets to which to devote your resources. In effect, a study commissioned by British Export Trade Research Organisation (BETRO) (Reference 10) in 1976 on this subject of key market concentration found from taking a representative sample of a quarter of British companies that the companies were spreading their resources too thinly over too many markets. Assuming a Pareto relationship where approximately 20 per cent of a company's markets could be found to account for perhaps 80 per cent of its exports, BETRO exhorted exporters to concentrate their resources on their 'best' markets. Newcomers to exporting, the report suggested, could build a prosperous export trade by dealing with five or six countries only. Concentration would also bring

- less administration
- better market knowledge
- more opportunity to compete on non-price factors
- less distraction
- higher market share

The BETRO Report concluded that British companies exported to too many markets, and this was a finding that was substantiated by the Barclays Bank Report on Export Competitiveness in the UK, France and West Germany in 1979 (Reference 11). Piercy qualified this theory of 'market concentration' by viewing this, not in terms of limiting the company as to market where it may sell, but to markets where it may market itself. By selling wherever demand arises but maintaining a certain selectivity over the use of marketing resources, Piercy (Reference 12) then confesses to a certain benefit in market concentration.

International market segmentation

Market segmentation follows the rationale of concentrating resources for the best prospects. In the pursuit of market segmentation, one is adopting a 'rifle' strategy at a given target market as opposed to the general market at large, which would constitute a 'shotgun' approach. Sometimes firing far and wide, the latter will strike a target but the 'rifle' strategy is probably the more effective of the two.

Three overall possibilities exist:

- market differentiation whereby competitors make different offerings across the entire market;
- market segmentation whereby specific target markets are identified and offerings are designed especially for these markets;
- market positioning whereby competitors position their offerings differently for each market segment.

There are degrees of segmentation, and so certain criteria have to be fulfilled:

1. *Measurability.* The target segment must be capable of some form of measurement, or at worst, a best guess.
2. *Size.* The target segment has to be large enough to make the marketing effort financially worthwhile.
3. *Accessibility.* Targeting is useless unless this group may be accessed by promotion and distribution.
4. *Responsiveness.* The group should react to any change in the marketing mix elements. Failure to do so indicates that this is not a proper segment that has been drawn.

If a company chooses to ignore the differences between consumers, it will be practising undifferentiated marketing. If, on the other hand, it segments the market on the basis of consumer differences, it can choose to practise either differentiated marketing – in which a marketing mix is used for each segment – or concentrated marketing – in which all or most marketing efforts are focused on one or a few segments.

Mandell and Rosenberg (Reference 13) mention also 'market integration' and 'market orchestration'. Market integration unites certain market segments, finds a basic characteristic that several otherwise different groups share in common, and designs a product that appeals to all of them. One example offered is in the area of snack foods. Market integration arose as a response to oversegmentation. Market orchestration arises where different market segments are to be included in the target range and lack compatibility. The price factor is therefore the most common means of orchestration since high and low prices will encourage some segments and discourage others.

Selecting a strategy then is by means of a review of five factors:

- *Company resources*, whether limited in terms of capital and/or marketing.
- *Product homogeneity*, degree of similarity within a product class.
- *Product age* (PLC theory of product phase and corporate response).
- *Market homogeneity*, depending upon where consensus needs are like/unlike.
- *Competition*, moving into several segments or a mass market will influence corporate response.

References

1. Business Environment Risk Review (BERI), Newark, Delaware USA.
2. Litvak, Isiah A. and Banting, Peter M., 'A conceptual framework for international business arrangements', in King, Robt. L. (ed), *Marketing and the New Science of Planning*, American Marketing Association Conference Proceedings, Chicago, Fall 1968, pp. 460–67.
3. Sheth, J. N. and Lutz, R. J., 'A Multivariate Model of Multinational Business Expansion', in Sethi, S. P. and Sheth, J. N., (eds), *Multinational Business Operations, vol. 3: Marketing Management*, Goodyear Pub., California, 1973.
4. Goodnow, J. D. and Hansz, James E., 'Environmental Determinants of Overseas Market Entry Strategies', *Journal of International Business Studies*, vol. 3, Spring 1972, p. 45.
5. Keegan, W., *Multinational Marketing Management*, Prentice-Hall, 2nd ed., 1980, Chapter 8.
6. Ryan, Michael, 'The Pan-European Survey Comes of Age', *Admap*, October 1981, pp. 533–36.
7. Barnes, W. N., 'International Marketing Indicators', *European Journal of Marketing*, vol. 14, no. 2, 1980, pp. 90–136.
8. Montgomery, David B. and Urban, Glen L., *Management Science in Marketing*, Prentice-Hall, 1969, pp. 4–6.
9. Ansoff, I., *Corporate Strategy*, Penguin, 1968.
10. BETRO Trust Committee, *Concentration on Key Markets*, London, BETRO, 1976.
11. *Barclays Bank Report on Export Development in France, Germany and the UK*, London, Barclays Bank, 1979.
12. Piercy, Nigel, *Export Strategy: Markets and Competition*, George Allen and Unwin, 1982.
13. Mandell, Maurice I. and Rosenberg, Larry H., *Marketing*, 2nd edition, Prentice-Hall, 1981.

Recommended further reading

D. J. Casley, D. A. Lury, *Data Collection in Developing Countries*, Clarendon Press, 1981.

4. *MARKET ENTRY STRATEGY DECISIONS*

To begin with, it has to be emphasised that there is no one, single universal 'best' strategy. The firm should consider all alternative channel strategies when entering each market. The 'best' strategy will be the one which is situationally best, it is optimal in that it satisfies – with regard to the conflicting pressures of the foreign and domestic operating environments – industry structure at home and abroad, and company marketing strategy.

It may be useful to think in terms of a company having to deploy a portfolio of international investments to deal with a diversity of market conditions worldwide. Conceptually, these forms of market entry which we describe below do not fit neatly into a sequential categorisation. It should not be assumed then that there is an incremental internationalisation process moving from export sales being part of domestic sales through to wholly-owned subsidiaries. In fact, research with one major British multinational established that thinking was moving towards the need to justify the existence of a wholly-owned subsidiary in preference to a free agent. Usually, ownership has been thought to be necessary to have control but control has a price, too, and so the optimal market entry choice has to be situational.

Selection of market entry method has an important bearing on strategy and can be limiting on future intended expansion of the company if care is not exercised.

Selecting a strategy

The factors to be considered in selection are:

1. *Speed of market entry desired.* If speed is required, building up a wholly-owned subsidiary will probably be by acquisition and licensing or use of an agent/distributor will be the likely ways to ensure access to distribution in the foreign market.

2. *Costs to include direct and indirect costs.* Subjectivity which is ever present may force a wrong decision. Savings may be outweighed by indirect costs such as freight, strikes or disruptions to output, lack of continuity with the power supply, or irregularity in the supply of raw materials. Against this, the cost of doing nothing has to be considered; this may be higher than the attendant risks of moving forward.

3. *Flexibility required.* The laws of a country exist to protect that country's nationals. There is as yet no such thing as international law and in disputes between two countries the domestic law of a third country is often

called upon, so that domestic law is used for a purpose for which it was never designed. Local laws invariably protect nationals, which means that agents are appointed or distributors given exclusive sales territory rights only where it is deemed unlikely that there will be very much future expansion by the company directly into that market.

4. *Risk factors* – including political risk as well as competitive risk. In a dynamic market, time is of the essence. No product remains 'new' forever. Getting the product to market is important but so, too, is avoiding the creation of a competitor, an accusation often levelled against licensing. Risk may be obviously diminished by minimising the investment stake in the company by, for example, accepting a local joint venture partner. Equally, investment activity in one market may lead to reprisals for the company elsewhere as has often been seen in the past with companies trading with Israel and then finding themselves subject to an Arab boycott.

5. *Investment payback period.* Shorter-term strategies are licensing and franchising deals, whereas collaborative joint ventures or joint equity ventures may tie up capital for a number of years.

6. *Long-term profit objectives* – the growth foreseen for that market in the years ahead. Here, the question of distribution channel policy is important for the future. A wholly owned subsidiary may build up its own technical service department alongside a small but growing sales team. Agents who have been hired but are no longer consistent with longer-term profit objectives have to be given *ex gratia* payments to dispense with their services and the contract which legally binds them with the company. Otherwise it may mean legal action and produce a punitive charge against the company if heard in a local court, with the added costs of local legal representation.

The alternative forms of foreign market entry may therefore be summarised before we begin to consider them in terms of being direct or indirect (see Table 4.1). Additionally a company may be perceived as being closely related to its country of origin in which case it will be ethnocentric; if based in a few countries with no visibly ethnic image it may be said to be polycentric; whereas, in the last category, those few companies such as IBM, Coca-Cola, or Pepsi-Cola – viewed as being globally co-ordinated with complex global sourcing, management reporting systems etc. – are labelled geocentric.

These terms ethnocentric, polycentric and geocentric are labels to describe outward manifestations of the company; they do not relate to corporate structure which is dealt with in Chapter 11.

In terms of structure, a company may have:

1. *A functional orientation* such as SKF ball bearings where the functional heads are also the functional heads for global operations as well as domestic Swedish operations. This type of structure is suitable for companies with either very extensive or very limited foreign operations. It is characterised by a highly concentrated structure with short lines of communication.

Table 4.1
Charting the possibilities for direct and indirect exports, production and
services

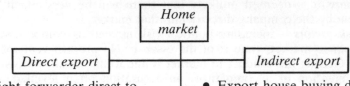

Direct export	Indirect export
• Freight forwarder direct to client	• Export house buying directly locally
• Agent who holds inventory	• Trading company of Japan or European trading nations, e.g. Britain, France, Germany
• Distributor who purchases inventory but holds exclusivity of sales	
• Consortium marketing group member	• Piggybacking uses distribution channel of another company in related field
• Overseas sales subsidiary	

Production moving abroad	Services moving abroad
• Licensing patented manufacturing process (often with know how)	• Franchising of brand name, logo (often with management contract)
• Know-how agreement for process production process	• Management contract for control
• Assembly of exported kits	• Industrial Cooperation Agreement (ICA) or contractual joint venture of fixed duration
• Industrial Co-operation Agreement (ICA) or contractual joint venture	
• Joint equity venture	• Joint equity venture of no fixed duration with capital investment
• Wholly owned subsidiary	• Wholly owned subsidiary

Source Adapted from Terpstra, *International Marketing*, Holt, Reinhart & Winston, 3rd
edition, 1983.

2. *A product orientation* whereby in the case of certain conglomerate
multinationals – e.g. ITT – there is little sense in combining highly
diversified divisions such as domestic electrical operations with insurance
services. Each division has responsibility for its product operations.
Separate product divisions are also found in ICI. The divisions are
autonomous but the international expertise may be spread throughout the
divisions and communication then becomes more difficult. This structure
ensures standardisation but the divisions may overlap.

3. *A geographical orientation.* Here, the company may have a fairly
narrow product range and it may make commercial sense to centralise
operations within a region in the international division, as British Leyland
does in North America. There may be more commonality between the

regions than between the various products in which it trades. Concentration of the area specialists is important when trading in areas with high potential risk.

4. *A matrix orientation* was the vogue in the 1970s and ensured that there was a country manager at head office level who acted as an 'overseer' of operations and liaised directly with the resident sales manager of one or more countries. The system allegedly yielded results in improved reporting procedures and co-ordination but also added to the bureaucracy and the ways in which different levels of the bureaucracy may be assessed.

Export-pull effect of indirect market entry strategies

The popular media is responsible for creating a distorted image of exporting as a pioneering activity which is noble in itself but also patriotic. It may be suicidal, if not also unpatriotic, therefore, to negate any of these groundless statements.

Companies do, however, find themselves being pushed into exporting and it is in this connection that we should first consider 'indirect' market entry strategies, remembering all the while that the rather grandiose term 'strategy' may equally apply to a strategy by default where a company faced with a certain market situation chooses to do nothing. Over time, an attitude and a strategy may be perceived. Those strategies termed 'indirect' are chiefly those whereby the domestic manufacturer is able to engage in the sale of his products abroad with minimal outlay or use of his own company resources. In this category, a company may even be unaware that its products are being exported. Foreign buying offices of department store chains (e.g. Myers of Australia have a London buying office) are a prime example of an 'export-pull' effect whereby goods are exported to a new market without the active participation of the producer himself. This may then create a demonstration effect within that foreign market which may lead to further export sales. Then, as envisaged by the Product Life Cycle for international trade, foreign production increases with an import substitution effect. Foreign production strength leads to eventual foreign production penetration and saturation of the domestic market which first launched the product.

As indirect market entry methods involve the use of intermediaries who handle all documentation, physical movement of goods, and channels of distribution for sale, indirect exports may take place either with or without the knowledge of the manufacturer himself. Indirect market entry may occur in a number of ways.

An *export house*, of which there are many in the City of London, will buy directly from you on behalf of a foreign principal in which case the sale will be a purely domestic one with the export house arranging the export of the goods.

The *trading company* is in a quite different league. Britain owed its strength in international trading to these trading companies such as the East India Company, Hudson Bay Company and others firmly established in what were then British colonies. Today, the United Africa Company,

Table 4.2

Stages of internationalisation

Stage	Activity levels	Conditions which make activity necessary	Strategic criteria met by activity	Responsibility of country manager
Export	Sell through agents	• Export small % of sales • No entry barriers	• Counter cyclicity • Distinctive economic envt • Access to similar growth	None
	Local sales office	• Local demand > capacity • Entry large % of sales • No entry barriers • Demand = capacity • Competition strong • After-sales service important	• Better growth • Extend demand life cycle • Economies of scale	Provide sale support
International	Local marketing	• Distinctive environment • Differentiated marketing strategies • Intensive competition	• Distinctive environment to sociopolitical	Maximise country sales
	Local production	• Barriers • Local cost advantages	• Access to resources	Optimise profitability of assigned projects
	Local R & D	• Distinctive marketing needs	• Advanced Technology • Extend Technological life cycle	
	Local diversification	• Local growth opportunity • Local financing	• Better growth • Critical mass • Synergy • Competitive advantage	Optimise profitability of assigned mission scope
Multinational	Global optimisation of Production/Resources/R&D	• Global competition • Global scale critical mass • Global scale synergy advantages	• Economies of scale	Contribute to global optimisation
	Global diversification Global portfolio management	• Competitive from globally optimised firms	• Long-term v. short-term portfolio balance • Global vulnerability balance • Global project optimisation	Contribute to global strategy

Source H. Igor Ansoff, *Strategic Dimensions of Internationalisation*, European Institute for Advanced Studies in Management, Working Paper 82–37, October 1982.

which is part of Unilever remains the largest trader in Africa. Elsewhere, the importance of the large Japanese trading houses such as Mitsui, each of which incorporates its own bank, is not to be discounted.

Piggybacking is a quite different affair. Piggybacking remains primarily an American phenomenon practised like sex between elephants: at a high level, with a great deal of roaring, and a long period to produce results.

Piggybacking is seen to be taking place amongst 10,000 or one-third of US exporting companies, who may have sound reasons e.g.

- The exporter may need additional products in order to sell a 'package' in foreign markets. These goods may widen his product range or extend the benefits or services previously on offer.
- Foreign customers may have asked the exporter to obtain specific merchandise not available in their markets. Here the exporter is simply making available his distribution outlets to another manufacturer. There is, however, a certain synergistic effect in that the goods are complementary and may aid sales of each other's products.
- Some US exporters want to sell additional products in foreign markets to increase their total export sales. In some cases, US exporters will ask a manufacturer to produce a product line with the exporter's own brand name.

Piggybacking seems to attract large companies rather than small, but it enables a non-exporter to exploit the distribution channels of an exporting company with a complementary, non-competing product. For the exporter, piggybacking offers the advantage of widening the product range carried, utilising the sales force to the full, and earning additional revenue from carrying products into distribution channels which would have to be served anyway. For the domestic company, there is the obvious advantage of a readymade overseas market with an experienced international exporting firm at the ready. There is less risk than going it alone and direct access to the market, as the channels of distribution already exist. With piggybacking there are two possible forms of payment: either outright full payment or a commission basis.

This relationship may therefore vary from an order-to-order basis to one of established permanence. Finding a piggybacker may prove difficult and once established there is also the problem of the nature of the relationship, the product selling price, and the potential disadvantage that since the products are subordinated to the other company's lines they may not be promoted as aggressively. The exporting manufacturer may feel greater loyalty to his own wares and he may be under greater pressure from his management to sell his own wares. Profitable business can, however, emanate from this kind of relationship although this relationship may mean either that A is purchasing from B to resell in foreign markets under his control, or else A is the agent of B and in return for providing suitable outlets for products complementary to his own, he receives a commission on sales. However, there is the added advantage also, though much less quantifiable, of increased sales resulting from augmented product range. The points to particularly note of a potential piggybacker are:

- The products the firm presently exports
- How your product will be promoted – in particular, who will handle your product, how often he travels abroad, etc.
- Type of distribution used in major foreign markets
- Exporting pricing policies
- Identification of others being 'piggybacked' (check with these firms to find out if they are happy with the arrangement)
- Estimated amount of export sales for your product
- Countries covered by the exporting manufacturer

The difficulty remains, however, of being stuck with an arrangement which could in the long term hinder your ability to expand your product range or establish your own export effort, or could not be changed if dissatisfied with the piggybacker's performance.

Direct exporting activities

These begin where the company may be actively involved in foreign sales but perhaps due to inexperience, arranges for all documentation and physical distribution to be handled for them by a freight forwarder.

Beyond this stage, the most popular form of direct entry is the agent and here the reader is recommended to turn to the 27 different types identified by McMillan and Paulden in their seminal work (Reference 6).

Agents

Agents are perhaps the most common form of low-cost direct involvement in foreign markets. However, there are a number of disadvantages. Firstly, although foreign embassies and national trade associations are able to supply lists of agents, it is often difficult for them to give a qualitative assessment or evaluation, or to recommend specific agents, perhaps for fear of libel. Quality is therefore variable and as an agent is paid commission only on sales, his loyalty may be questionable if it is seen to rest purely on the company currently providing him with the greatest earnings. As agents may represent a number of separate companies and product lines, this may be a problem. Meanwhile, the company holds responsibility for whatever unsold inventory is held by the agent, while at the same time being virtually deprived of market information.

No agent will willingly expose himself to the risk of being supplanted by a branch of the company's own sales organisation. In market situations where there is, in Boston Consulting Group terminology, a 'problem child' syndrome evident – i.e., slow growth for the company's product in a growth market – it may be difficult to determine exactly why this has arisen. On the other hand, where there is high market growth this creates pressures within the company to take over the foreign market from the agent. This may often require compensating the agent handsomely especially where local legislation exists to protect his position. Elsewhere, the situation may arise where the company wishes to expand its product line or else diversify into a quite different product and the local agent finds himself unable to meet this new expansion but holds a company agreement to exclusivity of sales territory.

Distributors

Distributors usually seek exclusive rights to specific sales territories but constitute yet another method of low-cost foreign market entry. The difference between the distributor and the agent is that the distributor will, like the foreign buying office, be placing an order similar to any other domestic purchase order in that the responsibility for the condition and sale of goods will end at some point to be agreed in the distribution channel between producer and distributor. The distributor actually takes title – i.e., owns the inventory which he carries – and represents the manufacturer in the sales and service of the products which he carries. Thus, in return for his capital investment he will usually seek exclusivity of supply and sales territory plus a reasonable turnover rate of the products handled.

Management contracts

Management contracts are quite different again in that they often subsume some other form of relationship in addition, such as licensing, franchising, or industrial co-operation (industrial joint venture). Management contracts emphasise the increasing importance of services and know-how as a saleable asset in international trade. Based on a contractual form, it will concern the transferral of management control systems and know-how involving personnel training. The demand arises mainly from those countries where there exists a 'managerial gap'. Essentially it is a 'software' package incorporating management and control systems, and frequently found in those industries where there is an expectation of quality, service, and attention. Hotels and hospitals are just two areas in which management contracts have been usefully explored. Management contracts do constitute big business, however. When the International Hospital Group of the UK won a twelve-year management contract for the 500-bed King Khaled National Guard Hospital in Jeddah, Saudi Arabia, this contract was valued at £150 million.

Franchising

Franchising is another means of selling a service, often to small investors with working capital. Franchising's origins go back two centuries to when brewers created the tied-house system to guarantee outlets for their beer. Three growing markets account for two-thirds of all franchises in the UK – home improvements and home maintenance (31 per cent), food and drink (18 per cent), and business services (17 per cent). Franchising transfers the legal right to a third party to use a registered company's name and logo, products, and packaging. For example, Kentucky Fried Chicken (part of the giant American RJ Reynold Tobacco and Drinks combine) have a standardised red and white corporate colour, a distinctive trademark, logo, and carton packaging for food. Kentucky Fried stipulate the sources from which the raw materials must be obtained, the recipes for the preparation of the food again to be strictly controlled, and the quantity to be served in each portion. The particular benefit which franchising confers is that it allows small independents with investment capital (average £26,000 in UK in 1985) but no industry or management experience, to enjoy the benefits of belonging to a large organisation whilst remaining owner-managers. Usually the franchisee is under 40, married with a couple of children but the franchise can cost between £5,000 and £250,000. Drain clearing is relatively low cost while fast food operations are considerably more expensive. The failure rate is low, about 2 per cent per annum in the UK, whereas 75 per cent of all small businesses fail in the first five years. This is partly due to the personal motivation of the franchisee as well as guidance from the franchisor. The return on initial capital invested is recovered on average in just under two years and the return on the full cost is just over three years. A large fast-food restaurant may take four to five years for the investment to be recovered. Franchising is rapidly increasing, as are the companies actively promoting it, e.g. Sheraton Intercontinental, Holiday Inns (hotels); Coca-Cola, Pepsi-Cola (soft drinks); Budget (car rental) and many of the fast-food companies; as well as others in drain clearing (Dyno-Rod), printing, and photocopying (Prontaprint). Coca-Cola is held to provide the classic example of a franchise strategy, with its independent bottlers around the world preparing soft drinks from concentrate according to specifications supplied by Coca-Cola which retains control over its trademark, recipe, and advertising. Franchising can often subsume a management contract and thus lead to profits from both royalties and management fees. It is still a relatively new concept in the international arena and the tax treatment for this form of trading has yet to be standardised. Cadbury-Schweppes who recently concluded a franchising deal with Asahi Breweries, part of the Sumitomo Group, to sell soft drinks in Japan, will benefit from the export of essences and concentrates from the UK.

An illustration of what can go wrong with a franchising deal is provided by the experiences of McDonalds, the American fast-food chain, in France. McDonalds have 7,000 restaurants worldwide but have been buying in franchises in the US. (All of its 126 British outlets are company owned). McDonalds franchised a certain individual in the early seventies to open a number of restaurants in Paris. The relationship soured when the US company charged him with not maintaining his restaurants to McDonalds' standards. There followed a long-winded lawsuit which was finally resolved in a Chicago court in 1982 in favour of the US company. McDonalds removed all names and references to the company from the franchised operation in Paris and set to work to catch up on the time lost to its rivals, including the US Burger King chain, on the flourishing Parisian fast-food markets. The franchisee renamed his restaurants O'Kitch. Meanwhile McDonalds selected for their re-entry to Paris an unusually stylish two-storey establishment which seeks to be very French, with granite bistro tables, art deco lights and lush plastic plants plus the innovation of loose chairs for the first time in a McDonalds restaurant.

The maintenance of standards and the need also for standardisation are two of the problems facing an international franchising operation. Meanwhile, it is interesting to note that the 126 McDonalds' operations now growing apace in the UK are wholly owned by McDonalds and not a franchise as found elsewhere among their 7,000 outlets worldwide. A legacy perhaps of their French experience. Kentucky Fried Chicken have called a temporary freeze on franchise recruiting and have just bought back 13 restaurants. Kentucky Fried Chicken own 60 stores out of 360 in the UK. Burger King again in the UK are negotiating to buy in the last of their UK franchises.

Licensing

Licensing confers only a right to utilise a company-specific and patent-protected process in manufacturing. This right is conveyed in the transferral of original blueprints and designs. Operational experience in production of the licensed technology is usually a separately negotiable item, as will be any subsequent modifications to the product transferred unless this has specifically been contracted and does not constitute 'new' technology. In its simplest form, then, it may involve the transmittal of original designs. Increasingly, though, use is being made of additional 'know-how' agreements which will include on-site training of supervisory staff plus an experience transferral in the operations of handling the licensed technology. 'Know-how' is estimated to save approximately two years on the tooling-up time for any major production plant. Where the licence does not include 'know-how' the buyer, while benefitting from a lower sales price, is hampered by the lack of available operational knowledge. The ability to cope with this situation depends upon the technical levels of competence of the buyer and seller respectively.

When licensing agreements do turn out to be far from successful there may well be subsequent recriminations against the seller, perhaps even at a national level, for his refusal to update technology without further fee particularly in the event of protracted delays in final production. Eastern Europe – which is on average slower than most to implement new technology as may have been witnessed in the case of the diffusion of Corfam by DuPont – is eager at the same time to reduce costs wherever possible, particularly as they are forever short of convertible currency reserves. This leads to money having to be saved on licensing which usually means buying the blueprints only, ensuring therefore that the technological gap between themselves and the West will always be maintained.

The 'advantage' incorporated in the licensing deal will in any event have a finite life. What licensors seek to do, therefore, is to protect the most secret part of their technology by continuing to export that particular component which embodies state-of-the-art technology. By so doing, they decrease the risk of creating a potential competitor – an accusation often levelled against licensing – while ensuring for themselves a steady revenue

Table 4.3
Essential characteristics of market entry methods

Market entry method (alphabetically)	Characteristics
Agents	Paid on commission usually with exclusivity of sales territory but handling more than one company and/or product line.
Consortium exporting	Encourages small companies to engage in joint representation in foreign markets. Assisted by government schemes in US and UK to encourage more small companies to participate in exporting.
Distributors	Differ in that they take title to the goods. This lessens risk and improves cashflow but weakens control as less is known about the final end-user or price charged.
Export houses	Approx. 700–800 of these in UK, accounting for 20 per cent of UK exports. Export House represent a buyer abroad. Trading Company buying and selling on own account following a particular Japanese strength.
Franchising	High growth of 10 per cent p.a. in UK. Estimated 230 active franchises in UK employing 71,000 people, with total turnover in excess of a billion pounds. Expected to employ 230,000 and have five billion pound turnover in UK by 1990. Transfers the right to use the company's name, logo and all that may be identifiable with the company. Examples abound in the fast-food industry. May also include a management contract.
Freight forwarder	Documentation and delivery service to foreign destination.
Joint ventures	Two distinct types: Industrial co-operation (contractual) and joint-equity. Contractual is of fixed duration; responsibilities and duties defined. Joint-equity involves investment, no fixed duration, and is continually evolving.
Licensing	Often regarded as second-best to exporting. It confers a right to utilise a company-specific process in manufacturing a proprietary product and may also include a management contract and continuing exports of components embodying advanced technology.
Management contracts	Transfer know-how and company-specific management control systems, and are widely evidenced in the services sector, e.g. hotel industry, private hospital management.
Piggybacking	Originated and still remains strong amongst one-third of US companies. Uses the distribution channel of another company. Returns achieved by means of commission or outright sale.

from export sales which can also be expected to increase as foreign production climbs. Licensing royalties, on the other hand, usually decrease over time and beyond a certain threshold. Licensing may also provide a strategic limitation as Xerox Corporation in the United States found when they granted Rank-Xerox, a British-American company, rights to all markets outside the US.

Licensing applies also to the increasing phenomenon of syndicating film personality and cartoon character rights to manufacturers of toys, clothing, stationery, etc. Disney cartoon characters perhaps started this trend many years ago with Mickey Mouse appearing on children's watches but the growth in this area of characterisation since then has been phenomenal. There have been the Smurfs displayed on petrol filling stations, the Flintstones on vitamin pills plus Garfield (200 licensees) and Snoopy on a range of coffee mugs and stationery, including posters and greeting cards. There is to be a calendar for 1986 of the '1986 James Bond 007 Calendar Girls', again produced under licence. More recently the stars of the American television programme *Dynasty* have been helping to promote the merchandise of 33 different firms which have paid to be associated with the series, with products ranging from 'Forever Krystle' perfume to Carrington House Carpets, plus jewellery and fashion wear bearing the Carrington family crest and including a $150 toiletry kit with a gold-plated toothbrush and razor and a shaving brush made of Chinese badger hair. The film industry, theatrical and dance companies, Olympic sports organisers, all seek to make additional revenue from the forward promotion of merchandise associated with either their current or forthcoming productions. If Cabbage Patch Kids merchandise was all to be handled by one company, that firm would rank no. 236 on Fortune's 500 list. Retail sales under the Cabbage Patch name were estimated to be worth $1.5 billion in 1984, and the sales of 5,000 products from these 150 licensees is expected to increase in 1986.

Where markets are fragmented and exporting the final goods is not possible, industrial process or product licensing remains a clear possibility. Where there is no direct investment permitted by law and no access to venture capital, etc. licensing remains a viable option. Curiously enough, there are no trade statistics on licences. The only organisation which seeks to collect information in this area is the UN World Intellectual Property Organisation (WIPO) based in Geneva.

Although criticised as being a 'second best' strategy to exporting, product or process licensing may prove to be the only way to enter a market. This was certainly true in previous years of Japan or Eastern Europe. Again, licensing may offer the best method of entry faced with a given level of risk. For smaller companies, licensing may hold many advantages such as lower level of capital required for market entry, lower risk, shorter-term payback period. For the larger company, licensing payments may prove to be an effective means of siphoning funds out of a country when exchange control regulations are in operation. A low transfer price rate from a high-tax country to a subsidiary in a low-tax country would have two effects. First, the manufacturer in the high-tax

Table 4.4

| | | Welcoming investment climate | | |
		High	Medium	Low
	High	Wholly owned JV	Assembly	Franchising
Cost of entry	Medium	Joint equity venture	Industrial cooperation	Know-how contracts
	Low	Sales subsidiary	Management contract	Exporting

country is only marginally profitable thus minimising his exposure to taxation. Secondly, the subsidiary overseas benefitting from a low transfer price will be able to record large profits in a low-tax country. For the company as a whole the strategy may make sense. What this equation leaves out, though, is the role of customs officers in exporting and importing countries and effect of unprofitability on the morale of the workforce. The disadvantages of licensing include then:

• creation of a potential competitor without the designation of specific sales territories.
• difficulties of maintaining control or 'leverage' over the licensee to avoid damage to trademarks or brand names as a result of the licensee's inferior quality control, after-sales service etc.
• increasing production by the licensee may result in lower royalties where there is a sliding scale in operation.
• the licensor is ceding certain sales territories to the licensee for the duration of the contract. Should he fail to live up to expectations, renegotiation may be expensive.
• problems involved in the transferral of funds, e.g. exchange control restrictions; exchange parities; plus of course, the refusal to pay!

For some processes particularly – and one may think of Du Pont's Corfam or Pilkington's float glass technique – exporting is not a practicable affair. Market entry and market expansion for the product or process can only be effected by a presence within the market. Territorial sales boundaries can also be agreed so as to defuse the criticism of the potential threat in licensing a potential competitor. This is the greatest single accusation levelled against licensing, yet masks the simple fact that much profitable business can be obtained via licensing. For a company which is small but technologically efficient, licensing has much to commend it, particularly as the royalties received on overseas production may well go to finance further expansion or fuel the research and development effort which created this invention, thereby maintaining the technological lead.

Table 4.5
Retail value of licensed goods

Year	Gross sales	Growth
1978	$ 6.5 billion	—
1979	$ 8.1 billion	24.6%
1980	$ 9.9 billion	22.2%
1981	$13.7 billion	38.4%
1982	$20.6 billion	50.4%
1983	$26.7 billion	29.6%
1984	$40.1 billion	50.2%

Figures based on annual industry survey by '*The Licensing Letter*'. Scottsdale. Ariz.
Source Marketing News (August 30 1985).

Direct investment activities

The company may decide to either:

- Build up representation in the foreign country as a wholly owned subsidiary. This is slow to achieve and expensive to maintain and slow also to yield any tangible results. If a very favourable growth market is envisaged, however, it may be the only real alternative because, although costly to maintain, it does allow flexibility.
- Acquire a foreign company. If speed of market entry is important then this may be more easily accomplished by acquiring a company already in the market. This effectively purchases market information, market share, and channels of distribution. It is not an optimal strategy, though, as the companies generally available for acquisition are those that have made themselves so with a high debt gearing, poor market performance, or lack of top management direction. Bad companies may be easily acquired whilst desirable acquisitions can only ever be bought at a premium.
- Enter into a joint venture with a local partner. Certain countries such as Nigeria, Japan, and some Middle Eastern countries discourage 100 per cent foreign ownership in all but undesirable sectors. A joint-equity venture may therefore be the only means of ensuring a market presence. In other countries, such as in the East European bloc, there is a growing trend towards a contractual form of joint venture which is being followed by industry itself in recent years as a result of ever increasing research and development costs and the critical mass required to achieve economies of scale in sectors such as automobile engineering.

To turn now to each of these in turn, the first issue which raises its head is the question of ownership and control. Although related, the words are not synonymous, and each of these three strategies above has to be examined in a situational context.

Wholly owned subsidiaries

A wholly owned sales subsidiary may provide a presence in the foreign
market but a sales presence alone is unpopular particularly amongst those
developing countries least likely to support production. Sales subsidiaries
are perceived as only taking money out of the country and contributing
nothing of value in return to the host country in which it is based.
However, it does ensure company control over all aspects of the marketing
mix in the foreign market, i.e. product, place (channels of distribution),
promotion and price. Problems arise in that local recruitment may be
required by host government legislation; long-term growth may be
encouraged which runs counter to the establishment of an agency base. In
these circumstances, establishment of a branch subsidiary may be the only
real alternative preceding local manufacture in the target market with the
establishment of sales, marketing, and servicing facilities.

The sales subsidiary will generally not be in existence long before calls
are made for some manufacturing or production base. Often the base does
not exist for a full scale manufacturing plant and so these developing
countries have to be satisfied with the provision at least of assembly
operations which at least to some degree provide employment, training,
and import substitution effects.

Company acquisition

The acquisition route was favoured for a period in the 1960s but it appears
now to be the reverse. Those companies which then diversified their
interests appear now to have divested themselves of their ancillary
activities and to have concentrated once again on their mainstream
activity.

In the same way as a tailored made-to-measure suit is preferable to a
readymade, so it is between acquisition and the steady development of a
wholly owned subsidiary. In return for a speedy access to the market one
has to make certain sacrifices, such as absorbing a company with suitable
distribution channels but heavily laden with debt or a weak product line, or
endowed for too long with an ineffective top management in which case the
change of corporate culture is likely to lead to tension. There is a further
problem always with a wholly owned subsidiary and that is the political risk
of expropriation.

Wholly owned subsidiaries in which there is 100 per cent investment
stake in a foreign country are becoming fewer in response to host
government pressure worldwide. Globally, there is a desire to both entice
and to control the multinational corporation as though it were a necessary
evil of our age. Foreign ownership and control of assets is an issue
constantly under review in all countries. Once the investment is made, the
company may then find itself subject to a local monopoly law or
governmental body applicable to all locally based companies. There is also
the greatest potential risk of expropriation of assets as there will be the
maximum level of investment with this type of foreign market entry. There

is also the highest degree of 'visibility' in that with no local ownership or control, the foreign subsidiary remains very 'foreign' and conspicuous, and will be correspondingly identified more closely with the home country of the parent company, whether it be British, American, or Japanese. Politically this may be undesirable. For globally integrated multinational corporations it may be difficult to undertake any other form of investment since it would involve not only the issues of ownership and control, but with control, the question of pricing components and sub-assemblies within the integrated multinational network, thereby upsetting a sophisticated global sourcing pattern. Recent years have seen increasing demands and host country legislation for local content whether in equity, employment or value deed. This is true of Japan, Nigeria, and other fast expanding world markets and is likely to continue.

Joint ventures

Joint ventures have been defined as 'the commitment, for more than a very short duration, of funds, facilities, and services by two or more legally separate interests, to an enterprise for their mutual benefit'.

The reasons for a joint venture, leaving aside for the moment that there are two types, include:

1. Explicit pressures by the host government which may include a definite ruling.
2. Implicit pressures by the host government which may include suspicion or fear of discriminatory action.
3. The desire to spread risk both:

   (*a*) normal business risks and
   (*b*) the risk of unpredictability of the environment, e.g. national political and economic uncertainty.

4. The need for local facilities and resources best obtained through a local interest with local influence and local knowledge of the customs and legal systems.
5. The opportunity to participate in any local project undertaken by the local partner.
6. Local identity – the benefits accruing to a locally identified operation.
7. Internal company reasons, e.g. goodwill, or the desire to spread corporate capital over a wide range of interests and markets.

In any event, the advantages must be strong enough to compensate for the initial lack of knowledge about economic, social, and legal conditions, and the market must be protected relatively well from entry by competitors. In an American survey, asking businesses to list the advantages of joint ventures the following points emerged:

1. The gaining of experience
2. Risk reduction
3. Capital saving

4. Access to lower-cost skilled labour
5. Improved government relations

In a study of the joint venture process in India and Pakistan (Reference 4), four clear stages in the investment environment could be noted:

1. *Unilateral antagonism.* The host nation fears the dangers of economic imperialism.
2. *Mutual suspicion.* Both foreign investors and capital-importing govern-ments may have considerable doubt over the mutuality of their interests. There is concern over the stimulus of economic development with scarce resources, so both foreign capital and technology are required. Imports are paid for by earning from extractive industry exports. Entry conditions for foreign capital and labour are relaxed but still constrained.
3. *Joint acceptance.* The social benefits are perceived to exceed the social costs, and as the needs of development create their own self-generating momentum, their relaxation continues.
4. *Sophisticated integration* – the logical extension of the relaxation mentioned. Foreign investors may be permitted entry in any form of operation which they desire. In so far as local collaboration and participation are felt to be desirable or even necessary, they may well be promoted through discriminatory fiscal and financial incentives, rather than through legislative prohibitions.

These phenomena are not unique to India and Pakistan but are universal truths. Grouping the possible reasons for partnership produced six situations:

1. *Forced partnership* – The choice is effectively forced upon the foreign investor either because of explicit host government direction, or indirectly because the partner pre-empts an exclusive licence.
2. *Convenience to the foreign partner* of local facilities under the control of the partner. Among these would be a site or plant, marketing or distributive facilities, or a strong market position where the partner was already in the same line of business as that of the proposed joint venture.
3. *Resources* – convenience of local sources of managerial and technical personnel, materials, components or local capital which can be contributed to the partner.
4. *Status and capability of the partner* in dealing with local authorities and public relations. This would also include status defined in terms of general financial and business soundness and standing.
5. *Favourable past association with the partner* when the latter had been an agent, licensee, major customer or partner in a previous joint venture. The category includes special cases in which there might have been strong personal contacts between individuals in the foreign and local parent companies, possibly individuals common to both.
6. *Identity* – a partner is chosen chiefly to obtain local identity, often through association with a potential 'sleeping partner'.

Nationality by itself was not enough justification in itself for entering a joint venture; a local partner would have to have something more to offer.
Joint ventures are of two types.

1. There is the familiar form of a **joint-equity venture** which is well known and documented, whereby each of the respective partners contributes a sum either in equity or technological know-how in return for a given stake in the operation of a joint venture. Unlike contractual ventures, these are open-ended and not of fixed duration.

2. There is also the increasingly popular **contractual joint venture** to be found in the aerospace industry and various other branches of engineering. It is to be found throughout the automobile industry as may be seen from Figure 4.2. In the Comecon bloc, these contractual joint ventures are referred to as 'industrial co-operation' and such agreements known as 'industrial co-operation agreements' or ICAs. Unlike equity ventures the investment stake may be in technology on one side only. The duration of the joint venture is laid down in the contract which designates the respective tasks and responsibilities of each party over the period of the joint venture. Any change or diversion has to be the subject of negotiation between the two partners.

Joint-equity ventures suffer in that the absorption of local equity capital from the foreign market will dilute the company equity base; whereas, an ICA or contractual joint venture on the other hand, is quite different in that the respective duties of both parties are clearly designated over a fixed period of years within a legal contract and the issue of ownership does not exist while control is still maintained. Both forms of joint venture seek to answer claims for local national ownership and involvement in foreign-based firms, yet the means by which they do so vary quite widely.

The particular attractions of the industrial co-operation include if we look at Eastern Europe (Reference 10):

1. The political and psychological attraction of an association with foreign investors which does not entail any degree of physical ownership of the host nation's resources. The latter remains in full legal control of its oil or copper deposits, while the foreign investor or consortium shares the capital expenditure, development costs, risks as well as profits, and contributes needed technical skill and equipment.

2. *Lack of choice* – Yugoslavia, for example, encourages joint-equity ventures with foreign capital but excludes contractual joint ventures.

For the Western company the responsibilities of a contractual joint venture are much easier to bear as it provides many of the advantages of a joint-equity venture without many of its attendant risks. Taking the example of Eastern Europe again, the following advantages obtain:

1. Royalties from sales in Eastern Europe.
2. Access to an increasing volume of low-cost output for marketing in the West.
3. No responsibility for management unless this has been specifically contracted for on a fee basis.

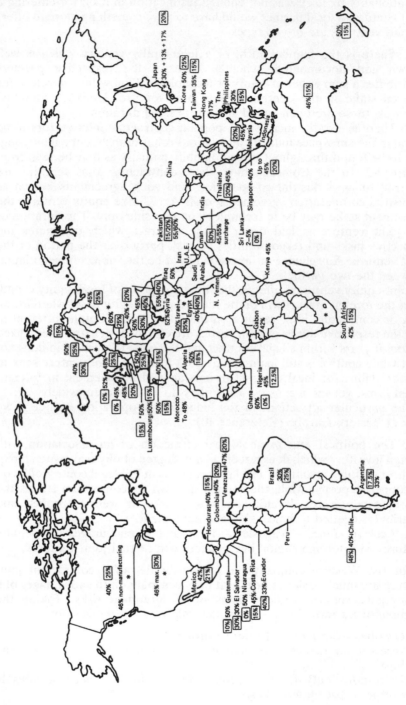

Figure 4.1 Foreign investment – host government support for business.

Table 4.6

Operational variable analysis contrasting industrial co-operation and joint-equity ventures

Operation variables	Industrial co-operation Possible advantages	Possible disadvantages	Joint-equity Possible advantages	Possible disadvantages
Ownership	None, no company finance involved	Lack of control	49% equity stake	Weakening of company equity base
Venture control	Contractual limitations, plant Eastern responsibility	Limited control	De facto control greater than equity share	Inability to reconcile objectives
Venture capital	No capital investment by company	ICA entails acceptance of goods made under licence	Capital and managerial investment	Commitment of company resources
Return on investment (ROI)	Fast	Speed of project rests with Eastern partner	Gradual ROI shows willingness to stay in market	Venture has to achieve profitability first
Risk sharing	Contractual liability only	Diminished risks diminish opportunity for spectacular profits	Half-share only	Eastern partner may refuse to kill-off an unprofitable joint venture
Venture duration	Fixed duration	Renewal or extension requires separate contract	Unlimited	Termination a possible problem
Western company repayment	Hard cash and goods	Adjustment to Western business cycles	Goods made under licence and hard cash	Subject to Eastern taxes
Manufacturing	Extra facility at cost	May flood market eventually	Extra plant at cost	Exposure to risk
Management skills	Limited, contractual obligations	Costs of this transfer may be greater than anticipated	Full access	Too great a dependence on the Western partner
Marketing	Lower cost goods made under licence	Co-ordination with Western business cycles	Lower cost goods made under licence	Investment in capital, machinery and management
Market expansion	Western access to CMEA and limited Eastern access to West via partner	Ability to vary deliveries according to demand	Western access to CMEA and limited Eastern access to West via partner	Sales priced only in 'hard' currency
Pricing	Lower costs	Western inability to forecast Eastern expectation	Lower costs	All costs priced in 'hard' currency only
Quality control	Goods to Western quality standards	Free access but geographical distance and costs of quality control	Goods to Western quality standards	Free access but geographical distance and costs of quality control
Research and development	May be included or may lead from an ICA	Dependent upon mutual capabilities	Ability to capitalise on Eastern strengths	Difficulties of co-ordination
Updating of technology transferred	Contractual	Ambiguity of contract act definition	Closer integration	Sharing of current company specific technology

Source S. J. Paliwoda, *Joint East-West Marketing and Production Ventures*, Gower Press, Farnborough (1981).

4. No company capital involved, and so the return on investment – limited to personnel and technology – may be very high.

In cars, commercial vehicles, computers, robotics, video, telecommunications, office equipment, aerospace and other key sectors, contractual joint ventures are on the increase. This movement, forced by competitive pressures is linking archrivals such as Philips and Sony; Volvo and Clark Equipment; Fiat and Alfa Romeo; ICL and Fujitsu; BL and Honda; Rolls-Royce and Pratt & Whitney to join forces to manufacture; sell, or conduct research and development.

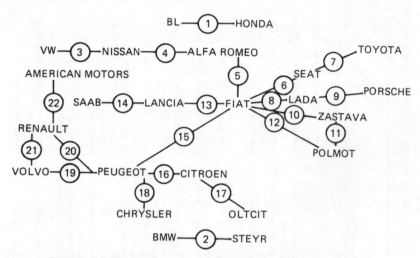

Figure 4.2 European car component co-operation deals.

Research and development costs for the automobile industry together with the critical mass required to achieve economies of scale ensured that this industry would be one of the first to find ways to make savings through joint collaboration. Figure 4.2 examines the number of existing car company contractual joint ventures. No one is particularly interested in ever owning any part of any other company. Instead, various links are forged between companies seeking to combine their engineering strengths in the development of:

- cars (BL/Honda)
- cars under licence (BL/Standard Motors of Madras, India)
- diesel engines (BMW/Steyr-Daimler-Puch)
- cars under licence (Suzuki-Maritu, India)
- cars (VAG/Nissan) Germany
- cars (Nissan/Alfa Romeo)
- car components (Alfa Romeo/Fiat)
- cars under licence (Seat/Fiat, Spain)
- cars under licence (Lada/Fiat, USSR)
- development work (Lada/Porsche, USSR)

- cars under licence/component exchange (Zastava/Fiat, Yugoslavia)
- component exchange (Zastava/Polmot, Yugoslavia/Poland)
- cars under licence/source of Fiat 126 for Europe (Polmot/Fiat, Poland)
- light commercial vehicles (Peugeot, Mohendira, India)
- commercial vehicles (General Motors/Enasa, Spain)
- commercial vehicle components (General Motors/Man, West Germany)
- joint development of automatic parts (Lancia/Saab)
- 1 million engines per year plant (Fiat/Peugeot)
- production of 130,000 new cars (Citroen/Olteit)
- diesel engines (Peugeot/Chrysler)
- V6 engine (Peugeot/Volvo/Renault)
- development work (Renault/Volvo)
- trucks 6–11 tonnes (VW/MAN, West Germany)
- medium duty transmissions (Iveco, Italy/Ecton, USA)
- truck axles (Iveco, Italy/Rockwell, US)
- CF6 – 80C2 aero-engines (Rolls-Royce/General Electric, USA)
- V – 2500 aero-engines (Rolls-Royce/Pratt and Whitney, USA)
- RB 211 – 535E4 series aero-engines (Rolls-Royce/General Electric, USA)
- CFM 56 aero-engines (Snecme, France/General Electric, USA)

There are of course some pitfalls associated with joint ventures. These include:

- difficulty of integrating into a global strategy with cross-border trading;
- conflict when corporate headquarters endeavours to impose limits or even guidelines;
- unacceptable positions can develop within a local market when the self-interest of one partner conflicts with the interest of the joint venture as a whole, as in the pricing of a single-source input or raw material;
- objectives of the respective partners may be incompatible;
- problems of management structures and staffing of joint ventures – nepotism may be the established norm;
- conflict in tax interests between the partners particularly where one may represent the local government interest.

A joint venture requires sharing rewards as well as risks. The main disadvantage is the very significant costs of control and co-ordination associated with working with a partner. An American study in 1971 revealed that more than one-third of the 1,100 joint ventures of 170 multinational corporations studied, were unstable, ending in 'divorce' or in a significant increase in the US firm's power over its partner. It was also found that joint ventures with a local government partner were more lasting. Research elsewhere has also shown that where business had the choice between joint-equity and contractual joint ventures, they were increasingly moving towards contractual joint ventures.

As an innovative form, contractual joint ventures assume complex forms and do not readily correspond to the known established forms of commercial contracts and so the UN Economic Commission for Europe in its *Guide on Drawing up International Contracts on Industrial Co-operation* (Reference 15) was forced to state:

. . . the drafters of contracts relating to industrial co-operation are obliged to use their imagination and to resort to legal innovation while endeavouring to conform as closely as possible to the economic, financial and commercial realities of industrial co-operation transactions.

Tripartite ventures

Tripartite ventures are few in number. Originally they developed as a means of third country market exploitation by a joint company owned by two separate foreign principals, perhaps also from different politico-economic blocs.

East-West *détente* of the early 1970s facilitated the trade exchange. During this period a few joint stock companies were established such as Polibur based in Manchester, England, a joint venture in the chemical engineering consulting and services field, owned equally by Petrocarbon Developments as a subsidiary of Burmah Oil and Polimex-Cekop of Poland. The expectations for the joint venture were that the Poles would be able to access Socialist countries with Western technology; the British partners would have lower cost Polish inputs to offer on Western markets. All profits would be shared equally. The identity and image of the company would change relative to the market which it was approaching. Unfortunately the downturn in the petro-chemicals sector which has produced overcapacity has created problems for this joint venture. Its success overall has been limited.

Industrialising nations continue, however, to make demands of the developed industrial nations to form partnerships. Recently, Indian engineering companies took an unusual step, which will undoubtedly create a precedent, in drawing up a list of ten major contracts totalling more than £120 million which had been won in third countries where the Indians would like to be awarded sub-contracts: Oman, China, Nigeria, and the Cameroon being four of the project locations listed.

References

1. Ansoff, Igor, 'Strategic Dimensions of Internationalisation', European Institute for Advanced Studies in Management, Brussels, *Working Paper no. 82–37*, October 1982.
2. Terpstra, Vern, *International Marketing*, 3rd edition, Holt Rinehart Winston, 1983.
3. Perlemutter, H. V., 'Some Management Problems on Spaceship Earth: the Megafirm in the Global Industrial Estate', *Academy of Management Proceedings*, New York, August 1969.
4. Conference Board, *Matrix Organisation of Complex Businesses*, Elsevier, 1983.
5. Roman, Daniel D. and Puett, Jr, E. F., *International Business and Technological Innovation*, North Holland, 1983.

6. McMillan, C. and Paulden, S., *Export Agents: A Complete Guide to their Selection and Control* 2nd edition, Gower, 1974.
7. Beeth, Gunnar, 'Distributors – Finding and Keeping the Good Ones', in Thorelli, H. and Becker, H., *International Marketing Strategy*, revised edition, Pergamon, 1980.
8. Brooke, M. Z., *Management Contracts*, Holt Rinehart Winston, London, 1984.
9. *Financial Times* 'The risks and rewards of plunging into collaboration ventures', 15 November 1982; 'McDonalds returns to the Paris Boulevards', January 24 1984 'After BL and Honda: who's linked up with whom', 1981.
10. Paliwoda, S. J., *Joint East-West Marketing and Production Ventures*, Gower, 1981.
11. Tomlinson, J. W. C., *Joint Ventures in India and Pakistan*, Praeger.
12. Killing, J. Peter, *Strategies for Joint Venture Success*, Croom Helm, 1983.
13. Bain, J. S. *Barriers to New Competition: their Character and Consequences in Manufacturing Industries*, Harvard University Press, Cambridge, Mass., 1965.
14. Franko, L. G., *Joint Venture Survival in Multinational Corporations*, Praeger, 1972.
15. UN Economic Commission for Europe, *Guide in Drawing up International Contracts on Industrial Co-operation*, Geneva, 1976, ECD/TRADE/124.

Recommended further reading

British Franchise Association, *Comprehensive Guide to Franchising*, Franchise Chambers, 75c Bell Street, Henley-on-Thames, 1986.
Tom Cannon and Mike Willis, *How to Buy and Sell Overseas*, Business Books, 1986.
W. H. Goldberg, *Mergers: Motives, Modes, Methods*, Gower, 1983.
M. Mendelsohn, *The Guide to Franchising*, 4th Ed., Pergamon Press, 1985.
M. Mendelsohn, *How to Evaluate a Franchise*, Franchise Publications, 1985.

5. EXPORTING AND THE SMALL BUSINESS

Defining a small business is a difficult task. *The Bolton Report* (Reference 1) which dealt with small firms in the UK, defined a small firm in the manufacturing sector as one employing 200 or less people. This is but one feature of the small firm; to arrive then at a more general definition, we will have to look elsewhere to pinpoint its essential characteristics which may have a bearing on the ability to export. For example, owner-management, and the fact that 'the people who run it are those that bear the risks of the enterprise' is one characteristic, but is not necessarily limited to small business as it is found also with Ford Motor Co., J. Sainsbury, Getty Oil, etc., which continue to be wholly-owned and controlled by the individuals who manage them. The importance of the small firm has then to be assessed in the light of other criteria which assess its absolute and relative size in the market place. We can define a small firm as one which:

1. has only a small share of its market;
2. is managed in a personalised way by its owners or part-owners and not through the medium of an elaborate management structure;
3. is not sufficiently large to have access to the capital market for the public issue or placing of securities.

Once a firm has grown significantly beyond any of these three thresholds it will cease to be a small firm.

There has been quite a marked change in company size and employment structure in the UK since the turn of the century. The percentage share of employment fell by half, i.e. from 38 per cent in 1935 to 19 per cent in 1968. The Census of Population shows also that the percentage of employers and self-employed fell from 25.5 per cent in 1911 to 7.5 per cent in the early 1970s. Against this, the 100 largest enterprises in the UK increased their share of net output from 16 per cent in 1909 to 40 per cent in 1970. Structural change has therefore occurred with more than 25 per cent of all world trade being between different units of a company.

In 1972 there were 10,495 US companies engaged in export; for Britain the figures are incomplete but over 85 per cent of exports in 1973 were accounted for by 1,568 firms (this includes all firms with over £1 million worth of exports that year) and the total value of British exports for that year was £11.5 billion: exactly half of that sum was made up by 82 firms. Only two of these firms were not part of groups with international investment and 30 were subsidiaries or affiliates of foreign concerns. As we shall see later in Chapter 18 figures for 1982 show a reduction in the number of companies accounting for half of the UK's exports.

British exporting is now dominated by large firms. In the UK, 20 per cent of the visible exports derive from the activities of a mere 10 firms. Although small firms account for 20 per cent of the GNP, an examination of six key industries showed that small firms accounted for 5 per cent of the exports of these industries. A study of small firms in the north-west of England reported in the *Bolton Report* (Reference 1) indicated that the small firms sampled contributed only 10 per cent of the total exports of all the firms in the sample. The report states:

The belief that small size is an insuperable disadvantage overseas has no doubt inhibited many small firms from entering export markets.

Mr Martin Rumbelow, Secretary of the British Overseas Trade Board (BOTB) captured the essential difficulty of persuading small companies to think big when he said that the encouragement of small businesses to export is always an uphill battle, one that you can never win, but one that you must always fight so as not to lose (Reference 2).

In Japan, the small company sector provides about 60 per cent of direct exports. In the UK, the figure is 8 per cent. The presence of the Japanese trading house makes it possible for small and medium-sized Japanese companies to regard their export markets as being just as accessible as their home markets, whereas some of their UK counterparts are unable to penetrate international markets at all. Japan may now be on the threshold of a new era in its relations with Europe, based upon on-the-spot manufacturing and assembly, rather than direct exports alone, and upon large-scale involvement in the economy of Europe rather than arms-length trading relations. There is the well publicised link between Honda and British Leyland in manufacturing, but more importantly there is the direct investment in the manufacture of domestic electrical equipment in the UK which has been made by Sony, Hitachi, and Toshiba.

For small businesses in the UK, the main outlet appears to be Europe. The EEC take 45 per cent whilst other European countries take a further 25 per cent according to a study conducted by Market Research Enterprises on behalf of British Telecom Europages.

The main features of the exporting activities of small firms include:

1. Export market research used by minority – The norm is for overseas orders to arise by chance and to be met, but that market is not then pursued further. Unexpected export orders do not generally give rise to market research.
2. Prime selling techniques are personal visits, use of fairs and exhibitions, and employment of agents.
3. Fairly low expenditure commitment in terms of total market research budgets and specifically export market research.
4. General ignorance of government support – little use made of BOTB services, with even less use made of management consultants, chambers of commerce and embassies overseas.
5. Limited resources lead to use of export houses and selling via UK buying offices of overseas department stores.

As already noted, the UK situation where small business accounts for only 8 per cent of exports as against the Japanese situation where the figure is 60 per cent, reveals not only a great disparity but a potential opportunity for small business in Britain to grow via exports, providing they are willing to accept the challenge. The following chart summarises the situation regarding exports in the UK, West Germany, and Japan.

UK	West Germany	Japan
Tradition of individual effort, therefore piecemeal and disjointed with separate negotiations with perhaps export houses, freight forwarders, insurance companies, banks, ECGD, etc.	*Each with a long tradition of highly co-ordinated exporting effort integrating separate functions.*	
	Banking strength; strong chambers of commerce overseas	*Sogoshosha (trading houses) including manufacturing, trading and banking combines with vast networks of overseas marketing offices.*

Problems for small exporters

Specific problem areas for small exporters include:

- A relatively large domestic market and lack of exposure to other cultures, making the selection of markets and identification of customers abroad difficult.
- The lack of management time and general resources.
- Reaching the foreign markets; selecting and motivating 'arm's length' commission agents.
- Controlling the foreign operation, channel policy, and physical distribution. The interest of principal and agent may often differ but small businesses because of their size may be more exposed.
- Paperwork and management of export operations.
- Cost of supervisory flying salesmen is often very high when costed per man year of effort in the field.
- Which language is the sales staff to learn if visiting many territories? Targeting key markets rather than spreading resources thinly over a number of territories has been a message of the BETRO Report, and Barclays Bank Report.
- Cost of overseas offices may not be justified by the sales potential of particular territorial markets. Going it alone retains independence of action but may be financially ruinous.
- Different safety and quality standards overseas may involve a small company in expensive modifications to achieve success.

- A long-term perspective has to be taken of many markets which may require a long company presence before achieving any payback.

The magnitude of these problems has been investigated in the US market (Reference 12) by asking respondents to rank order by relative importance, and this produced the following 'rank order' or 'league table' of difficulty:

1. **Paperwork**.
2. **Selecting a reliable distributor**. Lists available from embassies and trade councils do not offer a qualitative assessment, which is what may be required. Increasingly the British Clearing Banks are offering their services in this area.
3. Comparative disadvantages due to **non-tariff barriers**, e.g. health and safety standards used to exclude imports. Small companies do not always have the resources to modify and fight back.
4. **Honouring letters of credit**, although not where this has been endorsed by the local bank thus creating an irrevocable letter of credit (LC). LCs are still the most common form of payment.
5. **Communication with foreign customers**. Not only language but distance which may be both psychological as well as geographical.

Perceptions of non-exporting small firms

Very often perceptions are judgmental and not based on fact, thus creating psychological barriers to exporting. There may be an expectation of profit maximisation within a specific period. Although this expectation may be based on domestic market experience, international business does take longer to develop.

If a decision to sell or produce overseas is based on 'hunch', rather than substantiated by independent market research, unforeseen market limitation factors may come into play.

Companies may also consider an export effort to be too much trouble or they may believe that they could not cope with the resources required for overseas selling, assembly, manufacture, construction, engineering, consulting or licensing.

The geographical scope of overseas operations may discourage some firms, yet freight costs may not be the largest component in the foreign export price and telex and air travel can minimise distance as can the commonality of language.

There may be structural constraints emanating from company policy as devised by the board of directors. For example, there may be a policy limiting the company to certain types of trading relationships, such as wholly owned subsidiaries. Or there may be financial self-imposed constraints, e.g. refusal to seek external debt or equity capital.

Factors in the exporting success of small firms

Conventional wisdom states that the following factors may be important for a firm to achieve success in exporting, by exploiting an advantage in foreign markets whether in:

- High technology
- Substantial research and development (R&D)
- Sophisticated marketing
- Advanced forms of organisational design

A profile of successful small exporters in North America (Reference 8) adopted many of these points in its recipe offered for success. The successful firms were seen to:

1. Hold patents and/or have technological orientation
2. Have a price advantage in the market
3. Have already established fairly broad market coverage
4. Have sales volume in excess of $1 million per year (a measure too quickly eroded by inflation unfortunately)
5. Hold high profit aspirations

But another study took a different view, pointing out that the inputs which determine market effectiveness for the small firm could be different from those that apply to the large multinational corporation (Reference 10) (MNC). Stating then the factors which may contribute towards success, but including also a few rather general thoughts, we note that:

- Government assistance is a 'hygiene' factor in the Herzberg sense that it does not act as a motivator although its absence would be regrettable.
- Top management effort and backing are required.
- Pricing and promotion are most important.
- Firms with one or two products are more successful.
- Mature products, if modified for export, can compete successfully.
- Sophistication of a firm's manufacturing process is not an element in exporting success.
- Information for control reporting is vital – quality of information, frequency of reporting, closeness of monitoring of foreign operations.

This has been conceptualised into a model of small firm export sales (Reference 9) whereby export sales are a function of *Effort Opportunity Resistance* i.e.

$$S = f(E \times O \times R)$$

where R is represented by ability to compete outside home market; cultural uniqueness; logistical barriers; and government regulations. It is imperative that an exporter obtain whatever information he can about these three sales variables before entering the export field. The exporter not only needs to evaluate the opportunity that presents itself in the marketplace: he also needs to identify the resistance factors which may make it more difficult to take advantage of this opportunity and could even prevent him from capitalising on what might otherwise appear to be a lucrative market. Finally, the manufacturer must look at the *Effort* variable, objectively assessing the quantity and quality of inputs that he is capable of providing and willing to commit. After each variable has been analysed individually, some overall evaluation should be made.

The exporting consortium alternative

Assuming the size is an important variable in the exporting success of small firms, we wish now to consider the possibilities for small exporters to form themselves into export clubs or industry-wide export trade associations.

This is known as consortium marketing, federated marketing or grouping. Basically, the concept is simply one of strength in unity. Good agents need much backup supporting effort from home, which means frequent expensive visits are necessary, with management effort at a premium. Depending upon the number of participants, and the degree of government financial support, costs for a company in consortium have been estimated at about one-tenth of those which the company would otherwise have to meet for its own exclusive local presence, and about the same fraction for the equivalent cost of employing 'flying salesmen' to supervise agents.

Most importantly each member keeps his own identity and sovereignty, whilst sharing in the combined strength of the group; and small companies who constitute the growth sector of the economy and provide the new job opportunities, can in theory begin to sell into overseas markets as easily as they sell into the home market.

A union of three or four companies, offering complementary and non-competing products and services, collaborating through a joint organisation in an overseas sales facility provides the advantages of cost-sharing and risk-sharing for the individual companies (Reference 11).

Other advantages of such a union may include:

- The group can deploy resources beyond the budget limits of the individual companies, and with a joint turnover which will justify the expenditure.
- On-the-spot professional top calibre sales staff arrange feedback, after-sales service, local distribution, and provide permanent sales presence.
- Concentrating on specific markets minimises the language problem.

Forming an exporting consortium

Exporting consortiums usually develop along the following lines.

1. A target overseas geographical market is identified, in market and not product terms.
2. A group of two or three companies with complementary products/ services agree to co-operate in their export efforts. A group of companies thus formed can between them supply and design a service or package system, and in addition provide financial credits and working capital.
3. A jointly owned overseas marketing consortium is created and registered as a public company with limited liability.

4. The consortium is managed by a board of directors with one director appointed by each company. The consortium appoints its own general manager and overseas marketing staff.
5. Communications are established between the overseas offices or marketing staff, and the member companies. The role of the overseas posts is very important in agreeing and implementing plans, in collaborating, negotiating, and providing technical presence.
6. Local images may be all important. Equally a maintenance facility may be a prerequisite for sales, and the maintenance operation may in itself be very profitable.
7. The consortium will develop its own rules concerning managers and participants and third-party supplier's selling prices, stocks, publicity, and sales policies. All members are expected to quote fair prices to the consortium and not take unfair advantage of individual key inputs, e.g. raw materials.
8. A counter-trade member would supply financial credits for credit sales and provide working capital for contract operations.
9. The consortium appoints, if required, a consulting engineer as technical adviser so that it can take advantage of a strong consulting system.

Attracting more small firms into exporting

More small firms could be attracted into exporting by (a) improving the trading environment, and (b) simplify trading operations.

Improving the trading environment

This could be achieved by:

• Eliminating the distrust among small businessmen of government departments by making the latter more responsive to the needs of small business.
• Correcting the mistaken perception of non-exporters who view the cost factors – executive time, packaging and insurance costs, clerical time, shipping costs – to be higher than do exporters.
• Encouraging exporters to be proactive rather than reactive in their approach to international marketing, focussing on the profit advantage of international marketing activities over domestic sales, and moving away from the idea of a market of last resort.
• Encouraging trade associations to participate in exporting on behalf of their members, also to develop export market research databanks.
• Encouraging the development of voluntary export consortia which can provide the financial strength and marketing resources so many small firms lack.

Simplify trading operations

They key to this question is in simplifying and reducing paperwork. Arranging export credit and documentation may be a small task for the large company but for the small company taking perhaps its first large export order, the export preparations can be intimidating. In Britain, too, there is a polarisation of all financial services towards the South. This means that, firstly, in the North the general level of awareness of services will be lower, and that secondly, the expertise is mainly to be found only by travelling to London and the South since most bank branches feel quite out of their depth in trying to handle export credit assistance. The situation is changing, however, and the main clearing banks are beginning to move their financial services further north. Still, the banks impose a floor limit on the export credit facilities which they offer which they do not generally seek to go below. This may be of the order of £50,000. As this may well constitute a large order for the small company, it may feel, quite rightly, that its needs are not being served. Into this breech has stepped the confirming house such as the English Export Finance Association based in Rochdale. A licensed deposit taker by the Bank of England, it is not only physically present in its area but able and willing to handle a smaller scale of business.

With regard to paperwork particularly, much has been done by SITPRO (Simplification of International Trade Procedures), London to facilitate the processing of export documentation, also by providing task-specific pre-printed stationery, as well as occasional country reports. The Confederation of British Industry (CBI) helps with world regional area trade specialists as does the Export Credit Guarantee Department (ECGD) although it often encounters the criticism that its lines of credit are designed for large companies and the smaller size orders but which would probably constitute very large export orders for small businesses. With regard to the ECGD, too, a Matthews inquiry into its efficiency in March 1984 found a widely held feeling that the ECGD's service and premium charges to large exporters were adversely affected by the proportionately greater amount of time devoted by the department to servicing the small exporter. In the five years to 1983, all but the largest of the ECGD's comprehensive short-term guarantees failed to contribute enough to cover the cost of administration and claim payments. About 40 per cent of the smallest policies produced less than 3 per cent of premium income and accounted for nearly 20 per cent of administration costs. Matthews recommended that the ECGD should not have to meet the costs of services to small exporters beyond its obligation as an insurer.

The Department of Trade has centralised its services to exporters under the umbrella organisation of the British Overseas Trade Board (BOTB) which is now able to offer the following services:

- *Market Prospects Service.* This is used by companies sizing up an overseas opportunity. Carried out by the commercial department of the relevant overseas embassy it consists of a report on market conditions and established competitors plus an analysis of the specific prospects for the product and potential exporter. The £150 fee can be refunded as a contribution towards travel costs if an encouraging report stimulates an overseas visit by the BOTB's customer.

- *Export Marketing Research* funds are available to finance between one third and one half of the costs.
- *Export Representative Service* will help find a suitable agent, distributor or importer.
- *Overseas Status Report Service* offers assessments of these representatives.
- *Technical Help to Exporters.* Small firms can get up to £100 of help free. The service provides detailed information on foreign regulations and product standards and specifications.
- *Market Entry Guarantee Scheme*, designed for small and medium sized businesses offers loans between £20,000 and £150,000 to meet half the cost of overheads incurred by a company in setting up an overseas office, hiring staff and paying for travel and promotion. The BOTB charges a 3 per cent flat rate interest and makes a levy on sales with a view to getting its money back, but it also bears the loss if the operation is unsuccessful.
- *Export Intelligence Unit* offers a low cost (£45) subscription service to British exporters, matchmaking up to 150 enquiries from British consulates and embassies abroad with subscribing companies categorised by 18 different types, 7500 product and service headings and 165 markets. This has initiated £1 billion of British exports.
- *Export Services and Promotions Division*, based in London with regional offices.
- *Fairs and Promotions Branch* which supports groups of British firms at overseas fairs. This may be a relatively inexpensive and convenient way for a small company to take the opportunity to assess particularly difficult markets with the expert guidance of a mission.
- *Overseas Projects Group* which was established primarily to help cope with the complexities of forming a consortium in order to tender for large engineering and construction projects primarily in the Middle East.
- *Publicity Unit*, in conjunction with the Central Office of Information and BBC External Services.

Further incentives to small exporters include the Queen's Award for Exports, and although not specific to small exporters, many small firms have been successful in receiving this award in recent years. Additionally, in 1982 the Export Award for Smaller Businesses administered by Midland Bank International for small firms with less than 200 employees. The co-sponsors of this award include the British Overseas Trade Board, British Caledonian Airways and Thomas Cook. In 1984 this attracted 210 entrants, 127 manufacturers and 83 service companies vying for £25,000 of business travel to the first five winners.

References

1. Bolton, J., *Report of a Committee of Enquiry on Small Firms*, HMSO, 1971.
2. Gray, Frank, 'Encouraging Small Exporters to Think Big', *Financial Times*, 24th October 1985.

3. Bannock, Graham, *The Economics of Small Firms: Return from the Wilderness*, 1981.
4. Prais, S. J., *The Evolution of the Giant Firms in Britain*, Cambridge University Press, 1976.
5. Brooke, M. Z. and Remmers, H. L., *The International Firm*, Pitman, 1977, p. 32.
6. Cannon, T., 'Developing the export potential of small firms: the role of training', *Industrial and Commercial Training*, July, 1977.
7. *Financial Times*, 'Japanese in Europe', December 8, 1981.
8. Cavusgil, S. T., Bilkey, W. J. and Tesar, G., 'A note on the export behaviour of firms: exporter profiles', *Journal of International Business Studies* 10 (Spring/Summer) 1979, pp. 91–7.
9. Brasch, John J., 'Assessing Market Potential for Exports', *Journal of Small Business Management*, 17 (April) 1979, pp. 13–19.
10. Kirpalani, V. H. and Mackintosh, B. N., 'International marketing effectiveness of technology-oriented small firms', *Journal of International Business Studies*, Winter 1980, pp. 81–90.
11. For case studies of small firm export consortia see the *Director*, October 1977, pp. 84–6.
12. Rabino, S., 'Examination of barriers to exporting encountered by small manufacturing companies', *Management International Review*, 20 no. 1, 1980, pp. 67–73.
13. Wilson, Alexander and Lockhart, G. W., *How to start exporting – a guide for small firms*, Department of Industry Small Firm Information Service, no. 15. Leah Hertz, *Small Exporter's Guideline Sheets*, Small Business Bureau, 1986.

6. DECISIONS ON INTERNATIONAL PRODUCT POLICY

Before starting to consider international product planning, it is necessary to have a definition of what actually constitutes a product. The working definition which is to be used here is the definition offered by Kotler (Reference 9), namely:

A product is anything that can be offered to a market for attention, acquisitions, use or consumption; it includes physical objects, services, personalities, places, organisations and ideas.

A product may therefore be seen to embrace more than a branded, packaged good offered for sale. The definition has been widened to include the area of services selling which includes tourism, as well as the attendant benefits and services that products bring with them. Black and Decker is one company which has for many years had a marketing orientation which is evident in the way in which they perceive their customers. Asked about what business they are in, the company's response is that it is to sell solutions to clients who purchase their products with a particular problem in mind. Black and Decker do not see their mission as being to sell electrical drills but to make and sell equipment to meet client needs.

Competition is changing globally and important writers such as Levitt and Drucker have signalled this change in writing of the 'new competition'. Levitt (Reference 10) has stated for example, that:

. . . new competition is not between what companies produce in their factories but between what they add to their factory output in the form of packaging, services, advertising, customer service, financing, delivery arrangements, warehousing and other things that people value.

This emphasis on the attendant benefits and services that people value is what essentially separates the companies who practise the marketing concept from those who do not. If this is not provided by a local competitor the chances are that it will be provided by a foreign one. The internationalisation of competition is everywhere apparent with the established multinational companies chasing each other around the world in a never-ending search for market share. The multinationals have had to adopt a suitable 'positioning' strategy with regard to their products alongside local competitors but benefit immediately from the fact that their name or product is often already known, ahead of their actual arrival in that market, as a result of the effects of foreign travel, cinema, and television. For multinational companies the aim then is to seek to transfer product satisfaction across national boundaries.

Another important element of the 'new' competition is the arrival on world markets of the Japanese as a formidable trading nation. Using what has been termed as a 'cascading' strategy, (Reference 1) they will initially seek penetration of well-defined segments, then move to volume stimulation and segment domination, before cascading into other areas and moving across.

This raises the question, why do products fail? There are the problems of tariff barriers, of non-tariff barriers or 'invisible' barriers which seek to exclude products or services from a given market. Where access is granted, tariffs or subsidies to a local competitor may mean inability to compete or even match on price. Related to this also is the question of 'dumping' which may upset a market sufficiently to persuade existing local suppliers that there is no long-term future for them. Other reasons for failure would include cultural insensitivity; poor planning such that there is limited availability of the product in question; poor timing so that the regularity of supply or even first appearance on the market is ill-timed; misguided enthusiasm of top management concerned; product deficiencies with regard to the target market; and, finally, lack of Unique Selling Proposition (USP) generally, indicating that neither in the product, its accompanying benefits, nor its advertising, is there any criterion to differentiate this particular product from any of its competitors.

With regard to product suitability for foreign markets, this depends on the product itself; its stage in the product life cycle – whether introductory or not; and the intended host country and its economic life cycle stage – whether mature industrial, or one of the types of less developed country; as well as situation-specific characteristics such as the country's current product offering. Product life cycles have already been discussed, but it is important to remember also that this is only one part of the equation, and one must take cognisance of the state of development of transferor country and transferee. The example of McDonalds, the American hamburger chain, serves to illustrate this point with their entry to the UK. When this took place, the McDonalds mode of counter service and production line hamburger preparation was new to Britain so it meant that not only were McDonalds' American recipes being introduced but also the specifications for the catering equipment and polystyrene packaging. Once British suppliers were found, it made it easier for competitors to enter on the scene: profit-seeking suppliers now sought other potential clients for this equipment which they had developed.

Suitability is not, however, the same as acceptability and it is worth noting at this point the work done on international market segmentation by Wind and Douglas. They pointed out that segmentation could usefully be performed after first conducting a study of the enduring characteristics such as target market geography, topography, and demography. Little could be expected to change amongst these variables except over time. The second set of variables were the situation-specific characteristics and here they included factors such as buying patterns and consumption. Figure 6.1 is a flowchart of their basis for segmentation. At the same time, it should not be forgotten that prevailing local attitudes towards a particular product or product type should be monitored. Marketing can play an important role in influencing behaviour where stereotyped attitudes exist. Again, where the source of origin is deemed to have a positive effect, this may even allow a foreign product to remain competitive when not actually price competitive.

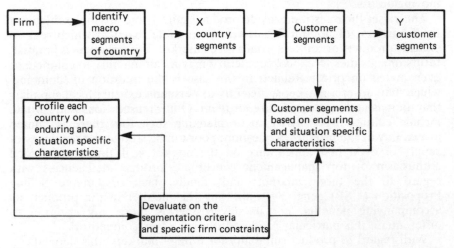

Figure 6.1 International market segmentation

Source Wind and Douglas, 'International Market Segmentation', *European Journal of Marketing*, vol. 6, no. 1, 1972.

Product modification or standardisation

The chairman of a US multinational corporation was once quoted as having said that, all things being equal, given that his company had universal, completely standardised products and given the economies of scale with their product line, he would ideally have only one worldwide production centre in the United States from which he would source worldwide. However, it is an imperfect world and so there were numerous obstacles in the way of what was for the company perhaps an ideal sourcing situation. Apart from a few companies fortunate enough to enjoy global products such as Coca-Cola or Pepsi, the question for the remainder is not single sourcing of a universal standardised product but, instead, the degree to which they will be able to standardise or bow to modification. Economies come from standardisation, but the local pressures may be in favour of some degree of local modification. We shall now examine these factors under the separate headings of standardisation and modification.

Product modification

Mandatory product modifications arise as a result of the following:

1. *Legal requirements.*
2. *Tariffs; 'invisible' tariffs.*

3. *Nationalism* as a response to lack of company presence on the market other than just in sales; unfortunate brand name; high perceived degree of 'foreignness' in the product offered.

4. *Technical requirements* are another means of excluding a product from a market until the technical specifications have been met. Regulations for such things as foodstuffs, drugs, electrical equipment are a few examples.

5. *Taxation* has to be considered. For example, with regard to cars, France has a system whereby the 'road tax' which is levied as a flat rate upon all users in Britain, is dependent in France upon engine size and age of the car. Indeed, it is a much more equitable system but is likely to add significantly to the running costs of luxury cars in France.

6. *Climate* plays a part, too, in that special modifications need to be made often with regard to higher working temperatures for machinery, or special packaging for consumer goods to ensure the freshness in actual use.

Other factors influencing modification include:

1. *Consumer tastes*. Traditionally, food has been held to be society's most culture-bound product but perhaps it is time to rethink this, in view of the fact that Kentucky Fried Chicken is now sold in Japan and that McDonalds and others are now to be found in France, the gastronomic capital of the world. Consumer tastes will have an important bearing on the name used; product features, labelling, packaging and materials; pricing and sales and advertising promotion.

2. *Low personal disposable income* in the target market will affect frequency of purchase as well as product sizes offered.

3. *Illiteracy and low levels of education* will necessitate product simplification with the use of symbols instead of words. Within the EEC, it has been the case for many years that all the instrumentation in the dashboard of the car is now labelled with symbols rather than words. It is presumably no reflection on the prevailing standards of education and general literacy levels within the EEC but a means devised by the multinational automobile companies of standardising their cars for all West European markets. Symbols travel more easily than does the written word.

4. *Poor maintenance standards* will necessitate product change perhaps prolonging periods between overhauls and regular servicing.

5. *Local labour costs*. Where these are low, they encourage a greater manual content in work carried out. Where labour costs are high, automation is always sought as an alternative.

Product standardisation

Factors which encourage product standardisation include:

1. *Production economies of scale.*
2. *Development costs*, as reflected in the increase in contractual joint ventures to counteract the escalating costs of new product development in the automobile industry or the aircraft industry.

3. *Stock costs* as a result of the maintenance of a wide range of products and high level of service.

4. *Components that are interchangeable* across product models.

5. *Technological content* is standard internationally for the industry.

6. *Consumer mobility* as a result of increasing travel opportunities which leads to familiarity with international products, such as perhaps Gillette or Bic razors; Coca-cola, Pepsi; and a wide range of clothing, toiletries and other articles.

7. *Market homogeneity* is increasing with the market concentration effects of the EEC for example. Concentration has taken place in many areas, leading to European industries rather than national industries. As the costs of research and development increase and as the needs of critical mass become apparent then companies begin to treat neighbouring country markets as an extended regional market rather than as a member of separate foreign markets.

The benefits of standardisation are:

- cost savings through experience-curve effects and economies of scale.
- consistency, with customers acknowledging consumer mobility and cross-border flows of television, radio, newspaper and periodical advertising.
- remaining barriers are common to all markets, such barriers as social conventions regarding product use, purchasing patterns.

Product standardisation and world product mandates

A world product mandate (WPM) is defined as the full development and production of a new product line in a subsidiary of a multinational company. It is rapidly becoming a major topic of public policy discussion although there still remain many unresolved technical and conceptual issues.

A world product mandate permits the subsidiary to be responsible for the development and worldwide marketing of a specific innovation. The subsidiary needs to bargain with its parent to secure a potentially profitable mandate but once it has it, the subsidiary can use the internal market of the multinational organisation to distribute and control the new process. It is necessary therefore to examine the cost benefits from the viewpoint of the three parties involved: host country, subsidiary company, and parent multinational.

Host countries seek employment, growth, and development technology and expertise from companies located within their boundaries. As was pointed out earlier in Chapter 4, host countries do complain about the perceived quality of investment made by multinationals within their boundaries. Such complaints may include:

- absence of, or insufficient, R and D at the subsidiary level, especially when the market size is small
- insufficient transfer or diffusion of technology
- employment of obsolete technology

Table 6.1
Obstacles to standardisation in international marketing strategies

Factors limiting standardisation	Product design	Pricing	Distribution	Sales force	Advertising and promotion, branding and packaging
Market characteristics					
Physical environment	Climate Product use conditions		Customer mobility	Dispersion of customers	Access to media Climate
Stage of economic and industrial development	Income levels Labour costs in relation to capital costs	Income levels	Consumer shopping patterns	Wage levels, availability of manpower	Needs for convenience rather than economy Purchase quantities
Cultural factors	'Custom and tradition' Attitudes toward foreign goods	Attitudes toward bargaining	Consumer shopping patterns	Attitudes toward selling	Language, literacy Symbolism
Industry conditions					
Stage of product life cycle in each market	Extent of product differentiation	Elasticity of demand	Availability of outlets Desirability of private brands	Need for missionary sales effort	Awareness, experience with products
Competition	Quality levels	Local costs Prices of substitutes	Competitors' control of outlets	Competitors' sales forces	Competitive expenditure messages
Marketing institutions					
Distributive system	Availability of outlets	Prevailing margins	Number and variety of outlets available Ability to 'force' distribution	Number, size, dispersion of outlets	Extent of self-service
Advertising media and agencies				Effectiveness of advertising, need for substitutes	Media availability, costs, overlaps
Legal restrictions	Product standards Patent laws Tariffs and taxes	Tariffs and taxes Antitrust laws Resale price maintenance	Restrictions on product lines Resale price maintenance	General employment restrictions Specific restrictions on selling	Specific restrictions on messages, costs Trademark laws

Source R. D. Buzzell, 'Can you Standardise Multinational Marketing?', *Harvard Business Review*, November–December 1968, pp. 102–13.

- inefficient subsidiary operation/no economies of scale
- high transfer pricing for goods imported from other sister subsidiaries
- downward pressure on the host's currency and drain on foreign exchange
- low local content ratio
- low or no exports
- negative or neutral effect on economic growth and development
- low, or no, adherence to host country's national goals.

For the most part, host countries have refused to bear a proportionate share of the cost or risk of developing technology, a product, or a market. Furthermore, they have been the primary source of environmental, sovereign, and political risk.

WPM is an arrangement whereby the MNC allows the subsidiary to transcend the restrictions of miniature or truncated operations by enlarging the subsidiary's mandate, and hence its associated responsibilities, above and beyond the geographical or political boundaries of the host country. The sphere of the new mandate's activity and coverage depends on the interactions between the costs and benefits of the mandate in terms of economies of scale and learning, transportation charges, added cost of logistics, cost of tariffs, non-tariff barriers, etc. For example, when economies of scale are reached at relatively low volumes or economies of learning are realised in comparatively short periods of time, the mandate is expected to be more limited in geographical scope than the global coverage implied in WPM.

It is possible to have regional product mandates (RPMs) especially when the demand of the contiguous region is larger than, or as large as, the optimal plant size. In that case, instead of a real WPM, a more limited mandate in terms of authority and responsibility with respect to at least one product is given to the subsidiary, but this is awarded on a competitive basis and a mandate must be earned.

From the host country viewpoint, there are the advantages of having relatively autonomous and internally directed institutions which are operating on a worldwide basis without much of the actual costs associated with developing such institutions.

World truck nears launch

Ford's 'world' truck will go on sale this year. It will have a European cab, a North American chassis and a diesel engine developed from one used by the group's agricultural tractor division. The components will be assembled in Brazil.

The first 'family' of designs for the new medium-to-heavy range is aimed primarily at the Brazilian and North American markets where the first products will go on sale in the autumn.

Mr Edson Williams, Ford vice-president and general manager of the group's truck operations, says: 'The Brazilian world truck takes the best we have within Ford and puts it together.'

The company has the capacity to build about 40,000 a year.

The cab will be adapted from the one used for the Ford Cargo range in Europe. Cab panels will be sent from the UK to Brazil for the new vehicle.

But the heavy cost of transport to Europe and the 14 per cent tariff barrier it would face before entering the EEC makes it unlikely that built-up trucks will find their way from Brazil to Europe, Mr Williams says.

However, Mr Williams reveals that other export markets are being considered and there seems to be potential in Asia.

Ford has invested about $100m in a new diesel engine plant in Brazil which will come into operation shortly, providing power units mainly for the domestic market. The engine is a six-cylinder, direct-injection 7.8 litre unit. There will also be an option of the existing Ford 6.6 litre turbo engine, but in a South American version. Output of 55,000 engines a year is envisaged.

The company will start by building what are known in North America as Class 6 and 7 trucks (medium-weight). Eventually heavyweight (Class 8) versions will be introduced – but using bought-in engines, because Ford has no intention of developing a 10-litre diesel engine of its own, Mr Williams points out.

The Brazilian project is part of Ford's response to the substantial over-capacity for heavy truck manufacturing worldwide.

Ford can simplify its heavy truck designs worldwide and establish those parts of the truck which could be made common to Ford vehicles the world over.

He looks ahead at the time when 'components for our heavy trucks will be of a single, world-class design and will be built in a number of countries. We will buy from those international suppliers who can supply in the countries where we assemble trucks and need the components.'

A locally-produced ZF gearbox will be used in the Brazilian-built 'world' truck for instance.

Ford began working its world truck programme in 1982. It will take another eight years to complete, says Mr Williams.

'We must prove it can work and that we can make money on heavy trucks.'

The company will spend about £1bn on truck development and production over the four or five years from 1983 out of its worldwide budget of £4bn. Britain will receive about 80 per cent of the £1bn for trucks.

This is because, although the group has truck plants in Australia and Brazil, the two big design centres are in the US and Britain.

Ford makes a profit on its total commercial vehicle operations but its strength is at the light end – with the Transit van and car-derived vans in Europe and with pick-up trucks and vans in the US.

However, the launch of the Cargo range in March 1981 at the cost of £125m was proof that Ford wants to win a much larger share of the European market for medium and heavy trucks.

The Cargo got off to an inauspicious start with many niggling problems and recalls by the company to put them right. Ford's share of the West European market for trucks of more than 3.5 tonnes, which stood at 7 per cent in 1980, has shrunk to just over 6 per cent.

With the full Cargo range in place and the initial technical problems behind it, Ford will concentrate on building sales, particularly in the UK, and getting some return on its investment.

Source: Financial Times, 16 January 1985

The parent MNC has very little incentive to grant a WPM to any subsidiary. Doing so defeats the very basic feature of MNCs – flexibility and freedom of choice with regard to source and location of supplies. In so far as worldwide procurement of the mandated product is concerned, a fully developed or natural WPM implies that the parent enterprise gives up this privilege and commits itself to the mandated subsidiary as the sole source in control of supplies for its worldwide markets.

In order to receive a mandate, a subsidiary must become highly competitive or find other sources of support. As a result of a mandate, the host country receives substantial benefits. Indeed there is such a great deal at stake for the host country that it cannot remain indifferent. It finds itself obliged to lend active support to the subsidiary to bid for and finally secure a mandate. Given the profound future benefits to the subsidiary (due to the mandate), a subsidiary finds it difficult not to accept the help and support from an old adversary in fighting for the mandate. In this process, a new coalition (i.e. subsidiary-host country) is formed and the old coalition (i.e. subsidiary-parent) is weakened. As a result, in order to receive, operate, and continue with the mandate successfully, the subsidiary will need the host government's continued active and substantial support.

A WPM restores a sense of power and accomplishment to the newly formed subsidary; it can produce a new coalition between the subsidiary and the host country; while it increases their interdependence with the rest of the MNC's system simultaneously.

In summary, WPM cultivates an environment which is highly conducive to efficient, complete, and co-operative operation for all the participants – the host country, the subsidiary, and its parent company.

Branding

Branding is important as a means of distinguishing a company offering, and differentiating one particular product from its competitors. To the company with a product with any commercial life left in it, branding is able to offer an advantage. Given all the other factors already mentioned – pricing, distribution, and promotion – branding is a means whereby the consumer can identify a particular product, and, if satisfied with it, ask for it by name. For the company concerned there are clear advantages to branding in that branding enables the company to differentiate its product more clearly but also to fetch a higher return than could be expected from generic products.

Ashton Chemicals is a Manchester company (whose name has been changed for the sake of this example) who specialise in manufacturing for export the kinds of pharmaceutical preparations which were common in Victorian England. A few of these have a brand name but many are generic and a few are packaged and presented to closely resemble the market leader in their particular field. Ashton's advantage in the export trade is that it is a long established company and it is based in Britain. Clients abroad still buy from Ashton although there may well be even a local competitor for these unexciting grandmother's recipes and their explanation of this is simply that where health is concerned, people are less exacting about price. Quality is much more important and here the fact that they are a long established company, able to boast a 'Made in England' on their labels, enhances their standing in the market place of many of the less developed countries.

Branding is perceived as a means of guarantee of quality offered by the manufacturer to the consumer. There is the expectation of standardisation, that each and every product will meet these same specifications. Where

Table 6.2

World product mandates from the points of view of the respective parties.

Host Country	Subsidiary	Multinational Corporation
1. Economies of scale and expertise	1. Reduced dependence on local market	1. Decentralisation of power
2. More efficient production, lower unit costs	2. Increased stability with market diversification	2. Loss of some control
3. Relative independence from local market	3. Market research information now required	3. Restricted to source of supply
4. Local content ratio up to 100%	4. Staff product support to sister subsidiaries	4. Need to protect the mandate and avoid duplication elsewhere
5. Creation of local suppliers	5. Interact with host government	5. Mandate must ensure continued competitiveness
6. Local purchasing eliminates transfer pricing disputes	6. Illustrate benefits clearly to host government	6. Safeguards to ensure product compatibility worldwide
7. High exports with low imports	7. Stronger management team required	7. Subsidiary needs now to be kept informed of product changes/legislation and market research
8. Ongoing R & D at subsidiary level	8. Subsidiary becomes a centre for that product's R & D	
9. Possible future exporter of technology	9. Convince parent MNC that benefits outweigh costs	8. MNC has to ask all subsidiaries to co-operate with the mandated subsidiary
10. Access to world markets		9. Mandated subsidiary must be fully integrated and accepted within the MNC organisation
11. Pressure to remain competitive supplier for a world market		
12. Improved relations with subsidiary		10. Smooth communications between sister subsidiaries
13. Improved relations with MNC		11. More intense planning and co-ordination necessary as options now reduced and dependence increased.
		12. MNC has to act as an adjudicator in the event of dispute.

Source Adapted from Hamid Etemad, 'World Product Mandates in Perspective' in Alan Rugman (ed), *Multinationals and Technology Transfer: The Canadian Experience*, Praeger, 1983.

there is this high degree of standardisation accompanied by a high degree of customer satisfaction, the brand is likely to become, if it has not already done so, the market leader. Occasionally, though, brands suffer the fate of being too successful in that they pass into the language and lose the distinctiveness which they once had. Sometimes this is due to market dominance because of patent protection, sometimes implying just market leadership. Where a brand becomes the name for all products of that type, it has become a generic. The German firm Bayer once had the rights to Aspirin which was a protected brand name until after the war. Indeed, the only country still to recognise protected rights to the name Aspirin as a registered brand name is Argentina.

Pharmaceutical products are likely to be standardised, but as reflected in Keegan's *Five Strategies for Multinational Marketing* (Reference 2), brand names often meant that although the name is the same, the ingredients may be quite different from the product sold in the home country. *The Economist* in 1982 (Reference 4) carried a report on how Bangladesh imposed a ban on 2,000 drugs. The aim was to both save foreign exchange and save also on drugs that did not work. For nearly three-quarters of these prohibited drugs had been listed by the World Health Organisation or by American or British drug authorities as useless, harmless, or both. A quite separate example entirely is that of cigarettes where high tar level cigarettes are freely available in some of the less-developed countries although now withdrawn from sale in the West. Branding may be international but the assurance of branding varies with national frontiers.

Branding lies behind the success of franchising. Franchising conveys only the right to use a name, logo, plus access to company-specific know-how including management systems. The key of this form of market representation is the importance attached to an important brand name, many of which are quite international: McDonalds hamburger chain, Budget rent-a-car; Kentucky Fried Chicken. All derive their income from the use of their names.

Marks and Spencer, the British firm with the quality image chain of department stores (Reference 3), has no manufacturing capacity of its own but nevertheless exports amounted to £58 million in 1982. Marks and Spencer have three strategies. The first is to grant the St Michael brand name franchise to freestanding sales outlets. The second is to establish shops within shops that sell the St Michael marque exclusively, as in Finland and Japan where Marks goods are sold within the Daiei department store chain. The last is to sell directly to selected retailers or to market through a wholesaler. The company policy is not to export to countries where they already have stores, i.e. France, Ireland, Canada and Holland.

International Harvester (IH) acquired two small but well-respected Lancashire lorry builders in Seddon and Atkinson, in 1974 (Reference 7). The Atkinson was a cult vehicle and dubbed the 'Knight of the Road', being quite identifiable with its trademark of the letter 'A' in a circle mounted on an old-style grille. IH merged the two companies and discarded the old imagery, but the old imagery is now returning. In Spain,

IH have bought into Enasa which makes the Pegaso which dominates the Spanish market and the Spanish are very proud of their product. The dilemma for IH therefore arises with the next expected generation of trucks, for not having a visible image in Europe in trucks themselves, they will be forced into a few decisions, as to which name to carry into Europe –British or Spanish? Or will it be American? What degree of commonality can we expect to see from these truck producers across their separate brand names? These are questions for the not too distant future.

Coca-cola and Pepsi-cola have licensed bottlers around the world who pay for the right to use the name. Pepsi is now based in 145 countries but they never patented their recipe as they feared they might lose it after the traditional 15–16 year period of first registration. Coca-cola dates back to 1893 as originally a cure for peptic ulcers. Although both Coke and Pepsi are seen as virtually interchangeable today to the majority of the buying public, 40 years ago the situation was quite different. Pepsi then was identified with the working classes and perceived as being better value than Coke. Pepsi first began to receive television advertising in the US from 1939 but the development of the two giants is fascinating.

Coca-cola benefitted from the Second World War when the US army took it with them overseas but Coke was still being sold in war-time Germany. There was a Coca-cola manager, Max Keith, who was head of soft drinks for all occupied Europe. Fanta was developed at this time because sugar was short in Hitler's Germany. Elsewhere, the US War Department was paying for bottling plants to be sent to the frontline.

Banking provides other quite different illustrations of the importance of branding. Travellers' cheques and plastic bank cards are now quite international. For travellers' cheques American Express and Thomas Cook were in at the very beginning, but the travel and entertainment cards at Diners Club and American Express were the first really international cards, and were followed belatedly by the various banking consortia of Visa International – who now issue travellers' cheques as well as credit cards – and Master Charge. These last two are consortia which allow the local banks to append their name to an internationally recognised and standardised card format. A local bank will acquires more respect from its clients when its travellers' cheques are readily accepted abroad at a wide variety of outlets instead of just correspondent banks. Here the power lying behind the name of the consortium constitutes the differential advantage. Interestingly, British television advertisements for travel and entertainment cards emphasise the freedom of international movement and purchasing power; the bank credit cards, the high number of outlets which will accept their cards. The approach in either case is quite different but here is an example of banks now being able to offer an international highly standardised branded product.

Selection of a brand name

Textbooks and management checklists often state that a good brand name should be able to meet a number of criteria such as legality of its use or description; suitability for the product; distinctiveness; and generally being short, easy to remember, and suggestive of the product that it represents. In the international marketing arena, many products fail to meet these criteria once transferred to the foreign market. An unfortunate branding example is GEC-Osram, a long and well-established lighting division of the British General Electric Corporation. Now although both GEC and Osram are well respected quality brand names in Britain, the name Osram in Polish means, quite simply and much less politely, excrement.

Products travel better than do brand names. General Motors sell a small hatchback car throughout Europe known as the Opel Corsa, using the German subsidiary name although the car is actually manufactured in Spain. In Britain, again with the same car, General Motors decided to use instead the name Vauxhall Nova as Vauxhall is the GM British subsidiary. Curious to relate then that 'Nova', in Spain, where this car is after all made, means 'doesn't work'!

Brand names take account of good commercial sense – making use wherever possible of a local subsidiary name; culture; and language. There is no good reason to explain why a Fiat Ritmo which sold well in Europe should not sell well in Britain or why it should sell better as a Fiat Strada in Britain when Strada means only 'Street'! The Japanese did have a car called the Cedric and a small truck in Japan which was not exported but known locally as the 'Little Bugger' (Reference 11). Sales of Tide in Denmark were low until it was deduced that it was the Danish word for menstrual flow. However, the Danes do sell successfully a hair product called Blackhead which obviously must have a different meaning over there.

The folklore of brand names is very rich – some companies use agencies to help them. Some will make a computer search but the difficulty always with a brand name is that unfavourable associations are usually because it is connected with a slang or colloquial usage and dictionaries do not usually provide any help whatsoever in this regard. The Japanese registered 3,000 names in 1983 which they thought would help them sell cars. 1,000 were names of Italian towns, rivers or regions.

Esso's 'Tiger in Your Tank' was undoubtedly a successful standardised campaign but it did undergo modification. To the French the concept of putting a tiger in the tank was bizarre and so it had to be translated as putting a tiger in your engine. Shell benefitted from French colloquial usage when they used their slogan in France *C'est celle que j'aime* a phrase used more to point out an attractive lady more often than a motor oil, but the closeness of 'celle' and 'Shell' made it effective. The point is that it is not just translation that is necessary but the transposition of a concept into another culture. Without checking back on the original, disasters do arise.

Types of branding

1. *Individual brand names.* This was a policy pursued by Rowntree-Mackintosh who only in the last few years introduced a corporate logo onto their packs. Products were stand-alone brands such as 'Smarties' or 'Kit-

Table 6.3
Concentration in grocery retailing: market share of main groups

Country	Major retailers	Percentage of grocery trade	Buying decision points
Austria	10	90.4	53
Belgium	10	64.4	21
Switzerland	10	87.6	14
Germany	10	38.6	30
France	10	75.1	188
Britain	10	58.0	10
Italy	15	46.9	450
Holland	10	73.5	30
Sweden	9	89.1	9

Source Martin von Mesdag, 'Europe's Brand Squeeze', *Management Today* (March 1985), pp. 70–3, 114.

Table 6.4
Shares of trade-owned brands in total grocery sales

Britain	21.5%
Sweden	20.5%
France	19.1%
Belgium	17.4%
Holland	17.1%
Austria	14.2%
Switzerland	14.2%
Norway	11.2%
Germany	7.9%
Italy	5.4%

Source Martin von Mesdag, *op. cit.*

Table 6.5
Growth in the market share of trade-owned brands and generics 1979–83

Sweden	+2.5%
Switzerland	+5.2%
France	+7.3%
Belgium	+12.3%
Austria	+21.4%
Holland	+24.8%
Italy	+25.6%
Britain	+31.9%
Germany	+107.9%

Source Martin von Mesdag, *op. cit.*

Kat' or 'After-Eight' with little mention of who the manufacturer was. It mattered little as they are all quality products but there was no association with the parent manufacturer. This has always been the case, too, with the promotion and sale of soaps and detergent washing powders with Unilever and Proctor & Gamble fighting an international battle for market share with competing brands in each sector.

2. *Blanket family name for all products* is what is practised by Heinz who used to emphasise 'Heinz 57 Varieties', although the total product range must extend now into hundreds. The phrase '57 Varieties' is attributed to the French philosopher Voltaire who on a visit to England commented favourably on the freedom of speech and the 57 varieties of religion.

3. *Separate family names for all products*. This is practised by department stores who may have different in-house brand names for different types of merchandise. Woolworth's and Littlewoods practise this.

4. *Company name and individual product name* is the strategy adopted by Kellogg's who emphasise their name strongly alongside all of their brands. Similarly, Ford Motors do likewise with each of their cars.

5. *'No-name', unbranded merchandise*. In grocery stores this has been adopted by Carrefour hypermarkets in France and Britain and by International Stores in Britain. Woolworths have introduced a range of generic 'no-name' products at discontinued prices. West Germany has experienced this effect quite markedly with cigarettes particularly where the 'no-name' cigarette packs made abroad now account for 40 per cent of the supermarket trade and has led to the market leader Reemstra having to slash its prices. The market had been rocked also by a rise of 39 per cent in the West German tax on tobacco which influenced smokers to trade down. The problem then for the established brands such as Peter Stuyvesant, Ernte, Marlboro, HB, etc. was to re-establish themselves as being value for money brands offering premium quality at a premium price.

Packaging

The example above of the movement on Western markets into plain, unbranded generic products is providing satisfaction for the consumerist lobby, long anxious about the size of advertising budgets and questionable promotional costs being added to overheads and hence final selling price. However, in Britain already, the packaging industry and the printing trades federation has made representation to trade and industry bodies about the effects that this is having on their industries.

Branded products fetch a premium over generic products. Aside from actual product qualities, there is the expectation of a 'no-nonsense' package which is purely functional rather than aesthetically or intrinsically appealing. Branded products offer the highest value-added to the packaging industry. Quality is implicit in the presentation of the product and that presentation is usually the package itself. Materials used are often laminated rather than single thickness. Lacquering of the printing inks gives an impressive sheen and means there is no smell or tainting from the inks. On generic products, this does not matter, it may even be expected as a result of lower price. Packaging then is no longer a promotional tool, but simply a barrier medium with generic products to protect the product as best it can and as cheaply as possible until final sale. Generic products display high-volume low-value unit sale characteristics, so specifications change quite dramatically over the branded products. There is need only for an identification label of the contents only, and as the lower priced product has a higher turnover rate the degree of protection may be reduced for a projected shorter shelf life. This will lower packaging costs further.

Packaging is often seen merely as a barrier property but for many products it is the product that you see on the shelf. Dehydrated soups for example are sold in sachets, or pouches as the Americans call them, but this container represents the product visibly to the buying public, whereas actual sight of the dried powder itself may not appear quite so appetising.

Packaging sizes change with personal disposable income but also with the available channels of distribution. There may be a clear split also in the infrastructure available to urban and rural dwellers. There may be special characteristics of the distribution channels such as a proliferation of wholesalers, or alternatively the large supermarket chains may effectively control distribution. These factors, in addition to the nation's topography, influence shelf life, and that in turn is affected by climate: again, a packaging problem. Packaging therefore has not only to act as a barrier but to come in what the end-user perceives as being the 'right' sizes; and to be easily identifiable in terms of contents and labelling. It is possible therefore to pursue a dual-brand strategy whereby the same product or very similar product is sold through two quite different channels of distribution as they are intended to be targetted at two or more quite different market segments. This is quite separate from the argument over 'own-label' manufacturing where the large supermarket chains in Britain now have manufacturers producing under their own label. Tesco and Safeway now both offer an 'own-label' whisky so their range is quite extensive. It is sometimes assumed that the contents are identical with the brand leader. This is a false assumption argument. Indeed it may be quite wrong to assume so, for both Nestle, with their Nescafe and Kelloggs with their Corn Flakes brand, have been advertising that they do not manufacture for anyone other than themselves nor under any other name than their registered brand names. British supermarket chains such as Tesco, Sainsbury, etc. have become both irritating to manufacturers over this issue but at the same time attractive because of the size of their market dominance. For manufacturers it may not be their first choice entering into 'own-label', but the volume considerations must surely make this a proposition worthy of consideration.

Brand name and trademark protection

Brand names operate under two separate conventions internationally – either prior use elsewhere of the brand name; or first registration, which would allow a private citizen to record all rights for one country to what were protected brand names elsewhere. A certain individual was reputed to have registered over three hundred brand names in the early 1960s and to have bartered furiously with multinationals subsequently seeking entry to that particular market.

Brand name protection therefore means registration in each country likely to be a market for the product concerned. It all depends on the market potential of the product concerned and the resources of the company. Nevertheless, these costs of brand name protection are expensive, amounting to 10–20 per cent of the development costs of certain new products. Du Pont had heavy registration costs with Corfam, the synthetic leather material for shoes, and only break even on its development costs when selling the process to the Soviet Union. Registration and protection therefore adds to total costs, while protecting the commercial advantage embodied in the product concerned from external competitions. This means though that either the product or the process itself has to be offered to a wider market in order to recover the costs of development. Ironically, this emphasises both the need to go abroad as well as the need for international protection.

Trademarks is a separate area from brand names yet although the name is what you would probably ask for or look for in a shop, the trademark is what would probably help you recognise the product even though a pack may be redesigned. A trademark can be any word, symbol, or device or any combination of these which identifies goods or services. Registration at the Patent Office confers upon the proprietor a statutory right to exclusive use of the mark. For example the style of a typeface can be registered. Consider the distinctiveness of the typefaces used in the Kellogg's logo or the IBM logo or the Wrangler logo on shirts and denim jeans. Trademarks are the manufacturer's way of assuring the consumer that he is purchasing an authentic product at a time when brand piracy is certainly on the increase and extending from the traditional areas of clothing into micro-computers from the Far East. A standard pack of Kellogg's Corn Flakes therefore has protected rights to the Kellogg's logo: the cockerel graphic; the slogan in 'the sunshine breakfast'; and the slogan underneath the brand name – 'the best to you'. Loss of control over any or all of these could invite product imitation which Kelloggs have been able to avoid completely in the UK until the advent of generic products.

It is interesting therefore to note how the Coca-Cola bottle was found not to be registrable as a trade mark in a reapplication by the Coca-Cola company to the Court of Appeal, January 23, 1985. From the early 1920s, the company had been selling Coca-Cola in unusually shaped bottles in the UK, and there was ample evidence to show that the public in the US, and in the UK associated the shape with Coca-Cola. The verdict was that a line drawing of a bottle may be registrable as the trade mark of a beverage if the bottle depicted is unusual and distinctive; but the bottle itself or its shape are not registrable in that they are not 'marks' capable of being applied to or incorporated in the beverage.

Goods are classified under different sections at the Patent Office, so a name in use under one category would not prevent registration of the same name by a different company in a different product category. Examples of names used by different companies for different products include Colt which can be a gun, a car, a lager, or ventilating equipment; Titan and Jaguar, both of which can be aircraft or motor vehicles; and Lloyds Bank and Lloyds, the insurance market.

Trademarks are protected by the Paris Union, known formally as the International Convention for the Protection of Industrial Property which allows a company registering in one country six months grace to register in any other he chooses. The Soviet Union is a member. The second agreement is the Madrid Arrangement, known formally as the Madrid Arrangement for International Registration of Trademarks. This is mostly European, has only 23 members and does not include the United States or Britain, but allows for registration in one country to be effective for all member countries.

Trademarks licensed to the sole distributors of pharmaceuticals and protected under national trademark laws, were in the past often used as a barrier against imports of identically branded goods sold by the manufacturer on another national market at a lower price. The EEC Commission has been waging a long and successful war against such trademark-assisted compartmentalisation of the Common Market, and has received powerful support from the European Court. The European Court ruled, in the American Home Products case, that two different trademarks must not be used for the same or similar product with the sole purpose of separating the national markets, or at least they must not be used to stop the parallel importer. The EEC Commission's project would go much further. It would lead to an automatic invalidation of trademarks if the protected goods were marketed in another member state under another trademark. The EEC has still to decide whether to have examination preceding registration, as in Britain and Ireland, or simply registration as elsewhere. If Britain and Ireland do give up the examination system this will bring them in line with the rest of the Common Market who are all members of the Madrid Arrangement whereby one registration is effective for all member countries.

The Trademark Registration Treaty (TRT) of August 1980 opened up the possibility of having simply one application for registration, channelled through UN World Intellectual Property Organisation (WIPO), and valid for all countries. However, to date this has attracted only five signatories, including the USSR and four developing countries: Burkina Faso, (formerly Upper Volta), Congo, Gabon, and Togo. The main obstacle is that Britain and the US presently enjoy strong trademark registration and while aware of the advantages which a common international system would bring, they view this as meaningless if the degree of protection conferred is to be in any way reduced. WIPO continues to act as the prime mover. In 1985, talks were held on what is called a Third Variant, i.e. a third variant of the Madrid Arrangement, the TRT being the second. The intention being to supersede the Madrid Arrangement and yet incorporate more flexibility to try to entice US and British participation.

The first change in trademark protection for more than fifty years came in August 1986 when Britain allowed owners of services to apply for statutory protection for their names and logos. With effect from 1 October 1986, banks, building societies, insurance companies, hoteliers, advertising agencies, car rental firms and the like have been protected and given the right to sue for infringement of their mark.

Industrial property rights

Licensing confers a right to produce under a company-specific technology. It allows access to an outsider to technology that has been protected by patents. Historically, industrial property rights which concerned technology have been the easiest to protect, but in today's world markets there is a great deal to be gained from product imitation or closely related brand names, sometimes even instituting a brand name that looks quite different but is phonetically identical in the local market abroad. Another large loophole at the moment is the question of computer software for the regulations have to be rewritten in order to encompass rights of authorship over computer software programs where development costs are high and duplication may be carried out with ease.

At the moment there are three international agreements on patent protection in addition to the Paris Union and Madrid Arrangement, which cover trademarks as well. The European Patent Convention encompasses sixteen countries; the European Community Patent Convention, its member countries; and the Patent Co-operation Treaty has 20 signatures including all the major Western trading nations. Registration in one member country is effective for all nations signatory to the agreement.

Brand piracy

At least five basic different types of forging famous trademarks have been identified (Reference 13):

1. *Outright piracy* – fake product in the same form and same trademark as the original and of comparable quality. Records and tapes are common examples.

2. *Reverse engineering* – stripping down the original product and then copying it, underselling the original manufacturer. This is happening currently in the computer industry with a myriad of IBM PC clones.

3. *Counterfeiting* which involves selling a product of lower quality with a falsified trademark. Clothing companies such as Levi Strauss and Co suffer heavily from this. Differences exist in product quality, e.g. stitching, seams, zips and studs.

4. *Passing off* – modifying both product and trademark, adapting a trademark that is similar in appearance, phonetic quality, or meaning to the original product. All that is normally associated with the product is copied including colour and packaging design.

5. *Wholesale infringement*. This involves the legal but rather question-

able registration of famous brand names overseas rather than the introduction of fake products, without the need to prove any title to the name or of usage elsewhere.

Brand piracy or product counterfeiting is becoming much more prevalent than ever before and entering into more and higher value-added areas such as microcomputers. A British response to this has been to establish the Anti-Counterfeiting Group (ACG) which is financed by 38 major companies seriously concerned with the growth of this activity.

Some of the activities of these product counterfeiters are comic such as the Asian manufacturer who promised Scotch Whisky made from real Scottish grapes and matured in the cellars of Buckingham Palace. There was also the Singapore manufacturer who tried to imitate the steering wheel covers of a West German company called Arus by even having a similar name, but his choice of 'Anus' in bold in the middle of a steering wheel met with some consumer resistance.

Elsewhere, the activities of these counterfeiters are not so funny. Levi's and Wrangler clothing have suffered from product imitations but this is spreading to higher value-added products as well such as heart pacemakers and birth control pills which were look-alikes for G. D. Searle's Ovulen brand but not so potent. G. D. Searle now mark their pills using more than one method. The House of Courreges which says that it only has 40 per cent of its 'own' market, worth $15 million a year; its image is so devalued by copies that most retailers have given up hope of restoring it. Other designer houses such as Gucci and Celine also suffer from this trade as do Cartier watches, Apple computers and Raleigh bicycles. Much of this sourcing is based upon the freeports of the Far East such as the export hungry 'Four Tigers' of Asia: Singapore, Hong Kong, Taiwan and South Korea. The ACG estimates that there are 30 different countries involved in product counterfeiting and that their output reaches most parts of the world. There is the obvious loss of revenue to the genuine company whose brand has been stolen but there is often a serious danger associated with the use of certain of these products. Heart pacemakers are said now to have been counterfeited, but imported brake linings and tyres of poor quality have long been a problem. The involvement of organised crime becomes apparent with the realisation that an estimated two-thirds of the video business in Britain is illicit, costing the industry £100 million in Britain alone.

Effective copying of the packaging where it is particularly distinctive helps pass off counterfeit products on an unsuspecting public. *Packaging Review* in September 1983, carried a report on how the whisky distillers Walker and Sons had been awarded £50,000 examplary damages against a former director of the Rockware Group for breach of its trading rights. The High Court judgement followed proceedings instigated in 1977 following the discovery of cases of counterfeit Johnny Walker Red and Black Label en route to Lebanon. The whisky was found in Walker-shaped bottles with forged labels in warehouses in Holland and West Germany. Investigations led to both civil and criminal proceedings against a former Rockware director and an interim injunction was granted on May 30, 1977 to stop any further breaches of Walker's rights. Final judgement in the civil action was made in November 1978 but the damages and costs totalling £116,000 were not assessed till May 1983. The criminal action against the former Rockware director and three others was heard in March 1982 and resulted in acquittals. The defence argued that prosecution could not be brought for conspiracy in one country to commit a crime in another.

Johnny Walker also suffered at the hands of the Bulgarian foreign trade enterprise Despred who were involved, as exporters, in 2,400 cases of counterfeit Johnny Walker whisky finding its way to the small Italian port of Aricoria. This was the first delivery of 22,500 cases destined for Africa. No explanation has ever been offered by the Bulgarians.

Counterfeiting is now being acknowledged to be damaging to Taiwan's national image. The fear is now real that foreign firms will be wary of bringing high technology to Taiwan if people can steal it with impunity. Even local firms may become reluctant to invest in expensive know-how if it can be lifted by competitors. Already the Taiwan High Court has overturned a lower court decision which has cleared two firms selling imitations of Apple computers. The Lower Court had argued that imitations of Apple's small computers were legitimate since Apple was not registered as a company in Taiwan. Whereas previously courts sided with local entrepreneurs, the government is keen now to introduce a new understanding. The penalty for making fake goods has been raised from two to five years' imprisonment. The High Court decision will help support this new drive. Plans are afoot also to introduce a special court to deal with cases involving infringement of trademarks, patents, and copyrights. Taiwan still remains the major base for counterfeiting but counterfeiting is increasing in South Korea and India. In 1985 US and UK vehicle-component and replacement-parts manufacturers established an independent investigation team in Taiwan to compile evidence against counterfeiters. The loss to the US car industry is estimated at $3 billion (£2.7 million) and £100 million to the UK. The fear is that Taiwan after a short period of overtly tough action against counterfeiters may once again relapse into a laissez-faire attitude. Extensive computerised dossiers are now being exchanged and legal action is being taken where the parties are identified while dossiers are being sent also to GATT headquarters in the hope that some internationally co-ordinated action might be taken to remove this menace. Converted to job losses, it means 6,000 jobs lost in Europe alone.

The difficulty for individual customs authorities, such as the UK Customs and Excise Department, is that they are mainly concerned with ensuring that consignments entering the country are property labelled and that duty is paid. Action needs to be taken by the company whose product is being counterfeited. For example, British Customs and Excise are willing to hold goods pending civil action but they are not empowered to seize. The losses therefore on tax revenue and lost company sales are almost impossible to estimate.

The EEC has joined with the US in pressing for firm action against counterfeiting under GATT, but has revealed a plan which will block and

possibly ultimately prevent counterfeit goods crossing community frontiers. Suspected counterfeit goods would be impounded for 10 days during
which time the trademark holder would be allowed to prove his case. If the
goods were found to be counterfeit they would then be confiscated and
'disposed of outside the normal channels of commerce'.

Five corporate strategies to handle counterfeiting

Kaikati, who has been one of the most important researchers in this area,
has advanced the following counter-strategies from his research of
counterfeiters and their victims:

1. Compete and attempt to overcome the opposition. A feasible strategy
   when the firm's stakes and power are relatively high. The objective is
   domination and forcing the counterfeiters out of the market. Many
   large companies now have a security force tracking down counterfeiters
   and pursuing them with legal actions wherever and whenever they are
   found.
2. Avoid conflict and withdraw from the fray. This is feasible where the
   firm's stakes and power are relatively low. The strategy objective is to
   throw in the towel or move on to greener pastures at the lowest possible
   cost.
3. Accommodate the opposition, where the objective is appeasement.
   Customers may switch to their brand if they knew their products were
   being faked. The company which is the victim of such action, is hoping
   that the problem will disappear. There is a further consideration in that
   pursuit of the offenders requires conclusive evidence which is a difficult
   and expensive proposition as it entails hiring private detectives for
   lengthy periods of time. Again, criminal action is speedier and more
   effective than civil action but loopholes in the law are being fully
   exploited by very professional criminals.
4. Collaborate. This is likely to be best when the firm's relations with the
   opposition are relatively positive. Fiorucci, an Italian jeans maker with
   outlets in the US has been charged with ordering cheap Korean copies
   of its own luxury jeans and marketing them as though made in Italy.
5. Compromise. The firm's stakes are moderate and power is slight. The
   trademark Persil is owned by Unilever in Britain and France and by
   Henkel in Germany, Belgium, Luxembourg, Holland, Italy and
   Denmark. Agreement had to be reached when Britain entered the EEC
   and there were price differentials between the manufacturers, Unilever
   being cheaper than Henkel. Also, price differentials between countries,
   which gave rise to parallel exporting opportunities. The two manufacturers agreed to respect each other's trademark and agreed that Henkel
   would use the name Persil in red inside a red oval whereas Unilever
   would use a green Persil trademark.

Distribution of counterfeit goods

Where goods are offered for sale by street traders, the public are right to
be suspicious when massive discounts are being offered, although even at

this level more professionalism has crept in. In the last few years there has been a problem with street traders in Britain offering supposedly French perfumes for sale at very low prices. To support their sales talk they flaunt glossy colour advertisements allegedly from quality magazines, which refer to these perfumes. In fact, these advertisements are also fake.

However, counterfeit goods are well beyond the level of just street trading but have entered many high street retailers in Britain and the United States. In the US alone it is a trade estimated at $20 billion in 1984 which is well up on the $3 billion estimate for 1978, but proposals to deal with the counterfeiters, including seizure of any goods suspected of being counterfeit, has run into opposition from America's cut-price retailers. K Mart is a large well known American chain of discount stores, who have a store in Los Angeles which was found by federal marshals to be selling 100 pairs of counterfeit Jordache designer jeans. Jordache refuses to sell to K Mart directly because it looks for outlets which reflect the image which it wishes to portray. K Mart therefore obtain their supplies from middlemen known in the trade as 'diverters', and it is these people whom Jordache are keen to pursue, although there is nothing illegal in the practice itself.

While opinions are divided as to what role government should have in this situation, 85 American corporations have meanwhile formed the Anti-Counterfeiting Coalition. An international code to let trademark owners intercept and seize shipments of suspect merchandise is the next step for the Coalition. The code being considered by the General Agreement on Tariffs and Trade (GATT) is opposed by Brazil, India, Hong Kong and Singapore because it is alleged that they fear that their trade in low-cost imitations will suffer. A few developed countries including Austria and Switzerland are opposing the code as well. Meanwhile, the Reagan Administration passed a law in 1984 which allows for goods to be confiscated, and distributors to be fined or even sent to jail. Technology provides another part of the answer in that companies, now more security conscious than ever before are expected to spend $50 million in 1985 on a variety of high technology gadgetry which provides a means of unobtrusively authenticating products with hidden magnetic or microchip tags, disappearing-reappearing inks, holographic images, and digitised 'fingerprints' of labels which read the unique pattern of fibres in each label. The verifiable label was developed by Light Signatures Inc. in 1981 and has been used by Nike Inc. (running shoes), MCA Inc. (records) and Levi Strauss, whose attorney Peter M. Phillipes was able to boast: 'We have virtually eliminated our counterfeiting problem in the US'.

After-sales service

There are obvious advantages where it is possible to standardise, if not globally at least regionally, the level of service accorded to customers. From cars to electronic hi-fi stereo systems, product guarantees and warranties are common in all parts of the world. Where previously these were national the clear trend is now international. In the past there may indeed have been valid reasons for separate warranties, region by region.

With cars, for example, servicing periods were at 3,000-mile intervals, whereas in recent years this has been extended to 9,000-mile intervals. Products have improved but alongside this, there needs to be a uniformity on the dealer network internationally. Standardised servicing facilities; availability of parts; even standard of training of mechanics and maintenance personnel; are all factors to be considered before internationalising a product warranty. It does add to company prestige and the consumer perception of product quality and reassurance in the event of breakdown. There may well, however, be instances of local market requirements, as in the case of the US or the EEC, but these needs can be incorporated within a standardised booklet. Production costs on the booklet can be reduced by producing it in large numbers, and comprehension can be aided by making it available in several languages.

References

1. Lorenz, C., 'How Japan "cascades" through Western markets', *Financial Times*, November 9, 1981.
2. Keegan, W., 'Five strategies for multinational marketing', *European Business*, January, 1970, pp. 35–40.
3. Cheeseright, P., 'St Michael and the crusade for overseas sales outlets', *Financial Times*, 9 July 1982.
4. 'Drugs on the run', *Economist*, September 11, 1982.
5. Haigh, P., 'Brand Rustlers', *Executive World*, April 1983, pp. 26–7.
6. Hermann, A. H., legal correspondent, *Financial Times*, 'The Perils of Harmony', March 24 1982.
7. 'IH buys itself a dual problem', *Management Today*, February 1982, p. 72.
8. Jennings, C., 'The Trade Mark Maze', *Marketing* 3 March 1983, pp. 31–3.
9. Kotler, P., *Marketing Management: Analysis, Planning and Control*, 4th edition, Prentice-Hall, 1980, p. 351.
10. Levitt, T., *The Marketing Imagination*, The Free Press, Macmillan Inc., 1983.
11. McLoughlin, 'Japan acts to avoid car clangers', *Guardian*, 6 December 1983.
12. Wind, J. and Douglas, S., 'International Market Segmentation', *European Journal of Marketing*, vol. 6, no. 1, 1972.
13. Kaikati, J. G., 'How multinational corporations cope with international trademark forgery', *Journal of International Marketing*, 1 (2), pp. 69–80.
14. Davies, Rachel, Barrister, FT Commercial Law Reports: 'Coke bottle not registrable as trade mark', *Financial Times*, 30 January 1985.

Recommended further reading

Brian C. Reid, *A Practical Introduction to Trade Marks*, Waterlow, 1984.
ICC *Business World*, special issue, July 1986; 'Corporate Security'.
Roland Rowell, *Counterfeiting and Forgery: A Practical Guide to the Law*, Butterworths, 1986.

7. PRICING, CREDIT AND TERMS OF DOING BUSINESS

Pricing strategies

Pricing has many publics to satisfy but for the corporate executive there is no such thing as perfect knowledge of perfect competition. For the company, pricing for a domestic market, there are strategic implications as to whether one chooses to price high, low, or merely be a price-follower. For example, pricing high and producing in low volume, skimming only the cream of the market, is the strategy employed by Rolls-Royce. However, when companies first introduce a new product and this also embodies a new concept or where there is no clear competition in price, there is the temptation to charge what the market will bear. In the initial stage at least, this helps create a certain exclusivity and helps build the image of the product which may subsequently be adjusted downwards when production increases.

At the other end of the pricing spectrum is market-penetration pricing which entails a low price but high volume market. This strategy is embodied in the dictum of Sir Jack Cohen, founder of Tesco supermarkets: 'Pile it high and sell it cheap!' This may be a valid strategy for a product that is either mature or reaching saturation whereupon lowering the price may draw in further sales. For the manufacturer, it may also help keep out competition partly because of low final prices and partly through the perception that low final prices are the result of economies of scale, and with mature products, that the cost savings are due to the experience curve effect (which produces cost savings of approximately one-third whenever production doubles). There are many examples that may be drawn of products now adopting penetration-pricing such as calculators and digital watches, now to be found in blister packs in supermarkets. As the product has become more established the volume has increased; the price has lowered; and the channel of distribution has changed also – for example, from specialist jeweller to supermarket. The jeweller is not redundant, however, since he now chooses to specialise in higher value added goods which means lower volume growth but provides a higher unit return. Again, calculators are an interesting product which have made themselves virtually indispensible to a public who did not know them one generation before. As a mass-market product, calculators fulfil a basic function and are difficult to differentiate, thus pricing plays a major role.

Appropriate pricing over the cycle depends on the development of three different aspects of industry (Reference 1) which usually move in parallel base paths:

114

1. *Technical maturity*, indicated by declining rate of product development, increasing standardisation among brands, and increasing stability of manufacturing processes and knowledge about them.

2. *Market maturity*, indicated by consumer acceptance of the basic service idea, by widespread belief that the products of most manufacturers will perform satisfactorily, and by enough familiarity and sophistication to permit consumers to compare brands competently.

3. *Competitive maturity*, indicated by increasing stability of market shares and price structures.

Somewhere in between the two strategies of skimming and of penetration, there is the flock of sheep who diligently follow the market leader, fearful of lowering prices and meeting retaliation, or raising prices and losing sales (Reference 2). The danger which often passes unrecognised is that the price follower may not have a true knowledge of his own costs, particularly in industries where there is a critical mass that has to be produced or economies of scale that may be reached beyond a certain level of production, and so there are inherent dangers always in basing market prices on someone else's costs. Skimming, penetration, and price-following or 'me-too' prices are features to be found in all domestic markets. What often happens though, is that when a product travels abroad it will, in seeking to position itself in the foreign market, allow itself to be influenced greatly by home country experience. At either end of the international marketing continuum there are products which may be identified with a certain pricing strategy internationally e.g. disposable razors, pens, and ladies' tights, where the price is cognisant of the fact that these products have a finite life. At the opposite end of this continuum would be those products which ignore the mass market but continue to appeal to the same market segment abroad as at home, such as Rolls-Royce. Essentially, a premium price is paid for a quality product.

Consumer sensitivity to pricing

It has been argued (Reference 3) that many desensitising factors operate to diminish the impact of price changes. Insensitivity will therefore be greater where the following conditions prevail:

- Personal selling, and therefore variation in point-of-sale effectiveness
- Promotion is local rather than standardised nationally
- Service after sale is important
- Consumer loyalties are significant
- Products are highly differentiated and difficult to compare
- There are multiple dimensions of product quality
- Unit price is low
- The product is sophisticated

A multi-stage approach to pricing

There are six major elements which have been identified (Reference 4) in a domestic pricing decision, which in sequential order are:

1. Selecting market targets
2. Choosing a brand image
3. Composing a marketing mix
4. Selecting a pricing policy
5. Determining a pricing strategy
6. Arriving at a specific price

However, the international pricing has to take many more variables into consideration.

International price standardisation

In an ideal world the same price for one's product would prevail everywhere, but this does not happen. When it does happen within a domestic market, it happens as a result of resale price maintenance (abolished many years ago in Britain by the Heath Government, but still practised in Japan). It cannot happen within international marketing because of currency fluctuations, different factor costs, different product requirements and governmental standards, plus official governmental limits on pricing and discounting. It is not always possible therefore to find exactly the same product available for sale across different markets for exactly the same price. The next best thing that happens is that this differential is contained within a few percentage points across markets. Otherwise, there is the ever-present danger of parallel exports taking place.

Table 7.1
Prices of new cars—excluding taxes—as a
percentage of Belgian prices:
October 25, 1983

	France	West Germany	UK
Austin Metro 1000L	106	109	149
BMW 320i	114	114	137
Citroën GSA Pallas	113	111	136
Fiat Panda 45	116	134	137
Ford Escort XR3i	115	116	132
Mazda 323 GT 1,5	126	112	147
Opel Kadett 1,6 SR	112	114	138
Peugeot 305 GL	109	112	135
Renault 5 GTL	109	112	136
Volkswagen Golf GTI	105	113	136
Average	112	115	138

Source: ICC *Business World*, January–March 1984, p. 9.

Parallel exporting is an illicit activity undertaken by intermediaries in the distribution channel who often find it more lucrative to export for sale rather than sell on the domestic market. By taking advantage of retail price maintenance and currency differentials elsewhere, these exporters – often wholesalers or retailers – are able to earn returns many times what they could have gained by selling in the domestic market. In so doing, however, they undercut the manufacturer's official prices in the market concerned, thus affecting his profitability but perhaps also bringing his brand into disrepute. Electrical equipment, for example, has to be constructed to different standards within Britain and the rest of Europe; pharmaceutical preparations may also be slightly different for different national markets but such differences are often glossed over in the search for price differentials and profit. This is not marketing that is being practised. (Parallel exporting is discussed more fully on pages 138–41.) As a strategy it is similar to encyclopaedia selling in that it requires a large pool of new customers as there may be all kinds of barriers to repeat business. Those who sell in this way lack the resources of the official organisation which they undermine. Product guarantees may therefore be suspect and reliability of subsequent deliveries doubtful and with the all-important price differential being subject to product availability on the domestic market plus the good fortune that currency devaluations do not take place to a degree to eliminate the differential. Occasionally though, there is room for humour in what happens, as when a Glasgow wholesaler decided to take it upon himself to export a Rowntree-Mackintosh product, 'Smarties', to the United States. To the best of his knowledge there was no known branded product on the US market of this name. Unfortunately for him, the product was already on the market but produced by Hershey and known there as 'M and M's'. The consignment of a few hundred pounds weight of 'Smarties' passed through New York customs and was met by the agent. No-one had checked the position with regard to the importation of confectionery into the US. Clearly, the colour red could not be used. It was specifically prohibited as it could be concealing hard drugs. The result was that the agent and his wife and children had to wade through this mountain to pick out the red sweets! Not knowing your market can be very expensive if you intend to stay in international marketing.

Export market overheads

Overheads arise with the sale of goods to their final destination, the consumer. In international marketing, there are the costs of freight and of distribution if the goods are simply to be exported; the problems of critical mass and economies of scale if the products are to be produced locally. The decision between exporting abroad and producing locally is often made more difficult by the frequent imposition by local governments of 'countervailing duties' which seek to ensure that foreign goods will not undercut local manufacturers in price, the price differential now being made up by the imposition of additional taxation.

The cost of market entry and representation is an overhead, as is any required product modification or any other modification such as to advertising and promotion. This type of modification is primarily for one market and cannot easily be replicated in whole or in part elsewhere. More will be said of this in Chapters 8 and 9. Bear in mind, though, that the exchange that is being effected between buyer and seller may often also require the use of an intermediary – whether an agent, distributor or even countertrade specialist – engaged to realise cash from the manufacturer's goods. Also, the terms agreed between buyer and seller may suddenly change the entire profitability of a contract.

For the moment, then, we assume that the product being exported is one which is already known to the home market. The company may, as the economists recommend, reduce the product price to the actual costs of production plus overhead contribution, i.e. it is assumed that research and development for the product is now a 'sunk' cost. Theoretically, the seller may price lower for a product. If he does, however, he is guilty of 'dumping' as he is no longer selling in foreign markets at a price comparable to that in his own domestic market. Where domestic demand is sluggish, this strategy of dumping may prove beneficial. Firstly, it does no damage to the domestic market. Secondly, the lower prices abroad are usually acceptable on a 'one-off basis' and seem to be preferable to the much longer-term damage implied in offering similar product discounts on the home markets. Once the precedent of domestic price discounts has been established, it is difficult to break. As a strategy, it may therefore protect the domestic price structure. Elsewhere, 'dumping' may be predatory, as when an exporting manufacturer often working with factor costs much lower than his local foreign market competitors, offers a low price in the foreign market with the intention of gaining market share.

Export quotation terms

International trade may be viewed as a 'trade-off' situation between an exporter and an importer. Either side wishes to maximise his return. The first problem is currency. The exporting firm may wish to quote in its own currency, particularly if it is inexperienced or it is a small firm uninterested in currency speculation and buying on forward markets. In any event, exporters will studiously seek to avoid inconvertible currencies and those which have experienced rapid depreciation and/or high inflation rates. The problem is lessened to some degree in that anticipated foreign currency earnings can be sold on the forward market at a premium.

The exporter can seek an export quotation which will lessen his responsibility or terminate it at the earliest opportunity. This can be done through a form of contract traditionally known as 'f.o.b.' (i.e. free on board) or 'ex works'. On this contractual basis, it is the foreign client's duty to collect the goods from the manufacturer and arrange shipment himself. The exporter's responsibility is probably less here than that of a domestic sale. Importers prefer a 'c.i.f.' (cost, insurance, freight) quotation or 'ex dock' with a named port of importation. Either of these means that the responsibilities of the importer begin only when the goods are in his own country. Importers prefer these two means because they provide an instant price comparison between competing exporting nations and local suppliers.

When the supplier company is faced with a cashflow crisis, money owing to them constitutes collateral and may be sold, i.e. 'factoring' or else 'discounted' or 'forfaited' – not for the full value, but at a discounted value, of which more will be said later. Risk may be covered by national export credit insurance schemes which cover governmental lines of credit plus commercial and industrial projects and exports worldwide for a fee based either on the company's global insurance business as in the case of the ECGD or on the risks inherent in the market concerned. The situation changes frequently with countries moving up and down the insurance scale either in terms of wealth (as happened with the Eastern European bloc, the Soviet Union now being classified amongst the wealthy nations). The insurance terms for a market will be influenced by exposure to risk in the market; or changed economic market conditions which affect the local market's ability to repay; as well as by the export credit agency's total portfolio.

Foreign currency invoicing and financing

When a UK supplier sells abroad he can either price in sterling, in which case he will be sure of receiving the exact price requested, or else price in a foreign currency and bear an exchange risk. The exchange risk arises since national currencies fluctuate one against another and even when one country will devalue, this will not be uniform against all other countries. So currencies may weaken and find themselves devaluing against stronger currencies, or, they may in fact appreciate relative to other currencies, or they may remain stable irrespective of currency movements elsewhere. Sterling experienced a 20 per cent devaluation against the US dollar within the first few months of 1985. Although this is an extreme case, and the more usual is for a few percentage points of difference, such a difference may be crucially important in high-value industrial contracts. The solution is therefore to consider forward foreign exchange markets.

Foreign currency is sold either at the spot rate, which is the daily rate prevailing on the day of the requested exchange transaction, or for any number of months ahead usually three, six, or nine. It is open to the exporter then to wait until he receives payment for his goods and then convert it at the spot rate. However, production and delivery lags often mean a few months have elapsed since the initial order was taken and while it is possible for an exporter to speculate on future movement of foreign currencies, he is as liable to lose as to win. Forward rates of exchange remove this uncertainty because the bank agrees to buy the exporter's foreign currency payment and change it into sterling when it falls due in six months' time. The important point to note here is that the rate of exchange is specified and known to the exporter when the forward contract is made. Accordingly, he can assure himself of his return plus perhaps benefit from an upturn in the value of the foreign currency relative to his own in the intervening six-month period. The forward rate usually therefore specifies a premium or discount over the spot rate, meaning that the financial markets expect that particular currency to appreciate or devalue over that given period.

The advantages of foreign currency invoicing include the following:

• The ability to invoice in international currencies such as the US dollar

Table 7.2

Main features of export credit systems in selected major countries

Country	Credit insurance	Export finance Short-term	Export finance Medium- & long-term	Cover/guarantees etc. Short term	Cover/guarantees etc. Medium- & long-term	Cost escalation	Performance bonds	Pre-shipment cover	Other facilities Local costs cover	Other facilities Exchange risk cover	Other facilities Investment insurance	Re-financing	Country
Australia	EFIC – Govt. Corp.	Commercial banks	Commercial banks, EFIC or official marketing boards.	Comprehensive; whole turnover or agreed group of countries.	Supplier and buyer credits.	No	Yes	Yes	Yes	No	Yes	Yes, by AER.	Australia
Canada	EDC – Crown Corp. Some private sector, independently.	Commercial banks	Commercial banks or EDC or both jointly.	Comprehensive guarantees; whole turnover of acceptable risk.	Supplier and buyer credits.	No	Yes —	Yes	(finance only)	No	Yes	No	Canada
Denmark	EKR – Govt. appointed representative council.	Commercial banks	Central bank organisation in co-operative with commercial banks.	No details available.	No details available.	No	Yes	Possible	Yes	Yes	No	No	Denmark
Finland	VTL – Govt. Agency.	Commercial banks	FEC, with bank backing.	Comprehensive.	No details available.	Yes	Yes	Yes	Yes	No	No	No details available.	Finland
France	COFACE – nationalised company.	Commercial banks	Commercial banks; BFCE (State agency) for maturities over 7 years.	Comprehensive.	Supplier and buyer credits.	Yes	Yes	Yes	Yes	Yes	Yes	Extensive facilities.	France
New Zealand	EXGO – Govt. Dept.	Commercial banks	Commercial banks. Also Export-Import Corp. and Govt. credits via Reserve Bank.	Political and other non-commercial risks.	Supplier and buyer credits.	No	Yes	Yes	Yes	No	Yes	Yes, from Reserve Bank.	New Zealand

Table 7.2 continued

Country	Export finance		Credit insurance	Cover/guarantees etc.		Other facilities						Re-financing	Country
	Short-term	Medium- & long-term		Short term	Medium- & long-term	Cost escalation	Performance bonds	Pre-shipment cover	Local costs cover	Exchange risk cover	Investment insurance		
Norway	Commercial banks	FFE (owned by commercial banks).	GIEK – Govt. agency	Comprehensive cover.	No details available.	No	Yes	Yes	Yes	Yes	Yes	No details available.	Norway
Sweden	Commercial banks	SEK Govt./ Commercial banks organisation (50–50).	EKN – State agency	Primarily political risks cover; choice of whole turnover, single transaction, country or buyer.	No details available	No	Yes	Yes	Yes	Yes	Yes	Yes, by SEK.	Sweden
United Kingdom	Commercial banks	Commercial banks.	ECGD – Govt. Dept. Some private sector, independently.	Comprehensive guarantees; whole turnover or acceptable spread.	Extended terms, (supplier and buyer credits).	Yes	Yes	Yes	Yes	No	Yes	No (but ECGD has contingent liability re foreign currency loans).	United Kingdom
United States	Commercial banks	Eximbank, or Eximbank/banks jointly. Also Private Export Funding Corporation (PEFCO).	Eximbank – Govt. agency jointly with private sector.	Comprehensive guarantees; whole turnover or acceptable spread.	Supplier and buyer credits.	No	No	Yes	Yes	No	No	Facility limited to some pre-agreed supplier credits.	United States
West Germany	Commercial banks	Commercial banks or KTW (State agency) or both jointly.	HERMES – Private Co. acting for Govt.	Comprehensive; whole turnover not compulsory – single transaction cover widely used.	Supplier and buyer credits.	No	Yes	Yes	Yes	Yes	No	Provided by AKA – bankers consortium – with some Bundesbank backing.	West Germany

Source 'Export Credit Facilities: An International Comparison', *Midland Bank Review*, Autumn 1980.

which may be more attractive to buyers in the country concerned.
- The buyer is relieved of exchange risk where the price quotation is given in his own currency.
- When sterling is at a discount on the forward exchange markets, an exporter can sell his expected foreign currency receipts forward for more sterling than he would receive at currently prevailing spot rates. This may enable him to quote a more competitive price in foreign currency or may provide him with a higher profit than would otherwise be the case.

Another point is that it is increasingly common for finance to be provided in foreign currency. One way of minimising exchange risk is to borrow the currency in which the contract is invoiced. Provided there is no default, this means that the debt outstanding will be covered. Financing in foreign currency may also allow the exporter to obtain cheaper supplies of finance credit, depending on relative interest rates. The UK government have actively promoted the use of foreign currency financing to ease pressure on the international role of sterling, and it will be found that the ECGD has had a ceiling on prospect finance, beyond which underwriting will only take place in a foreign currency.

Methods of payment

1. Payment in advance

Payment may be either cash with order (CWO) or cash on delivery (COD).

2. Open Account

This offers the least security to the exporter. 70 per cent of UK exports are now said to be paid for in this form. It saves money and procedural difficulties, but increases risk. It is popular within the EEC. Goods are sent to an overseas buyer who has agreed to pay within a certain period after the invoice date, usually not more than 180 days. Consignment Account is a variation of Open Account where the exporter retains ownership of the goods until they are sold.

3. Bills of exchange

A bill of exchange is defined as 'an unconditional order in writing, addressed by one person to another, signed by the person giving it, requiring the person to which it is addressed to pay on demand or at a fixed or determinable future time, a certain sum in money to, or to the order of, a specified person, or to bearer'. The exporter draws a bill of exchange on an overseas buyer or third party as designated in the export contract for the sum agreed. If the amount payable falls due on delivery of the goods, this is a 'sight' bill, i.e. payable on receipt; otherwise the variation is a 'time' bill which allows perhaps 30, 60 or 90 days before payment falls due.

4. Documentary Letter of Credit (Reference 5)

SITPRO estimate that 20 per cent of British exports are undertaken by letters of credit. However, letters of credit do not predominate in the countries of destination of the majority of British exports. Western Europe accounts for 56 per cent of British foreign trade; North America 15 per cent, and Australia 2 per cent. Thus 78 per cent of British exports fall outside of this means of facilitating payment.

A letter of credit (or documentary credit) is a conditional undertaking by a bank regarding payment. It is a written understanding by a bank (issuing bank) given to the seller (beneficiary) at the request and in accordance with the instructions of the buyer (applicant) to effect payment (that is, by making a payment, or by accepting or negotiating bills of exchange) up to a stated sum of money, within a prescribed time limit and against stipulated documents. A letter of credit offers both parties to a transaction a degree of security combined with a possibility, for a creditworthy partner, of securing financial assistance more easily.

The letter of credit is an undertaking by a bank and so the seller can look to the bank for payment instead of relying upon the ability or willingness of the buyer to pay. In its simple form, it is a conditional undertaking and so the seller must meet all his obligations. Only if all his obligations are met can he then demand payment. In its simple form, this is a **revocable credit** (now rare) which gives the buyer maximum flexibility as it can be amended or cancelled without prior notice to the seller up to moment of payment by the bank at which the issuing bank has made the credit available. An **irrevocable credit** is much less flexible and can only be amended or cancelled if all parties agree. A **confirmed irrevocable credit** means that a bank in the seller's country has added its own undertaking to that of the issuing bank and so while it guarantees the seller his money, it is much more costly to the buyer.

Letters of credit therefore have the following characteristics:

- They are an arrangement by banks for settling international commercial transactions.
- They provide a form of security for the parties involved.
- They ensure payment provided that the terms and conditions of the credit have been fulfilled.
- Payment by such means is based on documents only and not on merchandise or services involved.

However, it is worth pointing out that a Midland Bank International Division survey of 1,200 letters of credit showed that because of mistakes in documents and delays, one in every two transactions fails to retain its security and prompt payment, the documents being rejected by the bank on first presentation. In addition, over a quarter of all transport and insurance documents were wrong and one in seven invoices was incorrect. The total for this loss thus created (and this is for Britain alone) was £50m per annum in 1984 and means also that 10 per cent of business which was previously regarded as secure is not now so secure.

5. Leasing

Exporters of capital equipment may use leasing (Reference 6) in one of two ways:

1. To arrange cross-border leases directly from a bank or leasing company to the foreign buyer.
2. To obtain local leasing facilities either through overseas branches or subdivisions of UK banks or through international leasing associations.

The second is a more common arrangement. In both cases, it may also be possible to take advantage of ECGD facilities.

With leasing, the exporter receives prompt payment for goods directly from the leasing company and at the same time avoids any recourse. A leasing facility is best set up at the earliest opportunity, preferably when the exporter receives the order.

Bonding

In some countries, in the Middle East particularly (Reference 6), contracts are cash or short-term. Whereas this is an ideal situation for suppliers, it means that the buyer loses some of his leverage over his supplier as he cannot withhold payment as elsewhere where contracts are of a longer duration. In this situation a bond or guarantee is a written instrument issued to an overseas buyer by an acceptable third party, either a bank or insurance company. It guarantees compliance by an exporter or contractor with his obligations or the overseas buyer will be indemnified for a stated amount against the failure of the exporter/contractor to fulfil his obligations under the contract.

Bonds are of three types which may be either conditional or unconditional (known as 'on demand'). With a conditional bond, the onus is on the buyer to prove default by the exporter. 'On demand' bonds can be called for any reason at the sole discretion of the buyer, whether or not the exporter has fulfilled his contractual obligations. ECGD has a scheme designed to provide cover for the issue of all types of bonds for overseas contracts which are worth a quarter of a million pounds or more, and are on cash or near-cash terms. At the same time a recourse agreement is concluded with the contractor so that if he is held to be failing in his duties, ECGD may have recourse to him. The three types of bond, then, are:

1. *Tender or bid bond* which provides the buyer with an assurance that the party submitting the tender is making a responsible bid. If the contract is awarded to the bidder, the latter will comply with the conditions of the tender and enter into the contract. If he does not, the surety is liable to pay the costs incurred by the buyer in re-awarding the contract, subject to a limit of liability set by the amount of the bond. The amount may vary but generally represents between 2 and 5 per cent of the tender value.
2. *Performance bond* guarantees that the exporter will carry out the contract in accordance with its specifications and terms. The liability of

the surety is limited to the total amount of the bond, which is generally 10 per cent of the contract price but can be as low as 5 per cent or as high as 100 per cent.

3. *Advance payment or repayment bond.* A buyer often requires a bond guaranteeing that if the contract is not complete, the surety will make good any loss suffered by the buyer as a result of making the advance payment.

Discounting and factoring

The factors are mainly owned by the large banks. They offer two services – invoice discounting and factory. Invoice discounting (References 6 and 7) is a means of financing whereby the exporter sells his invoices to the factor at a discount in return for up to 80 per cent of purchase price in advance. This service is most suited to exporters selling on open account with charges normally at a margin above usual bank borrowing rates. Payments are made by the customers to the exporter and customers are usually not aware of the invoice discounting facility with the factor. Bad debt losses are taken by the exporter.

The second service is that of factoring (References 6 and 7). The types of business likely to be acceptable for invoice discounters will be the same as for export factoring. The factor investigates the creditworthiness of customers and establishes credit limits. The exporter sells within the credit limits and delivers and invoices to customers in the usual way, but sends a copy invoice to the factor. The factor maintains the sales ledger and also produces statements and reminders. If the exporter sells above the credit

Table 7.3
Factoring companies

THE ASSOCIATION OF BRITISH FACTORS
Results for 1983 (1982 figures in brackets)

	Number of clients	Volume of business £m
Anglo Factoring Services	110 (35)	96.4 (27.4)
Arbuthnot Factors	446 (343)	190.9 (147.1)
Alex Lawrie Factors (Lloyds)*	944 (1,078)	472.3 (345.8)
Credit Factoring Intnl. (NatWest)*	327 (377)	891.7 (784.3)
Griffin Factors (Midland)*	533 (435)	446.2 (391.0)
H & H Factors	260 (209)	154.6 (146.3)
Independent Factors (Lloyds)*	40 (43)	86.1 (77.8)
International Factors (Lloyds)*	515 (292)	444.2 (295.6)
Totals	3,175	£2,782.4

* Parent companies in brackets
Note Barclays Bank pulled out of factoring in 1983 and now use Anglo Factoring.
Source Financial Times, 17 January, 1984.

limit, this may be allowable but the factor then has recourse to the exporter in the event of non-payment by the customer. Customers are asked to pay direct to the factor.

With factoring, the exporter is able to sell his export debts and relieve himself of the task of credit checking, ledgering, some documentation, and collection as well as usually eliminating any risk of bad debt or currency loss. Factoring companies do not usually purchase trade debts on terms exceeding 120 days, but some companies will exceptionally accept debts arising from contracts which provide for terms of up to 180 days. Thus factoring is clearly most appropriate for exports on open account terms. It is used by exporters of all sizes and is particularly appropriate for those who are expanding rapidly. The factor charges a service fee of between 0.75 and 2.5 per cent of the sales value, depending upon the workload and risk carried by the factor. The factor agrees to purchase without recourse the exporter's debts as they are invoiced, on terms up to 180 days, and to pay a proportion of the invoice value to the exporter immediately.

The advantages to the exporter of factoring include:

1. Only one debtor – the factor
2. No sales ledgering necessary
3. No need to credit check or credit insurance
4. Non-recourse finance available
5. Regular cash flow
6. No foreign currency risk
7. Substantial savings in staff and collection systems.

The disadvantages are:

1. Factoring companies are inevitably selective in their choice of client and of the debts they will factor. The country of distribution will be a major consideration.
2. The service charge may be greater than the cost of employing own staff and systems.
3. Contact with customers is reduced or eliminated.
4. As the business grows and the factor's charge becomes unacceptable, the exporter will have developed no in-house experience.

Factoring is simply a method of exchanging book debts for cash on an agreed and regular basis. Apart from smoothing cash flow, it increases working capital. Factoring is not lending. It does not increase a company's debt so banks have found it an ideal source of new business while small businesses see in it a means of easing cashflow difficulties. Between 1971 and 1981 total UK-based sales factored by the nine members of the Association of British Factors (ABF) increased from £200 million to £2 billion a total which comprises the sales of more than 2,600 companies. Barclays Factoring pulled out of the factoring market in 1983. As Mr Burton of Barclays Factoring put it, 'In the recession climate factoring companies have to live with the problems of their clients'.

Forfaiting

This was developed in the 1950s primarily by the Swiss bank group Credit Suisse and is known correctly as 'forfait financing' (References 6 and 8). The word is derived from the French term of 'à forfait' which conveys the idea of a surrendering of rights. In Switzerland, 75 per cent of special trade financing is in the form of forfaiting while leasing accounts for 20 per cent and factoring for 5 per cent. Worldwide exports of between two and three billion US dollars are forfaited each year. It is estimated also that two-thirds are claims on the socialist countries of Eastern Europe and developing countries in Latin America, Asia, and Africa.

Forfaiting is an arrangement whereby exporters of capital goods can obtain medium-term finance, usually for periods of between one and seven years. Under this arrangement, the forfaiting bank buys at a discount bills of exchange, promissory notes or other obligations arising from international trade transactions. Promissory notes are the preferred instruments of payment because it is then possible for the exporter to free himself from all recourse obligations. The purchasing bank (forfaiter) may commit itself to buying promissory notes even before the supply contract is signed. A commitment fee is then payable.

For a transaction to be eligible for forfaiting, it has to carry an internationally known banking name as guarantor.

Unless the importer is of first-class undoubted financial standing, any forfaited debt must carry a security in the form of an 'aval', or unconditional bank guarantee acceptable to the forfaiter. This condition is of the utmost importance because of the non-recourse aspect of the business: the forfaiter relies on such a bank guarantee as his only security for lending. The bill or promissory note must also be unconditional and not dependent upon the exporter's performance, since the forfaiter has no right of recourse against the exporter. The forfait agreement then carries 80–90 per cent of the value of an export, as 10–20 per cent is usually paid in cash at the time an order for capital goods is placed. The forfaiter must consider risk, liquidity, and the fixing of the rate of return. To spread risk in terms of size and also geographical region, larger forfaiting transactions in excess of US$2 million are often syndicated.

When the forfaiter accepts the business he often gives a declaration waiving right of recourse to the drawer as by law the drawer always remains responsible for the payment of the bills. For the exporter the most important advantage is that he can sell his capital goods on credit and receive cash payment immediately from the forfaiter, who then assumes the rights and responsibility for collection of the debt. The only disadvantage is the high forfaiting rate but this is due to the fact that the forfaiter combines the service of a bank in financing with that of an insurance company in the assumption of risk so the forfaiting role must include not only a margin for financing but also a risk margin. Forfaiting is being seen as particularly appropriate for the export of capital goods. It is medium-term business, unlike factoring, and could range from one to seven years, although in practice a forfaiting financier will impose his own limits determined largely by market conditions and assessment of the risks involved for particular transactions.

Forfaiting is carried out by discounting in advance the interest for the whole life of the credit, and is done at a previously agreed fixed discount rate: thus the exporter receives immediate cash and is liable only for the satisfactory delivery of the goods, all other risks being borne by the forfaiter. It is primarily this latter fact coupled with the fixed-rate nature of the business which makes forfaiting generally a very attractive service to the exporter, although occasionally relatively expensive on a short-term view.

Accommodating countertrade in contract prices

Countertrade (Reference 9) is a genuine response to a difficult world trading environment. It is a means of payment for countries with reserves of convertible currency to purchase goods from the West, and pay partially in cash and partially in goods. GATT estimates countertrade to account for 8 per cent of total world trade which would value it at $2 trillion (i.e. million million), but this is held by bankers to be grossly underestimating the situation. The Organisation for Economic Cooperation and Development (OECD) estimates countertrade to account for 20 per cent of world trade, while Japan's External Trade Organisation believes the figure may be as high as 30 per cent. Certainly, whereas in 1975 there were perhaps only ten nations involved in countertrade, the figure now exceeds 90. For Britain alone, it is estimated to be worth just 5 per cent of British exports but this alone will represent £3 billion.

Countertrade (CT) has arisen because of:

1. Acute shortages of both foreign exchange and international lines of credit. Many developing countries are now no longer eligible for traditional medium and long-term export finance because of indebtedness to Western banks.
2. World markets for raw materials and low technology manufactures are weak.
3. CT can be used to fight protectionism in developed countries.
4. Fierce competition between Western exporters of manufactured goods and capital equipment.
5. Philanthropic and political attraction of bilateralism.

Countertrade is the generic term for a number of variants previously all collectively known as 'barter' (Reference 10). Before discussing the variants, it is as well to remember that countertrade produces its own problems (Reference 11). Payment in goods is always a poor substitute for cash and even where the countertrade goods may be utilised within the exporting firm, there is a potential threat created to existing suppliers as well as the continual danger implicit in using a new supplier with unknown reliability in quality, reliability, and continuity of supply.

The value of countertrade is also increasing. Kleinwort Benson, together with its partners Bank Handlowy of Poland and Banco di Sicilia, has, under the umbrella organisation Centro Bank in Vienna which they established in 1970, put together countertrade deals worth £100 million. Samuel Montagu, another British merchant bank, helped Downy Meco organise a £19 million countertrade deal in Indonesia. Of the clearing banks only National Westminster divulged information about its activities. It claims to have put together countertrade deals worth £2 million. The role of the banks is still unclear. Whether they will see themselves as principals in countertrade or confine their activities to the structuring of countertrade deals, certainly the UK clearing banks and US banks, such as Manufacturers Hanover, are emphatic that banks should not act as principals. Many 'blue-chip' companies such as Rolls-Royce are now seen to be involved in countertrade as witnessed in a $1 billion deal with Saudi Arabia involving the swap of ten 747s for up to 34 million barrels of oil, most of which has been delivered and sold on the spot market.

Bilateral trading

This occurs where an exchange of goods is effected under a mutual payments agreement between two sovereign states. It also involves the central bank or centralised foreign trade organisation which runs a clearing bank account in the name of the importing partner and a designated bank that in turn pays the exporting partner in local currency. This currency is inconvertible, and so termed 'soft', as opposed to 'hard' currency which is convertible. This gives rise to barter, and where an intermediary is required, to switch trading. Bilateral trading agreements between nations are on the increase and GATT voiced concern in 1983 that this trend threatened its very structure.

Bartering

Barter is a means whereby one partner trades with another and the existing balances are cleared by the movement of goods and/or services. Bi-lateral trade agreements amongst the developing nations have traditionally been hailed as examples, but in case anyone should think that this is a phenomenon of trading with African and Asian countries, it has been found often to exist in trade within Europe – with Greece and Finland to take but two examples. The Swedish pop group Abba when they performed on a tour of Poland received a rapturous welcome, but payment for their services in potatoes! Abba have done so much business with the communist bloc that they organised their own deals in Russian heavy machinery, Polish potatoes and Czechoslovakian glass amongst other things. Where the goods offered cannot be readily utilised for one's own consumption, the next best alternative is to employ the services of a specialist trader who will off-load these unwanted goods on a third market and realise cash for them. His services will cost about ten per cent and the goods handled may require to be heavily discounted by up to fifty per cent in the case of machine tools, for example.

Switch trading

This arises where one of the two parties to a bilateral trading agreement introduces a third party who then accepts the obligation to take either supplies or unwanted goods offered under the bilateral agreement and thus either converts them into cash or effects a further series of exchanges before converting them into goods which are desired.

Compensation trading

Compensation trading is another variant whereby the form of contract will usually allow part payment in cash with the remainder in goods from a restricted list. The goods available are limited, and are usually restricted to those which could not easily be sold elsewhere. Again, the specialist services of a trading house may be necessary to realise cash from these goods. The Soviet Union commonly requests compensation trading but where the Western goods which they seek are earmarked for a national priority project and/or are of a high technology nature, then they will pay cash.

Buyback

'Buyback' is now a specialist term to denote the relationship whereby payment for a licensed product or process will partly be made by means of the resultant product. The duration of these contracts is usually in excess of three years and can extend to 16 on occasion. This variant has been found in Eastern Europe where Polish factories producing International Harvesters crawler tractors discharge their obligations by sending back a certain volume of production to the original licensor. There are some advantages on either side. For the licensor it ensures a new production plant coming on stream with no investment and with product price and quality control assurances. For the East European country, it means the acquisition of new or state-of-the-art technology; access to 'know-how' which is often only contained in the minds of company personnel as in production, for example; plus softer terms on which to buy technology with guarantees of exports of a fixed percentage. In order not to conflict with corporate suppliers elsewhere, the contract would have to ensure either that new markets were capable of being accessed or that transfer prices to the licensor were on a part or lower than those of corporate subsidiaries elsewhere, a margin being allowed for freight costs.

Parallel trading

'Parallel trading' (or, counter purchase) is quite separate from parallel exports. Parallel trading is a phenomenon in East-West trade, whilst parallel exports occur in trade within the Western hemisphere. Parallel trading occurs when an East European country agrees to purchase a certain, usually much sought-after, item such as a computer. For desperately sought-after items, convertible currency is always available. What changes the situation slightly is that the convertible-currency contract will be dependent on a second contract whereby the seller must agree to repurchase a certain amount of goods available from within the importing country – the goods thus purchased to be of an agreed value, say 30 per cent of the initial contract price. There is no limit on the goods that may be selected, so goods which are easily exchangeable on Western markets, including commodities, may be included. This form of contract perhaps incurs the least penalties but is reserved for much sought-after imports by the East European nations.

Escrow account trading

This form of trading involves a third party. Exports are made only when sufficient funds have been raised from the sale of goods on behalf of the initial buyer. Payment is then made against the usual shipping documents from a blocked or trust account.

Offset trading

Two problems arise here. Either the exporter has undertaken a direct commitment to incorporate certain materials or components into his final products, sourced from within the importing country, or, in the second case, exports may be tied to a promise to assist a developing nation to earn hard currency and ease the cost of hard currency imports.

Transfer pricing

Transfer pricing essentially refers to the prices at which goods and services are transferred within the corporate family but across national frontiers, as they move globally – division to division or to a foreign subsidiary or minority joint equity venture. Transfer pricing becomes a problem at two quite different levels – within the company and with trade with the outside world.

Problems within the company

Where a profitable international division is an intermediary there will be an inevitable conflict over price when goods move from the manufacturing division to the international division and from there to the foreign subsidiary. For the manufacturing division, the price should be high enough to encourage a flow of products for export, and build up export trade. Where service or follow-up is needed, the prices fetched should make the manufacturing division willing to provide it. Low prices have the effect of showing poor returns for the manufacturing division, and losses can have a very bad effect on morale. However, from the viewpoint of the international division, the transfer price should be low enough to enable it to be both competitive and profitable in the foreign market. The international division also likes to be able to register profits and successes. Given these conflicting objectives the only outcome can be that of mutual antipathy and stalemate.

Possible solutions for this impasse include eliminating one of these divisions as a profit centre. The manufacturing division could be judged on the basis of costs and other performance criteria instead of profit. Secondly, the international division may operate as a service centre rather than as a sales centre, but this downgrading may also have a bad effect on morale. Finally, it may be possible to use the international division as a commission agent, purely on sales.

A second and more recent problem is that where transfer pricing within the corporate family includes also joint equity ventures. Should these ventures enjoy the same price levels as other fully owned parts of the corporation or be forced to pay a higher level of prices and invite political attack? This problem arises with the price paid for inputs from the corporation to the joint equity venture, as with supplies from the joint venture to the corporation. For the joint venture, which may well even be a minority joint venture holding for the corporation, price setting of components must be competitive with the corporation's subsidiaries elsewhere. The joint venture wishes to be profitable and to be successful in exporting. For the corporation this may occasionally present a dilemma over supplier choice. It may involve choosing amongst old, trusted suppliers; wholly owned suppliers; and untried, untested joint venture partners – the corporate objective being not to upset anyone and yet act in the best way for the group overall.

Problems in trading with the outside world

To the outside world, an important feature of interest to politicians, consumerists, and trade unions alike, is the ability of multinational corporations to source globally for their components and sub-assemblies. To cite but a few examples, IBM does it in the computer industry, and so, too, do the multinationals in the automobile industry such as General Motors and Ford.

Where this freedom exists, the possibility of abuse also exists. It is this that attracts the politicians. Host countries all over the world dislike losing tax revenue yet there is the prospect here, that since the component engineering and pricing structure is company-specific knowledge, with multinational sourcing it may be possible to move funds in the transfer of goods to a foreign country. Transferring at a low price from a high-tax country would allow a subsidiary in a low-tax country to make a larger than normal profit, and would best serve the interests of the firm. Some African countries such as Nigeria introduced import inspection procedures as a result of repeated allegations of over-invoicing on imports. This has the effect of withdrawing money from the country.

Equally, restrictions may exist with regard to repatriation of capital or the payment of fees for consultancy, licences etc., or there may just be the fear of losses through devaluation, high inflation, or impending tax legislation. In such circumstances, the prospect of being able to pay lower taxes in another country must seem enticing. In effect, it is difficult to establish whether these transfers are in fact taking place. For these reasons, customs authorities check values on imports more closely than exports but it is not always possible to have a reference point on the value of exports of either parts or components. Because there is an important political issue here, many multinationals including Exxon, IBM and Caterpillar actually publish a code of business ethics.

The strategic choices in transfer pricing are either then to transfer at direct manufacturing cost, which may seem suspect to the local country's customs authorities; at cost plus, at a percentage to be agreed – usually of the order of 10 per cent; and finally, at 'arm's length'. 'Arm's length' pricing means in fact that one is charging company divisions the same amount as one would an outside client. 'Arm's length' is therefore the term that is most often quoted by bodies such as the International Chamber of Commerce but it is also very difficult to narrowly define and to enforce, which probably also helps explain its popularity.

Conspiracy to fix prices

This is outlawed under anti-trust legislation in the United States and by the EEC under Section 80 of the Treaty of Rome. Even so, tacit collusion is much more difficult to establish than is an actual price cartel. A US lawyer writing in the *Harvard Business Review* (Reference 12) pointed out that even price fixers who do not get caught may not benefit by conspiring. His 22 rules on how to conspire to fix prices were:

1. Do not overlook the fact that the purpose of a price-fixing conspiracy is to make more money than you would have made had you not conspired in the first place.
2. Don't wink at a conspiracy unless it is a moneymaking proposition.
   a. Get your economists and analysts busy. Do not continue a profitless conspiracy. And, if you are not now conspiring, do not overlook this potentially profitable marketing technique.
   b. Price-fixing works best where no one conspirator has a substantial cost advantage over his co-conspirators.
3. Threaten a reluctant conspirator with anti-trust action in order to bring him into the fold.
4. Before conspiring, be sure that follow-the-leaderism and conscious parallelism are not in the cards. They are much less dangerous and work every bit as well.
   a. A successful leader-follower constantly repeats the incantation: 'A like price is a competitive price, a like price is a competitive price . . .'
   b. Conscious parallelism may be illegal but is certainly not as illegal as conspiring. Moreover, it is hard to prove.
   i. Get to know your competitors.
   ii. Develop effective lines of inter-firm communication.
   iii. Get in the habit of announcing policy and price changes in the press.
5. Do not have more active conspirators than necessary; do not have working-level meetings if not absolutely necessary; and do not include

personnel any further down the hierarchical ladder than is 100 per cent necessary.

6. Do not take notes; do not leave papers, work sheets, scratch pads, and the like lying around in hotel rooms and other meeting places; do not register under your real name; do not travel with your co-conspirators in public transportation to or from meetings; do not make conspiratorial telephone calls from your office (particularly if your efficient secretary keeps a log); in other words, do not keep records of any kind.

   a. If it cannot be done without writing it down, do not do it.

   b. If· you feel you must have something in writing, you are temperamentally unsuited to conspiring.

   c. Learn to take pride in a scratch pad well-burned or an alias well-rendered.

7. Do not meet in hotel rooms if you can avoid doing so.

8. Avoid complicated schemes.

9. Have some reason for meeting besides fixing prices.

10. Gripe a lot, especially about prices.

11. Develop a jargon.

12. Send up 'trial balloons'.

13. Remember that the line between overt price collusion and mere discussion of a common problem is fine indeed.

14. It is advisable to have at least one member in the conspiracy who has monopoly experience.

15. Do not be greedy.

   a. The share of each individual conspirator relative to the shares of any or all of his co-conspirators must be, by mutual consent, treated as irrelevant.

   b. If you are getting more than you would have gotten, stay in; if you are not, get out.

16. Do not overlook the possibility of dividing up sales revenues at the end of a prearranged conspiracy accounting period, irrespective of who actually made the sales.

17. Have an adequate contingency fund for educating (or eliminating) mavericks.

   a. Avoid giving the appearance of selling below cost. It antagonises the Federal Trade Commission.

18. Conspiracies work best on shelf items, but are least necessary. They work worst on special-order items, but are most needed in these areas.

   a. If you sell special-order items, do not allow your enthusiasm to conspire to get out of hand.

19. When the heat is on, get out.

20. Do not worry about being a good citizen and a respected member of the community. It will not help you.

21. Do not worry about avoiding identity of price. This will not solve your problem.

22. Get the advice of an experienced conspirator.

References

1. Dean, Joel, 'Pricing policies for new products', *Harvard Business Review*, November-December 1976.
2. Farley, J., Hulbert, J. and Weinstein, D., 'Price Setting and Volume Planning by two European Industrial Companies: a study and comparison of decision processes', *Journal of Marketing*, vol. 44, no. I, Winter 1980, pp. 46–54.
   White, J. and Niffenegger, P., 'Export Pricing – an investigation into the current practices of ten companies in the South West of England', *Quarterly Review of Marketing*, vol. 5, no. 4, Summer 1980, pp. 16–20.
3. Sampson, R. T., 'Sense and Sensitivity in Pricing', *Harvard Business Review*, November-December 1964.
4. Oxenfeldt, A. R., 'Multi-stage approach to Pricing', *Harvard Business Review*, July-August 1960.
5. SITPRO, *Letter of Credit Management and Control*, London, 1985.
   International Chamber of Commerce, *Guide to Documentary Credit Operations*, Paris, 1979.
6. Bank of England, *Money for Exports*, London, 1979.
7. Edwards, H., *Export Credit*, Gower, 1980.
   'Barclays pulls out of factoring market', *Financial Times*, 10th February 1983; 'Factoring: a means to a cash flow end', *Financial Times*, 30 March 1982.
8. Finanz, A. G., *The Forfaiting Manual*, 1979.
9. Bracher, R. N., 'If countertrade is inevitable make the best of it', *The Banker*, May 1984, pp. 69–71.
10. Kaikati, J. G., 'The Reincarnation of Barter as a Marketing Tool', *Journal of Marketing*, April 1976, vol. 40, p. 19.
    Paliwoda, S. J., 'East-West Countertrade arrangements: barter compensation, buyback and counterpurchase or "parallel" trade', UMIST Occasional Paper 8105, March 1981.
    Project Export Policy Division. Department of Trade and Industry, *Countertrade: some guidance for exporters*, London, July 1985.
11. *Purchasing and Supply Management*, 'Will counter-purchase deals bring economic suicide?', December 1980, p. 25.
12. Lawyer, John Q., 'How to conspire to fix prices', *Harvard Business Review*, March-April 1963.

Recommended further reading

Ian Gould, Rhodri Harris, *Forfaiting – an alternative approach to export trade finance*, Woodhead–Faulkner and Euromoney Publications.
Alan E. Branch, *Elements of Export Practice*, 2nd Ed., Chapman and Hall, 1984.

8. *LOGISTICS AND CHANNEL DECISIONS*

The meaning of logistics

Logistics is sometimes used as a suitable term to describe the movement of goods and services between supplier and end-user. Its range is, however, limited; so let us begin by tracing its origins. According to the Oxford English Dictionary, the term 'logistic' could be defined up to 1644 as 'pertaining to reason' then after 1706, 'pertaining to reckoning or calculations'. Its root meaning embraced the elementary processes of arithmetic. In its plural form, 'logistics' has become synonymous with distribution, but in this context it has strong military associations, it is 'the art of moving and quartering troops' (i.e. quartermaster's work), now especially of organising supplies. Military objectives such as speed and continuity of supply may be shared with marketers also, but the essential difference between the marketing profession and the military is that military strategists have never considered the satisfaction of the final consumer as being their main focus. Marketers also have to deal with competition and weapons of persuasion which may be forceful in their own way but are much less direct than armaments, take longer, are wasteful and so relatively more expensive when compared with military strategies.

Market entry decisions have already been discussed in Chapter 4 and so here the intention is to examine the decision areas involved in moving goods from supplier to end-user when this involves crossing international frontiers; also to compare channels of distribution within local markets for similar goods. It must be noted that the length of marketing channels, as a result of increasingly necessary cost reductions, are becoming shorter between supplier and end-user so this entails a reduction in the number of intermediaries who require price maintenance or recommended prices. Overall, SITPRO in 1979 estimated distribution costs in the UK to account for over 20 per cent of GNP. Distribution costs are not uniform across markets as may be seen from Table 8.1.

Transit systems have meant that European companies operating within the EEC can function for a European market rather than a national market as the border controls between member states have eased; regulations on packaging and labelling have been standardised throughout the community; and the ever-increasing volume of inter-state traffic has continually increased. The Unique Selling Proposition (USP) has to be evident in a foreign import but where this USP is not intrinsic to the product itself, it may be demonstrated by the level of customer service which the foreign company is able to offer alongside his local competitors, i.e. product availability, price being more difficult to promise unless there is a concentration of supply within the market.

Table 8.1

Comparative distribution costs as a percentage of sales in the UK (1976)

Country	US	UK	Japan	Australia
Transportation	6.4%	5.5%	13.5%	2.5%
Receiving and Dispatch	1.7⎫	2.5⎫		1.4
Warehousing	3.7⎭			1.8
Packaging and Storage	2.6	2.0⎫	13.0	1.7
Inventory	3.8	3.0⎬		3.6
Order Processing	1.2	1.0⎟		2.1
Administration	2.4	2.0⎭		1.0
	——	——	——	——
TOTAL	21.8	16.0	26.5	14.1

Source Peter Gilmour and Peter J. Rimmer, 'Business Logistics in the Pacific Basin', *Columbia Journal of World Business*, vol. II, no. 1, Spring 1976, p. 65.

Movement across frontiers

Speed employed in the transit of goods is an important consideration, as is cost relative to value-added of the item in question. Another is the packaging cost of the product for the export market plus additional export packing, although in recent years this has become greatly simplified by the use of low-cost polystyrene moulding to fit the shape of the product in question, with very little added weight. Packaging has also been simplified by palletisation which has moved into the computer stage with computer systems software now available and with packaging suppliers now designing individual product packaging to maximise the number of units per pallet. Palletisation with shrink wrap protection and containerisation have served both to protect goods against damage and diminish losses through theft.

Logistics is primarily an operations research tool to contain costs and optimise the flow of goods or services. However, within this channel between supplier and end-user, there are usually a number of intermediaries: there may be an importer who is an agent or distributor; a national stockholding centre; then regional warehouses; perhaps smaller warehouses; then retailers. The channel depends on the good or service itself, as much as local prevailing conditions, but the exporter will be seeking return on his product and accompanying services and his general investment. The uncontrollable elements with regard to distribution are the same as those facing international marketers generally, namely political and legal systems of the foreign market(s); economic conditions; degree of competition prevailing in the given market(s); level of distribution technology available or accessible; the topography, i.e. the geographical structure of the social market; and the social and cultural norms of the various target markets.

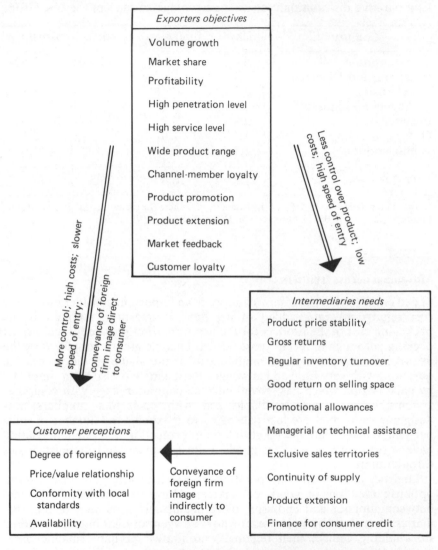

Figure 8.1 Foreign market distribution: corporate objectives and the needs of channel members.

Parallel exporting (see Figure 8.2) arises where domestic wholesalers begin to perceive greater returns available from the illicit exports of goods intended for the domestic market only. It undercuts the manufacturer's recommended price, upsets his foreign distribution channel members as well as doing damage to the corporate image where product specification between the two countries may be different as partly reflected in price. The dilemma for the manufacturer is whether or not to withdraw his product from sale in the domestic market where this traffic appears excessive. Alternatively, increasing the domestic product price may have a similar effect. The international product portfolio has to be planned, as with all elements of the marketing mix.

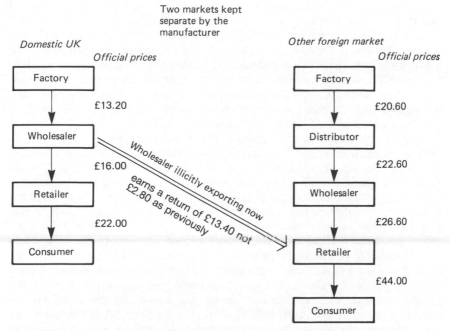

Figure 8.2 An example of parallel exporting

Note To understand parallel exporting one has to remember that many markets have recommended resale price maintenance structures – that is, it is virtually impossible for multinational corporations to standardise price structure completely – and that fluctuations in foreign exchange can create market opportunities.

The market is being upset by illicit exporting by wholesalers or retailers, but sometimes also by third party clients who then resell to the manufacturer's distribution outlets in another country. L'Oreal has suffered the embarrassment of cut-price outlets in France obtaining supplies from outside third countries and supplying French customers at levels lower than L'Oreal's officially recommended prices. In the UK there have been similar examples. In the Wilson Government era, Mallory Batteries, tried to raise prices in the UK to discourage parallel exports taking place and ruining its official market price and distribution structure in France and Germany. Johnny Walker Red Label, a product of the giant Distillers Company, was taken off the UK market for six years between 1977–83 before a change of heart restored it. Red Label had 12 per cent of the market when it was withdrawn. It is now being reintroduced to a stagnant market at the expense of Distiller's other brands (White Horse and Haig) and with no assurance that parallel exporting will not begin again. The EEC response to parallel exporting is clear from the case Hasselblad (GB) Ltd versus Commission supported by Camera Care Ltd. Significantly, Hasselblad was prosecuted by the EEC Commission in 1981 for infringing Article 35 (1) of the EEC Treaty, which relates to free trade. The Commission contended that Hasselblad acted in concert with six sole distributors to prevent, limit, or discourage exports of Hasselblad equipment between the member states and that the sole distributorships and selective distribution system operated constituted infringements. Hasselblad (GB) Ltd was fined £93,642. On appeal, this was reduced only to £45,218. The aim of the concerted practice had been to prevent imports into the UK of Hasselblad cameras intended for Camera Care and as such constituted a flagrant breach of the competition rules. Although corporate responses to combat parallel exporting may include withdrawing the product or raising its price in the domestic market, the practicality of EEC intervention has also to be considered.

In 1984, Waddington, the famous British games manufacturer, won an interim injunction in the Singapore High Court against a local importer involving the seizure of 559 sets of Monopoly and 531 sets of Cluedo purchased from a British export house and intended for sale at a discount on sets made by Waddington in Singapore. However, in January 1985 when the case for the injunction was heard before the Singapore High Court, it was ruled that the injunction could not be continued as there had been no misrepresentation. The case itself has still to come before the court, and Waddington have the right of appeal on the injunction hearing, but the overall situation is far from satisfactory for foreign companies manufacturing in Singapore. Although some consumers will enjoy temporarily the parallel importers' lower prices, there are important ramifications for foreign investment generally in Singapore; for the licensed distributors who have invested in goodwill; and the employment effects if Waddington chooses to leave the market as a response, particularly as this will likely be followed by others.

To turn to a more complex case of parallel exporting, which is that of the import of drugs, here we have a case where opinions are divided about the morality of behaviour on either side. Firstly, to take the industry case, the British pharmaceutical industry believes that it is losing sales worth about £100 million a year to companies which buy British-made drugs cheaply in Europe and bring them back to sell here. One large chemists' wholesaler, UniChem, which claims about 22 per cent of the wholesale market said that they are losing about 10 per cent of their sales to parallel importers, costing them about £3 million per month.

Not all wholesalers have the same view, for in 1984 32 wholesalers formed the Association of Pharmaceutical Wholesalers with the aim of establishing a code of conduct, lobbying MPs and mounting a public relations drive. Benefits obviously flow to the wholesalers and retailers who make better margins on these parallel imports. The drug manufacturers themselves have been active in trying to curb the practice by conducting a campaign emphasising the dangers to the public in being supplied with foreign language packaging or possibly differently formulated products.

One such wholesaler, Malcolm Town, and his company Maltown, were fined £6,360 in 1982 for illegally importing drugs which he then sold to health authorities and chemists for as little as half the manufacturer's list price. His solicitor argued the case that the interests of his client were very much allied to the public interest. Nine summonses related to the import and sale of three drugs: Septrin, used for treating bronchitis, manufactured by the Wellcome Foundation in Kent; Zyloric, prescribed for gout, made by the Wellcome Foundation in Spain was imported via Malaga and Gibraltar; and the Daonil, given to sufferers of diabetes mellitus, which was a Swiss drug, arrived in Britain via Hong Kong. The drugs were all being imported on a commercial basis and sold on a commercial basis. All drugs were sent for laboratory analysis before being sold on the British market.

The price structure in Britain which is an agreement between the National Health Service and the industry, allows for a 21 per cent profit margin to include advertising, promotion, research and development. However, this margin and this style of structure is sufficient to create disparities with other neighbouring European markets. Maltown has a list of about 300 imported drugs sold at prices substantially lower than the Health Service pays chemists for prescriptions. The trade price for 500 Septrin was £52.58 while Maltown obtained the same amount for £20.53. Zyloric was £14.34 for 100 milligrams while Maltown paid £6.34 and Daonil listed at £9.64 for 5 milligrams was only £4.37. Ventolin, an asthmatic inhaler, made in Britain by Glaxo Pharmaceuticals costs the Health Service £2.91 per prescription but Maltown reimports the drug at £1.45 from France, Belgium and Italy.

Although corporate responses to combat parallel exporting may include withdrawing the product or raising its price in the domestic market, government refused to act in the case of the drugs and was actually the one bringing the case against Maltown. The position of the EEC with regard to this phenomenon has therefore to be considered.

Marketing and logistics

This does not mean that companies which practise marketing cannot also implement logistics. General Motors who implemented an International Logistics Operation in 1977 differentiate between logistics and materials management (Reference 3). The generic term at GM is materials management whilst international logistics focuses on transportation, packaging, and handling of both inbound and outbound freight. GM has 48 major overseas operations with plants in 60 cities. Nearly 200,000 GM employees live outside the US and overseas activities are responsible for the employment of an additional 60,000 within the US. Outside of the US, the largest market is Europe where GM own Adam Opel AG of West Germany; Vauxhall Motors of the UK; assembly and component plants in Belgium, France, Ireland, Netherlands and Portugal; and major new factories in Austria, France and Spain. At present, virtually every European car manufacturer uses some GM components.

GM are found to practise the total-cost approach, i.e. material availability is accorded first priority followed closely by cost accordance or reduction. Alterations in transportation and packaging and the qualification of costs with possible alternatives leads to reasoned trade-offs being made, prejudgements being made on total corporate benefit rather than divisional benefit alone.

International logistics have been introduced within GM to a divisional structure and must be held to be a good idea at local level rather than be seen as a measure of centralisation but they have not been able to accommodate and analyse the data necessary to its operations other than manually. GM is also constrained by what may be termed 'local infrastructure deficiencies', namely the state of port and local transportation and warehousing facilities – limited or no container handling at dockside, lack of weather-protected warehousing, different national groups in different regions or across political boundaries, and largely impaired highway systems. Taken together, the effect of these factors is cost multiplication due to delay, multiple handling, and damage in transit or storage. These difficulties are compounded because of the lack of internationally standardised documentation such as with bills of lading or with invoicing.

On the one hand, customer service levels must always be attained or improved; on the other, the cost of GM logistical activities to support worldwide operations must constantly be reviewed. This leads then to the consideration of new institutional arrangements and modes of operation.

Table 8.2
Ten distribution myths

---

1. A channel of distribution is the movement of a product from the manufacturer to the ultimate consumer.
2. A channel's structure is determined by the characteristics of its products.
3. A distribution channel is managed by the manufacturer.
4. A firm should strive to maximise co-operation within its distribution channel.
5. The primary function of a warehouse is storage.
6. A firm sells to, or buys from, another firm.
7. Eliminating the middlemen will reduce distribution costs.
8. Administered channels are more efficient than non-administered channels.
9. A profitable channel is an efficient channel.
10. Planning distribution strategy is the responsibility of the distribution manager.

Source Michael M. Pearson, 'Ten Distribution Myths', *Business Horizons*, May-June 1981, pp. 17–23.

Cost of trade procedures and documentation

With regard to documentation, readers must be made aware of the work of SITPRO, the Committee for the Simplification of International Trade Procedures, who have achieved agreement on certain items of documentation including pre-printed computer paperwork for trade procedures, which they design, print and sell, and designed systems to complete multiple documentation tasks from one typing. The increasing availability of relatively inexpensive small business computer systems facilitates this and avoids the need for stocks of preprinted stationery and forms which may become obsolete. SITPRO systems are designed to Universal Nations' design standards, known as the UN Layout Key. Computer models specifically adopted to international logistics applications are yet to be developed.

Traditional information handling by traditional means has come under review because of questions over cost and efficiency. As to exactly what these costs amount to, SITPRO in their report, *Costing Guidelines for Export Administration*, commented:

In analysing the cost aspect of trade procedures and documentation, SITPRO has been able to draw upon a number of assessments of the overall cost of present systems. We have, for example, the US figures following a detailed examination of procedures in that country which showed that the costs of compliance with essential documentation and procedures in typical export and import transactions were of the order of $7\frac{1}{2}$ per cent of the average consignment value – that is 15 per cent for a full two-way transaction assuming that costs in other countries are not greatly different. As a very general indication of the possible orders of cost in the UK in export transaction, we would be quite ready to accept this ratio – viz one seventh of the value of the goods exported.

However, SITPRO now consider this to be out of date, and point to the following:

A SITPRO survey of multinationals trading in EEC found:

1. 1% of goods value to be a minimum attainable because of economies of scale and specialist systems.
2. EEC Commission consider cost to EEC companies trading with each other, of 'frontier crossing' is £7,000 million per annum, up to 5% of goods value.
3. SITPRO consider 3–4% realistic for medium sized companies, covering the door to door administration and related costs.

Costs arise due to:

1. Cost of complying with the procedures and documentation laid down for international trade. This may be reduced by good management and simplification of procedures, but is unavoidable.
2. Cost – direct and consequential of delay to the movement of goods, to paperwork or to the movement of money.
3. Cost arising from error. This can be substantial and includes not only costs of correcting errors in documents or procedures but also consequential costs such as demurrage on goods held in expensive quay areas, fines and interest costs on delayed payments. Most of these are avoidable.

Containerisation effects on freighting procedures

1. Road and ro-ro

The use of road haulage combined with roll-on-roll-off ferries has increased dramatically since British entry to the EEC and the continuing expansion of EEC membership since then. Road haulage means delivery to the customer, not to a dock; it involves freight forwarders who are transport operators as well as paper handlers.

2. Inland Clearance Depots

Small shipments are now normally sent to the nearest Inland Clearance Depot (ICD) or groupage depot and exporters deal with their local forwarder, or book directly with the shipping line at the local inland office. A container ship will call at only one, or at the most two, UK ports – possibly at the other end of the country from the exporter's place of business, but because the local ICD is responsible for delivery to the port, this restriction does not affect the export department. Recovery dates have been largely replaced by continuous cargo reception and joint services.

3. Less-than-container loads (LCLs)

Through local contact with carriers, arrangements can be made for local delivery of less-than-container loads (LCLs) and feeding into the through movement system, instead of awaiting planning. This alters rather than lightens the work of the export department. Instead of spending time on long-distance arrangements for booking and deliveries, the shipping manager needs to build extra checks into the routine, to make sure that LCL cargo is consolidated and shipped quickly rather than lying around in the depot. Instead of having to ensure that consignments catch a particular vessel, and sail from a particular port, in accordance with a documentary credit, the manager is better employed taking steps to see that credits are free of such restrictions in the first place. Trading terms may have to be changed from the traditional fob/cif to avoid elaborate calculations of cost allocation. More time can be devoted to routing and door-to-door freight costing, so as to take full advantage of the greatly extended range of shipping services. The whole emphasis of export office activites is moving from booking and dock delivery to the back-up and controls necessary to ensure proper delivery to the customer.

4. Full container loads (FCLs)

This change in emphasis is even more noteworthy for full-container-load (FCL) exports. In effect the ship comes to the factory. The empty container presented for loading is a miniature ship's hold. The exporter himself is responsible for 'stowage' – a new responsibility within the total export function – and the shipping line or combined transport operator collecting the loaded and sealed container takes charge of the goods at that point and issues the 'received' waybill or bill of lading – another example of the way in which the ship's rail has moved, in effect, to the exporter's premises. The goods loaded by the exporter will arrive at the customer's premises, or at least the destination port, in as good or as bad a condition as the exporter's own container loading allows them to be. It is often potentially unsafe to open a container for inspection or unloading, because poorly loaded cargo has shifted or been damaged and may spill out. In other words the exporter has a direct interest in and influence on loading and transport right through to destination. He is loading for a sea journey and not just for a road haul to the port. Container ship operators offer useful guidance on container loading techniques, especially for the safe loading of dangerous goods.

5. Free carrier (FRC)

Changes in terms of delivery are also necessary. 'FOB' (free on board) is becoming obsolete and is being replaced by the new Incoterm 'FRC' (free carrier) which refers to the point at which the seller hands over the goods to the carrier, for example at an ICD. Similarly, the other new Incoterms DCP (freight of carriage paid) and CIP (freight or carriage and insurance paid) are more appropriate to the now commonplace through transport of goods to the destination point than are the traditional 'C&F' (cost and freight) and 'CIF' (cost, insurance, freight) terms.

6. Combined transport (CT)

All these new routines are adjustments to the concept of 'multi-modal' combined transport in which the carrier (or combined transport operator) takes over the goods at a nominated point or near the seller's factory, and delivers them to or near the customer's premises. How the carrier does this is his business, and if damage or loss occurs he is liable on a uniform basis irrespective of the mode of transport at the time. The single combined transport document covers the total movement. Unless the export document is organised so as to work with this door-to-door concept, the department will become increasingly out of date. It cannot be properly effective if its routines or attitudes are not matched to current techniques.

Changes in approach and practice brought about by combined transport apply equally to ordinary through-container transport. Much of our deep-sea shipping trade operates on a port-to-port basis with optional pick-up and on-carriage. There is separate liability for each stage of handling. The operations of booking and delivering goods are the same as for combined transport, but when damage or loss occurs, the different system of separate liabilities is reflected in some special problems. Export staff need to be aware of whether they are dealing with goods under a full combined transport bill or lading/waybill, or through container bill of lading/waybill.

Air freight must now be seen as a form of through or combined transport. Air carriers themselves employ other modes. Goods are trucked for example from Manchester to Heathrow under a flight number and air waybill, for onward carriage by air to their ultimate destination. Some airfreight to Western Europe is ferried over by surface, often by airlines themselves, under flight and air waybill routines. Some long distance air-sea services are quicker than all-surface and cheaper than air alone. Any airfreight movement has by definition to be multi-modal as, unless both the exporter and importer are airport-based, a pick-up and delivery leg cannot be avoided. For all these reasons, export departments should see airfreight movement as door-to-door transport and organise their routines accordingly. For example, exporters should make sure that their air forwarders consolidate, fly, and break down at destination as promptly as possible.

In rail freight, as in air or other through/combined transport movements, the export department is concerned with the best way of delivering goods to the customer rather than the fact that part of the journey will be by a particular mode.

Foreign market channels of distribution

Distribution is an integral part of the marketing programme and so should always be considered in relation to product positioning strategy, price, and communications. On a comparative basis, little has been done since Bartels produced his work in 1963 on wholesaling and retailing in 15 countries. Direct comparisons are difficult between a home market and foreign target market because size alone is not an indicator of efficiency; competitive pressures between the two markets will differ; that there may well exist a very sophisticated 'black' market or 'dual economy' where goods officially banned from entering the country may be found to be easily and openly available. The same phenomenon occurs, too, where goods may be in short supply and not generally available at what may be officially determined governmentally controlled prices, but available nevertheless to those willing to pay a little extra.

Technology also imposes change upon channels of distribution as with containerisation in the use of freeports based near existing airports for the assembly and manufacture of duty-free goods for export only; and in electronic payments transfer which allows for instantaneous transfer of funds between countries. Technology also affects the distribution channel ranging from vending machines to goods material handling laser scanning of purchases at check-outs in large supermarkets or even larger hypermarkets. One example is the development of home shopping in Britain via a computer link through the public telephone system whereby it is possible to obtain anything from bank statements to household items. This works through the British Telecom service, Prestel, which gives a guide to goods on offer from the main retailing chains subscribing to the service. Technology is changing also in the home and marketers must take cognisance of this, growth in the percentage population with fridges and freezers, cars and other consumer durables affect not only what they buy but how they buy, in what quantities and how frequently.

Distribution is also affected by environmental change whereby changes arise within the society itself in terms of consumer attitudes, available means of distribution, and the role that distribution is expected to fulfil. In many of the developed countries the trend has been towards the inner city decline in industry and population and towards suburbia. However, with new zero growth in population, this trend has been arrested.

A state may decide that all importing has to be undertaken via a state trading enterprise. Alternatively, environmental change affects the profile of the channel: the respective role of the intermediaries who will be used, from importation or assembly down to final sale to the consumer or end-user; and the relationships between these intermediaries and the manufacturer.

Rising levels of personal disposable income in France created the postwar phenomenon of the hypermarket: a complex comprising usually of a supermarket and general household departments, all located on one level and located outside of the main towns but positioned well for major highway intersections. As a customer incentive, hypermarkets such as the major French chain Carrefour (which incidentally translates as 'crossroads') operate petrol filling stations at their out-of-town locations which offer low priced petrol for their customers.

This quantum leap which France has made since the war in her retailing structure illustrates the fact that in distribution there can never be a guarantee against obsolescence. The hypermarkets in France have changed not only the buying situation for consumers but also the selling situation for manufacturers, as the hypermarkets have become important customers for all the large manufacturing companies, and not just in food but for all the other items which they sell, such as domestic electrical equipment or clothing.

For the foreign company the question of location is important. There is the question of ownership and control, whether it is a matter of final goods inventory or assembly. Manufacturers can choose to extend into retailing, as some multinational companies such as Singer and Philips have done, or take part-ownership of the channel intermediaries whether wholesalers or retailers. It is also possible for the foreign company to engage in some other means of distribution, such as mail order direct to the customer which may be seen to involve lower cost in that the fixed costs of buildings and staff may be lower. However, against this are the heavy costs of postage in some countries together with the fact that there may be a significant gap between dispatch of goods and receipt of payment. This lead time may create a cashflow problem for the company and herein lies another problem. Interest rates are not equal between nations. If borrowings are expensive and inflation is high then there may be no advantages whatsoever in direct mail order. Other possibilities include exclusivity of sales for a retailer whether he is continuing with the manufacturer's name or having his 'own label' added, an area of operations that is significantly increasing over the last 10 years in Western Europe.

In terms of transit of goods there is a wide variation in the possibilities on offer, not only of the mode of transportation, as already discussed, but also in terms of whether the company should decide to lease plant, equipment, vehicles, etc. – as is common in France or the US – or buy, which would involve tying up capital. Aside from the relative advantages and disadvantages inherent in each respective method, there is always the guiding influence of competitive pressure to help shape the corporate decision.

It is accepted that to create sales it is necessary to have a communications package, but aside from the problem of devising a successful communications package that will make sense in a foreign country, there is the perennial problem of foreign market intelligence and feedback, other than in sales. Choice of distribution channel may inhibit or eliminate the flow of market information from the country concerned. One may expect to receive less information from an agent than from a sales subsidiary, and virtually no information to emanate from a distributor who has exclusive sales territory rights.

Questions as to packaging and the necessary barrier and promotional properties of products for export are dealt with separately in Chapter 6. For the moment, let us just bear in mind that for small retailers, the carton packaging is also the promotional material he is most likely to use within his shop window displays. For the manufacturer there are certain cost advantages in having a standardised carton cover acceptable for several markets: it eliminates the need for separate designs for each market allowing the firm to capitalise on its presentation which at the same time benefits the production area, facilitates transit and enhanced corporate image and brand awareness internationally, as well as helping small retailers with regard to product recognition, storage and display.

Use of freeports

Freeports are based on the concept of manufacturing or processing in bond free of all taxes, but whereas this has always been the case with whisky which needed three years at least to mature before being ready for sale whether on the home or export market, freeports exist only for the export market.

In 1982 there were reputed to have been more than 350 of these freeports around the world, of which more than two-thirds were in the developing world. They are estimated to have accounted for 9 per cent of world trade in that year and to have generated six million jobs. In a global economy experiencing little growth, this particular area of operations appears to offer some promise, and it is for this reason that the British Government in 1984 announced that six such freeports were to be established, each being based alongside an existing provincial airport to include Belfast Airport, Prestwick Airport, Liverpool Port, Southampton Port, Cardiff Port, and Birmingham Airport, none of which are important throughput centres in their own right. There is no Rotterdam amongst them. Elsewhere, examples of existing foreign freeports include: Hong Kong, Singapore, Hamburg, Amsterdam, Stockholm, Bombay, Sri Lanka, South Korea plus an estimated 40-plus in the United States. Manufacturers operating within a freeport are not liable to the import duties or the local or governmental taxes which manufacturers would pay immediately outside of the freeport area, but items which are assembled or produced within this area are not allowed to enter the domestic economy. They are produced solely for export and it is solely on this understanding that these tax concessions are made. Freeports other than those intended for the UK also have certain characteristics besides, such as relief from controls on planning, health and safety and employment measures. Wages are generally 10–30 times lower than in industrial nations.

Benefits of freeports

1. Better cash flow for firms located on freeports. Firms located on the zones do not pay customs duties or valued added taxes (VAT) on goods brought into the zone until they are released on to the domestic market. An exception to this arrangement is that VAT is payable on transactions between firms operating on the freeport, but this can be recovered if the goods are subsequently sold to customers outside the domestic market.
2. Freeports provide firms with a degree of flexibility in adjusting to market conditions. Goods can be stored on the zone without payment of duty until market prospects improve.
3. Freeports provide firms with freedom from paperwork and bureaucratic legislation.
4. Firms located on a zone can benefit from the concentration of facilities therein.
5. Firms located on a zone could benefit from savings in insurance and policing costs. Freeports are fenced-in areas policed and monitored by customs authorities and provide a safe and secure environment for firms.
6. Freeports could make a substantial contribution to employment. They could be a source of both direct and indirect employment opportunities. Increased investment from both home and foreign sources would make a direct contribution to employment. In addition, there would be indirect job creation in the form of jobs attached to storage, warehousing and servicing the zones.

The test for success of the freeport is whether it will be able to create investment additional to that which already exists, and avoid merely relocation of firms within the domestic economy. Another point is that intra-EEC trade is already exempt from duties and so it would have to be a manufacturing or assembly activity which relied on imports outside of the EEC. However, it does mean that British freeports would hold little attraction for Continental firms. As regards the VAT position this has changed recently in the UK whereby importers now have to pay VAT immediately on receipt of goods rather than when they are sold. As to the freeport, no tax would be paid on entry to the zone, only at the point at which freeport goods were to enter the domestic market. Thus should the strong export orientation fail to materialise, the future for the freeport is one only of becoming a bonded warehouse of imported goods awaiting entry to the domestic market.

The Malaysian part of Pasir Gudang is now operating in a freeport. Malaysian shippers will be able to store their goods at Pasir Gudang while waiting for prices of any particular commodity to pick up before exporting. It is hoped, too, that this freeport undergoing a $70 million expansion plan will take some traffic from neighbouring Singapore. Last year it handled 3 million tonnes with a capacity of 3.5 million tonnes but a projected capacity on completion of 7.6 million tonnes. Bausch and Lomb base their European distribution at Schipol airport in the Netherlands, which allows them day-to-day delivery throughout Europe. Similarly, periodicals such as *Time*,

Newsweek, *Business Week* are also distributed from this same base; getting information to the consumer on time necessitates air freight, but here there are the potential savings also of bulk distribution from the centre of a major European air network.

Channel interfaces

The exporter's overall objective is to achieve some target rate or return on investment. The first point to consider is that irrespective of whether we care to use middlemen, the intermediaries in the channel between us and our final customers, the functions of a convention or vertical marketing system do not change. In a vertical marketing system, the company is simply bringing 'in-house' certain activities which would be performed by others. It is still necessary to fulfil these functions, however. As we go down the channel, these functions change from design, production, branding, pricing, promoting, and selling, to a new set with a greater emphasis on functions such as stocking, promoting, display, selling, delivery, and finance. Whenever a manufacturer looks grudgingly therefore at discounts offered to intermediaries it is worthwhile remembering the functions that these intermediaries perform before deciding to bring these activities within the company. The cost savings once the discount structure has been abolished and the activities being brought in-house may then only be marginal.

The benefits of using intermediaries has to be set against the disadvantages of loss of control. Primarily, where speed of market entry is important there may be instant access to a number of outlets, low selling costs, and the advantage of an experienced distribution outlet; but intermediaries, whether agents or distributors, may not give a product the attention which the exporter would like. Given that some of these intermediaries may be handling products for a number of companies, their motivation may lie more with the product earning them the highest returns in commission. This loss of control of the company is difficult to quantify. They may not have established any reasonable marketing objectives or sales projection figures for the market in question and so the intermediary may simply be a low-cost presence for an anticipated low level of sales. Control, though, is lacking. Information, too, is likely to be limited or biased in view of the fact that if the market is booming then the intermediary will only commit economic suicide by admitting it to his principal and thereby invite the principal to bring in his own sales organisation and gear up for a future anticipated higher level of sales without intermediaries. Similarly, customer service may also be seen to be at risk. International warranties and brand awareness breaks down in markets where there is inadequate provision for service maintenance personnel and spare parts. Direct distribution avoids these problems but means a higher degree of investment is required and perhaps also a greater length of time before the local sales team is recruited and trained for the task. Avon Cosmetics maintain an approach of selling door-to-door wherever possible through a workforce of freelance agents who are also technically self-employed. Tupperware is an example of a company that has been successful in transferring its house-party style of selling to Japan. Elsewhere the pattern seems to be that wherever direct control is not possible or desirable, the next best alternative should be settled for. In this regard it is worth bearing in mind how Avon Cosmetics sell their cosmetics into the CMEA countries and how Marks and Spencer successfully export their name and branded product range into countries where they are not officially represented other than as a brand name administered by a distributor. Retailing, too, has become an international activity for many component groups.

Identifying the intermediaries

Intermediaries take various forms but may be acknowledged to be specialists of considerable experience often with numerous contacts in the trade in which they are based. The alternatives include importers who are wholesalers; importers who are cash-and-carry wholesalers; brokers; commission agents; exclusive distributors; sales offices; and international co-operative distribution groups such as the Dutch based VG and Spar purchasing associations in the grocery trade. VG has approximately 13,000 shops with 300 warehouses operated by 87 wholesalers. The cash and carry concept had approximately 1,800 outlets within the EEC in 1980 but this was perhaps only a 10 per cent or 180 total increase over a ten year period. Consideration should be given to the number, quality and type of outlets to be used, whether it would be possible for some of the distributive tasks to be absorbed at an acceptable cost or, if not, which form of channel intermediary has to be engaged. Retailing operators include door to door hawkers and street traders. Service levels too are important but these may be influenced also by the margins made available to the intermediary by the manufacturer. Where labour is cheap and plentiful, labour may be hired. Elsewhere, the drive is to mechanise. Allied to service level is the question of inventory: who exactly takes title to inventory, which is a cost to be borne in the foreign market. Finance and credit is another area for joint participation by both manufacturer and intermediary, as is promotional activity at the local level. A complete standardisation of distribution strategy across markets is difficult to achieve because of customer expectations as to service levels and the competitive pressures existing to ensure that one either responds to these demands or else leaves the market. Expectations with regard to customer service levels vary as do distribution costs. The problem for the company is one of demand management – developing a distribution mix which best serves each market in which the company is represented.

Product life cycle and distribution

Companies each have their own corporate culture and corporate ethic – a belief as to which product and geographic markets they should be in and which channels of distribution are available. However, the competitive culture does not respect this, and in a multi-modal channel situation a product may have to forge a new channel of its own. Some companies have remained in business through the maintenance of a highly individual channel of distribution such as Tupperware or Avon, as mentioned earlier. What is now being suggested is that the product life cycle works in two ways: firstly, with regard to the product itself and its stage in the cycle and, secondly, with regard to its distribution. Falling unit manufacturing costs leading to lower unit selling costs are signals of a mature product reaching into the saturation and decline phases of the cycle. Distribution therefore has to adjusted accordingly, to minimise costs but still ensure product availability, and this may lead to a change in the choice of channel used: perhaps from low-volume specialist retailer to high-volume general trader such as a department-store chain. Any differential advantage that may be identified when moving into a new channel or distribution away from the mainstream competition may not only provide a breathing-space, but a clear gain in profitability if it means leadership of a small but lucrative market segment now being accessed by means of this new distribution channel. Mature goods which are now being distributed in this way through new distribution channels include in Britain: spectacles and British Telecom telephone sets now available from department stores. Distribution channels therefore need to be reviewed periodically, and not just with regard to cost.

References

1. SITPRO, *The Effective Export Department*, London, 1982.
2. SITPRO, *Costing Guidelines for Export Administration*, 1979. British Business, 'Cutting the costs of international trading', 23 March 1984, pp. 560–4.
3. Kropfel, Robert E., Mentzer, John T. and Williams, Rex R., 'International Logistics Management at General Motors: Philosophy and Practice', *International Journal of Physical Distribution and Materials Management*, Vol. 11, no. 5/6, pp. 12–21.
4. Slater, Alan, 'International Marketing: The Role of Physical Distribution Management', *International Journal of Physical Distribution and Materials Management*, Vol. 10, no. 4, pp. 160–84.
5. Stock, James R. and Lambert, Douglas M., 'Physical Distribution Management in International Marketing', *International Marketing Review*, Autumn 1983, pp. 28–41.
6. Balasubramanyam, V. N. and Rothschild, R., 'Free zones in the United Kingdom', *Lloyds Bank Review* (October 1985). Basile, Antoine and Germidis, Dimitri, *Investing in Free Export Processing Zones*, OECD, 1984.
7. Davies, Warwick and Butler, Eamonn, *The Freeport Experiment*, Adam Smith Institute, 1986.
8. Dawson, John A., *Commercial Distribution in Europe*, Croom Helm, 1982.

9. *PROMOTION IN THE INTERNATIONAL CONTEXT*

Promotion and communications objectives

Communications affect every aspect of the firm – its public image; its particular product or service, its employee morale, its shareholders' perception of corporate efficiency. All may be affected, but the danger now is that improved communications, including telecommunications, alongside an increased level of trading activity worldwide since the last war, has reduced the importance of geographical frontiers. So-called 'psychic' or perceived distance may be felt to be greater between two neighbouring countries than two from different hemispheres. For example, British people may feel a closer affinity with Australians, because of a multiplicity of ties, than with the French. Yet, in a shrinking world or what has been called the 'global village', irrespective of where we live, we buy and use similar products which are directed towards us with messages that are now markedly similar worldwide. However, there is a great difference still between global products and global brands, and cultural convergence remains a distant and purely theoretical concept.

For a company in such a position, there are enormous economies of scale to be reaped, but there is also an inherent danger; that danger lies in rumour or misconstrued fact which may soon begin to gather its own momentum. One such example is provided by the difficulties faced by Proctor & Gamble in the United States, initially only in the southern states of America where the word began to spread that Proctor & Gamble through the use of their trademark encourage satanism. The supporting evidence was the Proctor & Gamble crescent moon and 13 stars, a registered trademark which no-one had probably examined too closely before, including most probably senior management of Proctor & Gamble themselves. In this particular case, Proctor & Gamble were being attacked from what is sometimes referred to as the 'biblebelt' of the Southern states. The news of this scare had first to reach Proctor & Gamble and to be taken seriously by its management but given the time lags of reporting market response even to sales, delay is inevitable, by which time considerable damage would already have been done to their market share. Next, what would be their competitive response? Ignore it and continue to promote individual brands or take it seriously, and take on the Devil? This example serves to show the difficult challenge that can sometimes be presented to those in charge of promotion. The scare started in 1980 and did not die down and by 1982, had reached a peak where Proctor & Gamble were receiving 15,000 calls per month routed through to their consumer services

153

department. Moving to the offensive, Proctor & Gamble then enlisted the support of one of the deans of the 'moral majority', Jerry Falwell; hired two detectives agencies to trace the culprits; filed six suits against people for spreading rumours and then set up a toll-free telephone number to handle anxious customer enquiries. The rumours, however, continued and calls were still pouring in at the rate of 5,600 a month when the company decided it had spent enough and suffered enough and was therefore discontinuing the use of its corporate logo on products over the next few years though they would continue with it on letterheads and at corporate headquarters.

In general, promotion may be said to include the following tools.

Personal selling

The use of the salesman particularly in high value-added industrial goods is unquestioned. A specific message delivered by person to those either taking or influencing the purchase decision is the objective. In international marketing, use of a flying salesman can be expensive and if he moves around too much he will be spreading himself too thinly over too many markets, only exhausting himself and representing his company badly. In some markets, such as Eastern Europe, there may be restrictions, as on a permanent sales representation and so the choice will fall between use of a flying salesman or of a state-owned representative agency. Personal contact may therefore be important to influence decision-makers but it is also expensive.

Exhibitions

Exhibitors also use personal selling but here one can often take advantage of specialised industrial fairs and symposia. There are specialist fairs for various goods and services, e.g. cameras and cinematographic equipment; building and construction machinery; footwear; packaging and many other industry sectors too numerous to mention. Details of these fairs may be obtained from the Department of Trade's Fairs and Promotions Branch or the Department of Trade publication, *British Business*. Exhibitions and fairs may therefore be general or specialist. Where specialist, the competition will be seen to gether together in that exhibition hall for the duration of the show to display their wares but also check on what everyone else is doing within the industry. Trade enquiries are more likely to be converted into sales at such exhibitions because buyers from different countries will usually congregate there. The expense of exhibiting therefore has to be set against the cost of not exhibiting. For British companies, the Department of Trade usually offers some financial assistance to encourage participation in the national pavilion. Industrially and internationally, these exhibitions provide some degree of image building for the participants, the value of which may greatly exceed the actual orders taken during the exhibition itself.

Public relations

Public relations is of particular significance to multinational companies. A favourable image of multinational operations in any particular market may be greatly enhanced by a free, unsolicited favourable mention in any of the media – television, cinema, radio, or press. Being seen to be open, generous, and an honest broker, may be thought to be fundamental but in actual fact what happens is that each of these large companies employs a public relations agency responsible for external relations. Press releases to all editors of newspapers and periodicals may detail important personnel changes or significant contracts that have just been won abroad, or technological breakthroughs that have just been achieved. The BBC television programme 'Tomorrow's World' exists to inform the public about the products of tomorrow. High technology companies such as Sinclair Electronics have often benefited from exposure of this kind which adds to their perceived public image, informs the buying public and reassures shareholders and other interested bodies at the same time. Public relations influences word-of-mouth reaction to the company and also media treatment.

Sales promotion

Sales promotion relates to those so-called 'below-the-line' services such as point-of-sale displays and demonstrations as well as leaflets, free trials, contests and premiums of one kind or another, e.g. 'two-for-price-of-one'. Targeting directly at the potential buyer, the sales promotion material seeks to encourage a response to action and to actual trial of the product or service concerned. In some countries, this area of operations may be quite constrained because the market is small or sluggish or because of political impediments.

Advertising

Advertising exists to inform, persuade, and remind a buying public of a particular product or service and it does so at a lower cost per head to the company than personal selling or exhibitions. Advertising may seek to create either a brand image for the product concerned or a corporate image for the company in general. With regard first to the product, emphasis would be on the brand, so selective demand stimulation would be sought rather than primary demand stimulation, which would be total demand for the product class. Where there is an oligopoly situation, advertising can create some confusion as to which one the advertiser is, e.g. whether the advertiser is Cinzano or Martini; nevertheless total sales are increased for both in this sector, and there is no real problem. More damaging, but difficult to avoid, is the situation which arises where branded products become so firmly entrenched in a market that they become almost a generic name in their own right. The brand name has then been greatly diminished if not lost through its own success. As we have already noted in

Britain it is common to hear people use 'Hoover' as a verb, meaning to vacuum carpets or as a noun, meaning a vacuum cleaner; a vacuum flask is known as a 'Thermos' flask; a roll of adhesive tape as 'Sellotape'.

Advertising seeks to stimulate demand for branded products and may do this in one of two ways either by means of a 'pull' strategy whereby a manufacturer might succeed in moving goods into retail shops by advertising to the end-users and ensuring that they ask for this particular product for their usual retailer. A 'push' strategy is where the manufacturer works down the channel of distribution 'pushing' the goods by means of financial discounts or incentives. Companies such as Nimslo with the revolutionary three-dimensional camera have relied upon the 'push' strategy; others such as Sinclair have used the 'pull' strategy moving to the retail channel of distribution once the product is being manufactured in sufficient quantity to meet demand.

With regard to advertising, choice has to be exercised as to the medium to be used whether press, television, radio, or other such as outdoor advertising. Points to note here are the reach, i.e. the *total number* of members of the target audience who are expected to receive this message at least once; *frequency* i.e. the number of times the target audience will be exposed to the message; *impact* dependent upon the medium used and the message, this depends on compatibility between the two. *Playboy* magazine always seems to attract advertisers for high value-added consumer durables, e.g. cars, hi-fi equipment, clothes that are geared primarily to a high-income male segment. Finally, there is *continuity* which relates to the length of time a campaign will run and the pattern of timing of the advertising within a campaign. Inevitably, therefore there has to be a trade-off between high-frequency low-reach or low-frequency high-reach. Certain products identify with one or other strategy, e.g. soap powders will appear on television during the day, occasionally during the evening. Advertisements for cars will be shown primarily in the evening. This is partly a question of value of purchase, partly a question of appealing to all the decision-makers as well as to their users. Husbands may wish to be involved in the purchase of washing machines or dishwashers even if they do not wish to be around to physically operate these machines once purchased.

The communications process

This seeks to transmit a message from a source such as a manufacturer through a medium such as television, press, or other to a receiver, an identified target segment audience. Known as the 'hypodermic model', it is subject to 'noise' i.e. external forces which limit the force of the message through the final receiver. In international marketing, this level of 'noise' is greatly increased through external forces which may be either competitive or environmental but which we can do nothing about. The feedback loop is the weakest part and this is usually sales, but the leads and lags of advertising make its direct effectiveness in achieving sales difficult to assess.

Success is most likely if the advertiser's goal is consistent with the goals of the target audience. Word-of-mouth advertising has been found to be important where one has been able first to influence those who in innovation studies are called 'opinion leaders'. These people are more open to the mass media than the people they influence. They are usually better educated and knowledgeable, they are the ones to turn to when seeking advice on a purchase about which you have no present knowledge either in terms of the meaning of product specifications or even in the recognition of reliable brand names.

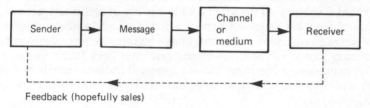

Feedback (hopefully sales)

Figure 9.1 Hypodermic communications model.

Actually changing attitudes is beyond the scope of most advertising, as was pointed out in the discussion on cultural variables. Nevertheless it is possible to influence behaviour where opinions are not strongly held and are not convictions. It is possible to persuade people to switch brands of toothpaste or to accept trial of a new product which embodies a new concept such as home computing for example. In all of this, reference groups play an important role as has been shown in innovation studies (see Figure 9.2).

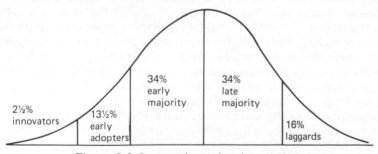

Figure 9.2 Innovation adoption cycle.

The lunatic fringe who desire to acquire all new products just introduced onto the market account for only 2½ per cent of those who will finally adopt it. They do not therefore constitute a viable market segment of their own. The early adopters are those opinion leaders whom it is crucial to have on your side. Their behaviour influences others. People are not sheep but are influenced by others particularly when nervous about the purchase of a totally new product concept or high-value item.

What inhibits the message from striking home is that each individual in the course of a day will be subjected to perhaps 300–400 messages. From early morning, one may rise to radio or television, have breakfast and read the morning newspaper listening all the while to the family perhaps discussing new acquisitions made by their friends. Walking along the street, there are billboards, posters and leaflets everywhere. On public transport, there are posters everywhere. Perhaps one may meet a friend or colleague and discuss his new car which was a personal import from Belgium and think 'strange, I didn't think it was so easy to import cars straight into the UK from Belgium and save 25 per cent on the British list price!' Again, at the office or place of work, the same is continuing even in a lunchtime visit to the bank since banks are now all active in a wide variety of secondary activities, and literature on their range of services may be everywhere apparent. The process is then repeated in a mirror image on the way home from work when an evening paper will be on sale, and one goes back home to listen to the family, listen about their day, what happened to their friends and perhaps watch television, read a newspaper or weekly television guide, or listen to radio.

As a means of self-protection, each individual exercises selective exposure which means exposure to messages that fit his existing attitudes and the avoidance of messages that are incompatible with his existing beliefs or attitudes. Secondly, individuals are guilty of selective perception, that is they may distort or misinterpret the intended meaning of a message when it differs from their attitudes. The greater the gap between attitudes held and messages presented, the greater the likelihood of message distortion. Thirdly, being exposed to such a vast number of messages in the course of a day, we could never be expected to remember them all. Each individual has a capacity only for selective retention, remembering better messages that reinforce their attitudes than those at variance with their attitudes. If it is of particular interest now or in the future, it is more likely to be remembered.

Another point to note is that of cognitive dissonance whereby the individual having made a high-value purchase will experience a period of doubt immediately afterwards. During this period, he will be seeking reassurance in his purchase and may for a time read the manufacturer's advertisements more avidly for false or misleading claims. To this end, car manufacturers, to take one example, seek in their advertising to both persuade people to buy and reassure those who have just made a purchase. Flattering the client by telling how wise he is in purchasing this particular model at this seasonal price, etc.

Advertising seeks to promote change by moving the individual through the following successive stages:

Unawareness		
Awareness		(that this brand exists)
Comprehension		(what this brand can do)
Conviction		(that this brand is supreme)
Action		(i.e. purchase)

Creating awareness is always the first step but secondly, one has to remind customers of the availability of existing products and their relative competitive strengths. Within the marketing channel, this message may have to be relayed perhaps in a different way to all members in the channel, perhaps through the trade press, perhaps through direct mail, perhaps through the salesforce. Advertising induces mental readiness, and pre-sells products. Cinema and TV films also help pre-sell branded products or product concepts that may not yet be available in that particular market. To be effective, advertising has to narrowly define its target audience and concentrate on the product or service's Unique Selling Proposition (USP), i.e. that which distinguishes this particular product or service from the competition, its relative strengths. Not all advertising is designed to produce sales as a certain percentage will be devoted simply to communication, as in the case of governmental health warnings on tobacco or road-safety or institutional advertisements about the good corporate behaviour of the oil companies investing in the North Sea. Both are current examples to be found in Britain today.

Advertising – the global situation

From 1976 to 1982 world advertising expenditure grew 122 per cent from $63 billion to $140 billion. At the same time, advertising billings for the multinational agencies rose 238 per cent from $8 billion to $27 billion. At the same time few brands are marketed on a worldwide basis because of language or lack or general transferability either because the product may be climactically or culturally unsuitable, too expensive, too large or too small. Smaller sizes may be required for poorer nations. One is left then to standardise only on what is left in terms of the common component parts. The famous Esso 'Put a Tiger in your Tank' campaign did create an image for an unromantic non-standardised product. In this search for product image, advertisers perceive the similarities more than the dissimilarities amongst global consumers (vindicating the Maslow Hierarchy of Needs) so potentially the same offering may be made to Malaysians or Nigerians as Americans or Europeans. This was held true for Hertz, Avis, Pepsi, Coke and McDonalds hamburgers, who are not representative of all multinational companies. A quite different experience was found by Ford of Europe when seeking to test consumer reaction to a new Ford Granada in Germany, UK, France and Sweden. Using a sample of 200–300 people in each of Germany, UK, France and Sweden to test the new Ford of Europe model against the 'next car', intended purchase on a number of variables provided a test bed for the international marketing standardisation of the product. Here there were quite important variations in the way in which consumers perceived an identical product and so the advertising was changed. This then meant segmentation of promotional strategies for international markets by allowing cross-country differences in product perceptions and product attribute preferences. See Table 9.4 on page 164.

This brings us onto Keegan's five strategies for multinational marketing (see Table 9.5 on page 164). In the above example, the product is the same worldwide and the communications are the same worldwide. This is the strategy employed by Coca-Cola and Pepsi. Food may generally be held to

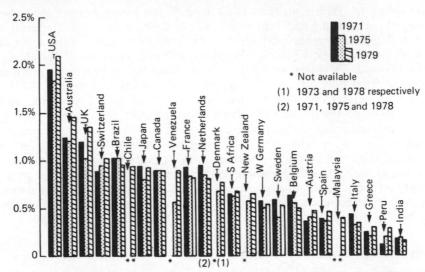

Figure 9.3 International advertising expenditures as a percentage of GNP.

be culture-bound but both these products are global with centrally produced advertising that incorporates local differences in language, etc. It coincides well with the production orientation because no differentiation is to be seen. This was true until Pepsico started to take a market share from Coca-Cola who then changed their formulation to suit this new market change. It suited some but not others so Coca-Cola effectively split their market between the new and classic Coke. In the second strategy, the same product can be communicated in different ways for different markets. Bicycles may either be for recreation or basic transportation; a small tractor may be a garden tractor in an affluent society or a small agricultural tractor in a less- developed country. Next, there is the third strategy where the communications remain the same but the product formulation changes. The prime example here is that of Esso with its 'Put a Tiger in your Tank' campaign which remained constant despite the fact that in some markets only 91 octane petrol was available, yet the advertising image employed throughout was the same as for 100 octane. In the fourth situation, the product and the communications both change; here the examples offered are greetings cards which vary with local holidays, feast days, etc. but also in nature because of different attitudes to colour, etc. Clothing too, Keegan held, is culture bound. However, in the last 10 to 15 years there has been the upsurge of multinational clothing led by the denim manufacturers behind Levi's and Wranglers, diversifying now into a range of casual wear. Similarly, the syndicated franchise behind the 'Snoopy' cartoon character has produced blank greetings cards for all occasions. One may well question whether the fourth case still remains applicable, as well as the examples offered. It includes no allowance either for the 'own label'/generic brand/acquisition or introduction of local brands. The final

Table 9.1
1981 total advertising expenditures, GNP and advertising expenditures as percentages of GNP, for 85 countries

Country	1981 advertising expenditures (Millions $US)	1981 GNP (Billions of $US)	Advertising as a % of GNP
Argentina	1,370.2	68.6	1.99
Australia	2,378.0	149.3	1.59
Austria	623.4	79.8	0.78
Bahamas	13.2	1.2	1.10
Bahrain	3.1	1.7	0.18
Bangladesh	5.6	8.1	0.07
Belgium	537.9	125.2	0.43
Bermuda	12.5	0.7	1.79
Bolivia	15.7	3.2	0.49
Brazil	2,589.1	267.6	0.97
Canada	3,529.4	253.2	1.39
Chile	405.0	24.5	1.65
Colombia	299.9	30.6	0.98
Costa Rica	27.9	4.1	0.68
Cyprus	16.8	2.2	0.76
Denmark	657.0	68.2	0.96
Dominican Republic	98.0	7.1	1.38
Ecuador	58.9	11.0	0.54
Egypt	265.2	26.0	1.02
El Salvador	16.3	3.4	0.48
Ethiopia	3.0	4.3	0.07
Finland	892.0	50.5	1.77
France	4,484.2	686.9	0.65
Ghana	8.3	5.2	0.16
Greece	127.8	44.5	0.29
Guatemala	74.5	8.1	0.92
Honduras	14.1	2.2	0.64
Hong Kong	173.2	23.5	0.74
Iceland	12.2	2.4	0.51
India	429.2	172.3	0.25
Indonesia	190.0	69.0	0.28
Iraq	73.4	43.2	0.17
Ireland	146.8	17.6	0.83
Israel	176.3	18.7	0.94
Italy	3,408.2	384.0	0.89
Jamaica	25.2	2.4	1.05
Japan	11,120.3	1,245.5	0.89
Jordan	21.2	5.3	0.40
Kenya	30.5	7.4	0.41
Kuwait	22.0	27.5	0.08
Lebanon	26.7	2.9	0.92
Liberia	1.5	1.0	0.15

Table 9.1 continued

Country	1981 advertising expenditures (Millions $US)	1981 GNP (Billions of $US)	Advertising as a % of GNP
Libya	34.9	29.1	0.12
Luxembourg	28.2	4.7	0.60
Malaysia	143.5	24.2	0.59
Malta	3.7	1.3	0.28
Mauritius	3.3	1.0	0.33
Mexico	820.6	149.2	0.55
Morocco	81.2	19.8	0.41
Nepal	1.1	2.1	0.05
Netherlands	1,822.1	169.3	1.08
Netherlands Antilles	9.9	1.4	0.71
New Zealand	294.2	22.4	1.31
Nicaragua	10.6	1.9	0.56
Nigeria	142.8	83.8	0.17
Norway	681.8	53.7	1.27
Pakistan	45.0	27.8	0.16
Panama	24.1	3.6	0.67
Paraguay	27.3	4.4	0.62
Peru	105.4	17.0	0.62
Philippines	111.3	35.7	0.31
Portugal	57.7	25.1	0.23
Puerto Rico	222.0	12.4	1.79
Saudi Arabia	103.2	129.0	0.08
Singapore	105.8	11.4	0.93
South Africa	821.9	68.9	1.19
South Korea	467.6	65.7	0.71
Spain	1,321.8	212.7	0.62
Sri Lanka	10.1	4.2	0.24
Sudan	9.4	7.8	0.12
Surinam	3.0	1.1	0.27
Sweden	1,090.4	114.8	0.95
Switzerland	1,235.7	105.5	1.17
Syria	31.0	9.4	0.33
Taiwan	329.0	28.7	1.15
Thailand	120.0	34.2	0.35
Trinidad & Tobago	34.6	5.4	0.64
Turkey	202.1	71.1	0.28
United Kingdom	5,925.1	453.3	1.31
United States	61,320.0	2,672.9	2.29
Uruguay	41.5	8.3	0.50
Venezuela	633.7	66.7	0.95
West Germany	5,536.0	867.6	0.64
Zambia	11.2	3.4	0.33
Zimbabwe	33.6	4.8	0.70

Table 9.2
The world's top 20 advertising agencies in 1985

Rank Group 1985	Gross Income (million $)	Billings (million $)
1. Young & Rubicam	536.0	3.58 billion
2. Ogilvy Group	481.1	3.32 billion
3. Dentsu Inc.	473.1	3.62 billion
4. Ted Bates Worldwide	466.0	3.11 billion
5. J. Walter Thompson Co.	450.9	3.01 billion
6. Saatchi & Saatchi Compton Worldwide	440.9	3.03 billion
7. BBDO International	377.0	2.52 billion
8. McCann–Erickson Worldwide	345.2	2.30 billion
9. D'Arcy Masius Benton & Bowles	319.5	2.18 billion
10. Foote, Cone & Belding Communications	284.2	1.90 billion
11. Leo Burnett Co.	269.4	1.87 billion
12. Grey Advertising	259.3	1.73 billion
13. Doyle Dane Bernbach Group	231.8	1.67 billion
14. Hakuhodo International	198.9	1.53 billion
15. SSC & B: Lintas Worldwide	190.9	1.30 billion
16. Bozell, Jacobs, Kenyon & Eckhardt	173.7	1.22 billion
17. Marschalk Campbell–Ewald Worldwide	150.1	1.00 billion
18. Eurocom Group	129.1	866.3
19. Needham Harper Worldwide	127.1	847.3
20. Dancer Fitzgerald Sample	121.5	879.3

Source: Reprinted with permission from 22 April 1986 issue of *Advertising Age*. Copyright (1985) by Crain Communications Ltd.

strategy is where no product exists but the needs exists. An example is when Colgate developed a hand-powered washing machine and then subsequently developed a communications package to accompany it. The realisation that 600 million women still washed clothes by hand provided a feasible market for a multinational who saw possibilities of increasing sales of detergent powders at the same time. However, an alternative could be as shown in Table 9.6.

Table 9.3
Europe's top 10 advertising agencies

Agency	Billings	Revenues
	Millions of dollars	
Saatchi & Saatchi, London	493	74
Publicis Conseil, Paris	254	37
D'Arcy MacManus Masius, London	238	28
J. Walter Thompson, London	237	34
Havas Conseil Groupe, Paris	177	26
Lintas, Hamburg	173	26
Team/BBDO, Düsseldorf	163	25
Roux, Séguéla, Cayzac & Goudard, Paris	154	23
Young & Rubicam Holdings, London	154	23
J. Walter Thompson, Frankfurt	150	23

Source Advertising Age's Focus

Table 9.4
Results of test of consumer reaction to new Ford of Europe car and 'next car'

Attributes	UK		France		Sweden	
	New model –high awareness	'Next car'	New model –high awareness	'Next car'	New model –high awareness	'Next car'
Luggage capacity	7.4	6.2	6.8	6.2	6.8	6.4
Technically advanced	7.2	6.7	6.6	6.6	7.4	6.6
Journey comfort	7.5	7.3	7.5	7.2	7.4	7.4
Styling	6.6	7.0	6.9	7.3	7.1	6.5
Prestige	6.5	6.9	7.0	7.2	6.6	6.4
Safety	6.8	6.7	6.3	6.5	5.8	6.4
Roadholding	7.0	7.4	6.7	7.7	7.0	7.5
Reliability	6.9	7.5	6.8	7.3	6.5	7.7
Purchase interest (%)	33		33		37	
Sample size	n=286		n=193		n=223	

Source Colvin, Heeler and Thorpe, 'Developing International Advertising Strategy, *Journal of Marketing*, vol. 44, Fall 1980, pp. 73–9.

Media availability

Media availability or its strengths in terms of coverage and reaching the target group is difficult in the home country and made much more difficult when one considers a foreign market. Tables 9.5, 9.6 and 9.7 summarise the position.

Table 9.5
Keegan's five strategies for multinational marketing

	Product strategy	Communications strategy	Product examples	Product function or need satisfied	Conditions of product use	Ability to buy product
1.	Uniform	Uniform	Coca-Cola, Pepsi	Same	Same	Yes
2.	Same	Different	Bicycles	Different recreation or transportation	Same	Yes
3.	Different	Same	Camay soap, Nescafé coffee, Petrol (gasoline)	Same	Different	Yes
4.	Different	Different	Clothing, greeting cards	Different	Different	Yes
5.	Invention	Develop new communications	Hand-powered Washing machine	Same		No

Source: Warren Keegan, *Multinational Marketing Management* (Prentice-Hall, 1984).

Table 9.6
International product/communications standardisation

	Generic/own label	Regional brand	International brand
Communications	No responsibility	Responsive and specific	Unresponsive and generalised
Distribution	No responsibility	Standardised	Varied
Pricing	No responsibility	Flexibility	No flexibility, fluctuations give rise to parallel importing/ exporting
Profitability	Only on volume	Premium	Premium
Product	No change ensures long production runs	Quality/value	Constant reviewed safeguards the marque
Development	No responsibility	Under constant review	Constant monitoring locally and by headquarters

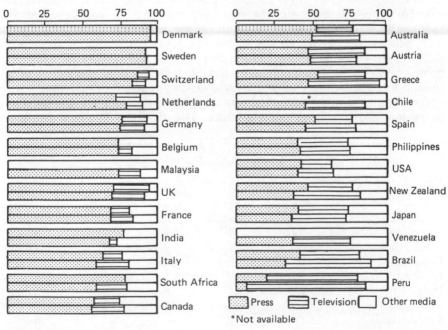

For each country, first column is 1971, or nearest available year (1973 or 1974); second is 1979 (1978 for Denmark)

Figure 9.4 Press and television shares of total advertising expenditure
Source: Trends in Advertising Expenditure in 25 Countries 1970–79, J. Walter Thompson. London, September 1980.

Table 9.7
Consumer media advertising expenditure 1979

| | Per capita | |
	$m	*$*
Germany	5,290	86
UK	4,611	82
France	2,662	50
Holland	1,630	117
Italy	1,078	20
Spain	1,004	27
Switzerland	907	144
Sweden	683	82
Austria	479	64
Belgium	473	48
Total	18,817	60

Source: Marketing, 21 October 1981.

More than half the world's households have at least one television set. For 1985 this was estimated to mean 473 million sets, and expected to increase to 500 million by 1986. Of the global total the US accounted for 84.9 million, the Soviet Union 82 million, Japan 30.2 million, Brazil 23 million, West Germany 22.1 million and the UK 18.9 million. The fastest growing market for television was where in 1974 the total was only half a million sets but by the end of 1984 had already reached 9.9 million.

Availability of television sets is but one side of the coin, the availability of commercial television quite another. Two-thirds of Western Europe

Table 9.8
Media used in 1979

| | Percentage consumer media expenditure | | | | |
	Print	*TV*	*Radio*	*Cinema*	*Outdoor*
Germany	79	11	4	1	4
UK ('80)	66	27	2	*	4
France	55	17	12	2	15
Holland	84	7	1	*	8
Italy	60	21	8	3	8
Spain	46	33	12	2	7
Switzerland	86	8	—	*	6
Sweden	93	—	—	2	5
Austria	61	23	9	*	7
Belgium	72	9	*	1	17

*Less than 1%
Source: Marketing, 21 October 1981.

Table 9.9
Commercial radio in Europe

	Stations	Coverage
Austria	1	National
France	5*	Regional – strong in Northern France, less strong South, weak North West
Germany	7	Regional – all areas
Italy	2	National
Luxembourg	1	National – English, French, German services
Holland	3	National
Spain	200	Local
UK	30	Regional – all areas

*Transmitted from outside
Source: Marketing, 21 October 1981.

may be said to be under-served in terms of programme choice, with government controlling the number of television channels, amount of broadcasting hours, and availability of advertising. No indigenous commercial television exists as yet in Denmark, Norway or Sweden, although each of them receive commercial television from their neighbours. Television reception like radio, often extends beyond its intended market coverage, which means that markets which do not allow the establishment of an indigenous or local station, but are unable to jam or block signals from a neighbouring transmitter, do in effect have a commercial station. Lastly, there are wide differences in television viewing rates where the West European average is between one and a half hours and five hours; the UK average of five hours and the US average of six and a half hours daily. Cable television varies from a penetration of 14 per cent in the UK to a high of 70 per cent in Belgium. Modern installation methods together with fibre-optic cable have significantly reduced the capital costs involved in cabling homes. However, penetration will increase slowly as it is still a slow and costly method of carrying television signals, particularly in rural areas. Cable television will remain complementary to satellite television rather than compete with it. Belgium has 55 licensed cable operators and for advertisers this allows a measure of targeting to a selected audience which satellite television can never hope to achieve.

Pan-European research: Readership data

There is generally no shortage of media data. The problem such as it exists is that surveys are restrictive, certainly national in character and usually sponsored by the publishers. There is little complementarity. A quite different means of sampling, and research methodology means that this plethora of national research material offers little insight into readership across nations. Just in Europe alone, there is for example:

West Germany
'Media Analyse' covers all media.
'Frauentypologie', deals with female demographic and psychographic categories.
'Soll und Haben' analyses private capital investment patterns.

France
'CESP' (Centre d'Etudes des Supports de Publicite) covers all media.
'SECODIP', consumer market orientated research.
'SOFRES', consumer market orientated research.

Netherlands
'NOP' consumer market survey.
'NOJ' consumer market survey.
'DMS' survey of decision-makers.

Italy
'ISPI' (Indagine Stampa Periodica Italiana) is the most comprehensive.
'Lancio' is much more recent and less tried and tested.

Benelux
'CIM' (Centre of Information about the Media) all media, similar to the British Target Group Index.
'SOBEMAP' for qualitative studies of page traffic and product interest.

Spain
'EGM', only reputable survey.

All sorts of problems arise in the study of the individual media in each of these countries. Benelux, for example, is not a country but a region incorporating Belgium and Luxembourg and with Flemish as well as French speakers. There are certain customs of buying newspapers or magazines which are regional or national. There is the question too, of literacy levels, and of reprographic capability both of which affect the demand for print media.

Since 1980, various initiatives have been undertaken to arrive at surveys which examine readership across nations and these include:

1. Fack Orvesto, a Swedish publication which undertakes a postal survey of top male income earners in Sweden which helps media planners evaluate relative merits of suitable Swedish and some international publications.

2. German, Swiss and Dutch surveys of decision-makers were all on an in-home personal interview basis but only the Dutch survey included women and each has a slightly different sampling framework.

3. 1980 European Businessman Readership Survey. (A postal survey covering 15 countries and including senior management in companies with more than 250 employees but the total universe is small, only 201,237.

4. Pan European Survey II (12 countries surveyed, not just top management). It identifies men of high status. This sample identifies a universe of 3,755,000 businessmen and a total universe of 6,258,333.

The use of international publications can benefit advertisers by helping to establish an international image. For most products, national media have had to be used to provide the range, frequency and level of coverage thought to be required for success.

Advertising agencies

Much of the myth surrounding the supposed dynamism of the advertising agencies was exploded in *Management Today*, December 1981. Some surprising facts emerged including:

1. The average account stays 9 years
2. Account switches relate to less than 3 per cent of billings
3. The three biggest agencies are more than 100 years old, and twelve are more than 50 years old.
4. The average advertising executive stays 12 years with the agency.

Nevertheless, once a move was made from one agency to another, the effects could be quite dramatic. Young and Rubicam decided to give up its international Procter & Gamble business when it was offered Colgate worldwide, Colgate firing its existing agencies to create space for Young and Rubicam.

Several options exist for agency selection:

1. Multinationals may select an international agency group with strong central control capable of imposing decisions on regional offices. Kodak and the Ford Motor Company both use J. Walter Thompson in all markets. Colgate use Young and Rubicam in all their markets.

2. Foreign marketing may require the services of an international agency federation with more decentralised control giving greater local autonomy. (This would include minority interest and associate partner relationships.)

3. For local selling an agency in each territory is considered best for that territory. It may lead to fragmentation but it is the strategy adopted by ITT.

4. A home market agency devises the campaign strategy and places advertising direct in the media of the chosen foreign target market.

5. A company can go it alone without an advertising agency and place advertisements direct or via local correspondents.

The final choice of agency would be very much influenced by the relative strengths of agencies measured against the following criteria:

1. Market coverage
2. Quality of coverage
3. Market research, public relations, and other marketing services available in-house
4. Definition of the respective roles of company advertising department and agency
5. Communication and control
6. International co-ordination
7. Size of company international business
8. Image
9. Company organisation
10. Level of involvement

Advertising standardisation versus local adaptation

The technology for standardisation including satellite television is now available but local tastes will still influence whether products will be successful or not. Food is held often to be the most culture-bound product. It is arguable whether this extends also to soft drinks but Coca-Cola's canned diet drinks did not have the success in Britain that was expected from US experience, not from lack of advertising but due to the British habit of drinking tea and coffee during the day and not canned drinks, as in the US. There is little chance of a brand achieving a coherent international image when there is fragmentation in the market response. Secondly, not all media are universally available nor to the same degree. Advertising messages have to be suited to their media. A verbose TV commercial is unlikely to travel on grounds of language alone. There is an added problem in that Marsteller's estimate that an English language ad runs 15 per cent longer in French and 50 per cent longer in German, sometimes creating unforeseen difficulties in translating one print ad into several languages. Nevertheless, a multinational such as Kodak is now starting to regionalise its advertising in Europe.

The media may be seen as:

Newspapers. Both national and international, e.g. *International Herald Tribune*, printed in Paris, or the *Financial Times* now printed in London and Frankfurt, with proposals for printing daily also in the USA. Few countries resemble Britain in this respect, however, and so it is more usual to find local or regional newspapers abroad.

Periodicals. Both national and international, e.g. *Newsweek*, *Time*, *Economist* carry advertisements to readers in the same social class internationally. Includes also TV programmes, papers, women's magazines, special interest publications and trade and technical publications.

The Cinema. A declining medium in Western countries for a number of years, but still very important in India, for example. Problems with this type of media are over the control of choice of cinema and the specific feature film which you wish your advertisement to accompany, and so this leads to lack of control over targetting, and quality of likely audience.

Increasingly, cinema makes use of international advertisements such as those prepared by Coca-Cola in their famous 'I'd love to teach the world to sing' advertisement. Not that this was an international advertisement as much as a blatantly American advertisement for a conspicuously American consumer product that has a vast international market precisely on those grounds. For more than twelve years, the advertising industry has held to this advertisement as an example of global advertising. The true effectiveness of this particular advertisement could, however, only be judged by recall tests of the person in the street paired alongside the advertising executive. Both may have recall but for different reasons.

Television. There are few markets today which do not receive television. More than half the world's households have at least one. The role of advertising in television will vary more from country to country. Exciting developments are taking place here which will retain television as the prime medium. Nevertheless, within Europe there are two systems in operation. PAL and SECAM exist in 95 per cent of Europe's 125 million households and plans for more direct-broadcast satellites will cover 44 million people in France, 55 million in Germany and 22 million in Scandinavia.

Again national and international advertisements are being used because of origination costs. Multinationals, particularly, reap the benefits of such economies with video recorded adverts. On the negative side, the adverts are usually very American in style and fail to have as high a degree of impact on a British audience as on an American one. New developments are taking place in satellite television broadcasting which are likely to increase the number of television channels. The first Pan-European satellite television channel, SKY, is already available. Broadcasting from London, it makes use of a low-power 20 watt solar EC51 satellite. This satellite's 'footprint' covers Europe but because its signals are coded they have to be decoded at the other end. This is being done by means of linking up with existing television cable networks. One point which must be emphasised then is its precision because of this cable link. It is possible to state exactly who is receiving this signal and where. Presently SKY Channel's audience exceeds 3 million across Europe but is expected to reach 7.1 million by the end of 1986. To this end the owners News International, have invested heavily in a two-part strategy. The first objective is to maximise potential existing cable links. A lower-powered satellite, as at present, would otherwise require the viewer to purchase a large dish in order to receive its signal. Using existing cable networks means that the channel is able to start life with a ready-made audience. The second objective is to use a high-power satellite in 1987 which will be a Direct Broadcasting Satellite (DBS) which will require only a small dish so cabling will not be necessary to receive SKY Channel.

Also developments in private subscriber cable television will create opportunities to target directly at selected market segments only; teletext services operated by the television companies provide free computer databank information on a variety of subjects including programme titles. Viewdata services such as Prestel operated by British Telecom which connects the television by telephone to a central computer and transmits pages of computer text back to the television screen at home, allows the viewer to interrogate the computer, order goods and withdraw, deposit or ask questions of his bank or building society account.

Radio. Availability differs considerably. This may be regional, national or international. In Britain, commercial radio is regional; only the BBC, which does not allow commercial advertising, is national, but within Europe there is also Radio Luxembourg, which broadcasts a strong signal across Western Europe and is a commercial station broadcasting in several languages.

Posters. Outdoor hoardings appear to be found everywhere apart, perhaps, from CMEA countries, where they are less common.

Leaflets which may be black and white, or colour, with or without photography. This form of advertising is dependent on the local sophistication of the printing industry as this requires local organisation.

Point-of-sale materials. These should be localised for the market concerned and are dependent upon prevailing customs as well as average sales and storage area of retail outlets.

Direct mail. Again, this is a localised form of advertising. The tendency may be not to use mail but the telephone. Mail may be slow and unreliable. People may not be used to receiving mail other than official letters which are usually bad news. There may be no special commercial mailing rates which would also make this method expensive.

Trade Fairs and Exhibitions. These are international in scope and seem to be expensive relative to the duration of the fair concerned, although official government support is always available for first-time exhibitors. It is up to the company to decide the relevance, size and quality of the anticipated audience relative to his target audience. There are high costs of space, stand construction, and manning.

In addition, we could add transport advertising; outdoor advertising at sports grounds including football matches; and neon signs and local attitudes towards their use. Against this listing, a few questions have to be set such as prevailing literacy levels. This would rule out printed advertising messages and would influence advertising more towards the spoken word on radio and on television. Reception coverage of television and radio may be open to some doubt, as may the reliability of circulation figures paraded for foreign newspapers and periodicals, unless there is a counterpart for the Audit Bureau of Circulation (ABC) which conducts an independent audit of magazines sold and therefore confirms circulation figures.

As countries differ, so must the way of putting the message across. The best approach is to 'preserve some covert multinationalisation in the campaign but to add a deft touch that is distinctly French or British or Italian'. A study of a select group of multinationals operating in Western Europe found that there was a high degree of standardisation in over 70 per cent of these enterprises. Companies sought standardisation without sacrificing the benefits of local entrepreneurship.

Pattern standardisation is a more planned, flexible form of standardisation. The overall theme and individual components of a campaign are designed originally for use in multiple markets, developed to provide a uniformity in direction but not in detail. A pre-planned effort is made to develop an overall corporate advertising strategy and to provide some of the benefits attributed to standardisations while permitting local flexibility in response to individual market differences.

The main objectives in standardising include:

1. To present a worldwide corporate image through media that are becoming increasingly international.
2. To reduce production and creative costs through economies of scale.
3. To reduce message confusion where there is media overlap or country-to-country consumer mobility.

One television film could be used in 25 or so markets. Also there is media overlap on the continent as, for example, among Dutch/Belgian/French/

Table 9.10

Issues in advertising and the countries where they are particularly sensitive

Issues	Sensitive countries
Advertising to children	Canada, Scandinavia, US, Greece, West Germany, Austria, Holland (toothbrush symbol in confectionery ads).
Class action by consumer associations	EEC Commission, US.
Comparative advertising	EEC Commission (encouragement), France (relaxation), Philippines (ban), US (encouragement).
Consumer protection in general	EEC Commission, Scandinavia, UN organisations, US.
Corrective ads	US, EEC Commission.
Feminine hygiene commercials (mandatory prior screening)	Canada (British).
Food, drugs, and cosmetics commercials (mandatory prior screening)	Canada, Mexico, Austria, Netherlands, Switzerland, West Germany.
Infant formula promotion	World Health Organisation/UNICEF.
Reversal of the burden of proof on the advertiser	EEC Commission, Scandinavia, US.
Sexism in advertising	Canada, Netherlands, Scandinavia, UK, US.
Use of foreign languages in advertisements	France, Mexico, Quebec Province.
Use of foreign materials, themes and illustrations	Korea, Moslem countries, Peru, Philippines.
Wording used in food and drug ads	Belgium, EEC Commission, US.
Cigarette advertising	Luxembourg, UK, Italy, Spain, Switzerland.
Alcohol advertising	Netherlands, Portugal, Spain, Switzerland.

Source: J. J. Boddewyn, 'The Global Spread of Advertising Regulations', *MSU Business Topics*, Spring 1981, pp. 5–13.

German channels. Multinationals tend to rely heavily on home-country agencies with overseas branches.

Greater standardisation is likely in the future as a result of the 1977 WARC TV-satellite agreement. Eutelstat launched the first of five European communications satellites in 1982, some for TV distribution, such as Sky Channel mentioned earlier.

Constraints on advertising

Substantiating advertising claims

False advertising claims will not be entertained and substantiation may be sought. Clearance is mandatory for all commercials in France, Australia, Finland and the UK, and for Canada in relation to advertising to children. Self-regulatory bodies exist in at least 14 countries including Denmark, Norway, UK, Spain, Sweden, and Venezuela.

Table 9.11
Advertising regulations and response to these regulations

Key regulatory factors	Major regulatory developments	Suggested business responses
Consumer protection (for example, against untruthful, unfair, misleading ads).	Prior substantiation of advertising claims is becoming the norm.	More self-regulation by industry.
Protection for competitors (for example, against the misuse of comparative and co-operative advertising).	Growing product restrictions affect the advertising of them. More informative ads are in order.	Collaboration with consumer organisations. Greater self-discipline by advertisers. Expanded lobbying and public advocacy.
Environmental protection (for example, against outdoor advertising).	Advertising language is being restricted. Vulnerable groups such as children are becoming the target of advertising regulations.	Revised marketing and promotion policies.
Civil rights protection (for example, against sexist ads).	More groups and people can now sue advertisers.	
Religion (for example, against the advertising of contraceptives).	Penalties are getting stiffer.	
Standards of taste and decency (for example, against sexy ads).		
Nationalism (for example, against the use of foreign languages, themes, and illustrations).		

Source J. J. Boddewyn, 'The Global Spread of Advertising Regulations' *MSU Business Topics*, Spring 1981, pp. 5–13; *Marketing*, 16 August 1983, p. 52.

Product restrictions

If the product is considered immoral, unsafe, or unhealthy, its promotion is likely to be restricted. Thus most countries ban or severely limit the advertising of cigarettes, alcoholic beverages, lotteries and pharmaceuticals because their use, misuse or overuse is considered undesirable.

Balancing information and emotional appeal

Slogans like 'Things go better with Coke' allow people to imagine themselves in new situations. Are they being sold the sizzle or the steak? Past awareness and interest move the audience to evaluation, trial and adoption. Comparative advertising is supported by the EEC and the US administration because it is more informative, identifying and contrasting brands.

Use of language

The US and the EEC are considering the use of words such as 'health', 'homemade', 'natural', and 'organic' when applied to food. The US does not allow 'cough remedies' but 'cough suppressants'. French xenophobia prohibits to a degree the use of English words which had almost successfully passed into the French language such as 'cash and carry', 'jumbo jet', 'supermarket', etc. French law now forbids the use of English in French advertising.

Vulnerable groups

The unwritten convention that is generally adhered to is that it is unfair to advertise to the young, old, poor, sick, recently bereaved, and ignorant and this is generally observed.

Legal action

The traditional view that only injured parties can sue is being eroded on the grounds that everyone has an interest in having false, unfair, and misleading advertising stopped before damage can be done. A draft EEC directive would allow customers and competitors as well as their legitimate associations, to start legal action against unfair or misleading advertising.

Penalties

In settling a suit brought by the United States' Federal Trade Commission (FTC), the STP Corporation – a company in the main producing oil additives was ordered to spend $200,000 to place notices in 35 newspapers and 11 magazines with an estimated readership of 78 million. The notices stated that tests conducted by STP cannot be relied upon to support its claim that its product reduces oil consumption.

An EEC draft directive on misleading and unfair advertising would permit courts to issue injunctions to cease and desist 'even without proof of intention or neglect or of actual prejudice'. Courts would be allowed to require publication of a corrective statement and of the court decision as well as to impose penalties taking into account the extent of the damage (this is already the case in France and the US).

Develop self-discipline

Some companies have their own code of ethics, and in general these would suggest that perhaps there are less untruths to be found in industry and commerce than in personal classified advertisements for house and car sales, or armed services recruiting campaigns and supportive literature.

Finally, the last word on multinational standardisation and regulation must go to George M. Black, Chairman of J. Walter Thompson's Frankfurt office, 'If I were to make a film for Europe-wide distribution, by the time we went through all the rules governing national advertising, we would be left with a poster'.

References

1. Anderson, R. D. 'Creativity and compromise in multinational advertising', *Industrial Marketing Digest*, vol. 7, no. 1, 1982, pp. 37–43.
2. Anderson, R. D., Engledow, J. L. and Becker, H., 'Advertising Attitudes in Germany and the US', *Journal of International Business Studies*, Winter 1978, pp. 27–38.
3. Boddewyn, J. J., 'The Global Spread of Advertising Regulations', *MSU Business Topics*, Spring 1981.
4. Brooke, A. S., 'Psychographic segmentation in Europe', *Journal of Advertiser Research*, vol. 22, no. 6, 1983, no. 19–27.
5. Incorporated Society of British Advertisers, *Guide to Advertising Overseas*, London, 1984. 'Advertising: Europe's New Common Market', *Business Week*, 23 July 1984, p. 65.
6. *Industrial Marketing Digest*, 'The marketing of a major contract', vol. 6, no. 2, 1981, pp. 89–98.
7. Johnsson, H., 'Sweden: rational approach to exhibition participations', *Industrial Marketing Digest*, vol. 5, no. 1, 1980, pp. 117–26.
8. Kaynak, E. and Mitchell, L. A., 'A Comparative Study of Advertising in Canada, the United Kingdom and Turkey', *European Journal of Marketing*, vol. 1, no. 1, 1981, pp. 1–9.
9. Leff, N. H. and Farley, J. U., 'Advertising Expenditures in the Developing World', *Journal of International Business Studies*, Fall 1980, pp. 69–79.
10. Moore, Derek, 'The Media bumping minefield', *Campaign*, 6 November 1981, pp. 65 and 66.
11. Peebles, D. M., Ryans, J. K. and Vernon, I. R., 'A New Perspective on Advertising Standardisation', *European Journal of Marketing*, vol. II, no. 8, pp. 569–76.
12. Samiee, J. K. and Ryans, J. R., 'Advertising and Consumerism in Europe', *Journal of International Business Studies*, Spring/Summer 1982, pp. 109–14.
13. Starch, Inra Hooper, *World Advertising Expenditures*, International Advertising Association, New York, 1982, 17th edition.
14. *Transnational Corporations in Advertising*, UN Centre for Research on Transnational Corporations, New York, 1979.
15. Wiechmann, U. E. and Lewis, G. P., 'Problems that plague multinational markets', *Harvard Business Review*, July-August 1979, pp. 118–24.

10. *INTERNATIONAL MARKETING PLANNING*

The international marketing plan

Planning is a process which logically we would expect to find taking place at all levels in the corporate organisation. Unfortunately the evidence which exists shows that companies exercise planning more in the domestic sales organisation than in the international. As an activity, planning should encompass all the factors which have been dealt with separately in this book so far, namely the marketing mix variables and the consideration of environments. So if there is lack of planning and consequent lack of control it is because top management motivation is lacking in knowledge of what to do next. A more positive approach is required of international marketing planning, planning to make things happen. As John Lennon observed, 'Life is what is happening to you when you are busy making plans'.

International marketing cannot succeed without the active support and commitment of top management, yet international market research, for example, is still dominated by subjectivity and lacks the commitment in time and resources devoted to domestic market research. Consequently, international marketing planning is pursued at a much lower level than domestic marketing planning. With international marketing planning, the purpose, form and methodology employed differs according to company size, organisation structure, length of involvement in international business activities, etc. International marketing planning as such may consist of no more than a sales budget or allocation handed to country managers by corporate management. Equally, it may also be more complex, recognising the higher-ordered interdependencies created by a global perspective of a truly multinational corporation. It is argued in fact, that co-ordinated plans and strategies are the hallmarks of the truly multinational company (Reference 1).

Mike Wilson, in *The Management of Marketing* identifies the following main elements of marketing plans:

- A statement of basic assumptions with regard to long- and short-term economic, technological, social and political developments.
- A review of past sales and profit performance of the company's major products by market and geographic areas.
- An analysis of external opportunities and threats by markets and products.
- An analysis of the company's and competitors' strengths and weaknesses in facilities, products, finances, customer acceptance, distribution, personnel, pricing, advertising, sales promotion, etc. This analysis will often include assessments of indirect competition.

177

- A statement of long-term objectives (marketing, financial, growth, etc.), and the strategies for achieving them.
- A statement of the objectives and strategies for the next year with a detailed breakdown in units and revenue for each product, each market, each geographical area, and each unit of the company's marketing force.
- A programme schedule which is carefully co-ordinated with the budgets for the units involved and which shows the sequence of all marketing activities for each product in each market and geographic area so that public relations, advertising, product publicity, sales promotion, and field selling can be co-ordinated.
- Statements of objectives for each of the following years similar to the statements for the next year but less detailed.
- A summary of how the company intends to capitalise on its opportunities and correct its weaknesses; key priorities, etc.

Table 10.1
International Marketing Planning Matrix

	Marketing planning variables					
International decisions	*Situation analysis*	*Problems– opportunity analysis*	*Objectives*	*Marketing programme*	*Marketing budgets*	*Sales vol. cost/profit estimate*
A. Commitment decision						
B. Country selection						
C. Mode of entry						
D. Marketing strategy						
E. Marketing organisation						

Source H. Becker and H. B. Thorelli, 'Strategic Planning in International Marketing' in Thorelli and Becker, *International Marketing Strategy*, Pergamon, 1980, p. 370.

International marketing planning is seen to have three levels: (Reference 2)

1. *Operational planning.* Shorter range (one- and three-year) planning is the responsibility of each overseas operating unit. The format in general follows that of US divisions and is supplied by the headquarters planning staff. Plans include sales, profit and cash-flow projections by product line, market share, capital requirements, etc. Although plans are integrated at regional levels, individual unit plans are forwarded intact to New York headquarters.

2. *Strategic planning.* Operating units – most of which are national in

scope – are asked to plan ahead on a longer-term basis for new products which might be developed from within or acquired. Headquarters deliberately provide only very general guidelines as to how far afield a local operation might explore. This is done to encourage the local managers to stretch their outlook. However, the scope normally is confined to the unit's country of operation, and plans are subject to review at headquarters.

3. *Corporate planning.* Worldwide plans are developed at international headquarters, tied closely to overall corporate objectives and plans. This planning takes two forms: 'protective planning' 'opportunity planning'. The first of these is strategic and long-range in character, anticipating worldwide changes in markets and business conditions relating to the present scope of operation. On the other hand, 'opportunity planning' is directed toward seeking new business directions for growth and diversification.

Overall corporate expectations of planning are that it has to:

1. Minimise the negative consequences of a variety of adverse exogenous and endogenous conditions.
2. Balance the available corporate resources against a set of global opportunities and alternatives.
3. Co-ordinate and integrate the activities of a necessarily decentralised organisation.
4. Create a framework for a communication system which ensures that all parts of the organisation are striving towards the same set of overall objectives and in their pursuit are using policies which are beneficial for the corporation as a whole rather than individual parts of it.

It is argued (Reference 3) that multinationals should concentrate on standardising the process of planning rather than standardising their marketing strategies. Planning is a decentralised activity not because of the geographic dispersion of the individual units or because their individual legal status frequently provides them with a high degree of autonomy, but because differences in local operating conditions demand a local response. Selectivity and distortion can, however, enter into the environment surveillance process via the data-gathering behaviour of the organisation. Perceptual bias can also enter the process at the stage of interpreting or evaluating the data, often performed by someone other than the data gatherer. Perceptual bias can occur at the data transmission linkage between the data gatherers and the interpreters and between interpreters and users. There is a pertinent question also as to whether data gatherers tend to ignore data which is essentially less quantitative and much more qualitative in nature, and so less easily verifiable.

The task facing a head office then is to obtain conformity within a set of overall objectives, performance criteria and company-wide policies to eliminate or at least minimise intra-company effects and inefficiencies. In many multinationals this situation has led to the institution of two distinctly separate long-range planning cycles which can be referred to as 'bottom-up' and 'top-down' planning. 'Top-down' planning may be a particularly

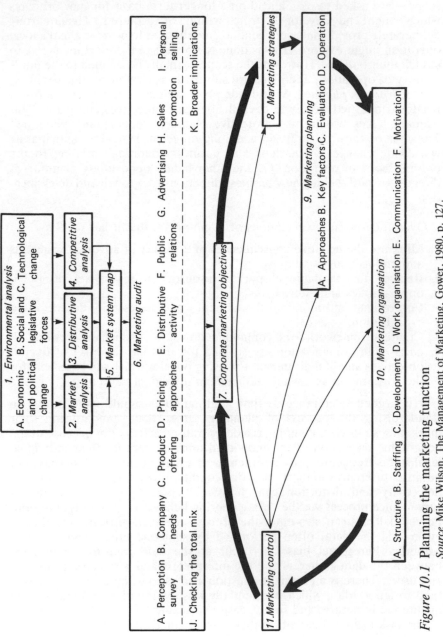

Figure 10.1 Planning the marketing function
Source Mike Wilson, The Management of Marketing, Gower, 1980, p. 127.

appropriate approach when subsidiary managers around the world are not very familiar with the concepts and practices of long-range planning. 'Bottom-up' may be particularly relevant where local conditions are sufficiently different to necessitate a local plan. Here there is management recognition of the local subsidiary manager as an expert in the corporate planning cycle. In many cases, locational decisions seem to evolve from the culmination of a series of apparently unrelated events rather than a specific plan. There are three broad sets of factors to consider here.

1. Country-related variables that characterise the business conditions in a certain country or region in terms of the political, economic, legal, competitive and tax situation, the market potential, cost and availability of manpower, local capital, and required supplies.
2. Product-related characteristics such as a product's typical life cycle, the degree of technical sophistication, and economies of scale that are associated with its production, the relative importance of transportation costs, etc.
3. Company-related variables which take into account such characteristics as a firm's size and its experience in international operations and policies as an expression of the firm's management philosophy.

Managerial decision making will result in specific marketing programmes on a global basis, with differentiated marketing programmes. This differentiation is in respect of both budget allocations and specific emphasis of marketing mix elements. The annual operating plan was found to be the planning keystone in virtually all multinational subsidiaries interviewed. For most it was the starting point for longer-term planning, typically for a five-year period. In the majority of cases, term planning was an exercise in extrapolation and very few companies practised strategic market planning.

Marketing programmes should be based on the concept of world segmentation. Unlike differentiating markets on a country basis, segmentation of urban dwellers internationally may reveal greater similarities than between local nationals. The most viable and profitable segmentation basis seems to be the examination of underlying factors which determine buyer demand. These factors can be broadly classified as **buyer expectations** and **buying climate**. The first is based on culture, social stratification, and family structure. The second refers to the specific situation in which consumers make decisions to buy and consume goods and services. It includes the economic, demographic, and physical settings in which buyers go about choosing and consuming products and services. It is based on financial factors (disposable personal income, asset holdings, etc.); geographical factors (temperature, humidity and altitude, tropical *v.* temperate climate, etc.); and demographic factors (size of family, age distributions of family members, life cycle of family, etc.).

In addition to difficulties often encountered in gathering information in the host country, there are sometimes delays in the communication of information within the multinational. If there is difficulty in communicating relevant information from one subsidiary to another, or from a domestic product division to an overseas subsidiary, subsidiary planning can be damaged. It may not be unusual for a subsidiary to be given a new product to introduce without adequate information on how that same product fared on launch elsewhere. Even more common are careless requests for information which emerge from head offices. Educating home-office personnel to the realities of subsidiary life may help, but companies must also pay more attention to the planning of intra-company communications flows. Procedures often need streamlining and more careful information management should result in a communication flow better co-ordinated with subsidiary needs. Similarly, there may be excessive emphasis by head office on short-term sales and product results. In either situation, strategic or long-term planning is neglected to the detriment of the company involved.

Culturally, we adopt value orientations which we have learnt. The following six categories help identify these values. Cultural patterns may therefore be identified by the degree to which people align themselves on the paired variables:

1. Egalitarian or elitist.
2. Laying stress on accomplishment or inherited attributes.
3. Expecting material or nonmaterial rewards.
4. Evaluating individuals or product in terms of objective norms or subjective standards.
5. Focusing on the distinctiveness of the parts (intensiveness) rather than the general characteristics of the whole (extensiveness).
6. Oriented towards personal or group gain.

A pressing desire to solve problems appears most readily in a culture that has strong egalitarian, material, and individual value orientations. There is the kind of orientation which causes contest mobility, a situation where individuals compete for, and win status and material rewards on the basis of performance. Rewards for performance in any society can be increased status, wealth or both. In the US, positional rewards are viewed as almost no rewards at all, whereas in Britain they are highly respected. Promotional information which supports products in culturally differentiated markets must also be individualised. Cultural values will strongly influence meaningful associations. They will control the types of product claims people are predisposed to entertain or consider plausible; they will influence the basis upon which claims can be rendered verifiable. To admit the relevance of cultural values is not enough; management must assess the significance of cultural attitudes and not just take into account 'comparative curiosities like polygamy and cannibalism, or merely study such consumer habits as the frequency with which people change their clothes'. Table 10.2 examines the differences in information used for marketing planning by nationality of subsidiary whilst Table 10.3 examines the relative importance of data sources for five environmental domains.

As to the conditions under which planning failed, a study into corporate planning failure of 300 companies in Europe and America revealed ten reasons (Reference 4):

Table 10.2

Information used for marketing planning by nationality of subsidiary

Source of information	Proportion of firms using American	European	Japanese	All firms
Distributors	43%	38%	33%	40%
Sales Force	75%	71%	83%	74%
Management of Other Subsidiaries	39%	54%	50%	47%
Marketing Research Dept.	57%	71%	0%	57%
Historical Data	75%	79%	33%	72%
Trade Sources	29%	29%	50%	31%
Commercial Suppliers	36%	8%	33%	24%
Official Sources	39%	58%	50%	48%
Home Office	14%	38%	17%	24%
Number of Firms	(28)	(24)	(6)	(58)

Source James H. Hulbert, William K. Brandt and Raimer Richers, 'Marketing Planning in the Multinational Subsidiary: Practices and Problems', *Journal of Marketing*, vol. 44, Summer 1980, p. 10.

Table 10.3

Relative importance of data sources for the five environmental domains (combined US and European samples)

Domains	Outside services	Outside experts	Home office staff	Home office top management	Business unit top management
Social	1.84*	1.11	2.41	2.80	2.27
Political	1.80	1.32	2.31	2.82	1.96
Ecological	1.77	1.51	2.49	2.06	2.27
Economic	1.67	1.65	2.86	2.60	2.07
Technological	1.47	1.58	2.79	2.30	2.46

Source Jeremiah J. O'Connell and J. W. Zimmerman, 'Scanning the International Environment', *Californian Management Review*, Winter 1979, vol. XXII, no. 2, p. 19.

- Planning is not integrated into the total management system.
- Only some levels of management are involved in the process.
- Responsibility for planning is vested solely in planning staff.
- Management expects plans to be realised exactly as planned.
- Too much detail is attempted.
- Management fails to implement the plan.
- Extrapolation and financial projections are confused with planning.
- Inadequate information inputs.
- Too much emphasis is placed on only one aspect of planning.
- The different dimensions of planning are not understood.

However, this related to corporate strategic planning rather than international marketing planning which is inherently more difficult again because of the extra variables to be considered.

Turning specifically to international marketing planning, the four most prevalent problems (Reference 2) for planning in the international arena may be said to relate to:

1. *Failure to 'take off'*. This may be due to distance, language, management climate, diversity and other factors unique to individual companies.

2. *Lack of acceptance by management*. It has been difficult for US companies to get overseas managers – whether nationals or Americans – to accept or use planning. This is often experienced when plans have originated solely at home base and do not reflect the 'real world' of the manager. As with planning anywhere, 'textbook' plans are doomed to failure.

3. *Quality of planning*. In many companies, foreign operating units have not yet attained the same quality of planning as their domestic counterparts. One reason for this is that planning data are neither as accurate nor as reliable as companies would wish.

4. *Lack of co-operation* among international units.

One of the accepted objectives of planning on an international scale is to realise synergistic benefits among various independent operations. While international planners must, and do, think synergistically, management abroad is inclined to think parochially.

With regard to the current practice of international marketing planning in the multinational corporation, it has been argued that (Reference 5):

1. There is no systematic and continuous assessment of buyer needs and expectations in the current practice of most corporations. Most of the marketing research is after-the-event: to find out whether a new concept or product developed by R & D will be acceptable to the customers. A continuous research effort to systematically monitor the current and changing needs of the market place is required.

2. Present practice is to perform marketing research on a country-to-country basis. In addition, most multinational business decisions are centred around the question of whether the company should extend its strategic programmes to new countries or adjust it to suit local conditions. While such a practice was probably quite appropriate in previous times, and may continue to be useful even today for exporting or trading companies, it is myopic in the long run. It is not difficult to trace a number of failures in multinational activities directly to this practice (Reference 5). A systematic and continuous worldwide assessment of buyer needs and expectations is likely to point out that:

(a) potential markets are mostly in the metropolitan areas especially in the less developed countries;
(b) clustering metropolitan areas both within and between countries is more meaningful from a marketing viewpoint;
(c) we shall probably find greater similarity between metropolitan areas across countries than within countries.

3. The assessment of customer needs and expectations should be based on data collected at the micro level, namely the household or business unit.

The focus on customer needs is a more enduring concept and tends to avoid the myopic tendency which a company is likely to fall into as its products become mature in their life cycle.

Concentration on key markets

The study entitled *Concentration on Key Markets*, undertaken by the British Export Trade Research Organisation (BETRO), was published by the British Overseas Trade Board (BOTB) in 1975 and in revised form in 1979. The basis objective of this study was to establish where exactly companies were successful out of all the export markets in which they were represented. Reviewing the allocation of resources to markets, the recommendation was made that companies should concentrate on those areas which amounted for the bulk of current export sales.

The BETRO study claimed a representative sample of 25 per cent of British exporters. This was broken down approximately into the following groups: one-third selling to less than 30 countries, exporting some 75–80 per cent of their output in the range ten million pounds or more, yet with a surprisingly small salesforce of some two to four men. A further one-third sold to between 30 and 60 countries, but here the large number of countries included some seen as insurance in case existing markets elsewhere turned sour. The final one-third were selling to between 60 and 180 countries but were suffering from the marginal effort expended which proved a poor utilisation of resources for the company concerned.

The issues which the BETRO Report addressed specifically were:

1. Is it right to dissipate the efforts of a small selling organisation over 154 countries with relatively modest returns?
2. Would it be wise to have a fresh look at the 10 countries taking 90 per cent of company exports and ask 'Which are the four or five where we stand the best chance of increasing substantially our market share?' and when the answer is found, to deploy there all the marketing and technical talent that the company can muster?

Behind this was the principle of 'reinforcing success', and fighting against overextending the company resources. Nevertheless, the resources in finance and manpower required to develop a prosperous export business are surprisingly modest; they are well within the reach of the small company employing no more than 100 people. Advantages of market concentration following through this principle of 'reinforcing success' included:

- A span of control especially when conditions become tough.
- Greater market knowledge in total and to a wider spread of people within the organisation.
- Ability to identify the best markets and concentrate on them solely.
- The belief shared by 80 per cent of respondents that exports will grow faster than domestic sales in the next four to five years.

Inexperience in exporting was no more a barrier to success than was size. As the Betro Report stated:

as far as newcomers to exporting are concerned, it can be stated with a fair measure of certainty that they can achieve just as good or even better results by never selling to more than 10 countries as other companies who sell to 160.

There were in fact particular advantages of the small operation:

1. It needs a smaller organisation with fewer staff and lower overheads.

2. It can acquire more detailed knowledge and a better understanding of agents' and distributors' capabilities. The small company has a chance to get to know them personally through close contact and so it has better knowledge of their needs and market requirements. This is primary information quite different from secondary, published sources of information. Here there was the ability to know what competitors were doing and how to adapt to market conditions.

3. Products may be sold less on price than on other factors such as:

- reliability of delivery
- after-sales service including technical support and spare parts
- credit and discount terms
- brand loyalty amongst customers
- manufacturer's image within the trade and amongst customers
- ability to establish whether competition is primarily on price, quality, design, etc.

4. No potential distractions at least from various sources, as is the case with large organisations. The organisation structured instead for maximum effectiveness.

5. Concentration will lead to a rise in sales if a decision to concentrate is made during a period of boom and long delivery dates, and a company can gain a lot of goodwill by giving better delivery to its most important key markets. In periods of declining sales a 'concentrating' company will be in a better position to secure orders than those trading in a haphazard manner (even in a depression, when many companies lose market shares, some do gain a bigger share. This is more likely to be the company that knows its market and can seize the opportunity rather than others whose contacts are more superficial).

The recommendation for all companies irrespective of size is to:

- Concentrate scarce resources of talent, effort, and cash on a few markets.
- Invest manpower in export markets on a par with home markets.
- Maintain frequent personal contact with overseas customers.
- Invest in areas geared towards export growth.
- Undertake, as continuing company policy, comparative cost studies of home and export activities.

Planning and Third World markets

Third-World markets are notably dissimilar as will be seen in Chapter 16. Basically, these fall into the following categories:

1. High-volume, low-value raw material exporters but with infrastructural base.
2. High-volume, low-value raw material exporters with little infrastructural base.
3. Low-volume, low-value traditional exporters but with infrastructural base.
4. Least developed nations.

It is not possible to segment on the basis of being single commodity exporters as this would apply to many in the first three categories. There are therefore those in category 2 with little infrastructure but with new-found wealth and so able to make a quantum leap by buying in expertise from abroad to provide education and technical services wherever necessary.

Political risk is one of the most obvious dangers to international business. 'Political risk is the likelihood that political forces will cause drastic changes in a country's business environment that affect the profit and other goals of a particular business enterprise'. Risk of this kind may apply to an industry as a whole or to one company in particular. The most frequently encountered risk arises from political forces hostile towards foreign enterprise for philosophical reasons that diverge sharply from prevailing government policies (Reference 6). Other risks are social unrest and disorder; the private vested interests of local business groups; recent or impending independence; new international alliances; and armed conflicts or terrorism. Less predictable, and political only in the sense that it is a tool of politicians, is the exposure of corruption or scandal. This is often linked to a government official who might well have provided influence for a foreign firm.

Market access is another problem and investment has taken place by multinationals in the past in order to produce goods within the protection of tariff walls. Market access may be restricted by the local government. Alternatively, for those choosing to enter there may be the attendant benefits of supplying a captive market, further protected from the entry of foreign competition. This has enticed some multinationals in the automobile industry for example to make investments which otherwise would not have appeared quite so attractive.

Market access implies not only entering the country and meeting the standard tariff and duty barriers, the various so-called 'invisible' tariff barriers relating perhaps to areas as diverse as health and safety but providing also for distribution to the final consumer. There may in fact be more similarity between city-dwellers across nations than between nationals themselves. Marketing must identify this where it exists and make full use of this advantage.

Capital is not always the missing factor and this is why we began with a classification of developing countries. For oil-rich countries with new-found wealth the new problem is one of learning how to manage wealth after years of planning for poverty. Income from the oil industry may be seen too, as in the Boston Consultancy Group (BCG) Product Portfolio

Matrix, in terms of a 'cash cow' to be used and to be milked for cash to produce new 'stars' high in relative market share in high-growth markets. To diversify, technology and management are both required, and marketing is subsumed within these, as partly a social act, partly a technical science. To cite Drucker: (Reference 7)

Marketing is generally the most neglected area in the economic life of developing countries. It is manufacturing or construction which occupies the greatest attention in these countries. Its effectiveness as an engine of economic development with special emphasis on its ability to develop rapidly much-needed entrepreneurial and management skills needs hardly any elaboration. Because it provides a systematic discipline in a vital area of economic activity it fills one of the greatest needs of a developing economy. . . . Marketing occupies a critical role in respect to underdeveloped 'growth' countries. Indeed, marketing is the most important 'multiplier' of such development. It is in itself in every one of these areas the least developed, the most backward part of the economic system. It is development above all others, that makes possible economic integration and the fullest utilisation of whatever assets and productive capacity an economy already possesses. It mobilises latent economic energy. It contributes to the greatest needs: that for the rapid development of entrepreneurs and managers, and at the same time it may be the easiest area of managerial work to get going . . . it is the most systematised, and therefore the most learnable and the most teachable of all areas of business management and entrepreneurship.

Marketing therefore has a special niche in the area of technology transfer from North to South or East to West and this becomes noticeable with the number of contractual arrangements including management contracts, which allow for manufacture under licence in a given country but for the licensor himself to buy back a given quantity of output. In this way, the host country is able to deal with shortcomings in marketing knowledge and lack of contact with, and general experience of, free world markets.

Capital has diverse roles to play. Establishing within the host nation perhaps as a joint venture with a local partner may enable the joint venture to take advantage of its new local identity to compete for local contracts and for local finance. Multinational subsidiaries worldwide export under the terms and assurances of national export credit guarantees departments –ECGD in the UK, Coface in France, Hermes in West Germany, Eximbank in the US (see Table 7.1 on pages 120–1).

Competition in developing countries is usually minimal and so the greater risk of competition arises from the potential threat of entry by a Western competitor. This is one way in which a local host government may maintain leverage on a multinational subsidiary. Where an investment is large, though, there may well be governmental undertakings to exclude further outside competition and grant certain exclusivity of supply to governmental departments etc.

Reconciling the multinational enterprise (MNE) and the host government

The situation which is most often depicted is one where the multinational subsidiary is faced with certain demands by the host government.

Increasingly, though, because of the extraterritorial reach of US legislation and of the US administration, a multinational subsidiary may find itself subjected, as we have found earlier, to demands by the host government and by the home government as well. Figure 10.2 summarises the situation.

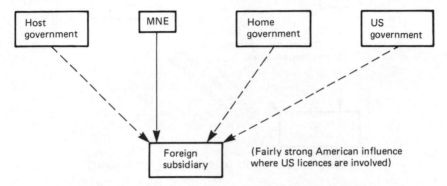

Figure 10.2 Pressures on the multinational subsidiary.

The host government seeks greater self-reliance, industrialisation, import substitution and an increasing export activity which will also employ and train its workforce. The size of certain of these projects being indentified by host governments as national priority plans makes it feasible only for companies with multinational expertise to compete for tenders.

For the MNE, the search is for economic and political stability; necessary market size; reassurance on fulfilment of contracts; available workforce; co-operative governmental attitude; and the ability to repatriate earnings back to head office. Difficulties arise here because the subsidiary is after all only one part of the multinational group and may be subject to Head Office rulings which do not take into account its best interests or continued viability in the foreign market. This may also engender conflict.

The pressure remains on the foreign subsidiary as to whom it recognises as its master. It is partly for this reason that the issue of staffing is also important. Many multinationals deemed ethnocentric because of a strong home-country orientation evidenced by the nationality of their foreign top management may in fact only be acting in their best interests as they perceive it. Alternatively, those with a polycentric orientation who have appointed local nationals as managers may therefore be seen to be storing up trouble for themselves, putting local nationals in the position of serving either foreign head-office or national government interests. In practice, the situation is not quite so anxiety-ridden as may be depicted but presents one aspect of the dilemma involved in staffing fringe subsidiaries.

Some countries allow the MNEs to make the bidding for investments. Others have reserved for themselves the right to develop by themselves certain economic sectors. This is true of Mexico, Brazil, India, Venezuela, Nigeria and Indonesia but it is also true that these countries have a relatively high average income compared to the least developed nations.

The issue of multinationals and host governments is complex and may best be summarised as a love-hate relationship as typified in Chapter 1 when we cited the 'dilemma of the multinational: a force for good or evil?'

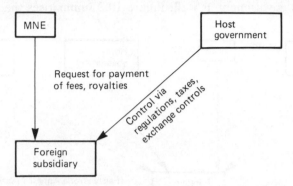

Figure 10.3 Pressures on the foreign subsidiary.

The multinational enterprise: the good citizen

It was IBM who coined the phrase 'corporate citizenship' when they stated that their aim was to be a good citizen in each country in which they were represented. Few organisations are of the size of a geocentric multinational such as IBM, nor have the immediate visibility of such a large corporation and hence the need to produce a statement on corporate ethics. Many multinationals do, however, produce a leaflet on their corporate policy and business ethics.

Ethics do enter into the question of international business. Again, the extraterritoriality of US legislation, such as the Foreign Corrupt Practices Act of 1977, is making this issue more problematic. The Act prohibits companies from engaging in 'questionable payments', with penalties ranging from a million dollars for each corporate offence to $10,000 per offender and up to five years in prison. This Act affects not only American companies but also multinational corporations with representation in the US. Therefore it is open to the US to pursue a British or German multinational for unseemly activities in an African country through its US representative base.

The practice of business is not uniform the world over, and although shareholders or members of the public in an industrialised Western country may be shocked to hear that one of their largest companies has been active in bribery and corruption, these terms of trading may not have the same emotive appeal in the host country as at home. Payments may be made as 'dash', a fairly innocuous but generally almost standard payment in Nigeria, to ensure that the bureaucracy will deal with an application. The term is 'dash', not bribery or corruption. It ensures that papers on a crowded desk will be moved from the bottom of the pile to the top of the pile for action. In bureaucratically infested countries this may be a common means of expediting business.

The OECD has developed guidelines for the multinational firm as part of a broader understanding on various investment issues. The OECD Ministers have signed a *Declaration on International Investment and Multinational Enterprises*, which includes several interrelated elements.

- A reaffirmation by OECD members that a liberal international investment climate is in the common interest of the industrial nations.
- An agreement that they should give equal treatment to foreign-controlled and national enterprises.
- A decision to co-operate to avoid 'beggar thy neighbour' actions, pulling or pushing particular investments in or out of their jurisdictions.
- A set of voluntary guidelines, defining standards for good business conduct which the Ministers collectively recommended to transnational enterprises operating in their territories.
- A consultative process under each of the above elements of the investment agreement.

The mutual benefits of partnership

What often occasions anxiety between multinational and government are the questions of ownership and control and the transfer of technology. The multinational is best placed to meet the needs of the lesser developed countries. Mutually beneficial arrangements can therefore be struck between the two parties which convey respective benefits to either.

In dealing with nationalistic tendencies, the long-range planning effort should be influenced by the two main considerations. Firstly, joint ventures with foreign partners are an obvious and frequently recommended strategy, but generally not the best strategy for countering nationalistic pressures on international firms. Secondly, a large part of the demands that arise from nationalistic sentiments can and should be met by a corporation's strong commitment to a truly geocentric or cosmopolitan management philosophy which enables a corporation to react to environmental differences on a strictly functional basis.

References

1. Hulbert, James M., Brandt, William K. and Raimer Richers, 'Marketing Planning in the Multinational Subsidiary: Practices and Problems', *Journal of Marketing*, vol. 44, Summer 1980, pp. 7–15.
2. Cain, William W., 'International Planning: Mission Impossible?' *Columbia Journal of World Business*, July-August 1970, pp. 53–60.
3. Shruptine, Kelly, F. and Toyne, Brian, 'International Marketing Planning A Standardised Process', *Journal of International Marketing*, vol. 1, no. 1, pp. 16–28.
4. Ringbakk, K. A., 'Strategic Planning in a turbulent international environment', *Long-Range Planning*, 9 June 1976, pp. 2–11.
5. Jagdish and Sheth, N., 'A market-oriented strategy of long-range planning for multinational corporations', *European Research*, January 1977, pp. 3–12.
6. Robock, Stefan H. and Simmonds, Kenneth, *International Business and Multinational Enterprises*, Irwin, 3rd edition, 1983, p. 342.

7. Drucker, Peter F., 'Marketing and Economic Development', in Thorelli, H. and Becker, H., *International Marketing Strategy*, Pergamon, 1980, p. 392.
8. O'Connell, Jeremiah J. and Zimmerman, J. W., 'Scanning the International Environment', *California Management Review*, Winter 1979, vol. XXII, no. 2.
9. Goldmark, Frances M., 'Strategy: Worldwide Long Range Market Analysis', *Columbia Journal of World Business*, Winter 1974, pp. 50–53.
10. Schollhammer, Jans, 'Long-Range Planning in Multinational Firms', *Columbia Journal of World Business*, September-October 1971, pp. 79–86.
11. Sommers, Montrose and Kernan, Jerome, 'Why products flourish here, fizzle there', *Columbia Journal of World Business*, March-April 1967, pp. 89–97.
12. McDonald, M. H. B., 'Marketing planning in an industrial and international context', *Cranfield Research Papers in Marketing and Logistics*, vol. 5, no. 23, 1978/9.

11. ORGANISATION FOR MULTINATIONAL MARKETING CONTROL

Patterns of organisational development

The intention here is not to study organisation *per se* but to look inquisitively at the way in which the company operating internationally modifies its organisational structure to accommodate markets, products, and its consumers. This will be the path along which transactions take place between the firm and its customers. Literature on the subject of multinational organisation development has in the past questioned whether structure influenced strategy and vice versa. Let us state now that it is transactional considerations, not technology, that are typically decisive in determining which mode of organisation will obtain in what circumstances and why (Reference 1). As this is a marketing text, this is the line of enquiry which we shall follow.

Related issues are the level and quality of communication between the head office and not just the subsidiary as is often supposed, but what now amounts to an international portfolio of different investments from wholly owned to joint venture to licensing or franchising (Reference 1), consortium marketing, etc. Williamson traces the chronology of these changes which have been taking place. In the beginning there were markets, and progressively more refined forms of internal organisation have successively evolved. First, peer groups, then simple hierarchies, and finally the vertically integrated firm in which a compound hierarchy exists, have appeared.

In the quest to optimise resources in the light of stated company objectives, close monitoring has to take place with regard to the level of interaction between head office and its subsidiaries and affiliates. There is no correct solution to this problem. The choice of organisational form must be situational, i.e. that which best suits the company concerned given the characteristics of the industry, the product range, customer characteristics, and national markets in which it is trading. Each company finds its own solution. There is no 'industry' solution either, for some companies have changed their corporate structure more than once as has Massey-Ferguson, for example, from a product structure to a regional structure and back again. Another point to bear in mind is that over time no variables are held constant. Companies divest themselves of certain product lines or subsidiaries or else acquire by takeover, merger, and slow and gradual build-up of market presence.

Corporate organisation has therefore to take into account a certain degree of flexibility for growth and product extension. Against this, there are often governmental barriers inhibiting foreign direct investment for example, or pressure – explicit as well as implicit – towards industrial co-operation and contractual joint ventures. There may well be variations to the trading environment peculiar to one particular trading region. Governments may impose political and philosophical strictures on the forms of organisation which it will countenance within its own jurisdiction. The question of corporate culture – whether the firm is ethnocentric, polycentric, or geocentric – can also be a barrier as this will influence the degree of freedom granted to the subsidiaries and affiliates in their reporting procedures to head office.

Degree of centralisation	Organisation type				
	A (direct)	B (geographical)	C (project)	D (matrix)	E (project)
High					
Medium					
Low					

The shaded squares are the most common

Figure 11.1 Organisation types.

Source Michael Z. Brooke, *Centralisation and Autonomy: A Study in Organisation Behaviour*, Holt-Rinehart-Winston, 1984.

As Figure 11.1 shows, there are five main groups of international company organisation (Reference 8).

Type A – the direct type

The most senior staff of the company have a direct relationship with the foreign subsidiary. Multinationals such as the Swedish SKF ball-bearing company have traditionally been organised along these functional lines which transcend national boundaries.

Type B – the geographical type

This relationship is mediated through managers of the geographical projection, whether international, regional or national titles.

Type C – the product type

Product group managers have direct control over the subsidiaries operating in their product area.

Type D – the matrix type

The matrix organisation in which the subsidiary managers report along both the product, group, and geographical lines, sometimes even functional lines as well.

Type E – the project type

The application to the total organisation of the project organisation devised for large-scale assembly operations like aircraft buildings. The company is organised into a series of project groups which bring together staff drawn from any relevant projection and are constantly changing.

In general, the B type (geographical) is more frequently decentralised; the C type (product) more usually centralised; the E type (project) almost always centralised; while A (direct) and D (matrix) may be either.

Williamson refers to the issue of vertical specialisation along product lines as the unitary form of organisation or the U-form enterprise. He summarises the difficulties that the large U-form enterprise experiences in terms of indecomposability, incommensurability, non-operational goal specification, and the confounding of strategic and operating decisions. Incommensurability makes it difficult to specify the goals of the functional divisions in ways which clearly contribute to higher-level enterprise objectives. Indecomposability makes it necessary to attempt more extensive co-ordination among the parts; for a given span of control, this naturally results in a greater loss of control between hierarchical levels. Moreover, to the extent that efforts at co-ordination break down and the individual parts suboptimise, the strategic interconnectedness between them virtually assures that spillover costs will be substantial.

The inherent weakness in the centralised and functionally departmentalised operating company becomes critical only when the administrative load on the senior executives increases to such an extent that they are unable to handle their entrepreneurial responsibilities efficiently. Unable to identify meaningfully with, or contribute to, the realisation of global goals, managers in each of the functional parts attend to what they perceive to be operational subgoals instead.

Six-way classification scheme for company organisation

Unitary (U-form). This is the traditional functionally organised enterprise. It is still the appropriate structure in most small to lower middle-sized firms. Some medium-sized firms in which intercommunications are especially rich may continue to find this the appropriate structure. A variant on this structure occasionally appears in that the enterprise is of U-

Table 11.1
Key problems identified by headquarters executives

	Rank (out of 182)	Score (in per cent)		Rank (out of 182)	Score (in per cent)
Lack of qualified international personnel			**Too little relevant communication between headquarters and the subsidiaries**		
Getting qualified international personnel is difficult	1	73	The subsidiaries don't inform headquarters about their problems until the last minute	5	65
It is difficult to find qualified local managers for the subsidiaries	1	73	The subsidiaries do not get enough consulting service from headquarters	13	61
The company can't find enough capable people who are willing to move to different countries	15	60	There is a communications gap between headquarters and the subsidiaries	31	51
There isn't enough manpower at headquarters to make the necessary visits to local operations	22	57	The subsidiaries provide headquarters with too little feedback	33	50
Lack of strategic thinking and long-range planning at the subsidiary level			**Insufficient utilisation of multinational marketing experience**		
Subsidiary managers are preoccupied with purely operational problems and don't think enough about long-range strategy	3	71	The company is a national company with international business; there is too much focus on domestic operations	25	56
Subsidiary managers don't do a good job of analysing and forecasting their business	5	65	Subsidiary managers don't benefit from marketing experience available at headquarters and vice versa	28	53
There is too much emphasis in the subsidiary on short-term financial performance. This is an obstacle to the development of long-term marketing strategies	13	61	The company does not take advantage of its experience with product introductions in one country for use in other countries	36	49
Lack of marketing expertise at the subsidiary level			**Restricted headquarters control of the subsidiaries**		
The company lacks marketing competence at the subsidiary level	4	69	The company lacks central co-ordination of its marketing efforts	45	46
The subsidiaries don't give their advertising agencies proper direction	8	63	The headquarters staff is too small to exercise the proper control over the subsidiaries	8	63
The company doesn't understand consumers in the countries where it operates	8	63	Subsidiary managers resist direction from headquarters	17	59
Many subsidiaries don't gather enough marketing intelligence	17	59	Subsidiaries have profit responsibility and therefore resist any restraints on their decision-making authority	36	48
The subsidiary does a poor job of defining targets for its product marketing	20	58			

Source Ulrich E. Weichmann and Lewis G. Pringle, 'Problems that plague multinational marketers' *Harvard Business Review*, July–August, 1979.

Table 11.2
Key problems identified by subsidiary executives

	Rank (out of 120)	Score (in per cent)
Excessive headquarters control procedures		
Reaching a decision takes too long because we must get approval from headquarters	2	58
There is too much bureaucracy in the organisation	5	55
Too much paperwork has to be sent to headquarters	6	54
Headquarters staff and subsidiary management differ about which problems are important	17	46
Headquarters tries to control its subsidiaries too tightly	22	45
Excessive financial and marketing constraints		
The emphasis on short-term financial performance is an obstacle to the development of long-term marketing strategies for local markets	1	65
The subsidiary must increase sales to meet corporate profit objectives even though it operates with many marketing constraints imposed by headquarters	7	50
Headquarters expects a profit return each year without investing more money in the local company	10	49
Insufficient participation of subsidiaries in product decisions		
The subsidiary is too dependent on headquarters for new product development	13	47
Headquarters is unresponsive to the subsidiaries' requests for product modifications	22	45
New products are developed centrally and are not geared to the specific needs of the local market	22	45
Domestic operations have priority in product and resource allocation; subsidiaries rank second	31	43

	Rank (out of 120)	Score (in per cent)
Insensitivity of headquarters to local market differences		
Headquarters management feels that what works in one market should also work in other markets	2	58
Headquarters makes decisions without thorough knowledge of marketing conditions in the subsidiary's country	12	48
Marketing strategies developed at headquarters don't reflect the fact that the subsidiary's position may be significantly different in its market	13	47
The attempt to standardise marketing programmes across borders neglects the fact that our company has different market shares and market acceptance in each country	27	44
Shortage of useful information from headquarters		
The company doesn't have a good training programme for its international managers	7	50
New product information doesn't come from headquarters often enough	22	45
The company has an inadequate procedure for sharing information among its subsidiaries	27	44
There is very little cross-fertilisation with respect to ideas and problem solving among functional groups within the company	27	44
Lack of multinational orientation at headquarters		
Headquarters is too home-country oriented	17	46
Headquarters managers are not truly multinational personnel	17	46

Source Ulrich E. Weichmann and Lewis G. Pringle, *op. cit.*

form character but the firm has become diversified to a slight degree and the incidental parts are of proven semi-autonomous standing. Unless such diversification accounts for at least one-third of the firm's value-added, such a functionally organised firm will be assigned to the U-form category.

Holding company (H-form). This is the divisionalised enterprise for which the requisite internal control apparatus has not been provided. The divisions are often affiliated with the parent company through a subsidiary relationship.

Multidivisional (M-form). This is the divisionalised enterprise in which a separation of operations from strategic decision-making is provided, and for which the requisite internal control apparatus has been assembled and is systematically employed. Two sub-categories should be distinguished: type D_1 which denotes a highly integrated M-form enterprise, possibly with differentiated but otherwise common final products; and type D_2, which denotes the M-form enterprise with diversified final products or services. Comparing these two forms, it is seen that a more extensive internal control apparatus to manage spillover effects is needed in the former.

Transitional multidivisional (M-form). This is the M-form enterprise that is in the process of adjustment. Organisational learning may be involved or newly acquired parts may not yet have been brought into a regular divisionalised relationship in the parent enterprise.

Corrupted multidivisional (M-form). The M-form enterprise is a multidivisional structure for which the requisite central apparatus has been provided but in which the general management has become extensively involved in operating affairs. The appropriate distance relation is thus missing, with the result that M-form performance, in the long run, cannot reliably be expressed.

Mixed (X-form). Conceivably a divisionalised enterprise will have a mixed form in which some divisions will be essentially of the holding company variety, others will be M-form, and still others will be under the close supervision of the general management. Whether a mixed form is likely to be viable over the long run is perhaps to be doubted. Some 'exceptions' might, however, survive simply as a matter of chance. The X-form classification might thus be included for completeness purposes and as a reminder that organisational survival is jointly a function of natural and chance processes. In the long run the rational structures should thrive but deviant cases will appear and occasionally persist.

In the multidivision structure (M-form), the co-ordinator's office has to be transformed and an elite staff needs to be supplied to assist the general office in strategic decision-making responsibilities, including control. Relieved of operating duties and tactical decisions, a general executive is less likely to reflect the position of just one part of the whole. The characteristics and advantages of the M-form innovation is summarised by Williamson in the following way:

1. The responsibility for operating decisions is assigned to essentially self-contained operating divisions or quasi firms.
2. The elite staff attached to the general office performs both advisory and

auditing functions. Both have the effect of securing greater control over operating decision behaviour.
3. The general office is principally concerned with strategic decisions, inviting planning, appraisal, and control, including the allocation of resources among the competing operating divisions.
4. The separation of the general office from operations provides general office executives with the psychological commitment to be concerned with the overall performance of the organisation rather than become absorbed in the affairs of the functional parts.
5. The resulting structure displays both rationality and synergy: the whole is greater, more effective, more efficient, than the sum of the parts.

Divisionalisation

Operating decisions are no longer to be found at the top but are resolved at the divisional level, which relieves the communication load. Strategic decisions are reserved for the general office which reduces partisan political input into the resource allocation process. The internal auditing and control techniques which the parent office has access to, serve to overcome information-impactedness conditions and permits fine tuning to be exercised over the operating parts. Cash flows in the M-form firm are not automatically returned to their sources but are instead exposed to an internal competition. The usual criterion is the rate of return on invested capital. This assignment of cash flows to high yield uses is the most fundamental attribute of the M-form enterprise.

Optimum divisionalisation thus involves:

1. The identification of separable economic activities within the firm.
2. According quasi autonomous standing, usually of a profit-centre nature to each.
3. Monitoring the efficiency performance of each division.
4. Awarding incentives.
5. Allocating cash flows to high yield uses.
6. Strategic planning.

The general management of the M-form organisation usually requires the support of a specialised staff to discharge these functions effectively. The performance potential in divisionalised firms frequently goes unrealised because general management 'either continue to be overly responsive to operating problems – that is, non-strategic but interventionist – or reduce the size of the corporate office to a minimum level at which no capacity exists for strategic and structural decision making'.

Hierarchy in the organisational framework

With regard to hierarchy, Williamson points to the affirmative ways in which hierarchy affects each of the factors in the organisational framework:

Bounded rationality. Hierarchy extends the bounds of rationality by permitting the specialisation of decision making and economising on communication expense.

Opportunism. Hierarchy permits additional incentive and control techniques to be brought to bear in a more selective manner, thereby serving to curb small-numbers opportunism.

Uncertainty. Interdependent units are allowed to adapt to unforeseen contingencies in a co-ordinated way and furthermore hierarchy serves to absorb uncertainty.

Small numbers. Small-numbers bargaining indeterminacies can be resolved by decree.

Information impactedness. Hierarchy extends the constitutional powers to perform an audit, thereby narrowing, prospectively at least, the information gap that obtains between autonomous agents.

Atmosphere. As compared with market modes of exchange, hierarchy provides, for some purposes at least, a less calculative exchange atmosphere.

It is interesting next to compare Ouchi's *Theory Z* alongside Williamson's writings on hierarchy. Ouchi's 'theory Z' companies were those which had developed naturally in the US but with many characteristics similar to firms in Japan. Theory Z organisations do have hierarchical modes of control and so do not rely entirely upon the self-direction of the workforce. Nevertheless, self-direction does replace hierarchical direction to a great extent, which enhances commitment, loyalty and motivation.

Ouchi differentiates between a hierarchy or bureaucracy and type Z, in that the Z organisations have achieved a high state of consistency in their internal culture. They are, according to Ouchi, most aptly described as 'clans' in that they are intimate associations of people engaged in economic activity but tied together through a variety of bonds. Clans are distinct from hierarchies and from markets which are the other two fundamental social mechanisms through which transactions between individuals can be governed. In a market, each individual is in fact asked to pursue selfish interests. In a clan, each individual is also effectively told to do just what the other person wants. In the latter case, however, the socialisation of all to a common good is so complete and the capacity of the system to measure the subtleties of contributions in the long run is so exact, that individuals will naturally seek to do that which is in the common good. Despite its remarkable properties, the clan organisational form in industry possesses a few potentially disabling weaknesses. A clan always tends to develop xenophobia, a fear of outsiders. At the extreme, Theory Z companies will express the 'Not invented here' mentality – 'We have most of the top people in the field so why should I?' The trouble comes if the company starts to slip. They will not know it since they have no external point of comparison. Building an organisation, is, says Ouchi, not like building a house but more like building a marriage. An organisation constantly in the process of development will degenerate without attention.

A theory Z culture has a distinct set of values – among them long-term employment, trust, and close personal relationships. No area or facet of a Z company is untouched by that culture, from its strategies to its personnel – even its products are shaped by those values. Corporate cultures are not easily changed. Significant corporate cultural change may take between six and fifteen years according to one source, but according to Ouchi, it takes two years to persuade managers but ten to fifteen years to allow for this new work ethic to percolate through an organisation at every level. Taking a parallel with the acceptance of marketing within British industry it may be seen that despite labour slimming and labour confrontation, which may have been a necessary precursor to intended corporate cultural change, there is little evidence that British Leyland post-Michael Edwardes, British Steel post-Ian McGregor or British Airways under Lord King, have taken any significant steps at all to move more towards a marketing orientation.

In most businesses, the strategic tensions created by balancing the economic and political imperatives for the multinational managers to work with a variety of hybrid structures. Whether organised by area or product the hierarchy dominates. The hierarchy (References 5 and 6) determines:

1. The nature of the information that managers collect and use, or their 'world view'. In a geographical structure this may be information that is relevant to national portfolios of diverse businesses, while in a product structure it may be information that is relevant to business portfolios consisting of diverse countries.
2. The way managers decide to compete – on a local for local basis (geographical structure) or by global rationalisation (product organisation).
3. The people who have the power to commit strategic resources (area managers or product managers).
4. The basis for administrative procedures, such as career progression (across businesses in a geographical organisation or within a business across geographical organisations).

If one understood the hierarchy, one could understand the organisation, its capabilities, and limitations. However, as MNEs are frequently complex organisations rather than 'pure' in product, functional, or geographical structure, then the following four orientations may usefully be considered, as by suitably modifying them, strategic direction can be altered.

1. *Cognitive orientation* or the perception of the 'relevant environment' by individual managers within the organisation. The relevant environment of a business is constructed of an understanding of the key competitors, the competitive structure and the forces that are likely to mould the pattern of evolution of that business. We have to recognise that in a complex organisation, different types of managers (area, product, or functional) and managers at different levels can have very different perceptions of the relative environment. In other words, their cognitive orientations can be very different.

2. *Strategic orientation*, or the competitive posture and methods of competition that the various groups of managers are willing to adopt. If the

various managers have different cognitive orientations, then they will have different perceptions of an appropriate strategic orientation to cope with the threats or to exploit the opportunities inherent in their different world views.

3. *Power orientation* or the locus of power among managers in the organisation to commit resources – financial, technological, and managerial – to pursue a strategy.

4. *Administrative orientation*, or the orientation of support systems such as the accounting system and the personnel system. Accounting data, for example, may be consolidated along product lines or along national subsidiary lines.

The mechanisms which managers in the hybrid or matrix structure can use to influence these four orientations include:

1. Data management mechanisms.
2. Manager management mechanisms – power to assign managers to key positions.
3. Conflict resolution systems – mechanisms to resolve conflict including decision responsibility assignments are necessary.

These mechanisms can exist within four strategic control situations: fragmented, dependent, autonomous or integrated.

Relevant control systems

The Boston Consulting Group (BCG) Product Portfolio Matrix

It is a commonplace to raise questions such as 'Where are we now?', 'Where do we want to go?', 'How do we get there?'. It is infernally difficult, however, to answer these questions, particularly as to which business the company sees itself being in. In one case it was substandard gas pipes sold as scaffolding which opened up a new market for an existing product. Other existing products are finding new applications with the development of North Sea oil which, as an industry, has spawned many new developments of its own in welding, pipes, drilling, and construction.

A study of the market would be expected to examine sales trends; previous forecasts in relation to performance; assessment of the general market situation and competitive environment; problems and opportunities envisaged in the marketplace; planning assumptions and constraints. A distillation of this data combines with company strength and weaknesses and is moulded by corporate policy and the corporate view of the direction the company should take, so as to set marketing objectives in realistic terms, e.g. sales volume in money terms and in units and market share in percentages.

The BCG Product Portfolio Matrix has attracted a lot of attention amongst managers because it seeks to compartmentalise the company's entire product range into a 2 × 2 matrix where the respective axes are relative market share and market growth. The theories underpinning the BCG Product Portfolio Matrix include the Product Life Cycle hypothesis;

the Experience Curve Effect whereby a doubling of production volume will produce attendant cost savings of 25–30 per cent; and the correlation between relative market share and profitability which BCG stress strongly.

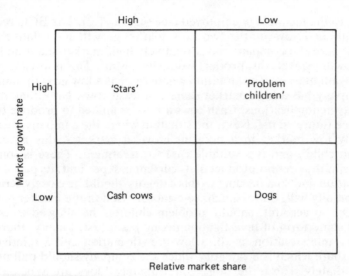

Figure 11.2 BCG Business Portfolio Matrix – implications for investment.

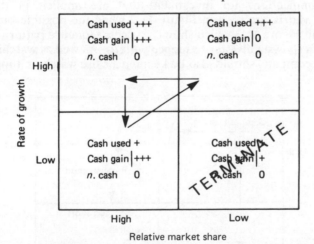

Figure 11.3 BCG Business Portfolio Matrix – success sequence.

BCG makes an important distinction between actual market share and relative market share. Relative market share means a particular manufacturer's product market share relative to that manufacturer's largest competitor. Two companies may have the same actual market share but BCG would argue that there was a difference in the competitive position between two companies if one had a relative market share of 5 per cent and the other 15 per cent. A general rule is that relative market share would be deemed 'high' if in excess of 10 per cent. An example of market growth is that of word processors estimated to be growing at a rate of 34 per cent in 1984.

Next, to the technology employed (see Figure 11.2). The BCG recognise only 'high' and 'low' on the two axes, market growth and relative market share. Where the company has a relatively high market share and is in a high growth market, this product would be a 'star'. This is a rising product in a buoyant market. The situation where there is a low growth market but the company has a high market share is a 'cash cow'. Note that each cell has strategic implications. Cash cows are to be milked to produce the cash to finance future 'stars'. Next, the situation where the company is enjoying relatively low market in a buoyant growing market – this is termed a 'problem child', and is a suitable case for treatment. There is something wrong with the present product in its current cost per unit, its packaging, or presentation and so a product in this category should be closely scrutinised and hopefully will, on relaunch, re-establish itself in the market place as a 'star'. On no account, should 'problem children' be allowed to continue without some form of investigation taking place first. Finally, there is the least enviable situation of all, a low growth market and a relatively low market share which is a category which the company should pull itself out of immediately. This is the 'dog'. Unfortunately, 'dogs' are to be put down, there is never any stay of execution for a 'dog'.

The ramifications for investment that are implicit in the Product Portfolio Matrix are seen in Figure 11.2 while the possible outcomes are depicted in Figure 11.3 which shows a success sequence pattern and Figure 11.4 which shows a disaster sequence pattern. As well as watching product sales, the company should also be keeping a close watch on those products

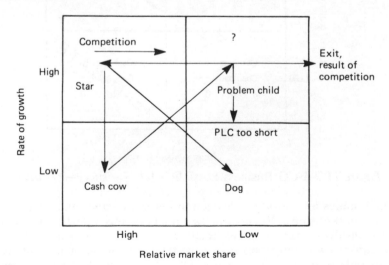

Figure 11.4 BCG Business Portfolio Matrix – disaster sequence.

consuming rather than generating funds although there are definitional problems (Reference 7):

the BMW Company of West Germany would be a dog company if its relative market share were relative in all motor cars produced and its marketing segment was the 'motoring public'. However, if the BMW Motor Company's market segment is regarded as, fast, high quality, prestigious saloon cars, then its relative market share appears much higher.

There is perhaps too rigid a comprehension into only four cells and this is what gave rise to the Directional Policy Matrix (see Figure 11.5). This recognises that products may actually be on the fence between 'dog' and 'cash cow' or any two categories. Besides this, there was, too, the fact that there was room in the market for the company that either could not be number one or wished only to be number two, due perhaps to size or technological capability, etc.

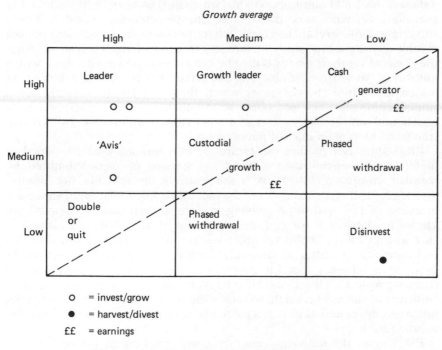

Figure 11.5 Shell Directional Policy Matrix.

If the market is growing it may be relatively easy to acquire market share, but in a static or declining market, market share can only be bought at the expense of competitors who are likely to retaliate perhaps with price reductions, thereby jeopardising the market for all concerned.

The matrix is as viable in an international context as in a domestic one, the only reservation being that governments may take notice of 'cash cows' being milked in their particular country to finance some 'stars' being nurtured in an overseas freeport. In the same way as Wells and Vernon showed how the PLC theory could be used for international markets, the same is true here of the BCG matrix. It has the same roots after all in the PLC theory but the experience curve emphasises product unit cost advantages, and relative market share serves to emphasise this commercial advantage under the BCG guidelines. Whereas the PLC offered a post-mortem rationalisation for American investments, the BCG offers strategic alternatives as a result of the data-gathering exercise, e.g. market segment concentration, market share holding, harvesting (taking the cash), and termination.

PIMS database

PIMS is an acronym for Profit Impact on Marketing Strategy. Based in the Strategic Planning Institute, Cambridge, Massachussets, PIMS has a database of 1,800 subscribers who are mainly American though it has subsidiary branches now throughout Europe, including London. For a subscription of several thousand dollars per annum, subscribers do not receive any 'omnibus' study or industry or product report. Instead, what they receive for their money is the ability to interrogate the database with a number of 'what if' questions. The subscriber inserts some key data about his company into the computer which then searches its memory for a similar company. The computer would then be able to respond to a question about the likely effect of a 4 per cent price increase, or to reveal trends, or to explain market phenomena.

PIMS does not predict the future. It tells instead what happened in highly similar circumstances based on millions of facts submitted by member companies. PIMS is based entirely on real life not theory. Academics and researchers decry the fact that it has a long list of variables, in excess of 120, and so, in arriving at a given point there is the problem known to statisticians of multicollinearity; in other words, we cannot be sure which of the 120 plus variables was responsible for this situation. No two companies are after all identical, so this is a weakness. However, PIMS exists as a business tool for businessmen and as such it apears to be receiving wide acclaim. Even if it cannot explain all the answers it is getting sufficient of the answers right to satisfy the businessmen who are generally much less interested as to how a particular solution was arrived at, than the solution itself.

PIMS make the following generalisations based on their experience:

1. Higher profitability is accounted for by

   - lower capital intensity (investment)
   - high market share
   - high product quality.

2. High market position and high product quality

   - are very profitable
   - can be used as substitutes for each other.

3. If market is weak

   - do not use high prices
   - do not do R & D, imitate other products instead.

4. If market position is strong increase R & D expenses
5. If one's product is of low quality do not advertise it
6. To be profitable

   - introduce new products at the bottom of a recession (a most difficult theory to put into practice)
   - do not spend more than 10 cents of the sales dollar for marketing.

References

1. Williamson, Oliver E., *Markets and Hierarchies: Analysis and Antitrust Implications*. Macmillan, The Free Press, New York, 1975.
2. Williamson, Oliver E. and Bhargava, N., *Market structure and competitive behaviour: theory and empirical analysis of the firm*. Keith Cowling (ed.), Gray-Mills Publishing Ltd., London, 1972, pp. 127–48.
3. Ouchi, William, *Theory Z – How American business can meet the Japanese challenge*, Addison-Wesley, 1981.
4. Wiechmann, Ulrich E. and Pringle, Lewis G., 'Problems that plague multinational marketers', *Harvard Business Review*, July-August 1979, pp. 118–24.
5. Pralidad, C. K. and Doz, Yves L., 'An approach to strategic control in MNCs', *Sloan Management Review*, Summer 1981, pp. 5–13.
6. Doz, Yves L. and Prahalad, C. K., 'Headquarters influence and strategic control in MNCs', *Sloan Management Review*, Fall 1981, pp. 15–29.
7. McNamee, Patrick M., *Tools and Techniques for Strategic Management*, Pergamon, 1985.
8. Brooke, Michael Z., *Centralisation and Autonomy: A Study in Organisation Behaviour*, Holt-Rinehart-Winston, 1984.

12. *THE JAPANESE TRADING ENVIRONMENT*

Economic and social background

Japan has the world's third largest GNP, which has grown 18-fold since 1960. It accounts for 10 per cent of the world's GNP. Japan consists of four main islands: Kyushu, Shikoku; the main island Honshu; and Hokkaido. Others lying to the south of Kyushu such as Okinawa and others were administered by the US up to May 1972.

The land mass is almost double the size of the UK, comprising 143,000 square miles (94,000 square miles in the UK). The country is mountainous and volcanic, with short fast-flowing unnavigable rivers.

The country is influenced by the Chinese who introduced their script into Japan in 400 AD. From the twelfth century, political power lay with the military rulers, the Shogun. First European contact came in the sixteenth century from the Dutch at Nagasaki, which broke Japanese isolation. The overthrow of Tokugawa Shogun and restoration of the Emperor Meiji followed. The latter moved from the traditional imperial capital of Kydo to the Tokugawan Shogun's capital at Edo which was renamed Tokyo which means 'Eastern capital'.

Japan annexed Taiwan in 1884–5 and acquired Korea as a colony in 1911. It joined the Allies in World War 1, and has had a growing determination to dominate China. In 1941 Japan attacked the US and later there was the US bombing of Hiroshima and Nagasaki which ended the war for Japan. The Peace Treaty which ended the occupation was signed at San Francisco on 8 September 1957 and came into force in April 1952. Neither the USSR nor China was a party to this treaty.

Japan has since looked to the US for security, as her largest market and supplier of foodstuffs. Relations with the USSR have been cool because of the Soviet annexation of four small islands off Hokkaido at the end of the War. The USSR has also criticised the Japanese treaty of peace and friendship with China as being 'anti-Soviet' in nature. Previously Japan supported Taiwan but after the Nixon visit to China, recognised the People's Republic of China. Article 9 of the Japanese Constitution renounces war as a sovereign right and declares that war potential will never be maintained. There is a self-defence army, navy and air force but the country spends a total of only 1 per cent of GNP on defence.

Religions are not mutually hostile nor mutually exclusive. The main religions are:

Shinto. An indigenous religion which worships a deity as manifested in works of nature or man which inspire feelings of awe or respect.

Figure 12.1 Map of Japan

Buddhism. This was introduced from China in the sixth century. There are a number of different sects but this is the most common religion now in Japan.

Christianity and **New Religions**. Christianity is a minority religion. The Soka Gakkai or Value Adding Society combines the pursuit of material benefit combined with an intolerant form of Buddhism (Nicheren Shoshu Sect).

Internal market conditions

Japan is the second largest consumer market in the free world – roughly 40 per cent larger than West Germany and 2.8 times that of Great Britain.

The Gross National Product of Japan is the second largest in the industrialised world after the US, and even if the Comecon countries are included Japan still ranks as number three. It is more than twice as large as that of the UK and is expanding at a much faster rate than that of any other advanced industrialised country. Japan is a market of 118.7 million people

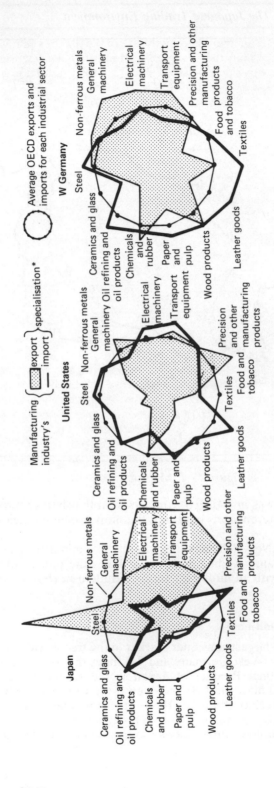

Figure 12.2 Comparing export-import profiles: Japan, US and West Germany
Source The Economist, July 9, 1983.

(1982 figures) and has an average growth rate of 0.5–0.6 per cent with a per capita income higher than that in the UK. Imports have been increasing fast but have tended to slacken (see Table 12.1 for Production and Price Indicator(s) in the last two years).

Table 12.1
The rise in Japanese production and prices

	Average % change in 1971–83	
	Real GNP	*Prices**
USA	2.6	7.0
Japan	4.5	5.0
'West Germany	2.1	4.7
France	2.8	10.4
UK	1.6	12.5

*GNP deflators
Source OECD

While the world economy was expanding Japan was not unfavourable to trade liberalisation but the oil shock of 1973/74 and successive oil shocks since then have changed this. Against a backcloth then of a static world market, the law of comparative 'disadvantage' holds sway over that of comparative advantage. In Japan, it has been particularly noted that the terminology of trade has taken on military overtones in the usage of such terms as 'trade war', for example. Export earnings as a percentage of GNP show Japan's exports in 1977 to contribute 12 per cent of GNP; the equivalent figure for the UK is 24 per cent. Japan's production costs

Table 12.2
Relative measures of competitiveness (percentage changes per annum)

	Productivity (of which EEC Germany)		US	Japan	Relative unit labour costs National currency (of which EEC Germany)		US	Japan	Relative unit labour costs Common currency (of which EEC Germany)		US	Japan
Manufacturing industry												
1960–70	+5.0	(+4.8)	+2.7	+10.7	+1.1	(+0.5)	−1.2	−0.4	+0.9	(+2.2)	−0.9	−0.2
1970–75	+3.1	(+3.2)	+3.4	+4.6	+1.8	(−2.9)	−5.4	+4.2	+2.5	(+1.6)	−8.6	+5.9
1975–80	+4.0	(+3.3)	+1.7	+8.2	+2.1	(−3.1)	+0.9	−8.3	+2.7	(+1.7)	−0.6	−3.9
1980–84	+3.1	(+2.8)	+3.7	+3.9	+0.8	(−3.8)	−1.1	−3.9	−6.5	(−2.5)	+7.6	+2.4
Whole economy												
1960–70	+4.5	(+4.4)	+2.0	+9.1	+0.2	(−0.3)	−0.8	+0.3	+0.1	(+1.5)	−0.5	+0.5
1970–75	+2.8	(+2.8)	+1.5	+4.1	+1.1	(−3.1)	−4.6	+4.7	+1.9	(+1.4)	−7.8	+6.4
1975–80	+2.7	(+3.1)	+0.4	+3.8	+1.1	(−5.3)	−0.2	−3.9	+1.7	(−0.6)	−1.7	+0.7
1980–84	+1.7	(+1.8)	+1.4	+2.1	+0.9	(−4.6)	−0.6	−3.4	−6.5	(−3.4)	+8.2	+3.0

Source 'The Japanese Banking System', *Barclays' Bank Review*, August 1984, p. 67.

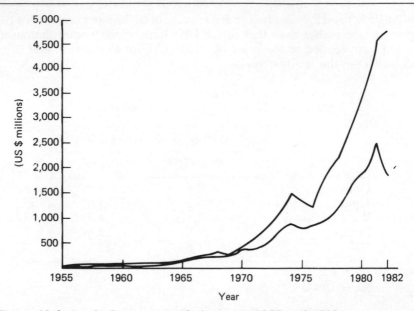

Figure 12.3 Anglo-Japanese trade between 1955 and 1982
Sources Ministry of Finance *Economic Statistics Annual '82*; Research and
Statistics Department, The Bank of Japan.

remain low and its productivity is improving whilst the UK seems to show
both low productivity and low investment. (See Table 12.2 and Figure 12.3.)

Insatiable world demand for Japanese exports, limited capacity to
import, low inflation rates, an embarrassingly large $114.2 billion surplus
(in 1984), and $8.96 billion in the first quarter of 1985, a fairly steady rate
of GNP growth, have all combined to make Japan's record appear
unavoidably good compared with that of any of its partners or competitors
in the West.

Approximately 60 per cent of Japan's imports are fuels and raw
materials with only 27 per cent accounted for by manufactures. Japan,
however, claims that its strategy was to implement a domestic demand-
oriented economy. The yen is presently artificially weak. The US are
currently demanding that Japan does more to bolster and internationalise
the yen. 97 per cent of Japanese imports and 60 per cent exports are priced
in US dollars. Pressures of high inflation and interest rates do not exist in
Japan. An examination of the stability of the yen/dollar bears this out e.g.

230Y	= US $1	Oct 1981
264.2Y	= US $	Oct 1982
246.20Y	= US $9	Nov 1983
249Y	= US $17	Oct 1984

It was previously boasted that Japanese industry could withstand a 25
per cent worsening of the yen relative to the dollar and still be competitive
but as we have seen, Japanese industry is dependent on the small firm. The

period September-November 1985 saw a 20 per cent appreciation of the yen to 203 yen to the dollar and MITI's survey of small firms with export ratios over 20 per cent found about half either reporting foreign exchange losses or contraction of new export business.

Japan's export performance is due to:

1. **Stable prices** – the impact of an artificially low yen exchange rate on the price of its exports.

2. **Slack domestic demand** holding down imports of raw materials and fuel as well as manufacturing goods, plus soft prices for imported energy.

3. **Interest rates**. The Ministry of Finance cannot lower interest rates because lowering interest rates would probably weaken the yen, thus further making Japanese exports even more competitive and Japan's trade partners more unhappy. Western nations should continue to press for the internationalisation of the yen, forcing yen export prices higher at least in the short term.

In the longer term, Japan should attract foreign direct investment (FDI). It presumably restricts FDI but the strength of the economy is to be seen in the lowest inflation rate of any major industrial country at 1.8 per cent. Slowly Japan is moving to the point where its own capital markets are open enough to play a greater role in the international financial system. Pressure

Table 12.3
Japanese exports to the UK

The top twenty	Dec 1982 £'000	Jan-Dec 1983 £'000
Telecom. & sound equipment	48,285	725,401
Road vehicles	16,230	579,348
Electrical machinery n.e.s.	17,355	199,729
Misc. manufactures	9,916	199,175
Office, data processing machines	15,656	172,163
Photo & optical; watches, clocks	7,672	114,193
Textile yarn, fabrics etc.	5,909	72,094
Power generating machinery	4,817	71,513
Specialised industrial machinery	4,613	64,355
General industrial machinery	4,244	63,079
Metal manufactures n.e.s.	4,305	43,696
Scientific, controlling etc. installations	2,806	32,550
Metal working machinery	1,760	32,596
Organic chemicals	2,014	29,266
Iron & steel	1,156	28,571
Inorganic chemicals	874	26,341
Coal, coke & briquettes	2,095	24,290
Non-ferrous metals	289	19,783
Non-metallic mineral manufactures	1,077	17,448
Transport equipment n.e.s.	49	15,678

Table 12.4
UK exports to Japan

The top twenty	Dec 1982 £'000	Jan-Dec 1983 £'000
Beverages	4,673	69,858
Textile yarn, fabrics etc.	4,106	51,817
Medical & pharmaceutical products	4,202	48,876
Miscellaneous manufactures	2,727	39,851
Power generating machinery	3,065	36,922
Non-ferrous metals	3,200	33,350
Organic chemicals	2,963	31,168
Electrical machinery n.e.s.	3,703	26,938
Clothing	733	25,932
Scientific, controlling etc. installations	2,098	25,225
Specialised industrial machinery	2,243	25,104
General industrialised machinery	1,151	20,022
Photo & optical; watches, clocks	1,999	17,711
Non-metallic mineral manufactures	1,182	16,777
Office, data processing machines	1,277	15,333
Dyeing & tanning materials	1,043	14,183
Transport equipment n.e.s.	486	13,300
Chemicals n.e.s.	1,026	12,489
Textile fibres & waste	1,403	12,072
Metal manufactures n.e.s.	549	11,744

is now on Japan. Already it has been taking steps since 1980 to revise its formerly rigid exchange control laws.

Nevertheless, Japan continues to make striking gains in its industrial competitiveness, and in so doing attracts foreign investment capital. It is worth mentioning at this point the 1985 annual survey of industrial competitiveness by the European Management Forum, which is an independent non-profit foundation. The survey includes interviews with more than 1,000 business executives in the 28 countries and judges competitiveness on 302 criteria in ten groups.

The EMF *Sixth Annual Survey on International Competitiveness* published in 1985 showed that Japan had for the first time fallen from the top of the table on competitiveness and productivity. Japan was now third behind the US and Switzerland, partly because of low levels of natural resources but chiefly because of a fall in Japanese business confidence. For the preceding five years, Japan had been top of the table but the top four places continued to be dominated by the US, Switzerland, Japan and West Germany.

Reasons for the Japanese moving into foreign markets

1. Satellite manufacture became profitable because of yen revaluation.

2. Commercial and other services required to support satellite manufacturing increased the outflow from Japan.
3. Strategic overseas investment in the extractive industries safeguards the supply of essential basic materials, e.g. copper, iron ore, bauxite, and coking coal.

Reasons for Japanese growth

As perceived by Westerners, an aura of mysticism surrounds the East and Westerners are unable to understand a religious reverence for the Japanese imperial family. The culture and value system is different in Japan from that practised in Britain. Nevertheless there is the danger of unquestioning acceptance of Japanese invincibility stemming perhaps from the unity of mind and body found in Japanese exports such as the martial arts.

A rapidly growing proportion of Japan's population is over 65 thus creating opportunities for retirement and leisure as well as automation, roboticisation, retraining, and health care programmes. Japan's strengths lie in innovation not invention, and not in the labour cost either, for Japan is demanning heavily. Yet as Martin Beresford noted in *Management Today*, October 1981, pp. 60–6:

much of Japan's success has resulted from just 'doing things better' i.e. applying quite unexotic technology steadily to improve product design or productivity in existing industries.

The Japanese have an organisational system known as 'keiretsu' which is the engine behind their growth. These we shall deal with later but it is important to note their history, centralisation, family ties, cross-holdings, debt ties and managerial exchanges, also the closeness of banks to Japanese industry. Next, it pays to examine the Japanese strategy in entering Western markets (Reference 1). This has been said to resemble a cascading strategy pattern. They enter into carefully selected small segments and then gradually move across the entire market. An examination of Japanese marketing strategies since the 1950s shows how in numerous cases – transistor radios, televisions, cars, stereo, hi-fi – the Japanese have consistently used essentially the same strategy. The strategy is to launch a single product into the foreign market. This will be aimed at a small but well-defined market segment. It therefore does not arouse competitive reaction. The gradual build-up of parts, maintenance, and after-sales is taking place. Meanwhile, once this has been done, the product range is extended, 'cascading' into the market with new lines of products.

Company size alone is not the reason as we shall see. The Mitsubishi group, with a 1978 turnover of $106 billion, is more than a dozen times the size of Britain's ICI whilst five others – DKB, Sumitomo, Mitsui, Fuyo and Sanwa – with sales in 1978 ranging from 9 billion dollars to 64 billion dollars, outsold even General Motors and Royal Dutch Shell. Japan's automobile industry is now the largest in the world. European multinationals such as Philips, Hoechst, and Nestle fail also to compare with these Japanese giants. Against this, over 80 per cent of the country's labour force of 34 million work in small or medium-size companies which are just as dynamic and competitive as their larger counterparts. At the same time Japan is experiencing a very high level of company failures, a record 20,841 in 1984 and only a slightly lower figure is expected for 1985. Five of Japan's listed stock market companies failed in 1984, the most in twenty years.

Psychic distance appears then to be creating an advantage in favour of Japanese businessmen vis-a-vis UK businessmen where, by way of comparison (Reference 2).

An attitude born in the British Empire and corner-store tradition seems to prevail amongst many of best doing business with people who think the same way as they do. One effect is this failure to realise that much good business can be done with countries with different economic systems – consequently there is defensiveness where there should be aggression.

Meanwhile the Japanese hold continues to spread from electronics and motor vehicles to numerically controlled machine tools, tractors and construction machinery.

During the 20 years from 1953 to 1973 Japan invested more per unit of added value than its major Western competitors, i.e. 24.2 per cent compared with 13.3 per cent for the UK, and taking base index as 100 for Japan in 1953, the 1973 figure for the UK is 40 (Reference 3)! It must also be conceded that Japan has earned a reputation for an ideal relationship between government and industry in backing innovation.

28.8 per cent of Japanese export trade is accounted for by sales of automobiles followed by VCR's and radio communications equipment. Twenty-five years ago in 1960 crude oil accounted for 28.7 per cent of Japan's imports. In 1985, crude and refined oil was responsible for 28.7 per cent of imports, followed by natural gas and oil products. By way of further comparison, the US which developed the automobile industry at the turn of the century, sells 2,000 cars into Japan each year but takes 2 million cars from Japan. Nevertheless, Japanese industry has de-manned wherever possible. Citing the case of the Japanese electronics industry, for example, as having multiplied its output 3.4 times between 1968 and 1978 while its exports increased 5.2 times, its production finally became 25 per cent larger than the combined production of West Germany, France, Italy and the UK. Again there are colour television assembly lines nearly 70 per cent of which are now fully automated, lowering production times from 6 man hours to 1.5, and reducing power consumption per 20-inch set from 325W in 1972 to 95W in 1977. A 1984 survey of 763 Japanese companies showed the proportion allocated to basic research to be an average 5.2 per cent of total outlay. While 117 firms replied that they spent over 20% on basic research, 291 stated only 2 per cent. This survey also showed heavy dependence on universities, etc.

There was little Japanese investment in the EEC in the 1960s except for areas like zips and stationery. In the 1970s this came to include ball bearings, colour televisions, chemicals, and synthetic fabrics. In the 1980s Nissan and Honda began car production in Europe. 36 Japanese companies are now operating or about to operate in Britain as against more than 1,500 from the US.

Eleven ingredients of the Japanese recipe

The following have been advanced by Professor Ronald Dore, Assistant Director of the Technical Change Centre.

1. The Japanese have a strong ethic and this is so of their managers and technologists.
2. The Japanese are well educated, over 90 per cent stay at school until 18, and 40 per cent then proceed to college or university where a fifth of undergraduate degrees and half of master's degrees are in engineering.
3. Japanese work co-operatively in large corporations.
4. There is extensive use of subcontracting in manufacture.
5. Japan's is a managerial, production-orientated capitalism, not a shareholder dominated form of capitalism.
6. Japan has the most effective form of incomes policy outside of Austria and Sweden.
7. Japan has a high savings rate and low rates of interest and her corporations invest 15 per cent of GNP, as also do government and households combined.
8. Japan is still a relatively 'small government' country where the tax is around 24 per cent of national income as compared with 40 per cent in Britain.
9. Japanese corporations are very good at forming cartels.
10. The Japanese value and honour the public service, and an intelligent industrial policy is one consequence of this.
11. By contrast, the Japanese do not much honour politicians, whose role in running the economy is small.

The Sogo Shosha: Japan's international trading houses

In post-war Japan the Sogo Shosha were divided up into many different and separate companies. Mitsui, then the largest (now it is Mitsubishi), was divided up into over 200 companies but by 1959 it had reassembled and now handles approximately 10 per cent of Japanese exports on its own. Mitsui is now the fourth largest US exporter after Boeing, General Motors and General Electric.

The nine big Sogo Shoshas account for an estimated 50–60 per cent of Japan's external trade. The Sogo Shosha have an impressive pedigree going back more than a hundred years. Their strength lies in their integration of trading, manufacturing, and banking affiliates. Mitsubishi is linked with Mitsubishi Bank; Mitsui with Mitsui Bank; Marubeni with Fuji; C. Itoh to Dai-Ichi Kangyo Bank. These banks rank among the largest in the world in asset terms. At the end of 1981, the nine major Sogo Shoshas had a total of approximately 57,000 personnel. Of these, about

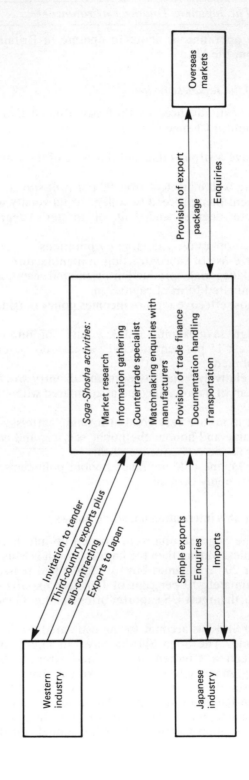

Figure 12.4 Activities of the Sogo Shoshas

Within the image:

Western industry

- Invitation to tender
- Third-country exports plus sub-contracting
- Exports to Japan

Soga-Shosha activities:
- Market research
- Information gathering
- Countertrade specialist
- Matchmaking enquiries with manufacturers
- Provision of trade finance
- Documentation handling
- Transportation

Overseas markets

- Provision of export package
- Enquiries

Japanese industry

- Simple exports
- Enquiries
- Imports

23,900 (including 6,300 expatriate personnel) were working at a total of 1,044 overseas offices including wholly owned affiliates and joint ventures.

It is usual to read of obituaries for the Soga Shosha – only 20 per cent of Japan's domestic wholesale trade now goes via the top ten trading houses compared with a majority situation in early 1950. The threat derives from the increasing independence of Japanese car manufacturers and others; from Japanese banks lending directly to the small company rather than via them; and from the fact also that gross profit margins for the traditional business of Sogo Shoshas is falling, signalling stagnant turnover and rising costs. Against this, it should be noted that the Sogo Shoshas are moving increasingly into third-country trade, acting as an intermediary for other Western companies, whilst at home they are being seen to be active in new investments, e.g. cable television and data communications.

Sales of the big nine Sogo Shoshas to March 31 1983 were valued at 349 billion US dollars of which domestic sales accounted for 40.2 per cent; exports 21.5 per cent; imports 24.1 per cent; and offshore trade 14.2 per cent. Third-country business as a percentage of total sales has almost trebled since 1971.

Imports into Japan

Japan is said to still retain an ancient complex distribution system that has evolved from agricultural produce. This poses a problem for domestic as well as foreign companies. Japan has more wholesalers and retailers per capita than any other industrial nation. It is explained by the 'Keiretsu' system in which producers, importers, distributors, and retailers are all financially linked with each other either directly or through a bank or Sogo Shosha. This results in close ties and bonds forged by mutual obligation and service.

Technically, all imports require licences under Article 52 of the Japan Foreign Exchange Law. However, most goods enter unrestricted and with nominal formality. This can be done under the Import Declaration Scheme (IDS) or under the import quota scheme. Under the Import Declaration Scheme the only requirement is to report to the Ministry of International Trade and Industry (MITI) through foreign exchange banks on the remittance of payment abroad. Under the import quota scheme certain goods are subject to a specific quantitative restriction. Under Articles 21 and 22 of GATT the Japanese government is allowed to restrict imports for security, public health, revenue or other reasons (including heavy aircraft, aircraft engines, explosives, arms, swords, tobacco products, and narcotics). Under this system an importer must first obtain an Import Quota Allocation Certificate from MITI which entitles him to receive an import licence on application to an authorised foreign exchange bank. The size of import quotas are decided by the Japanese authorities on a global basis but the amounts are not made public. Allocations are made to importers on the basis of their past performance, usually twice a year.

Table 12.5
Outline of measures taken to open the Japanese market

	Economic measures for foreign trade (12/16/82)	Market-opening measures (5/28/82)	Promotion of urgent economic measures for foreign trade (1/13/83)
1. Reduction or abolition of customs tariffs	• Government accelerates by two years all tariff cuts agreed to at the Tokyo Round negotiations	• Implementation in 1982 of accelerated tariff cuts noted at left. Tariff reduction or abolition carried out on an additional 17 agricultural products and 198 industrial products starting in fiscal 1983	• Tariffs lowered or abolished on 47 agricultural products and 28 industrial products in addition to tobacco products, chocolate and biscuits, starting in fiscal 1983
2. Easing of import restrictions	• Review of residual import restricted items	• Import quotas raised for herring, port products, high test molasses and canned pineapple	• Import restrictions eased for beans and peas, peanuts, fruit puree and paste, non-citrus fruit juice, tomato juice, and tomato ketchup and sauce
3. Reform of import inspection procedures	• Government decides to review import inspection procedures • Measures taken to make import inspection procedures more appropriate	• Full use of O.T.O. • Customs clearance and import formalities made simpler and speedier • Openness and clarity ensured in the formation of standards and criteria	• Inquiry meeting held by O.T.O. • Proxy declaration system introduced at O.T.O. • Liaison and Co-ordination Headquarters established for discussions on the standards and certification systems

	Reform of import inspection procedures (1/30/82)	Reform of standards and certification systems (3/24/83)
	• O.T.O. established in order to provide a better system of dealing with complaints from foreign countries	• Measures taken to legally guarantee non-discriminatory treatment for foreign companies applying for certification

	Economic measures for foreign trade (12/16/82)	Market-opening measures (5/28/82)	Promotion of urgent economic measures for foreign trade (1/13/83)
4. Import promotion measures	• Government begins emergency foreign currency lending for import • Import missions sent overseas to hold product shows and engage in other import-promotion activities	• Phased implementation of plan to trade in foreign tobacco products (by 1985) • Continued implementation of emergency foreign currency lending for import • Promotion of exports of Alaskan oil and other products to Japan	• Distribution of foreign tobacco products further encouraged • Efforts made to expand imports of manufactured goods
5. Reform of distribution structure and business practices		• Decision made to discuss problems at the Manufactured Imports • Strict application of the Anti-Monopoly Law with respect to the distribution of imported goods • Mediation system established for individual transactions	

Source MITI, 'White Paper on International Trade 1983', Tokyo, November 1983.

Tariffs

Except for certain raw materials, essential items of industrial equipment, antiques, and a few other manufactured goods, imports are liable to customs duties. Most are calculated as a percentage of the value of the goods. Of the 2,576 headings in the Japanese Customs Tariff 412 are duty free, and these are mainly raw materials which represent almost 50 per cent by value of Japanese imports. The tariff rates then are:

1. Basic rate
2. GATT rate
3. Temporary rate (reviewed annually)
4. Special rate under Generalised Preferences

Japan's tariffs are on average lower than those of most industrialised countries but 'non-tariff barriers' constitute a problem. Toyota produce a booklet to help foreign suppliers around the maze of bureaucracy which, combined with long distribution channels, can be a barrier to entry to the market. Import regulations include:

Duty assessment on the basis of the declared c.i.f. value. On this basis the customs may increase the basis for assessment of duty in order to bring the c.i.f. price up to the value which an independent buyer would have to pay, assuming he had no special relationship with the supplier. This 'arms length' concept is introduced here and is in fact a countervailing duty to ensure that imports do not gain over domestic products.

Duty is normally levied 'ad valorem'. However, for wool and Scotch whisky a specific duty may be levied solely on the basis of the quality.

Internal taxes operate, regardless of whether they are for domestic or foreign goods, from 5 per cent on cosmetics to 30 per cent on motor boats, etc. but there are also excise duties.

Import documentation. Certificates of origin are not required for goods for which conventional or beneficial rates of duty are claimed, such as goods entitled to GATT or MFN status. A declaration of origin in the commercial invoice is sufficient.

Transit and bond. Although there are no designated free ports as such, certain factories and warehouses have been designated for the processing in bond of imported materials and goods for ultimate re-export. These are of five types:

1. Designated bonded area owned or administered by the Japanese Government, local public bodies, or Japan National Railways.
2. Bonded sheds.
3. Bonded warehouses.
4. Bonded manufacturing warehouses.
5. Bonded exhibition sites.

Storage for imported goods is for up to 24 months but may be extended. The total number of bonded facilities in Japan is 3,300, located in 9 areas – Tokyo, Yokohama, Kobe, Osaka, Nagoya, Moji, Nagasaki, Naha and Hakodate. Each contains all forms of bonded facility.

Product testing for imports. With motor vehicles, individual units may be tested on arrival or they may be subject to an exhaustive test when import is first undertaken, after which a model is given 'type approval' which permits further imports of that model without testing. Testing can take several months and cost 20,000–200,000 yen. (Often test cars are not in a saleable condition afterwards.) There are a number of Japanese safety and environmental protection regulations for vehicles.

In the case of pharmaceuticals all drugs or medical devices imported into, or manufactured in, Japan must be tested and then registered by the Ministry of Health and Welfare before being put on sale in Japan. The registration period is often lengthened to between six months and one year by regulations which require double blind testing of new products, ethical testing, and even supplying the authorities with vaccine serum in the case of new vaccines. These testing requirements also involve the exporter in costs which often reach several thousand pounds sterling. All importers of pharmaceuticals must be licensed by the Ministry of Health and Welfare to handle pharmaceuticals. This entails having at least one employee who is a registered pharmacist.

Electrical appliances have to be tested by the Japan Electrical Testing Laboratory and can take from one to three months. Gas appliances must be tested and approved by the Japan Gas Appliance Inspection Association before they can be sold in Japan.

Processed cheese is subject to an import quota and so the Japanese authorities may, in cases of doubt, test imports of natural cheeses in order to check that they are not processed ones, in spite of the fact that natural cheese is not on the import quota. In the case of natural cheeses, it is possible to avoid such testing provided the consignment is accompanied by an official public analyst's certificate to the effect that the import in question is a natural cheese. Elsewhere, one has to beware the Japanese creativity in creating new national standards as for skiing equipment where Japan seemingly believes its snow is different from everyone else's!

Market prospects for exports to Japan

The prospects for exports to Japan are outwardly good but direct exports are difficult. In high value areas such as cars or microelectronics, Japan exports at least four times as much as it imports.
1. Distance and resulting high costs where there is a ratio of high bulk to value on exports.
2. Tariffs and certain non-tariff barriers estimated to number 258 in all, including the designation of scheduled air traffic.
3. Distribution – in Japan this is said to be the major reason for the Western failure to infiltrate the Japanese market. This is often more difficult than entering Japan (Reference 4). This is seen as a non-tariff barrier because of the high number of small firms, doubtless aided by the retention in Japan of retail price maintenance. There are 300,000 wholesaling firms (Tonja) who keep on selling to each other and atomistic competition among its 1.6m retailers. A particular point to

note is that retailers and wholesalers demand a lot from manufacturers. This has the following effects:

- Necessitating substantial capital investment by the manufacturer.
- Limited freedom on pricing, given that only wholesale selling prices can be determined by the manufacturer.
- Frequent price changes are best avoided partly due to the depth of the distribution channel. A Japanese manufacturer summarised it thus: 'We cannot consider our growth without our dealers' growth, and our dealers' growth cannot be considered without ours.' This perspective engenders harmony but inhibits change taking place.
- Rebates (traditional in the Japanese food business) – the largest rebates may be higher than the normal margins allowed.
- Supply (prompt delivery is essential).
- Promotional assistance and budgeting are required.
- Sales – frequent personal visits to customers at all levels are most important.
- Training support for education, management, technical staff is required.

4. Royalties for manufacture under licence. Quick approval is usually granted. Previously licensing was the only method of entering Japan.
5. Capital investment in a joint venture manufacturing arrangement.

From the British perspective Japan is the number one market for worsteds, number two for quality knitwear and number three for Scotch whisky, although this has been dropping from 3 million cases p.a. to 2.5 million. Parallel exporting has done some damage to established brand pricing and image. The overall picture which emerges, though, is of a commodity trade pattern with British exports to Japan being quite unlike Japanese imports into Britain, gauged either in overall value or unit value, as well as technological input.

Considerations before exporting

1. Japanese rules governing technical agreements and the establishment of joint venture branches and wholly owned subsidiaries.
2. Japanese regulations on the remittance of profit and capital.
3. Tax situation.

Advertising in Japan

Advertising is seen to be creative rather than a sales tool. Bert Marsh of Young and Rubicam (Reference 5) defined three main types of advertising in Japan: follow-the-leader; use of celebrities; and use of mood. The key to sales is distribution not advertising. Following the competition is not particularly frowned upon. Celebrities are often used to position a product. Since Americans are considered to be great coffee drinkers then it follows that American actors such as Kirk Douglas and Peter Fonda are in demand for coffee commercials. The actor's image is important to the positioning of the product. Direct confrontation or 'knocking copy' is not used. Mood is very extensively used, depicting perhaps the beauties of nature and only at the very end of the commercial, introducing the product in question. To Westerners, this is not effective advertising but to the Japanese this form of advertising adds to the image of the company. Commercial films are left to the film producer rather than the agency and different agencies may be used for different media. Advertising is still secondary to good distribution in effecting sales in Japan.

Trademarks and Industrial Property Rights

The Department of Trade recommends that the registration of trademarks be considered by any company seriously intending to do business in Japan, as it is relatively simple and inexpensive. Inventions should also be protected, although the processes are more complicated. For companies with a large range of designs the protection of all of them could be very expensive and they might consider protecting only those designs which have greater potential in Japan. The Japanese classification is different from that in use in most European countries and makes no provision for service marks.

For application for registration to be successful the inventions and designs must not have been known publicly or worked publicly in Japan; nor should they have been described in publications circulated in Japan or in any other country prior to the application. The first person to apply for registration of a patent or trademark obtains the right. Unlike the UK and some other countries, proof of prior use does not confer priority rights. The Japanese Unfair Competition Prevention has given some protection to unregistered designs and trademarks provided that they are 'well known' to Japanese consumers or dealers of the products concerned. However, under the Paris Convention for the Protection of Industrial Property to which both the UK and Japan are signatories, an application made in one of the signatory countries is treated as if it were made at the same time in other signatory countries provided that the application claiming priority under the convention is made in those other countries within twelve months of the first application in the case of inventions, and within six months in the case of designs and trademarks. (Reference 6)

Japan and the UK did not become parties to the Trademark Registration Treaty which came into force in August 1980 but failed. It would have meant that to register a trademark in the signatory nations designated by the application filing one application to the UN World Intellectual Property Organisation (WIPO). Unless the government of a designated country refuses to register it within 15 months of the publication by WIPO, it automatically becomes registered in that country. Applications are published by WIPO as soon as they are filed. It is not necessary to use the trademark in order to register it, but it will cease to be protected if it is not used within three years of registration.

Licensing

British companies have been slower than others to enter into licensing in Japan. Of 1,755 agreements (with a duration of more than one year) in

Table 12.6
Leading examples of foreign-capitalised businesses in Japan

Company name	Country	Industrial area	Location in Japan
Shipley Far East Ltd	USA	Semi-conductor materials	Sasagami-mura, Niigata Prefecture
MRC	USA	Machinery for manufacturing semiconductors	Kunisaki-cho, Oita Prefecture
Sanyo Duracell Co Ltd	USA	Dry batteries	Iwami-cho, Tottori Prefecture
Morex	USA	Electric machinery	Shioya-cho, Tochigi Prefecture
Ferrofluidics	USA	Electric machinery	Yokaichiba-shi, Chiba Prefecture
Spraying Systems Far East Company	USA	Spray nozzles	Yokaichiba-shi, Chiba Prefecture
CRI	USA	Chemicals	Miyako-shi, Iwate Prefecture
Union Carbide	USA	Chemicals	Kozuki-cho, Hyogo Prefecture
Sumitomo 3M Ltd	USA	Chemicals	Oyama-cho, Shizuoka Prefecture
Roussel	France	Pharmaceuticals	Shirakawa-shi, Fukushima Prefecture
Pharmacia Japan K.K.	Sweden	Pharmaceuticals	Hokota-cho, Ibaraki Prefecture
Hoechst Japan Ltd	West Germany	Pharmaceuticals	Ogasa-gun, Shizuoka Prefecture
Merck Japan	Switzerland	Pharmaceuticals	Iwaki-shi, Fukushima Prefecture
Ginma Japan	USA	Medical instruments and machines	Gotemba-shi, Shizuoka Prefecture
Novo Industry	Denmark	Enzymes	Ishikariwan-shinko, Hokkaido

Source MITI, op. cit.

1978 the number of agreements entered into by UK companies was 135, compared with 870 for the US; 186 for West Germany; and 206 for France.

Foreign investment in Japan

Foreign direct investment

Well over 1,000 foreign investors have already established a direct stake in Japanese industry. The MITI study of 1979 showed that half of these were US companies and there were only 77 UK companies with a stake of less than 20 per cent in equity of Japanese companies. Other findings included:

- 52 per cent of all foreign investors in Japanese firms were in manufacturing industry with a particularly heavy preponderance in the chemical and general machinery section.
- Of a total of 655 foreign-affiliated manufacturing corporations in Japan, 42 per cent (273 corporations) are 50 per cent foreign owned; 26 per cent (172 corporations) are less than 50 per cent foreign owned and 32 per cent (210 corporations) are more then 50 per cent foreign owned.
- Although foreign affiliated Japanese firms were responsible for only 2.2 per cent of total sales of all Japanese enterprises in 1977, their share of certain business sectors has been increasing steadily and average profitability is consistently greater than domestic Japanese enterprises.

Joint ventures

Until the early 1970s wholly owned subsidiaries were discouraged. It was much easier to establish with 50 per cent or less of the equity. Measures in 1973 and 1975 allowed foreign investment of up to 100 per cent by new enterprises but still controlled certain activities (e.g. nuclear energy, power, light and gas supply, manufacture of aircraft, arms and explosives) and restricted other activities (e.g. agriculture, forestry and fishing, petroleum and mining, leather and leather products manufacture). Even so, approval was automatic up to an ownership level of less than 10 per cent for a single foreign investor and less than 25 per cent for all foreign investors (15 per cent in the case of fisheries) provided that no one designated by the foreign investors was proposed as a director of the new company. Approval was also automatic up to a foreign ownership of 50 per cent in a new enterprise in the mining industry. The amended law on foreign exchange and foreign trade control came into effect in 1980, introducing a prior reporting procedure, with in-depth examination of foreign investments confined to the restricted industries. Joint ventures still remain popular because they utilise the Japanese company's existing distribution network and leave personnel problems to the Japanese partner. However, the partners must agree on marketing methods; pricing policy; and definition of export areas. Joint ventures have tended to move away from distribution towards semi-processing to supply local manufacturing capacity. Provisions of the Anti-Monopoly Law and Fair Trade Commission should be given close examination in relation to each stage of an expanding joint venture. The majority of investments receive clearance from the Bank of Japan in two weeks. Remittance of profit or capital requires the permission of the Bank of Japan, but no difficulties should normally be encountered over this. Tax on the income of branches follows the same general lines as that on joint ventures or wholly owned subsidiaries.

Industrial co-operation: a better alternative to protectionism

Much of the response of the Western industrialised nations has been spent in terms of debating the merits and demerits of protectionism. The Japanese have been embarrassingly successful in their global trade of

Table 12.7
Direct Japanese overseas investment by country and region

Country or territory	1981			1982			Cumulative total 1951–1982		
	No. of cases	Amount ($million)	Share (%)	No. of cases	Amount ($million)	Share (%)	No. of cases	Amount ($million)	Share (%)
USA	896	2,354	26.4	859	2,738	35.5	9,995	13,970	26.3
Canada	65	167	1.9	52	167	2.2	599	1,255	2.4
North America total	961	2,522	28.2	911	2,905	37.7	10,594	15,225	28.7
Brazil	53	316	3.5	31	322	4.2	1,215	3,545	6.7
Panama	225	614	6.9	260	722	9.4	1,064	2,022	3.8
Mexico	16	82	0.9	12	143	1.9	207	1,042	2.0
Peru	2	4	0.0	8	185	2.4	91	679	1.3
Bermuda	6	32	0.4	2	5	0.1	65	410	0.8
Cayman Islands	1	26	0.3	4	6	0.1	48	215	0.4
Argentina	12	58	0.6	9	45	0.6	106	145	0.3
Chile	1	3	0.0	6	13	0.2	50	140	0.3
Puerto Rico	3	15	0.2	2	6	0.1	37	140	0.3
Venezuela	6	7	0.1	5	8	0.1	76	129	0.2
Antilles	—	—	—	3	31	0.4	28	113	0.2
Others	28	24	0.3	27	19	0.2	440	270	0.5
Latin America total	353	1,181	13.2	369	1,503	19.5	3,427	8,852	16.7
Indonesia	88	2,434	27.3	84	410	5.3	1,148	7,268	13.7
Hongkong	178	329	3.7	161	400	5.2	2,002	1,825	3.4
Singapore	164	266	3.0	154	180	2.3	1,373	1,383	2.6
Republic of Korea	33	73	0.8	26	103	1.3	1,105	1,312	2.5
Malaysia	41	31	0.3	77	83	1.1	720	764	1.4
Philippines	28	72	0.8	19	34	0.4	583	721	1.4
Thailand	52	31	0.3	66	94	1.2	853	521	1.0
Taiwan	98	54	0.6	65	55	0.7	1,225	479	0.9
Brunei	—	5	0.1	—	—	—	19	100	0.2
Others	30	43	0.5	17	25	0.3	316	180	0.3
Asia total	712	3,338	37.4	669	1,384	18.0	9,344	14,552	27.4
Saudi Arabia-Kuwait	—	50	0.6	—	41	0.5	4	1,113	2.1
Iran	—	0	0.0	—	0	0.0	108	1,002	1.9
Saudi Arabia	10	45	0.5	13	57	0.7	73	225	0.4
Others	7	1	0.0	7	26	0.3	89	139	0.3
Middle East total	17	96	1.1	20	124	1.6	274	2,479	4.7
UK	49	110	1.2	64	176	2.3	829	2,296	4.3
West Germany	55	116	1.3	76	194	2.5	604	808	1.5
France	31	54	0.6	35	102	1.3	529	540	1.0
Netherlands	20	138	1.5	24	73	0.9	201	509	1.0
Belgium	15	107	1.2	10	64	0.8	202	462	0.9
Switzerland	12	67	0.8	16	79	1.0	145	337	0.6
Luxemburg	5	104	1.2	6	127	1.6	56	336	0.6
Spain	11	39	0.4	11	19	0.2	111	231	0.4
USSR	—	—	—	—	—	—	6	193	0.4
Ireland	7	21	0.2	2	6	0.1	50	176	0.3
Italy	9	28	0.3	11	19	0.2	109	114	0.2
Others	15	14	0.2	17	17	0.2	181	145	0.3
Europe total	229	798	8.9	272	876	11.4	3,023	6,146	11.6
Liberia	68	466	5.2	69	434	5.6	483	1,692	3.2
Zaire	6	12	0.1	5	11	0.1	56	267	0.5
Nigeria	4	1	0.0	5	2	0.0	83	156	0.3
Zambia	2	55	0.6	1	20	0.3	15	120	0.2

Table 12.7 continued

	1981			1982			Cumulative total 1951–1982		
Country or territory	No. of cases	Amount ($million)	Share (%)	No. of cases	Amount ($million)	Share (%)	No. of cases	Amount ($million)	Share (%)
Others	24	39	0.4	19	22	0.3	286	274	0.5
Africa total	104	573	6.4	99	489	6.3	923	2,507	4.7
Australia	108	348	3.9	138	370	4.8	972	2,882	5.4
New Zealand	41	56	0.6	50	31	0.4	178	212	0.4
Papua New Guinea	16	7	0.1	11	10	0.1	159	177	0.3
Others	22	13	0.1	13	10	0.1	169	98	0.2
Oceania total	187	424	4.7	212	421	5.5	1,478	3,370	6.3
Grand total	2,563	8,931	100.0	2,552	7,703	100.0	29,063	53,131	100.0

Source Ministry of Finance, 'Direct overseas investment registered during fiscal year 1982', Foreign Press Centre, Japan, Report R-83-2, June 1983.

technologies which they have originally imported and developed themselves. One such example in machine tools is Fujitsu Fanuc which controls half the world market for numerically-controlled machine tools although they did not invent them. Another is the House of Fraser decision to open a Harrods shop within Tokyo's giant Mitsukoshi store. Marks and Spencer Plc faced initial success with their range of products in 50 Daiei stores but then sales peaked and thought had to be given as to how to increase sales to the consumer. M & S are now developing St Michael boutiques in Japan for a Daiei chain which is seeking to move up-market. Such cases of startling Japanese export success are found alongside domestic non-tariff barriers and a domestic currency which defies international pressure for revaluation. This has led to the creation of a trade ombudsman to handle complaints concerning imports. It remains to be seen whether this is simply a delaying tactic or a sincere response. As things stand, each and every official Japanese movement – whether Cabinet changes or an economic mission of the leading Japanese industrialists to Europe – is scrutinised for meaning whilst in such areas as car exports, the Japanese are asked to exercise what is termed 'voluntary restraint'. By restricting the Japanese manufacturers to approximately 11 per cent of the British market, shiploads can be planned to the point where a Japanese car sold on the UK market is new – because of the voluntary quota – whilst a British car, because of having stockpiles of unsold inventory, will generally be at least 15 months old at the time of sale. Protectionism in this case has turned to disadvantage.

Consider next the argument for co-operation, part of the official Japanese response to reduce the EEC deficit with Japan of 10.7 billion dollars. Industrial co-operation is a phenomenon born of our times. Market development costs plus the size of market required to ensure a return on investment have led to the bringing together of industrial producers in a number of different areas, the most highly publicised of which has been the Honda–British Leyland agreement.

Table 12.8
Direct Japanese overseas investment by industry and region (cumulative total end 1982)

	North America		Latin America		Asia		Middle East	
	No. of cases	Amount ($million)	No. of cases	Amount ($million)	No. of cases	Amount ($million)	No. of cases	Amount ($million)
Manufacturing industry								
Foods	311	367	96	154	335	176	1	0
Textiles	115	217	142	372	635	1,002	3	4
Lumber-pulp	73	426	38	189	252	162	—	—
Chemicals	151	384	112	521	637	990	21	1,009
Iron-nonferrous	100	435	83	1,037	510	1,487	10	59
Machinery	294	417	111	296	545	367	6	10
Electrical machinery	301	1,141	105	273	859	643	5	12
Transport machines	59	614	42	488	180	350	5	4
Others	313	250	98	103	990	623	16	39
Total	1,717	4,250	827	3,435	4,943	5,800	67	1,137
Non-manufacturing industry								
Agriculture/Forestry	136	233	173	163	321	235	3	2
Fisheries	62	85	80	83	140	83	5	1
Mining	210	776	134	1,404	164	5,383	9	39
Construction	151	166	62	142	260	128	45	28
Commerce	4,188	5,332	478	651	1,664	652	48	12
Finance/Insurance	124	1,546	92	470	182	360	15	50
Services	696	627	126	237	472	1,115	12	4
Shipping	46	25	447	1,140	52	78	3	2
Real estate	138	426	12	10	14	39	—	—
Others	856	1,182	850	1,060	505	500	31	85
Total	6,607	10,398	2,454	5,359	3,774	8,573	171	223
Establishment/expansion of branch offices	265	92	47	35	465	142	35	1,117
Real estate	2,005	485	99	23	169	37	1	2
Grand total	10,594	15,225	3,427	8,852	9,344	14,552	274	2,479

	Europe		Africa		Oceania		Total	
	No. of cases	Amount	No. of cases	Amount	No. of cases	Amount	No. of cases	Amount
Manufacturing industry								
Foods	32	44	29	8	42	57	846	806
Textiles	81	156	50	39	8	6	1,034	1,795
Lumber-pulp	1	0	1	0	75	122	440	899
Chemicals	68	158	8	16	18	99	1,015	3,176
Iron-nonferrous	295	171	25	82	84	338	1,107	3,608
Machinery	99	145	—	—	21	30	1,076	1,265
Electrical machinery	87	226	7	5	11	21	1,375	2,322
Transport machines	15	115	5	8	12	242	318	1,822
Others	102	166	8	6	25	70	1,552	1,258
Total	780	1,181	133	154	296	985	8,763	16,952
Non-manufacturing industry								
Agriculture/Forestry	2	0	12	7	164	84	811	723
Fisheries	4	2	72	57	101	46	464	358
Mining	9	859	126	556	187	1,274	839	10,291
Construction	16	40	13	19	13	12	560	536
Commerce	1,364	1,455	21	5	353	376	8,116	8,482

Table 12.8 continued

	Europe		Africa		Oceania		Total	
	No. of cases	Amount	No. of cases	Amount	No. of cases	Amount	No. of cases	Amount
Non-manufacturing industry								
Finance/Insurance	173	1,288	13	3	31	85	630	3,802
Services	94	125	53	520	77	90	1,530	2,717
Shipping	7	1	97	396	6	6	658	1,649
Real estate	9	37	—	—	14	9	187	521
Others	221	947	351	777	155	385	2,969	4,937
Total	1,899	4,755	758	2,340	1,101	2,367	16,744	34,016
Establishment/expansion								
of branch offices	164	171	11	1	11	10	998	1,568
Real estate	180	38	21	2	70	7	2,538	595
Grand total	3,023	6,146	923	2,507	1,478	3,370	29,063	53,131

Source Ministry of Finance *op cit.*

Outlining the basis for an agreement – to ensure a community of interests and like benefits and to define the respective duties of either party – is an essential prerequisite. A case study investigation of two Japanese factories matched with one British factory and one American, found that the implications for public policy were:

1. Direct investment of Japanese companies is not likely to have an immediate or substantial effect on local development.
2. Once Japanese multinationals establish their factories, they are less likely to shift their operations to some other region.
3. New investment in modernisation and automation of production will not be able to make domestic companies competitive against Japanese.
4. A licensing agreement with, or takeover by, the Japanese would not be effective measures to revive competitiveness of the domestic industry.

In so far as Britain is concerned, the possible avenues for Japanese participation in British manufacturing industry have been reduced to joint venture or acquisition with public anxiety over the Japanese challenge to European industry, as in the case of Hitachi in Britain.

Meanwhile, the reverse flow of foreign direct investment into Japan is increasing. The April – September 1981 half-year forecast reported 482 cases as opposed to 388 for the comparable six months the year before. The value of the investment had also risen 77.5 per cent to 213 million dollars. Amongst the West European countries West Germany and France had eight investments in the half-year; UK six; Switzerland five; and Italy three. General Motors is collaborating with Toyota to produce small cars to be sold as Chevrolets. Thorn-EMI, Telefunken and Thomson have all sought JVC's designs for video cassette recorders and use Japanese components in their new European production plants. More recently, Kodak announced its plans for combined 8 mm video cameras and recorders, buying in machines from Matsushita and tape from TDK but using the Kodak brand name. Nachi-Fujikoshi, the third largest Japanese ball-bearing manufacturer has switched its capital expenditure into robot production and is looking for high growth in overseas markets for robots. It has entered into a joint venture with Advanced Robotics of the United States whereby it hopes to sell about 300 arc-welding robots in the US and Canada over the next few years. Another Japanese company, Fujitsu Fanuc has joint venture agreements with Siemens of West Germany, the British 600 Group, and with General Motors in the United States. The Fujitsu-Fanuc-GM venture is to design, manufacture, and sell robotic systems and GM is presently known to be keen to modernise its production plants. Elsewhere, Samkyo Seiki Manufacturing and IBM entered a joint venture, whereby IBM will market a low-cost Japanese manufactured robot in the United States under the IBM name. Other ventures known to exist include Westinghouse Electric with Komatsu and Yaskawa Electric Manufacturing with Machine Intelligence Corporation and Hobart Corporation. In France, Toray and Elf Aquitaine have formed a joint venture to go into carbon fibres. Fujitsu, Toshiba, and others are also getting ready to start European production of integrated circuits. Japanese investments have created approximately 26,000 jobs within the EEC.

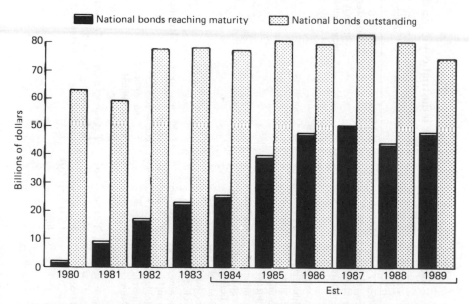

Figure 12.5 Japan's need to refinance its massive debt will drive up interest rates

Note Japan's budget deficit in 1983 was 13,345 million yen or 4.77 per cent of GNP in 1983.
Source Business Week, 5 March 1984.

Another much publicised venture has been the Honda link with British Leyland to produce a new model to replace the ageing Triumph Dolomite.

Table 12.9

Recent examples of major industrial co-operation projects involving Japan

	USA	UK	W Germany	France	Italy	Netherlands	Belgium
Consumer electronics	I. Colour TV sets, microwave ovens, audio equipment, refrigerators	I. Colour TV sets, VTRs	I. VTRs	I. Audio T. Transfer of technology for image orthicons and VTRs			
Computers, ICs and communications equipment	I. ICs, telephone switchboards, information processing equipment T. Communications equipment cross-licensing, extension of OCR production technology	I. ICs T. Transfer of computer technology O. Semi-conductor button telephones	I. ICs O. Computers		T. Transfer of design technology for semi-conductors, joint development of logic circuits		
Industrial machinery	I. Machine tools T. Transfer of technology and joint development in robotics	I. Robots T. Transfer of robot technology	I. Machine tools, ceramic conductors T. Transfer of NC equipment technology	I. Machine tools	T. Technical tie-ups for MCs		
Automobiles	I. Motorcycles, compact cars, small trucks	T. Transfer of automobile technology O. Battery fork lifts	T. Co-operation in the passenger car field	T. Transfer of motorcycle technology	I. Compact cars, motorcycles T. Technical tie-ups involving assembly and manufacture of passenger cars		

Table 12.9 continued

	USA	UK	W Germany	France	Italy	Netherlands	Belgium
Aircraft	T. Joint development of civil aircraft (3-country joint project involving Japan, USA and Italy)	T. Development of jet engines for civil aircraft (five-nation joint project involving Japan, USA, UK, W. Germany and Italy)	T. Joint Development of helicopters				
Others	I. Automobile air conditioners and headlights, automobile tyres and inner tubes T. Introduction of space technology, cross-licensing of ion-exchange membranes O. Ultrasonic diagnostic equipment	I. Videotapes T. Introduction of production technology for silicon carbide sintered products M. Hydroelectric power plant, fertiliser project	T. Treatment technology for waste products or nuclear fuel, introduction of electro-magnetic valve technology M. Factory for cold rolled sheet, dam, harbour facilities	I. Videocassette tapes, carbon fibre M. Thermopower plant, petroleum refining plant	T. Introduction of technology for polypropylene moulding machines M. Gas pipeline	I. Plate glass, film T. Transfer of soda plant technology	I. Glass, plate glass T. Transfer of manufacturing technology for vaporisation equipment M. Thermopower plant, fertiliser project

Notes
1. I – Investment exchange; T – Technological exchange; M – Market co-operation in a third country; O – OEM agreement.
2. 'Investment exchange' takes the forms of local production by Japanese firms and joint ventures undertaken with a foreign partner.
3. The term 'OEM agreement' refers to an arrangement under which a Japanese manufacturer produces and exports a certain category of product under the brand name of its foreign partner.
4. This table lists projects undertaken from fiscal 1978 through the end of fiscal 1982.

Source MITI, 'White Paper on International Trade 1983', Tokyo, November 1983.

As a former vociferous critic of Japanese car imports into the UK, the British Leyland received some wry comment over the deal. One commentator contrasted BL with 'the vicar, whom having spent months preaching about the evils of adultery, finally runs off with the curate's wife'. For BL, the financial stake in production of this new much-needed lower medium sector Japanese car, the Triumph Acclaim, the investment is only £70 million, most of which involves a paint factory at Cowley which can be used for other BL cars. This compares favourably with the £240 million which, it is estimated, would be required to develop a new model from scratch. For Honda, there are the benefits of exports of engines and transmission systems plus a royalty on each car sold plus a manufacturing facility within the Common Market. Whether, as has been maintained, the Acclaim will prove to be a one-off market filler remains to be seen. The car industry is such that negotiations are constantly taking place over possible joint ventures and industrial co-operation on the development of engines and gear-boxes. A close association with Honda may therefore blossom into a more permanent relationship, as has happened with industrial co-operation ventures elsewhere. Meanwhile, a test case in Italy has already established the Honda-BL Acclaim to be a British car, by virtue of the last substantial part of production, amounting in this case to 60 per cent by volume or 70 per cent by price.

Another example of co-operation is that between ICL with Fujitsu. This venture provides for co-operation in marketing, technology and semi-conductor purchasing. ICL, in return for agreeing to market Fujitsu computers, receives early access to the Japanese group's computer technology. Under this deal ICL would also purchase substantial quantities of microchips. For ICL, it presents an opportunity to restructure and complete its product range without over-reaching its already thin resources. For Fujitsu, there is the obvious advantage of market access, technology sharing and exports.

Rowntree-Mackintosh exports its more expensive boxed confectionery through Dodwell, the Inchcape trading subsidiary which also handles a number of other British firms including Royal Doulton. Other Rowntree-Mackintosh lines such as Polo, Golden Toffee Wafer, and Kit-Kat which now sells 2,000 tons a year in Japan, are manufactured locally by the Fujiya Confectionery Company. British confectionery is said, though, to be too sweet for the Japanese palate and so some product modification may still be required.

In other industries such as industrial robotics, petrochemicals, and tele-communications, agreements have been signed between Hitachi and GEC; ICI and Mitsui Petrochemical; Hitachi and Thomson; and Fujitsu and Siemens. TI and Fairchild are establishing semiconductor plants in Japan.

The potential for industrial co-operation

Yet further possibilities present themselves if one considers the importance of the Japanese Soga-Shoshas, the trading houses, with their worldwide network of offices and speciality in Eurodollar lending. Mr Ikeda of

Marubeni Corporation, the fourth largest Japanese trading company has gone on record as having 17 per cent of his corporation's turnover in the form of 'third-country' trade, i.e. where Marubeni trade the products of, say, a Western supplier to a third country in, say, West Africa (Reference 7).

Whilst a recession lasts and while interest rates in the West are double those prevailing in Japan, reasons abound for inertia amongst Western nations. Interest rate differentials provoke massive international monetary displacements. Japan, again peculiarly with a large amount of savings deposits, is relatively insulated from such shocks. By way of comparison, Britain, with its network of building societies, would appear to be investing its savings in unproductive investments.

The first advantage to the Japanese then is in capital and, secondly, in their dominance of the technologies which they have acquired and developed. For meaningful co-operation to develop there has to be a mutually profitable exchange. At the moment, there is the universal impression of the Japanese being interested only in selling, not buying. Given a more outward-looking breadth of perspective, opportunities for Anglo-Japanese co-operation exist in the following areas.

Ongoing research and development and technology improvements. Already this is taking place as we have seen in computers, but scope exists to do likewise on other sectors of electronics or automotive engineering, an area in which the UK is particularly skilled.

Marketing and distribution in third markets is about to be embarked upon by BL with 10,000 Triumph Acclaim sales per year in continental Europe.

Joint entry into third markets was hinted at as a possible means of developing Anglo-Japanese trade and reducing a trade imbalance. Presently, this does not exist but could certainly do so.

Co-production and specialisation of production. Co-operation is true of BL, manufacturing 70 per cent by value of the Triumph Acclaim. Specialisation is also included but to a lesser degree as this particular agreement is of a shorter nature to that of the ICL-Fujitsu co-operation where there is clearer product line specialisation taking place over time.

Financial services offered by the Sogo Shoshas would imply a certain synergy with those of our own institutions. As yet this remains to be developed although banking institutions are finding Japan to be an attractive site for location, given that Tokyo will soon emerge as a world financial centre on a par with London and New York.

The West has been demanding, and has had their request sustained, for an ombudsman for Japanese foreign trade in view of the complex Japanese administrative blocks, and major non-tariff barriers (57 non- tariff barriers including import inspection, guarantees, testing, etc.). Tariffs were reduced on 323 items including chocolate, biscuits, agricultural tractors and tobacco as of April 1983. Simplification and improvement of import inspection procedures and the strengthening of the Office of the Trade Ombudsman are also being sought.

The anachronism of the Japanese financial system

Pressures for change in the Japanese financial system arise due to:

1. **Plentiful supply of capital**. Japan is awash in capital, and exports it. Japan was the largest single supplier of savings for the world in 1984, now OPEC is no longer a source of new cash.
2. **Domestic dissent**. Affluent savers want higher yields, corporate borrowers want more choice, and the strongest banks and brokerage houses are chafing under restrictions unlike those found in any other major market.
3. **High Debt**. In 1983 this amounted to 425 billion dollars. A mountain of outstanding government debt reaches maturity in 1985 and that makes it impossible for monetary authorities to continue controlling domestic interest rates by government fiat.
4. **Impatient foreigners**. The patience of foreign banks and businessmen with Japan's closed capital markets has run out. Unless some reciprocal privileges are offered soon, they are threatening to hold up the expansion of Japanese banks in their markets.

Japan has been inching its way towards financial liberalisation since it passed a major revision of its Foreign Exchange Law in 1980. The revision abolished formal controls that enabled the government to regulate all foreign-currency transactions by Japanese residents. In theory, the new law allowed a free flow of funds in and out of Japan, but in practice the government used administrative guidance with its banks to make sure they restricted flows.

If capital flows were free a huge rush of money would quickly leave Japan at current interest rates. In the short term, the yen would weaken but Japanese interest rates set by the market would then go up and capital would flow back into Japan. Unfortunately, the yen would be stronger than it is and Japanese companies would have to compete on the same basis with the same finance costs as Western companies.

Freer yen flows would also bring wider use of the currency. Only 2–3 per cent of Japan's imports and 42 per cent of its exports are denominated in yen as against 43.7 per cent and 82.5 per cent for West Germany in Deutschmarks (Reference 8). Although Japan accounts for 10 per cent of the free world's GNP the yen accounts for just 3.6 per cent of reserves held by foreign countries: Thus compares with 71.4 per cent held in dollars and 11.6 per cent in Deutschmarks. Yen-denominated assets accounted for only 1.4 per cent of total Euromarket business in 1983.

Structural change in the Japanese economy

Growth of the service sector together with the appearance of new electronics industries has served to keep the Japanese economy moving during the past few years while traditional pillars of the economic system have been crumbling (investment in services sector more than double that of either the auto or steel industries). However, the new 'soft' industries, as they have been called by government ministers, have brought problems as well. According to the Finance Ministry which created the term 'softnomics' (in a book on the Japanese economy issued in early 1983) the new trend means first and foremost that the government has become seriously short of information about what is happening in the economy.

Service sector companies as well as many of the small high-technology companies, as the major users of robots and numerically-controlled machines, tend to be small enough to attract the attention of Japanese tax authorities and they are unlikely to be invited to become members of the various industry associations through which Japanese economic ministers keep in touch with different sectors of the economy.

A further problem posed by the growth of the new soft sectors is that of statistical definition. Japan's Industrial Taxation Index which generally has been regarded as a key economic indicator is based overwhelmingly on the product of the traditional 'hard' industries. A new industrial production index which makes due allowances for soft sectors of the economy is seen as an urgent necessity by the Ministry of Finance and is in fact in the process of preparation.

Services require less, but more frequent, investment than steel or shipyards. Thus the questions arise as to whether they are more stable and whether it is possible to plan the necessary investment cycles more accurately than has been possible with other industries.

References

1. Lorenz, C., 'How Japan "cascades" through Western Markets', *Financial Times*, November 9, 1981.
2. Paliwoda, S. J., *Joint East-West Marketing and Production Ventures*, Gower, 1981.
3. Wright Boulton, J. and Jenney, B. W., 'Secrets of Japanese Success', *Management Today*, January 1981, p. 64.
4. Shimaguchi, Mibucki and Lazer, W., 'Japanese distribution channels, invisible barriers to market entry', *MSU Business Topics*, Winter 1979.
   Czinkota, M. R., 'Distribution of consumer products in Japan; an overview'. National Center for Export Import Studies, Georgetown University, Washington DC, USA, *Staff Paper 17*, February 1985.
5. Wagenaar, Jan Dirk, 'Advertising in Japan', *Marketing Trends*, No. 2, 1980, pp. 4–5.
6. *Financial Times*, 'Japanese Industry Survey', 12 December 1983; 'Japan Survey', 23 July 1984. *Import Procedures and Industrial Property Rights in Japan*, BOTB, London, 1979. MITI, *White Paper on International Trade 1983*, Tokyo, November 1983.
7. Keizan Koho Center (Japan Institute for Social and Economic Affairs) KKC Brief No. 15, January 1984, *Sogo Shoshas Spearhead a Growth Area – Third Country Trade*.
8. *Business Week*, 'A wary Japan starts to open up its financial markets', 5 March 1984, pp. 30–3.

Recommended further reading

Financial Times, 'Japanese ski makers freeze out the opposition', 11 August, 1986.
Mark Smalley, 'Through Japan's half-open door', *Management Today*, October 1986, pp. 88–94.

13. *MARKETING TO NIGERIA*

Nigeria is essentially a raw-material supplying LDC (least developed country) since it is dependent on oil for 94 per cent of exports. There is a scarcity of data on Nigeria. *The Economist* in a special survey commented that 'This is the first survey published by *The Economist* in which every single number is probably wrong, there is no accurate information about Nigeria', and then went on to say that nobody knows how many Nigerians there are and that according to cynical government officials, nobody ever will. The total is therefore somewhere between 80 and 120 million. Needless to say, this makes life for the country's environmental planners virtually impossible, as no one can say with any certainty how many schools, hospitals or houses are needed, nor how much food or water or electricity is required. Nor can there be any agreement about what should be the appropriate political representation if there is no agreement as to the size of the constituencies.

A population census was held in 1973 but its findings (79.7 million) were annulled after allegations of rigging. There are no plans as yet for another official census mainly because the problems of surmounting election malpractices remain. The official 1963 count, two years after independence, gave 55.7 million, and averaging 2.5 per cent growth p.a., this would yield 88 million by the end of 1981; but since Nigerians have large families a more feasible growth rate of 3.5 per cent would give 113 million, plus immigration from Chad (civil war), Niger (drought) and Ghana, a much poorer economy. A similar extrapolation of the 1973 figure would give 106 million today. The Nigerian Census Board issued an official estimate of 94 million in 1984. By year 2000 a population of 200 million is likely at current rates of growth, which will consume twice today's oil production plus twice the food currently produced. The future therefore is a bleak one of impending catastrophe.

Nigeria is the most populous and economically powerful nation in Black Africa, but remains a developing country struggling to come to terms with its oil wealth. It is the giant of Africa, one of the world's 10 most populous nations, strategically vital, and rich in natural resources, especially oil.

Foreign trade

In the years immediately after World War II agricultural products provided 78.7 per cent of Nigeria's export earnings while more than 60 per cent of its imports came from the UK. By 1980 oil accounted for 96.1 per cent of export earnings with the UK providing 22 per cent of Nigeria's imports.

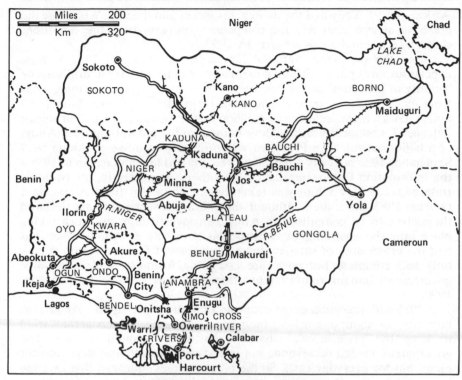

Figure 13.1 Map of Nigeria

Behind these figures are the fundamental shifts in Nigeria's trading. Its range of suppliers has widened largely to embrace more West European countries but the spread of its earnings has narrowed. It remains a mere exporter of raw materials and importer of manufactures. Various attempts have been made towards a national development policy but these have been at risk for the following reasons.

1. Smuggling – imports officially came to $16.7 billion in 1982 but the true figure must have been higher (despite the M Form, explained later).
2. Government has only limited control over the size of its export revenue and so responds to its rise and fall with import restrictions.
3. Government is committed to growth of manufactured exports and sees the Economic Community of West African States (ECOWAS) as the most accessible channel but only limited tariff reductions have been agreed and deep-rooted problems like the convertibility of currencies remain. Also, Nigerian non-oil exports which constitute less than 5 per cent of exports have declined sharply.

Oil development plans

With the takings from oil, Nigeria's leaders were going to build a new

African power. They had the money, resources and the will. What they did not have at any level was the competence to carry their fine ambitions through, e.g. building 44 airports by 1990.

Under the projected National Development Plan, for 1981–5, total expenditure was put as 82 billion naira and agriculture was put firmly as the 'priority of priorities' as the best means of diversifying the economy away from its dependency on oil. The main recipients were agriculture (10.7 billion naira); manufacturing (6.4 billion naira); housing (2.7 billion naira); defence (7.3 billion naira) and development of the federal capital at Abuja (2.5 billion naira). The President was originally to move to Abuja by 7 September 1982 but only a partial movement had taken place up to 1985 – the Information Department and a few others. Significantly, the National Independence Day salute was taken by the President from Abuja on 1 October 1983. Since then, although the military government have declared themselves to be committed to Abuja, an investigation has been taking place into the awarding of construction contracts in Abuja which has had the effect only of slowing down development further. Abuja is now only half complete but costs are escalating furiously while successive governments remain committed to a three-phase move to be completed by 1990.

In 1981 with recession in the countries that buy Nigerian oil – Americans buy most, or about one-fifth of their imported supply – the Nigerians tried to keep the price above what the customers wanted to pay. The government needed oil revenue not just to sustain ambitious development plans, but for everyday cash. So the oil companies squeezed that revenue by cutting exports from Nigeria from a high in 1980 of around 2 million barrels a day to a low in August 1981 of approximately half a million barrels a day. Non-Opec Britain briefly overtook Nigeria as a supplier to North America.

Nigeria's profile as a development-hungry oil giant is less likely to attract lenders especially as Nigeria refinanced $2 billion foreign debt in 1983. Debt servicing will account for one-third of exports in 1985 ($12 billion). Medium term debt is estimated at $11 billion with short-term obligations of some additional $6–8 billion. Meanwhile reserves have fallen to $1.3 billion barely one month's import cover. Nigeria has been producing oil at 1.6 million barrels per day above its growth of 1.3 b/d, a level which will be hard to sustain as negotiations continue with the IMF over a $2.5 billion loan but have been sticking over the issue of naira devaluation. Inflation in 1984 was 38 per cent but is quickening under the domestic impact of heavy government expenditure plus the rise in minimum wage and the international oil glut. Countertrade has risen sharply from $500m in 1984 to $2 billion in 1985 and almost 15% of 1984 exports and most of its export growth.

Nigerian economic potential

In developing a wide industrial base, Nigeria is looking toward turning itself into Africa's manufacturing giant. Investment in steel plant alone has been running at £1 billion at Ajaokuta where a Russian-designed steel mill based on outmoded technology below the Benue-Niger confluences produces expensive poor quality steel from low-grade local ore and coal. One day when the rivers have been dammed for year-round navigation and power this may seem a good idea.

Other major infrastructure projects include ambitious programmes for power, telecommunications, roads, water supply, and oil-related plants producing such products as nitrogenous fertilisers. To date, nothing has been done to tap the natural gas reserves of Nigeria estimated to be 85 trillion c.ft of proven reserves in the oil rich Niger delta. Gas exploitation projects have either been stalled or are making little progress.

In 1980 the UK share of the Nigeria market was worth about £1.2 billion with exports alone almost doubling compared to 1979. But most of the giant development projects are going to other European countries and the US and Japan. Increasing pressures for countertrade have changed this situation jettisoning Brazil forward from a 1.5 per cent market share to being one of its main suppliers in 1985 as a result of a $1 billion countertrade oil deal which involves the use of an escrow account. The French are actively engaged now in countertrade negotiations and are the only Western nation to have experienced an upturn in sales to Nigeria in recent years. The UK share has been stagnating.

Regulations on exporting

The 'M' form and Pre-Shipment Inspection are two facets of selling to Nigeria that deter exporters (Reference 2). The Société Générale de Surveillance (SGS) the world's largest trade inspection group is no longer the agent of the Nigerian government but the system which they helped create is an integral part of the Nigerian government's system of import controls.

The licensing system decides what the country should buy abroad and the M Form system introduced in 1979 by the Central Bank has given the government for the first time some measure of what Nigeria spends in foreign currency, and their inspection agents act to check that the country buys what it requires at reasonable prices. That is the theory but there is no means of establishing exactly how successful this approach has been.

Meanwhile in 1984 the foreign exchange limit on expenditure was $10.4 billion, 15 per cent down on 1983 import levels and 38 per cent down on 1982 and 60 per cent down on 1980 levels. With all imports placed on licence and the Ministry of Commerce and Industries only issuing these licences in the middle of the year, this was a further curb to imports. Furthermore, the government limited the amount of foreign exchange available to each bank on a strict pro rota basis according to its assessment of need. By the time companies had secured an import licence their banks had exceeded the monthly foreign exchange allocation.

The total effect of these increases has been to allow government to reach its financial targets but as Nigerian industry depends on raw materials and parts, this has cut production by up to 50 per cent. The size of her population plus import dependency makes Nigeria still the most important export market in black Africa. The main benefit of the regulations for Nigeria is that export regulations act as a deterrent to those seeking to make overpriced sales into the Nigerian market or to make fraudulent sales. Lagos businessmen claim that it has had some success.

It is the deterrent which then attracts the Nigerian government. A Central Bank report noted that SGS estimated that savings on the import bill through deterrents would be at least five times the visible savings. Visible foreign exchange savings in 1980, the second year of SGS's Nigerian operation were 176.8 million naira or 163.5 per cent more than in 1979. This saving constitutes 3.5 per cent of the f.o.b. value of the goods inspected by SGS. So the Central Bank estimated that the cumulative savings on foreign exchange in 1979 and 1980 through the deterrent effect was 1.2 billion naira. This is the rough equivalent of one month's import bill. But against this has to be set the charges of SGS, calculated as a percentage of the value of the goods it inspects. These came to 36 million naira in 1980 and 16.6 million in 1979. In 1982, the estimated savings were N409.7 million.

When the SGS inspection procedures before shipment were introduced in 1979, they caused confusion among importers and those selling to Nigeria, but the system has now bedded down and the sharp edge of the system has been blunted. The pre-shipment inspection scheme is just something else the trading community has to live with. It cuts out the worst abuses of Nigeria's insatiable desire for imports and can check that basic materials are not over-priced. For imports with a high technological content, and where there is a high level of added value, the ability of this scheme to secure prices is much less effective.

Without a correctly completed M Form (and the Central Bank maintains tight control) the exporter cannot be paid. But difficulties often occur because exporters are unaware that the M Form has to be completed by the importers and requires comprehensive information on the goods. The onus therefore lies with the exporter to pass the correct information to his buyer. The information covers f.o.b. price, freight, and ancillary charges. In addition, the importer is required to produce tax clearance and (in the case of raw materials) approved manufacturer certificates.

Once the M Form has been approved by the Central Bank the importer can open a letter of credit and confirm the order. Some goods are subject to pre-shipment inspection but it is as well to check with the inspection agency beforehand. Exporters shipping prior to the M Form gaining Central Bank approval or without PSI (pre-shipment inspection) are liable to forfeit payment or to have the goods confiscated.

The Comprehensive Import Supervision System (CISS)

Following some dissatisfaction and allegations against the operations of the SGS, the new Federal Military Government which seized power on 31 December 1983 decided to terminate the contract of SGS on the 30 September 1984. A new Comprehensive Import Supervision Scheme

(CISS) which zoned the world into three regions for pre-shipment inspection purposes was established (Reference 3). Under the new CISS arrangement, three new pre-shipment inspection agents were appointed as against one in 1979 when the system was first introduced. Each of the agents or group of agents was given the responsibility to carry out pre-shipment inspection in one of the zones as shown in Table 13.1. The three regions into which the world was divided are designated as Zones A, B and C. Clearly, each zone covers two continents except Zone A which includes, in addition, the United Kingdom. This suggests that, in addition to proximity of the continents as a basis for zoning, the volume of imports from each of the continents was also considered. This latter reason explains the extraction of the United Kingdom from Zone B where it naturally belongs, into Zone A whose other constituents export much less to Nigeria compared to Zone B.

Table 13.1
Zonal responsibilities of Nigerian pre-shipment inspection agents

Zone	*Agents*
A	
United Kingdom	Cotecna, Inspection, SA, Switzerland
Ireland	Cotecna International comprising
Australia	Overseas Merchandise Inspection
Asia	(OMIC), Japan; Daniel C. Griffiths, UK
B	
Europe (excluding the UK)	Bureau Veritas/
Africa	Thionville (for food imports)
C	
North America (including Canada)	Swede Control/
South America	Intertek

The inspection agents

The new arrangement provides for five inspection agents from different countries. This compares sharply with the terminated contract in which SGS was the sole inspection agent. The new arrangement thus introduces a fair degree of competition as against the total monopoly of SGS.

Cotecna International was a new company comprised of three agents from Switzerland, the United Kingdom and Japan. Cotecna is based in Geneva in Switzerland, and incorporating D. C. Griffiths a British company, and OMIC (Overseas Merchandise Inspection Company) a Japanese firm. The agent responsible for inspecting imports from the UK and Ireland is Cotecna International (UK) Ltd, 2 Perry Road, Witham, Essex, CM8 3TV. The agent for Zone B, Bureau Veritas/Thionville Inc. is a French company while the agent for Zone C, Swede Control/Intertek Services Ltd., is a Swedish firm.

Though engaged on the 1 October 1984, the new agents were expected to commence effective operation by 1 November 1984. This one-month interim fuelled concern about the change and awakened old worries relating to disruption of trade. It took, for example, more than 12 months for the SGS contract to work relatively smoothly because of the need to train enough personnel, to expand offices, and for the Central Bank of Nigeria to master the operation of the M Form. The new agents, therefore, require time to come to terms with the additional requirements of the new contract upon their resources.

Why the change?

From the point of view of the Federal Military Government the change to a new inspection arrangement was necessary to introduce competition and terminate the monopoly of SGS. This would effect a higher degree of efficiency in performance and hence lead to the achievement of the foreign exchange saving objective of the government. The new system would also be cost effective and thus financially beneficial to Nigeria.

Behind these, however, are other reasons for the change. SGS was accused of refusing to train Nigerians to take over complete control of pre-shipment inspection as provided in the contract. It was also alleged that the company was less efficient than it projected itself to be and did not make significant foreign exchange savings for Nigeria. Government officials also claimed that SGS 'showed unacceptable arrogance' to the Military Government and refused to competitise the contract by sharing it with others (Reference 4). Perhaps also in the mind of the Federal Military Government was the scandal that SGS gave bribes to some members of a committee of the defunct House of Representatives of the ousted civilian administration of President Shehu Shagari, to sustain its contract when Shagari's government attempted to review the contract because of its monopoly conditions. Whatever the pros and cons of the change, the question still remains – is pre-shipment inspection, especially by foreign firms, worthwhile? Is there no other way of achieving the required goals?

Advice for British exporters to Nigeria

- Visit the country to get a feel for the market.
- Get to know customers; credit agencies are few and not always reliable.
- Appoint a good agent. Many agents, but not all perform well. Choose carefully.
- Be aggressive and persistent in marketing. Our competitors are not put off by similar problems.
- Do not confine yourself to Lagos – our competitors don't.
- Do your homework; business in Nigeria is hedged about with regulation.
- Be adaptable.
- British companies start with an advantage – capitalise on it.

Joint ventures

Foreigners can now have majority participation (60 per cent) in the production of metal containers, fertilisers and cement, sugar plantations, and processing, as well as agricultural plantations for cash crops. Up to 40 per cent of the equity can be owned by foreigners in insurance and in the manufacture of jewellery and clothes, clock repairing and rice milling. Above all, it was hoped to discourage smuggling (alleged to account for one-third of cigarette consumption in Nigeria).

In the past the Government has not stuck by its promise of protection; import licences are still being issued for imported finished models of some cars.

Under the agreement of increasing local content of their finished product over a given period – usually 10 years – in return for protection for imports, some manufacturers entered. Designated manufacturers in the car sector were VW and Peugeot while commercial vehicles are assembled by BL, Fiat, Mercedes and Steyr–Daimler–Puch. Recently, Ford decided to join Steyr in supplying 2,000 kits a year for trucks. Each of the factories was set up in a different part of the country to spread the benefits of generated employment.

Apart from not keeping its promise, there is the problem of the difficulty of keeping to the schedule of increasing local content unless more component factories are established.

Nigerian stock exchange

The stock exchange is less successful as an aid to companies seeking to raise equity finance; most of the 90 quoted companies in the exchange represent foreign companies that were forced to make flotations as a way of attracting Nigerian majority owners, and since the value of their shares is artificially depressed, these companies have no incentive to issue more shares while others have no interest in going public.

Mobil Nigeria justified a three dollars per share price when 18.6 million were put on sale in December 1978 but the price was set at 1.25 dollars by the Government so shares were quickly taken up, but at a loss to the company, in both equity value as well as control.

Bribery and corruption or 'dash'?

Nothing so annoys and worries foreigners as the unusual demand for bribes called 'dash'. People's deepest loyalty is to the home village and community from which most of them have very recently moved and with which even the most urban maintain strong personal links. The wants of families – infinitely extended through aunts, uncles and cousins in a way incomprehensible to Europeans – are very real. The richest and best-educated Nigerians feel this pull of the home community at least as strongly as the poorest, perhaps because their fathers were village chiefs, with feudal obligations. There is a real and admirable collective solidarity extending beyond the village to the tribe and the whole language group (of which Nigeria has approximately 200) but not to the nation and society as a whole. English therefore remains the national language.

Getting power or money for yourself means sharing within the group. The poorest relation basks in the glory, and may even get some of the money, attained by the successful. Getting rich confers collective merit. Other loyalties – to the public service, the private firm, etc. – can never be as strong as that to the family and its tribal or ethnic extensions. To use a British parallel, the Nigerian who takes bribes sees himself as Robin Hood and not as the Wicked Sheriff of Nottingham.

Summary

Nigerian society

- Tribal divisions are still strong.
- Severely overcrowded Lagos had 0.5 million people in 1960, 4.5 million in 1984.
- Lagos by 2000 AD will have 15 million people if growth continues.
- The new federal capital, Abuja, is as yet incomplete and behind target.
- Societal divisions continue – 'religious' rioting took place in Kano in Dec 1980 and claimed 4,000 dead.
- The population figure is unknown but continues to increase, begging the question whether Nigeria is experiencing Malthusian growth.

The immediate future

The future is uncertain, with continued political instability, and a military regime. Depressed world oil markets are making it difficult for Nigeria to maintain her status quo, never mind expand. It is likely therefore that Nigeria will expand into further oil-related countertrade deals with her trading partners.

References

1. *Economist*, 'Special survey: Nigeria', 23 January 1982.
2. SITPRO, *Nigeria*, London 1984.
3. Central Bank of Nigeria, *Circular Ref. ECD/AD/211/84* of 29 September 1984.
4. *West Africa*, 8 October 1984, p. 2043.
5. Offered by Sir Mervyn Brown, British High Commissioner to Nigeria.

14. *MARKETING TO THE EEC COUNTRIES*

Today the EEC is a market of 270 million people in about 90 million households, a workforce of around 105 million, and so represents a market comparable in size to the USA, and yet to envisage the EEC as a single market is more of a hope than a reality. The EEC is a difficult animal to describe fully. The situation is similar to that of the half-consumed bottle of whisky: does one say that it is half-empty or half-full? Similarly with the EEC, being born out of a post-war Europe dedicated to growth in peace, many of the judgements made about it are clouded. In fact, in terms of meeting its objectives, the EEC is similar to the half-consumed bottle of whisky. It has perhaps met half of them. Andrew Shonfield, in a BBC Reith Lecture in 1972, summed it up rather nicely when he said

This is more like a bag of marbles than a melting-pot, the marbles are soft on the surface and made of some sticky substance, like putty, which keeps them clinging together as they are pushed around and constantly make contact with one another inside the bag. It does not sound very attractive; it certainly is not very coherent. It is much less satisfactory to describe than the simplified version of a supranational European government which was the ideal of the founding fathers of the Community.

Background to the EEC

Many attempts were made in the years immediately after the War to create alliances which would make war a thing of yesteryear. However, the Soviet refusal to remove itself from the lands which it had just liberated from the Nazis, inevitably soured this atmosphere and made Western Europe fall back on itself. Thus in 1948 the creation of the Brussels Treaty Organisation, which was the forerunner of the North Atlantic Treaty Organisation (NATO), created an immediate need for the defence of democracy. Also in 1948, there was the creation of the Organisation for European Economic Co-operation (OEEC), and the Council of Europe in 1949. However, by this time, the regional organisation of the United Nations, the Economic Commission for Europe, established only two years before, for the purpose of economic reconstruction in Europe had been rendered inoperable by the very real division now of two camps within Europe: East and West and the onset of the Cold War between them.

Economic integration began properly in 1951 with the establishment of the European Coal and Steel Community (ECSC). Initiated by the French, it sought to end the historic rivalry between France and Germany, who shared the Ruhr Valley and to make war between the two nations not only 'unthinkable but materially impossible'. The plan was to create, by the removal of trade barriers, a common market in coal, iron and steel, with free access to all members – West Germany, France, Italy, Holland, Belgium and Luxemburg. This was therefore the creation of a grouping to be known for years thereafter as the Six. The EEC came into being on 1 January 1958.

The Treaty of Rome established the EEC. This called for a free trade area eliminating internal trade barriers; a customs union creating a common external tariff; a common market with free movement of the factors of production; and an economic union aiming at a unification of monetary and fiscal policy. Common policies were also to be established in agriculture and transport. It also established the European Social Fund (ESF) and the European Investment Bank (EIB). A common commercial policy was also a declared aim, to make special and separate trading arrangements for the former colonial territories which were still under-developed.

Assuming that there is a spectrum of international integration (Reference 2) at one end of the scale there is the independent national economy and at the other end is the economy which has become so completely integrated that it amounts in practice to a region in another wider economy. Between these extremes are five main stages of integration including:

1. A free trade area in which internal tariffs are abolished but countries' previous tariffs vis-à-vis other countries are maintained.
2. A customs union where a common external tariff on products is established, in addition to internal tariff abolition.
3. A common market in which restrictions to the movement of labour and capital between member states are abolished.
4. An economic union in which some national policies are harmonised in spheres other than tariffs, or labour and capital movements, but remain administered by the constituent member states.
5. Economic federalism in which certain key policies are administered by a central federal authority, rather than by the member states, and in which the previously independent national currencies are merged in a single common currency (or, on a weaker definition, bound in rigid and nominally invariable exchange ratios).

The period 1958–69 was a so-called transitional period but by this time, although the mechanism was still suffering from a number of imperfections it had also had its successes. Thus, in 1970 the members voted for the Community to have a source of income of its own. The first enlargement took place in 1973 with the UK, Ireland and Denmark. Greece then joined in 1981 and Portugal and Spain are members with effect from 1 January 1986. Each new member has, on accession, been given a number of years to make the transition to full membership of the EEC; this transition meaning the dismantling of trade ties and tariff barriers.

The Community today

The Community has conspicuously failed so far to reduce the inequalities amongst its present members. Unemployment remains unacceptably high in peripheral areas. The second expansion of the EEC means taking in countries where the average GDP per head is not much over half that in the Community in general (Reference 3), though at purchasing parities rather more. This means any serious policy commitment on equalisation of incomes requires transfers from north to south.

In population, Greece, Spain and Portugal add 21 per cent to the population of the Nine whilst in 1973 the UK, Denmark and Ireland added 33 per cent to the then Community of Six. However, they bring no Commonwealth and fewer cheap food complications (Reference 3). At the same time it has to be recognised that their accession into membership comes in time of recession rather than boom, and that these three countries are poorer and therefore ostensibly more demanding partners than the UK, Denmark and Ireland. Greece, Spain and Portugal are highly competitive in traditional industries, extending in the case of Spain to steel and ships as well as textiles and leather goods. Spain and Greece are at an important stage in their industrial growth when they need to move from reliance on the traditional industries, such as textiles, to more advanced ones influenced by product innovation and specialisation. Spain, which is in many ways comparable to Italy with a time-lag of a few years, is well advanced in this direction, but is still relatively weak in capital goods and the more complex chemicals, let alone the high technology area. Greece has much further to go; and there is general agreement that for Portugal the distance may be too great to cover without substantial aid and time.

There are problems pending over:

Migrant labour, given income differentials between the member states.

Agriculture with the Mediterranean region including many underprivileged areas. There is the problem of a present wine surplus added to the fact that Spain is, too, a major wine producer. In fruit and vegetables, it is likely also that Spain and Greece will make inroads into this market which has been the preserve of Italy, France and Holland.

Finance. One could view the southern enlargement as a useful way of forcing a rich Europe to transfer large sums to the poorer states on its periphery. With regard to finance, there are a number of unknowns such as the direct and indirect costs of the accession of the three; and whether the problem of the Community Budget will resolve itself or whether there will be a radical re-alignment of the CAP.

Foreign policy. An EEC policy requires uniformity and conformity. It will require the new members to discipline themselves. There can be little scope for opportunistic foreign policy on behalf of one member state.

Marketing by population concentration: the 'Golden Triangle'

Over three-fifths of the Community population and of its GNP are found in a comparatively small area outlined in Figure 14.1, which is some five to six times better off than some outlying areas of the Community. This is obviously of interest to companies geared towards the mass market. Most important languages within the EEC are English and French. Radio Luxemburg broadcasts in both of these languages plus others as well, to an audience which encompasses nearly all the inhabitants of the most populous and wealthy conurbations forming the 'Golden Triangle' (Reference 4).

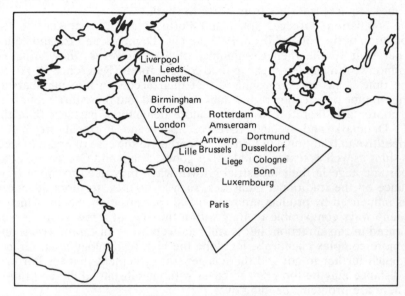

Figure 14.1 The 'Golden Triangle' of the EEC

Source John Drew, *Doing Business in the European Community*, 2nd edition, Butterworths, London, 1983, p. 83.

From a British perspective, this so-called Golden Triangle could well be challenged for including Leeds, Liverpool, Manchester and Birmingham. The most affluent areas are in London and the South of England. Liverpool has had very high levels of unemployment relative to any other city since the mid-1970s. Its industrial base has been much eroded as has its port which now only handles a fraction of the tonnage which· it used to. Leeds and Manchester are slightly different. Both have suffered from the slump in the world textile trade while Birmingham, being more dependent on the automobile industry, although also in recession, has perhaps suffered slightly less than the rest of this group, all of whom are struggling manfully to recover from this recession.

Political risk

Within the EEC, companies investing face a different form of political risk relative to other markets. There is little risk of expropriation, more from nationalisation, which has been a policy of socialist governments in Britain and France. Perhaps, too, the EEC country in question has never really known stability. This, too, ought to be considered as well. Italy, for example, changes governments with a monotonous frequency but with an imperceptible effect on her foreign policy.

National governments do vary in their attitude towards industry and investment. France takes the view, for example, that the onus is on the company to prove that a medicine does positive good, whilst in the UK it is sufficient to show that it does not do any harm. Aside, though, from national governments and their official opposition parties, the Commission now also has to be consulted with regard to large investments, mergers or takeovers which are likely to affect market positions and the normal conduct of trade.

The Commission is working towards the easing of conditions relating to industrial co-operation between companies based in different member countries, whereby they would be able to jointly pool their resources without merging financially. Freedom of movement of both funds and labour is written into the Treaty of Rome. With regard to wage rates, these still differ and so too do the levels of direct and indirect taxation, although VAT, to take one example, is now collected on a common basis throughout the Community. Local or regional investment incentives therefore require close inspection.

Decision-making bodies

These are (References 5 and 6) the Commission; Council of Ministers; Court of Justice; Parliamentary Assembly; and the Economic and Social Committee. In addition, there are said to be 2,000 committees, sub-committees and working parties. In normal practice, the Commission would consult with COPA, the grouping of agricultural organisations and with UNICE, the industrial association.

Commissioners are appointed by the member governments for four-year renewable terms, and are resident in Brussels. The main duty with which they are entrusted is to make proposals for Community action to the Council of Ministers. The President and Vice-President are chosen from amongst the 14 and hold their offices for two-year renewable terms. The UK, West Germany, France and Italy each nominated two Commissioners whilst the smaller states: Belgium, Holland, Ireland, Denmark and Luxemburg nominated one each. Spain is to nominate two, and Portugal and Greece one each.

Each Commissioner is responsible for a portfolio, although some will carry more than one portfolio. Each has a private office (cabinet) to which he makes the appointments. Invariably, the members appointed are of the same nationality as the Commissioner. His deputy is known as the *chef du cabinet*. Beneath the Commissioner, there will be one or more Director General – similar to the permanent head of a ministry – who is responsible for a broad policy area, and he will, in turn, have below him, Directors and Heads of Division. The need for Commissioners to be impartial at all times is enshrined in the Treaty of Rome, article 157, which requires that

Commissioners 'shall neither seek nor take instruction from any Government or from any other body'. However, as the Commission staff only employs 11,000 (including translators, interpreters and some 2,600 in the separate scientific and technological Joint Research Centre) as against perhaps 20,000 for a British Ministry it is not hard to see that the Commission can only hope to be effective if the governmental departments of its member states agree to administer its policies. If the Commissioners approve of the draft directive drawn up by a Directorate-General, after any necessary amendments, it is then proposed by the Commission as a draft directive to the Council of Ministers. This gives member states, through the Council of Ministers, the final say on whether the directive becomes law or not. It can, however, take years before legislation is accepted and becomes law.

The Council of Ministers consists of a minister from each member-state government, and the ministers change according to the subjects on the agenda. Ministers represent the interests of their own governments, but try to arrive at agreements which are in the Community interest. There is a system of qualified voting so that France, West Germany, Italy and the UK have ten votes each; Holland, Belgium and Greece five votes; Ireland and Denmark three; and Luxemburg two. For a qualified majority, 45 votes are required, but when the Council votes on a proposal that does not emanate from the Commission, then, in addition, the support of six states is also necessary. The Council of Ministers meets only for a certain number of days in the year, and are not resident in Brussels. Each member state takes a six-month turn to chair Council meetings, a national minister of foreign affairs being President of the Council during that period. There is a small permanent staff in Brussels but the main preparatory work is undertaken by the ambassadors and their embassy staff.

The ambassadors or representatives act as a link between the member countries and the Community. They meet in the Committee of Permanent Representatives (known as COREPER), prepare agendas, agree non-contentious proposals so that when the ministers attend much has already been agreed and only matters still in dispute need to be negotiated.

The European Council is a meeting of the heads of government and takes place three times per year. Contentious issues which have not been resolved at the Council of Ministers are discussed in the European Council. At the end of each Council, a communiqué is issued giving the broad outlines of what has been agreed. Scope for progress exists as the heads of governments are often also heads of state in certain cases. If the political will also exists for agreement to take place, then the Council is capable of meeting this challenge. Mrs Thatcher has tested the efficacy of this system on more than one occasion over the issue of British payments to the EEC budget.

The Court of Justice is the ultimate interpreter of the treaties on which the EEC is based and the final arbiter of disputes concerning secondary legislation whenever there is a query or disagreement about the meaning of a particular regulation, directive, or decision. It is situated in Luxemburg with a staff of 460. It arose out of the European Coal and Steel Community

(ECSC) but now has a much wider brief. There are eleven judges, each appointed for six years. Hearings are in public but deliberations are in secret. A judge can only be removed by the unanimous vote of his colleagues to the effect that he is no longer capable of carrying out his duties. A quorum consists of seven judges; there must be an odd number sitting and decisions are reached by simple majority. The Court produces its own reports containing the basic facts of the case, the summing up by the Advocate-General, and the judgement. Companies on whom the Commission has imposed fines may appeal to the Court. The Court also gives preliminary rulings for the benefit of national courts. It may proceed against member states if a member state is not fulfilling its legal obligations. It reviews the legality of Community acts, and it settles disputes.

The European Court (Reference 7) set a precedent in May 1985 when it gave a ruling against the Council of Ministers, finding them guilty of breaching the Treaty of Rome by failing to ensure freedom to provide transport services across the Community. The complaint has been made by the European Parliament supported by the Commission and it establishes for the first time that the Parliament can take the Council to court. It will be seen by parliamentarians as opening a new door to extending their influence over Community politics and policies. It was not an unqualified success, however. The Court did not support the contention of the European Parliament that the Council was at fault for failing to agree a common transport policy. The Court said that the Council has failed to take measures to comply with the Treaty of Rome which stipulated that freedom of services should be established within the 12-year transitional period after the Treaty signature in 1957. It is a moral victory for the Parliament although impossible to enforce. The Council has been told that it is its duty to agree, but is can hardly be forced to do so. The Council therefore remains free to deal with most of the Commission's 14 pending specific training proposals as it pleases. The Court did not accept the view of Advocate General Lenz that the Council had a duty to reach a decision on such proposals as the weights and measurements of heavy goods vehicles, co-ordination of taxation of such vehicles, and harmonisation of social measures in inland shipping. Nor did the Court accept the Dutch government's proposal that it should transform freedom of transport services from a Treaty objective into directly applicable law, enforceable in national courts.

Until 1981 the European Parliament held one-third of its sessions in Luxemburg and two-thirds in Strasbourg, in Eastern France. In 1981, it decided to hold no more sessions in Luxemburg, and this was upheld by the Court of Justice. However, more than three-quarters of the Parliamentary secretariat of approximately 2,600 are based in Luxemburg which means that they have to travel between the two points regularly. The first direct elections to the European Parliament were held in June 1979. There are 434 members of the European Parliament who control 15 important committees which scrutinise Commission proposals and prepare reports. They have the right to dismiss the government i.e. the Commissioners, provided over half the members vote. They also have the final vote on part of the European Community budget allocation, and can reject the budget as a whole. They give an opinion, which is not binding, on European laws sent from the Commission to the Council of Ministers.

The Economic and Social Committee is purely consultative. Its membership is appointed for four years and currently numbers 156: 24 from France, West Germany, Italy and the UK; 12 from Belgium and Holland; 9 from Denmark and Ireland; and 6 from Luxemburg. Its membership is wide: producers; workers; farmers; merchants; the professions; universities; consumer organisations; transport operators; or any appropriate interest group. Its members are selected by the Council from lists submitted by member states. No particular importance is assigned to its role. Its functions are more like an in-house opinion poll for the Council and Commission. Its decisions are reached in open debate in full sessions rather than by lobbying.

Companies likely to be affected by the growth of intra-European trade

Businesses that may benefit (References 4, 8 and 9) include:

1. The UK company which sees the need to enter the Community market for the first time. Its manufacturing and marketing operations can no longer be confined to one-sixth of the potential home market of 270 million consumers and it needs to change that situation by either exporting or investing. Many UK companies appreciate that their costs are considerably lower than those of most Community countries in spite of above-average inflation and recent movements in exchange rates. While an increasing number have taken advantage of this to develop European operations, there are still considerable numbers of medium-sized companies which have not adapted to the new patterns of trade. Some of them have well-established marketing operations or investments abroad but for historic reasons these are in other parts of the world, often Commonwealth countries.

2. The UK company which has a traditional set of activities within the Community, whether of a marketing or production nature, but which has not looked carefully at this historic situation for some time. It may be in the wrong market or selling the wrong product.

3. The third type has its main centre of operations outside the Community. Until now it has seen Europe as a number of different national markets. It must now consider the best ways of doing business with a group of countries surrounded by a tariff wall and which negotiates any exceptions to these tariffs centrally from Brussels.

Patents and trademarks

A new European Patent Office was established in Munich in 1978. It is anticipated that a Community-wide patent will replace national patents before too long. The Commission opposes the use of trademarks, patent licences and know-how agreements as a means of market protection (Reference 8).

EEC industry

Large companies with annual sales of over 200 million units of account make up over 50 per cent of all Community sales. Europe's 50 largest companies alone account for 25 per cent of total sales. The Commission is therefore keen to be involved in the approval of mergers before they take place.

Harmonisation: the common commercial policy

Up to 1980 the Council of Ministers had adopted about 136 directives relating to industrial products and over 50 concerned with foodstuffs. The industrial products include motor vehicles (approx. 40); metrology, i.e. measuring equipment; cosmetics; solvents and other dangerous substances; and electrical equipment. In the case of foodstuffs, directives govern their labelling, durability, additives as well as packaging (restriction on the use of PVC), presentation, advertising and composition. Additives have been subject to provisions specifying maximum levels. Much has therefore been done but there is still a long way to go since the Commission estimates that in the industrial field alone 300 directives will be necessary. It is a very time-consuming process. Also, technological progress renders existing standards obsolescent and therefore effort has to be diverted into bringing them up to date. The Community has therefore been forced to adopt a speedier process in respect of amendments to standards.

The EEC has also taken action with regard to the continuation of personal car imports which it supports (see Chapter 7); anti-dumping measures (see Chapter 2); and local government authority purchasing (see Chapter 2).

Since 1970 the Community alone has been responsible for negotiating tariff agreements with third countries and with GATT. When a bilateral agreement between one of the member states and a third country lapses, the Commission takes over responsibility for negotiation.

Competition policy within the EEC

The foundation stone of the EEC being free trade, it is not surprising then to find the Commission implacably opposed to all forms of cartel and collusion which 'have as their object or effect, the prevention, restriction or distortion of competition within the common market'. This may take various forms (Reference 8), e.g.:

1. **Market sharing agreements** which create protected markets, often in one member state. The Commission in 1969 banned a quinine cartel and imposed a fine, and in 1973 acted against a sugar cartel.
2. **Price fixing agreements** such as the dyestuffs cartel which controlled

80 per cent of the European market. Producers had agreed to raise their prices by the same amount and at virtually the same time. This was the first occasion when companies headquartered outside the EEC were fined for their actions within its territories.

3. **Exclusive purchase agreements** to buy from specified manufacturers or importers, or exclusive supply agreements to sell to certain buyers. Such agreements, which have arisen in areas as diverse as records and heating equipment, are usually proscribed by the Commission, as they create unfair advantage and act to distort free trade.

4. **Agreements on industrial and commercial property rights**. The exclusive use of patents, trademarks and works of art is not necessarily excluded from competition rules.

5. **Exclusive or selective distribution agreements**. Selective distribution arrangements are sometimes permitted if they improve the quality of the service provided. Discrimination against retailers for their pricing policies can be severely punished. However, it also encourages positive developments particularly with regard to co-operation between small and medium-size firms. Escaping the general ban are the following types of agreement:

- Exclusive representation contracts with trade representatives.
- Small scale agreements, taking account of turnover and market share (which must not exceed 5 per cent).
- Subcontracting agreements.
- Information exchanges between companies, joint studies and joint use of equipment.

Finally, with regard to mergers, the position is less clear. The Commission is able to act only with respect to mergers which arise under the European Coal and Steel Treaty. The Commission did seek extra powers in this regard in 1973 and again in 1981, asking that the largest mergers be subjected to its scrutiny. The Commission also asked for the power to ban mergers which, in its view, pose a threat to effective competition in the Community.

In 1962 there were 18 national trading monopolies in the Community covering goods ranging from potassium, gunpowder and explosives to alcohol and tobacco. Partly by negotiation and partly by taking recalcitrant offenders to the European Court, the Commission has frequently achieved the objective laid down by the European Treaties, namely the abolition of discrimination between nationals of the member states in the procurement and marketing of goods. Despite recent advances, minor problems still exist, notably in the marketing of tobacco in Italy and France. In Greece, which joined the EEC in 1981 the dismantling of state monopolies has yet to begin.

Common Agricultural Policy (CAP)

The objectives of the CAP, as detailed in Article 39 of the Treaty of Rome are:

(*a*) to increase agricultural productivity.
(*b*) to ensure a fair standard of living for the agricultural community.
(*c*) to stabilise markets.
(*d*) to provide certainty of supplies.
(*e*) to ensure supplies to consumers at reasonable prices.

Approximately 70 per cent of the Community's total budget (Reference 5) is accounted for by the CAP. The most important prices fixed at Community level are:

1. Indicative or guide prices which are the expected prices for the producer.
2. Intervention price which is a lower price at which the Community is obliged to buy products from farmers, traders and co-operatives if they cannot be sold in the Community markets or be exported. When production exceeds demands there are surpluses, and in agricultural production, there are many such surpluses within the EEC.

CAP also benefits the larger farmers since the more a farmer has to sell, the more he benefits from the revenue-enhancing effect of the policy. To reduce milk production, slaughter premiums were granted but this did not meet with success as the farmers collected the premiums and invested them in ever more productive dairy cattle.

The Community has been trying to change towards a more viable farm size to improve the economics of its agricultural production and support schemes. The Mansholt Plan which was not adopted, was for a farm of 200–300 acres for wheat production, 40–60 cows for milk, 15–200 head of cattle for beef and veal production. Its aims was not to coerce but to create financial inducements for adopting its recommendations.

Thanks to subsidies, the Community farm prices remain high by world market price levels, and guaranteed prices only stimulate further supplies thus exacerbating the situation further. In the 1979/80 season, wheat and barley prices were about 60 per cent above world levels whilst beef was over 100 per cent and butter 280 per cent above. The problem lies with CAP itself. Its objectives, as outlined above, include terms which are outwardly agreeable but practically expensive to maintain. For example, providing certainty of supplies is usually a feature only of the public utilities: gas, water and electricity. To offer a 100 per cent level of service means inevitably that you have to be overstocked by up to 10 per cent on occasion. As for the rest of its aims, it is open to question whether they are mutually exclusive, whether indeed it is possible to provide a fair standard of living, stabilise markets, and ensure supplies at reasonable prices, and all at the same time.

The Lomé Convention

This is an arrangement which has established a special relationship between the Community and over 60 African, Caribbean and Pacific (ACP) countries. A new convention came into force in 1981 for a period of five years, replacing the earlier convention signed in 1976.

The Lomé Convention has been hailed as a breakthrough in relations between developed and developing countries. It brought together the old Yaounde states, usually referred to as the AASM and less developed Commonwealth countries in Africa, the Caribbean and the Pacific. There were 19 AASM – 18 in the old Yaounde plus Mauritius – and these were now joined by 21 Commonwealth countries. In addition there were five outsiders and Guinea. In all therefore there were 46 less developed signatories (the Bahamas was added later).

The Convention covers:

1. **Trade co-operation**. Practically all products from the ACP countries may be imported freely into the EEC, but the arrangement is not reciprocal. ACP countries may charge import duties provided that they do not discriminate between member states.

2. **Financial and technical co-operation**. The common unit of currency for conversion purposes is the ECU (European Currency Unit). Note, though, that Thomas Cook have announced that they will soon be launching ECU travellers cheques for their European clients. Funds of nearly 6,000 million ECU were set aside for use up to 1985. These funds were to finance investment projects by the ACP countries and will be managed jointly. Four major sectors share most of the aid: rural development, industrialisation, economic infrastructure and social development. There is also provision for regional co-operation of two or more ACP countries and support for small and medium-sized firms.

3. **Stabilisation of export earnings**. The STABEX system compensates ACP states for losses if the volume of exports in their most important products falls below a certain level. The poorest countries do not have to repay the compensatory amounts, but other countries do if the situation improves. The scheme is intended to even out large deficit and surplus positions which have caused such wide price fluctuation that, in some instances, the rational planning of a developing economy has become almost impossible.

4. **Industrial and agricultural co-operation**. The intention is to grant aid to help ACP countries to develop and diversify their industrial production, in particular through the transfer of technology. This policy will raise the important question of the Community's obligation to buy the goods which the industries of the Third World produce. This will put pressure on Community industries, in particular very heavy pressure on labour-intensive, low-technology industries. It will accelerate their decline and push industry within the Community into higher technologies and more sophisticated services. Co-operation will be stepped up in areas such as new energy sources. Private investment will also be encouraged.

5. **Institutions**. The Lomé Agreement is implemented by a Council of Ministers aided by a Consultative Assembly of representatives of the ACP countries and the European Parliament. In each of the countries – totalling over 60 – there is a representative of the Community, whose task is to manage the operation of the Convention. Although at present only trade relations are involved, there is clearly present the germ of the idea of

Community representatives acting more as ambassadors to the ACP countries. It could make individual embassies largely redundant in time.

The principal agreements between the Community and the Mediterranean countries are:

1. With Maghreb countries – Algeria, Morocco, and Tunisia.
2. With the Mashreq countries – Egypt, Jordan, Syria and Lebanon.
3. The agreements with Israel, Cyprus and Malta.

The commercial aspects of the agreements involve free access for industrial goods to the Community and concessions covering some agricultural products. The agreements are not reciprocal, although in the case of Israel there will be a free trade area for industrial products by 1989.

Arrangements have been made in the agreements to ensure that the nearly one million Maghreb workers in the Community benefit from the same pay and conditions of work as Community nationals. A Council of Ministers determines the policies behind the various treaties, but the negotiation and renegotiation of the treaties is the responsibility of the Commission, and in particular of a Directorate-General, who co-ordinates the views of other Directorate-Generals.

The second enlargement of the EEC

Greece and Portugal are not seen as important markets for Britain but Spain offers great possibilities, which will depend on her ability to dismantle her tariff and non-tariff barriers rapidly and effectively. Spain has a more highly developed industrial structure than either Greece or Portugal. The Spanish car market is heavily protected at the moment; imports of pharmaceutical products are almost zero because of non-tariff barriers, and yet the size of the pharmaceutical market in Spain is larger than that of the UK.

Spain has maintained high tariff protection; local content requirements; and export complementation. With regard to the automobile market, Spain (Reference 10) is attractive because of the low density of car ownership; the export market access now to the EEC; and stable labour relations combined with a relatively low wage level.

References

1. Shonfield, Andrew, 'Europe: Journey to an Unknown Destination' an expanded version of the *BBC Reith Lectures 1972*, Penguin, 1973.
2. Holland, Stuart, *Uncommon Market*, Macmillan, 1980.
3. Seers, Dudley and Vaitsos, Constantine, *The Second Enlargement of the EEC*, St Martin's Press, New York, 1982.
4. Drew, John, *Doing Business in the European Community*, Butterworths, 2nd edition, 1983.
5. Swann, Dennis, *The Economics of the Common Market*, Penguin, 5th edition, 1984.
6. Overton, David, *Common Market Digest*, Library Association, London, 1983.

7. Hermann, A. H., Legal Correspondent, 'Precedent set by Court ruling on EEC Ministers', *Financial Times*, 23 May 1985.
8. Evans, Dennis, *Trading within the European Community: a United Kingdom Executive Guide*, Tolley Publishing Co. Ltd, Croydon, Surrey, 1983. Stanley A. Budd, *The EEC – A Guide to the Maze*, INRO Press, Edinburgh, 1985.
9. *Export Europe, Selling to Western Europe*, BOTB, London, 1982.
10. Komissar, Gerson, 'From Closed to Open Competition: the Car Industry in Spain on its way to the EEC', Norwegian School of Management, Oslo, Paper to the European International Business Association, INSEAD, Fontainebleau, France, December 1982.

15. MARKETING TO EASTERN EUROPE

'Eastern Europe' is a convenient term to describe certain of the countries of the Soviet-led Council for Mutual Economic Assistance (CMEA) which share not only geographical proximity but certain other market characteristics such as control planning. The countries which are commonly held to comprise the Eastern European bloc are Bulgaria, Czechoslovakia, East Germany, Hungary, Poland, Romania and the USSR. Yugoslavia is not a full member of the Eastern bloc as it has only associate membership of the CMEA (known also as Comecon). However, in addition to the above-named countries, the CMEA also includes Vietnam, Mongolia and Cuba, which lack commodities, aside from central planning with the rest of this political bloc.

Despite the population size of the bloc its share of global foreign trade does not match its productive potential. Economic growth rates in Eastern Europe have continued to exceed those of the developed market economies. The Centrally-Planned Economies' percentage of world trade has increased as follows:

1973	9.7%
1978	9.6%
1979	10.7%
1981	9.2%
1982	10.3%
1983	10.9%

but this is from a very low base. It should, however, be remembered that the term 'Centrally-Planned Economy' includes much besides Eastern Europe, but these UN figures exclude Albania, China, North Korea and Vietnam. Apart from a dip in 1981, these figures reflect an increase. There may, however, be several factors to explain this increasing trend besides general growth at home. Firstly, certain of these East European nations have been hard strapped for the convertible currency to repay outstanding borrowings (Reference 1). This influenced Hungary and Poland to apply for membership of the IMF as a potential source of additional liquidity. (Romania was an early member of the IMF). Meanwhile, anything that was capable of being sold on Western markets was sold there, and while attention has been focused primarily on Hungary, Poland and Romania, it is worth noting that all of the East European nations reduced their imbalance in trade with the West in the period 1979–83 by either selling more on Western markets and/or reducing Western imports.

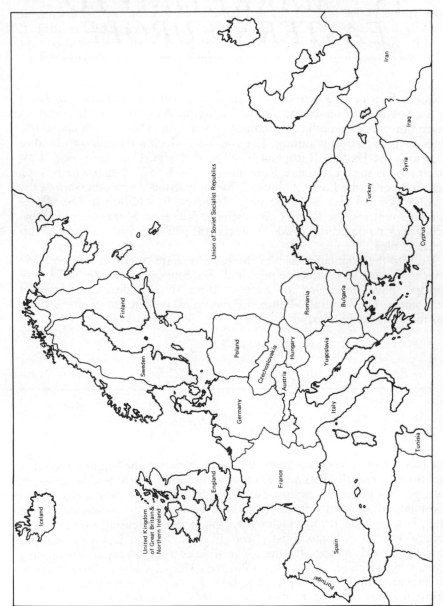

Figure 15.1 Map of Eastern Europe

The Eastern bloc manifests common characteristics in terms of foreign trade, where, in each member state, foreign trade is a state monopoly. (Reference 1) There is, though, a latitude of freedom in the degree of centralisation/decentralisation applied to the management and control of the foreign trade system. Between the two extremes of centralisation and decentralisation there are a number of mixed systems. Thus the position on this gradient or stage in the centralisation/decentralisation spectrum does have significant meaning for the marketing function: Authoritative; Directive; Mixed-Middle system; and Integrative. A laissez-faire system is incompatible with the very nature of socialism.

Foreign trade as a centrally planned state monopoly: the foreign trade enterprise

Needs and priorities are determined not only domestically but for the entire Comecon bloc as a region. Planning periods are chiefly five years integrating the national Five Year Plans for the region; and each member state reviews the progress of its plan on an annual basis.

The Government is a single party in power. Planning is undertaken by a Commission which includes planning experts as well as the Council of Ministers. Jointly, they determine national priorities. Finance for foreign trade is then determined by the State Bank for Foreign Trade who then communicates this information down the structure to the industrial association enterprises and Foreign Trade Enterprises (FTEs), who alone are responsible for all imports and exports for their respective industries. Perspective plans are also drawn for a 20-year period, the difficulty here being not only the length of the period but the degree of cohesion amongst the CMEA members. Romania is a famous example of a country who refused to specialise in agriculture on behalf of the CMEA, but went ahead to develop its oil and industrial assets. Specialisation, whereby only one country is designated to be a supplier of a given product or commodity, has run into problems chiefly because of national pride amongst the individual states and eagerness amongst all to produce industrial and high-technology goods; so licence sales take place with countries other than those officially designated by the CMEA to specialise in that particular industrial branch.

The Foreign Trade Enterprise

Each sector of industry has its own Foreign Trade Enterprise (FTE) which controls all imports and exports for its own sector. It is generally difficult to cross over to another industrial end-use sector without having to approach another FTE. This generally applies whether buying or selling. FTEs generally use their monopsony purchasing power to play off potential suppliers against each other to obtain maximum price advantage or other contractual concessions which is at the heart of the 'whipsawing' accusation often labelled against the FTEs. There is no understanding of the concept of project management or venture management as practised quite commonly in the West which requires the co-ordination of all interested parties in the commissioning and establishment of a new industrial undertaking. Instead the separate and independent FTEs will seek to fulfil their obligations to a national industrial project according to their own schedule and financial budgets. Where their purchasing budgets are low and their own sales are low, they will then seek countertrade proposals from potential suppliers but this usually only has the effect of extending the duration of a project and making it overall more expensive.

Western embargo on strategic exports to the Eastern bloc

The embargo is applied by each member state of CoCom (or Consultative Committee) which functions as a branch of the NATO military alliance as a response to the Eastern bloc's Warsaw Pact alliance. CoCom is based in Paris but includes France which is not a member of NATO.

CoCom has not been entirely successful as it requires each member state to draw up its list for the UK. This list is embodied in the 168 page Export of Goods (Control) Order 1985 which does not require parliamentary approval. The United States on the other hand has a 700 page fine-print list of 200,000 sensitive items. Some nations' lists are shorter than others, allowing for 'leakage' of technology if shipped via a subsidiary abroad in a more lax CoCom-member country or a neutral one such as Austria, Sweden, or Switzerland which account for a considerable amount of East-West trade. In addition, there are now a multitude of developing countries in the Far East producing sophisticated electronic equipment such as Taiwan, Hong Kong and Singapore. These currently escape the controls. However, Singapore has become the first country outside NATO, France and Japan to say publicly that it is ready to co-operate to prevent the diversion of sensitive high-technology products to Soviet-bloc countries. The CoCom list as such is also open to political manoeuvring in that what is considered to be a strategic, and hence prohibited, export seldom remains constant, but varies with the prevailing diplomatic climate of *détente* or frigidity. New CoCom procedures provide for revision of 25 per cent of the CoCom list of revision of all items every four years. Political influences also cause government-backed credits to be awarded 'in the national interest' where there would be no clearly identifiable commercial criteria for so doing. Similarly, political influences also cause them to be withdrawn, and the preferential 'Much Favoured Nation' status that may be accorded a trading partner under GATT rules is also a political endowment.

Eleven expectations of East-West trade

The following may be said to be expectations of doing business in Eastern Europe and the Soviet Union. However, these are generalisations and so will therefore be true more of some countries rather than others. The degree to which this may be applicable relates also to this degree to which the individual economies are either centralised or decentralised.

1. East-West trade is slow to reap rewards and executive-intensive so therefore expensive.
2. Since there is a single buying point for each industrial sector, the foreign trade enterprise (FTE), this concentrates buying power in a

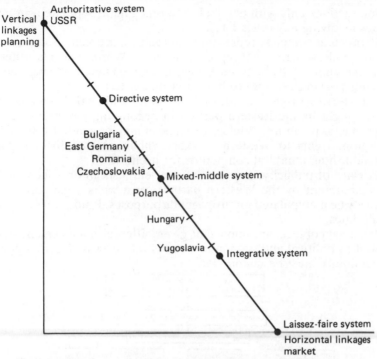

Figure 15.2 Spectrum of macroeconomic systems. Adapted from A. C. Samli and W. Jermakowicz, 'The stages of marketing evolution in East European countries', *European Journal of Marketing*, vol. 17, no. 2, p. 29.

monopsony, which leads in turn to the FTE playing off between potential suppliers for better terms. It should also be noted though that major industrial producers are being accorded industrial foreign trade enterprise status.

3. Where a product is required to fill a national priority need, identified in the five year plan, convertible currency will be made available and paperwork expedited.
4. Where a product lies outside of the national five year plan priorities, it is likely that requests for countertrade will be made.
5. It is generally difficult to find market and product supply information particularly total industrial consumption or unit value of purchases.
6. It is generally difficult to indentify decision makers in Ministries and the industrial associations, which group all factories within an industry sector, and in certain countries it is expressly forbidden to communicate with the end-users in the factories.
7. Expect protracted, frustrating negotiations because of a sluggish and unco-ordinated bureaucracy. A few countries such as Hungary and the USSR allow countertrade purchases to be made across FTEs, others, including Poland, do not. In this case, it is possible to conduct

transactions only with one FTE at a time and as separate transactions not involving any other FTE.

8. Permanent company representation can be a problem. Some countries do not allow permanent representation nor Western agents either, and so the choice falls between having a state agency, choosing one from among several, or else to have a visiting salesman only.

9. Sales territory rights outside of the domestic and CMEA boundaries will be sought by the Eastern partner in negotiating any licensing or co-production venture. While a concession may be made for the CMEA region, rights to Western markets will mean that the company is establishing a natural competitor for itself.

10. A glare of publicity, a degree of over-enthusiasm or a seeming over-commitment by the Western partner, or a weak legal contract may easily be manipulated for propaganda purposes. Prudence is required at all times.

11. Personal contacts are important given different management styles as well as political and economic systems with clearly different goals, so continuity must be maintained.

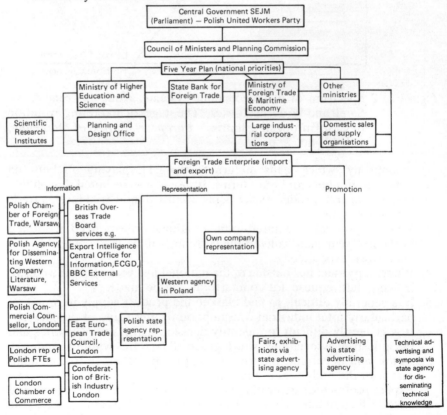

Figure 15.3 A Western company's bird's eye view of the Polish foreign trade structure

Source Amended from S. J. Paliwoda, *Joint East-West Marketing and Production Ventures*, Gower, 1981.

Market entry methods

In the past, licensing was the most appropriate alternative to direct exports. Not without dangers of creating a political competitor, licensing remained the most popular because of inability until the 1980s of engaging in more complex longer lasting ventures. Politically, ownership of the means of production could not be in the hands of foreigners so direct investment was curtailed and there was little enthusiasm on either side for joint ventures. However, since the 1970s there have been more than a thousand such joint ventures in Eastern Europe (Reference 3). Often incorporating a management contract alongside a licensing agreement, these contractual joint ventures or industrial co-operation agreements, as they are called, create a means whereby the Western company is able to secure a higher value-added return for his technology than before.

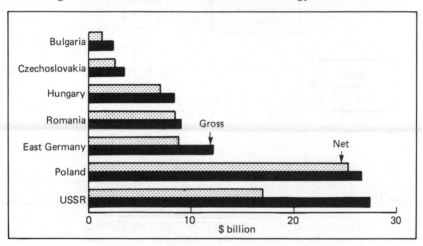

Figure 15.4 Comecon debt, end of 1983

Source UN Economic Commission for Europe

The lack of up-to-date reliable information

The lack of up-to-date reliable information is a common problem, compounded by the fact that different statistical bases are used, which reduces the scope for comparability. Some possible sources are indicated in Figure 15.3. It is also usually difficult to contact the actual end-user to improve upon a published specification emanating from the Foreign Trade Enterprise. The difficulty is that the FTE is an administrative organ frequently lacking the technical expertise or even the application knowledge of the end-user concerned.

Internal markets

Internal markets within Eastern Europe are in effect sellers' markets. Central planning is responsible for shortages and the poor phasing of

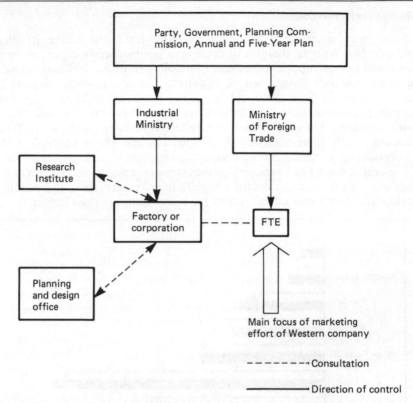

Figure 15.5 An illustration of the organisation of the Polish Buying Centre
  Source: S. J. Paliwoda, *Joint East-West Marketing and Production Ventures*,
  Gower, 1981.

production to meet seasonal needs. Centralised planning is at odds, too,
with the concept of promotion as practised in the West, for, increasing
levels of consumption beyond the previously planned levels would only
mean diverting resources from some other part of the economy.
Advertising and promotion is practised very little and generally available
only for foreign companies wishing to make their wares known in the
domestic market. For foreign companies, there is little media choice and
many restrictions on advertising; there is a requirement, for example, that
the message must be educational in nature rather than simply a sales
message. There is little Western advertising to be found in the East
European press. Fairs, promotions, and technical symposia are often used
instead and since buying power is concentrated in the FTE it is easy enough
to contact them directly. Technical fairs and symposia are the responsibility of a separate agency which handles science and technology including the
technical press and is always quite separate from, and often cheaper than,
the single state advertising agency.
  Distribution within Eastern Europe is generally poor. There is a

shortage of vehicles to actually move the goods from producer to consumer. Again, with regard to consumption, the average size of retail outlet is surprisingly small for the neighbourhood it is expected to serve, and so, again, this invites shortages as there is a lack of both shelf selling space and storage space. Shortages are however, endemic to the Eastern European system and occasionally create opportunities for Western firms, where gaps are created in targets essential to the fulfilment of a national priority plan.

Branding is at an excessively low level. There appears to be no coherent policy here. The Eastern Europeans prefer to waste their money in exchanging what are often good products in low-return countertrade whilst the same goods could be sold directly in Western markets with some degree of investment at a much higher return. There seems little interest on their part in doing so, preferring instead simply to take the money in a strategy dubbed as 'disaster pricing'. The pattern has been to ask Western partners to undertake this marketing and promotion for them on Western markets. Slowly, the situation is changing. Polish foods in Britain are now branded 'Pek' or 'Krakus'; there is the Polski-Fiat car now renamed the FSO and another more recent one, the Polonez; the Soviet Lada car which in late 1984 introduced a number of 'add-ons' produced by the Soviet factory to create a customised finish, e.g. front spoilers, aerodynamic sills, etc. – a most unusual step for a centrally planned economy to take towards satisfaction of a consumer in the West, particularly as Western manufacturers would not normally undertake this themselves but leave such car customisation to specialist suppliers instead.

Potential for East-West trade

Convertible currency reserves and import needs

Convertible currency reserves are insufficient for all import needs. This means two things: firstly, loans or 'soft' government-backed credits when available, and in recent years with Afghanistan and the imposition of martial law in Poland, these have not been available; secondly, there will inevitably be requests for the Western seller to accept Eastern bloc goods as part- payment. The Eastern bloc is particularly sensitive to high interest rate levels even if these are less than the currently prevailing interest rates. In the past, this has meant artificially camouflaging the real cost of borrowing in the total contract price but once interest rates began to rise into double digit figures, this was no longer a viable strategy.

There have been few government-backed credits in recent years, due to the overall political situation and difficulty with external funding due to the fact that some of the East European nations are facing problems with the repayment of outstanding indebtedness, as illustrated in the following Table 15.1.

Having already outlined the foreign debt/foreign earnings structure, the situation is not a very optimistic one apart from perhaps in Bulgaria, Czechoslovakia and East Germany. Bulgaria recently agreed to the

Table 15.1
Four stages of marketing evolution in East European countries

*Stage 1   Totally planned and controlled distribution systems
            (authoritative economic system)*
- National economy is treated as a big nationwide enterprise.
- All decisions about structure of production and directions of investment are made at the central governmental level in the planning council.
- Directive form of management
- Ration-card type distribution system.
- Nationalised retailing structure with virtual monopoly of sales in urban areas.
- Nationwide seller's market.

*Stage 2   Directly planned and controlled distribution systems
            (directive economic system)*
- An enterprise is regarded as a ministry association.
- Some competition among ministries.
- Some pressure on the producers to attract customers.
- Introducing of input-output analysis at the governmental level.
- Large-scale advertising of an ideological character is utilised.
- Better method of estimating, thanks to input-output analysis where, when and what the consumers will buy.
- Increased choice for the ultimate consumer.

*Stage 3   Partially planned and more indirectly controlled distribution
            systems (mixed-middle system)*
- An enterprise is regarded as an industrial association.
- Some competition among the industrial associations.
- Moderate degree of decentralisation.
- Planning of market consumption goods and services is decentralised.
- Some product differentiation – particularly free market mechanism for individual consumption products.
- Increased availability of consumer credit.

*Stage 4   Indirectly planned and controlled distribution systems
            (integrative economic system)*
- The focal point in the economy is the enterprise.
- Competition among the enterprises.
- Government influences the behaviour of enterprises indirectly only by the use of economic parameters.
- Free market mechanism for all goods and services.
- High autonomy for enterprises to improve their marketing efforts.
- High product differentiation and market segmentation.
- Ability to fluctuate prices.
- Increased discretionary income and luxury items.

Source A. C. Samli and W. Jermakowicz, 'The stages of marketing evolution in East European countries', *European Journal of Marketing*, vol. 17, no. 2, p. 29.

establishment of joint ventures with foreign principals whilst Czechoslovakia and East Germany are the two oldest established industrial countries of the Eastern bloc who have not traditionally traded to any high degree with the West, particularly after the 1968 Soviet invasion of Czechoslovakia. Elsewhere, demand will continue to arise, but the problem will be in helping to effect payment whether by product-related terms which are difficult to accept in a trade recession, or leasing which may signify foreign ownership of the means of production or some new acceptable method yet to be devised. Ingenuity will continue to be required and applied in the pursuit of East-West trade more than before.

The future possibility remains nevertheless of market expansion via tripartite industrial co-operation, i.e. Western partner and Eastern partner working together on a joint project in a third country, usually one of the less developed African or Asian countries amenable to a socialist presence. Whilst world interest rates remain punitively high, it is not only difficult for the LDC's without collateral or promise of earnings to borrow, but to do so without incurring heavy rates of interest. Thus the potential remains but the means of suitable financing has yet to be devised so as to tap what is a very large market. Nevertheless, the UN Economic Commission for Europe estimated that there were approximately 749 industrial co-operation agreements in force in 1983 (966, if Yugoslavia is included).

References

1. Paliwoda, Stanley J., 'Marketing in Eastern Europe', in Erdener Kaynak, *International Marketing Management*, Praeger, 1985, pp. 286–304; Price Waterhouse, *Doing Business in Eastern Europe*, 1982.
2. Samli, A. C., *Marketing and Distribution Systems in Eastern Europe*, Praeger, 1981.
3. Paliwoda, Stanley J. and Liebrenz, Marilyn L., 'Expectations and outcomes of multinational joint ventures in Eastern Europe', *European Journal of Marketing*, vol. 18, no. 3, 1984.
   Liebrenz, Marilyn L., *Transfer of Technology: US Multinationals and Production Ventures*, Praeger, 1984.
   Paliwoda, Stanley J. and Liebrenz, Marilyn L., 'Transfer of Technology to Eastern Europe' and 'Transfer of Technology within Eastern Europe', in A. C. Samli, *Technology Transfer*, Praeger, 1985.

Recommended further reading

Andrew Freris, *The Soviet Industrial Enterprise: Theory and Practice*, Croom-Helm, 1984.

Malcolm R. Hill, *East–West Trade, Industrial Cooperation and Technology Transfer*, Gower, 1983.

East European Trade Council, *Contemplating Commerce*, 2nd edition, London, 1986.

East European Trade Council, *Register of Commercial Houses trading with Eastern Europe*, London, 1983.

Linda Malvern, David Hebditch and Nick Anning, *Techno-Bandits*, Houghton-Mifflin, 1984.

16. *CHINA*

The People's Republic of China was established in 1949 but it chose to maintain an isolationist policy until the early 1970s when it joined the United Nations and became involved in world affairs. In 1972 China signed a treaty with Japan, and in 1975 with the EEC. In 1980 China joined the IMF and the World Bank. China set itself the goal in 1978 of transforming the country into a powerful, modern, socialist state by the year 2000 and quadrupling its GNP. Countertrade is likely to play a large role in this modernisation programme.

China is an underdeveloped country and a market unlike other communist countries, partly due to its size, housing one-quarter of the world's population, which means approximately one billion inhabitants, of whom 800 million are peasants, but partly due to its politics which ensured its isolation from the rest of the world. Arriving now with the intention to spend on industrial investments, China is being openly welcomed by world trading, banking and financial communities. Per capita income in 1979 was $253. In 1979, the Bank of China signed numerous agreements with leading banking institutions in the West and Japan for both private commercial credits and government backed export credits, although its foreign trade represents a very small share of its national income. China needs to both encourage exports and lower tariffs. China borrows more than a billion dollars a year and has become the third largest recipient of World Bank financing after India and Brazil. The largest single area of lending is in the area of energy.

China's foreign trade in 1983 (exports and imports, US $billion):

Japan	9.077	22.3 % of total
Hong Kong and Macao	6.980	17.1
EEC	5.722	14.1
US	4.027	9.9
CMEA	2.165	5.4
Other	12.729	31.2

Total exports 22.2 = 1.25% of total world exports
Total imports 18.5 = 1.04% of total world imports

Domestically, China underwent profound change as a result of the death of Mao Zedong in October 1976 and the pre-eminence of Deng Xiaoping in December 1978, and since then has known only dynamic change. These changes extend to five areas. Firstly, in the political arena, many Chinese citizens who were alienated under former regimes have been rehabilitated. Moves are taking place which, taken together, are very significant. For example, direct election of representatives at the county level, and a greater role for legislation, developing a basic criminal and civil code as well as laws relating to the operations of foreign firms in China. In the absence of commercial law, trade took place on trust. Secondly, intellectual liberalisation is greater than before but not yet complete. The Party adheres rigidly still to four basic tenets: the leadership of the party; the guiding role of Marxism, Leninism and Maoism; the maintenance of the 'people's democratic dictatorship' as China's form of government; and the pursuit of a socialist road to economic development. Thirdly, since 1978 there has been 're-adjustment' of the Soviet model of development which was transplanted wholesale into China and strongly advocated during the decade of the Cultural Revolution in the late 1960s and 1970s. In 1981 the reforms extended to 6,000 enterprises accounting for about 60 per cent of industrial output. The policy encouraging people to save and be satisfied with no wage increases, which gave China a ratio of investment to national income of 36 per cent pre-1978, has since dropped to 27 per cent but there was also a 5 per cent real increase in wages between 1979 and 1981.

China has a technology gap in most of its basic industries of up to ten years. It does have some industrially advanced regions but reforms are needed to increase the productivity of investments, meet the multiple objectives of a modernising economy and the diversified needs of the people. This new China has set lower industrial targets but higher targets for light industry which produces consumer goods. This is intended to absorb greater purchasing power, and meet new consumer demands seen in declining sales of plain clothing characteristic of the Maoist period, and the desire for more fashion. However, although productivity changes have been taking place, the share of old people in the population is rising alongside these other social trends. Whereas previously bicycles, sewing machines and watches have been the most important, now this has changed to televisions, tape recorders, cameras and washing machines. Politically, there is no longer the need for China to be so self-reliant and so China's new leaders have expanded greatly trade with the West.

There are three types of economic enterprise permitted in China – individual, collective and state. Economic reform allows farmers as well as industrial enterprises to sell their surplus or to swap their produce for other products. Industrial enterprises are being made responsible for their own profits and losses. Unprofitable enterprises have been closed or threatened with closure (small iron plants run by prefectures and counties have been reduced from 466 to 276) whilst profitable ones have been allowed to retain a greater part of their net income to use for bonuses, benefits and new investments. In the Shanghai region in 1980 this was reportedly an average 8 per cent of profits whereas in Sichuan province, it varied between 10 per cent and 20 per cent. Meanwhile, the state is no longer providing investment capital to industrial enterprises free of charge. This is now available in the form of bank loans, carrying interest charges and a term of repayment. In 1980, 810,000 individuals started their own businesses. The state provided work for only 29 per cent of 6 million newly employed urban workers in 1981 whereas collectives accounted for 49 per cent, private businesses for 5 per cent, with the remaining 17 per cent being temporary labour. Chinese society remains rooted around the concept of the commune which consists of a cluster of villages around a traditional market town with a population which varies between 15,000 and 50,000. Below the commune is the brigade and there may be twelve brigades per commune. These resemble large villages. Next down the scale is the co-operative, and there may be eight or ten of these per brigade. However, even here change is taking place as responsibility shifts to smaller units and the family groups, the households classed as self-employed, which are so important for China's agricultural output. In total, six kinds of businesses are permitted under the individual enterprise form (Reference 5):

- Commercial – retailing items purchased wholesale from collective and state enterprises.
- Handicrafts making and selling simple items such as toys or baskets or art works; some forms of art work, such as painting, can only be sold to the state for resale by the state.
- Transportation – primarily 'pedicabs' or three-wheeled bicycles with a seat for one or two passengers.
- Repairing – shoe repair, bicycle repair, etc.
- Services – barbering, hairdressing, tailoring etc.
- Food preparation – from street stands to small restaurants.

With the permission of the Industrial and Commercial Bureau, and by contracts approved by the Bureau, individual enterprises may hire up to five apprentices and up to two assistants. The reasons offered for this are to better serve the needs of consumers and to help alleviate the pressing problem of unemployment.

Recent research (Reference 3) pointed to the following conclusions:

1. The commune system should be seen in a historical perspective as a product of evolutionary adaptation and not as an immutable institution created during a heroic period of socialist construction.
2. Experimentation with alternative institutional arrangements has always been part of the Chinese style of rural development and thus the recent innovations and experiments are consistent with past approaches to development problems.
3. There is an economic logic to the commune system that can best be understood when the household economy is regarded as the base of the system and the fourth tier of a four-tiered institutional hierarchy.
4. The essence of the new reforms is a shift of responsibility for crop cultivation from the production team to the household economy, but not to the private sector. This shift does not imply the imminent disbandment of the commune system although in some circumstances the commune system could be severely weakened and even destroyed.
5. Some aspects of the new reforms if not corrected, could lead to greater inequality, lower levels of capital accumulation and slower long run rates of growth of output, but these consequences are not inherent in the reforms.
6. Such evidence as exists indicates that the distribution of collective

income in rural areas, including collective income originating in the household economy, continues to be relatively egalitarian.
7. Moreover, in the few cases where comparisons over time are possible, there is no evidence that the reforms have been associated with an increase in the degree of inequality at the local level.

Table 16.1
China's joint equity ventures, 1979 to spring 1981

Venture	Chinese partners	Foreign partners
Approved solely by FICC (Equity shares in parentheses)		
1. Beijing Air Catering Co. Ltd.	Civil Aviation Administration of China (51%)	China Air Catering, Hong Kong, Ltd. (49%)
2. China Schindler Elevator Co., Ltd., Beijing and Shanghai	China Construction Machinery Corp. (75%)	Schindler Holding AG, Switzerland (17%); Jardine Matheson & Co., Ltd., Hong Kong (8%)
3. Tainshan Woolen Textile Co., Ltd., Urumqi	Urumqi No. 1 Knitwear Mill, and the Urumqi People's Knitwear Mill (51%)	Peninsula Knitwears, Ltd.; Rawcott International, Ltd.; Hong Kong & Tokyo Boshi Kogyo Co., Ltd. (49%)
4. Jianguo Hotel, Beijing	China International Travel Service (51%)	Zhong Mei Hotel Development Venture, Ltd., Hong Kong (49%)
5. Great Wall Hotel, Beijing	China International Travel Service (51%)	E-S Pacific Development & Construction Co., Ltd., Bermuda (49%)
6. Palace Hotel, Beijing	China International Travel Services	Yick Ho, Ltd., Hong Kong
7. Guangming Overseas-Chinese Electronics Co., Ltd.	(Unknown)	Electronics Enterprises, Ltd., Hong Kong
8. Name and activity of joint venture not disclosed by mutual agreement of partners	(Unknown)	(Unknown)
Approved by FICC and provincial or municipal authorities		
9. Westlake Rattan Co., Zhejiang	Zhejiang Furniture and Sundry Goods Industrial Corp.	New Arts Enterprises, Hong Kong
10. Orient Optical Factory, Zhejiang	(Unknown)	Fada (Prosperity) Optical Factory, Hong Kong
11. Yanhua Standard Battery Co., Hebei	(Unknown)	Standard Battery, Ltd., Hong Kong
12. Jinhua Watchdial and Watchhand Corp.	Tianjin Watch Components Factory (70%)	Wah Hing Watch Component Factory, Hong Kong (20%); Wah Sing Corp. (10%)
13. Sino-French Joint Venture Wine Co., Ltd., Tianjin	Tianjin Wine Factory (62%)	Remy Martin, France (38%)

Table 16.1 continued

Venture	Chinese partners	Foreign partners
	Approved solely by FICC (Equity shares in parentheses)	

Approved by provincial authorities according to FICC guidelines

14. Guangming Pig Farm, Guangdong	(Unknown)	Overseas United Co., Philippines
15. Jiangqiao Enterprises, Fujian	(Unknown)	Jin Gang, Ltd., Hong Kong
16. Yiguang Colour Photograph Studio, Fujian	(Unknown)	Minhua (Fujiang) Trading Centre, Hong Kong
17. Fujiang Erzhou Crafts Factory	(Unknown)	Jiahua Trading Co., Hong Kong

Approved by FICC according to unofficial press reports

18. China Orient Leasing Co.	Beijing Machinery & Electrical Equipment Co. (30%); China International Trust and Investment Corp. (20%)	Orient Leasing Co., Japan (50%)
19. China-Otsuka Co., Ltd., Tianjin	China Pharmaceutical Corp. (50%)	Otsuka Pharmaceutical Co., Japan (50%)
20. Fujian-Hitachi, Ltd., Fuzhou	Fujian Electronics Import and Export Corp. (40%); Fujian Investment and Enterprise Corp. (10%)	Hitachi (38%); Hitachi Sales Co. (10%); Toei Shoko, Ltd. (2%)
21. Name not disclosed, but is in the area of vacuum pumps	Shanghai General Machinery Co. (50%)	Bush KG, West Germany (50%)
22. Name not disclosed, but is in the area of electronic instruments	Shanghai Instrumentation Industry (51%)	Foxboro Instruments, USA (49%)
23. Name not disclosed, but is in the area of pneumatic instruments in Zhaoqing, Guangdong	Guangdong Instrument Factory (51%)	Foxboro Instruments, USA (49%)
24. Computer World Publishing Services	Enterprise name not disclosed (60%)	US company name not announced (40%)

Source F. W. Wu, 'The political risk of foreign direct investment in post-Mao China: a preliminary assessment', *Management International Review*, 22(1), 1982, pp. 13–23.

China's party and state bureaucracies are in need of reform. Bureaucracy is being reduced with planned decentralisation and the average age of officials to be reduced whilst their expected level of education is increased. The present economic system is highly centralised with:

(*a*) Decision-making confined to the leading central economic organs.
(*b*) Highly centralised planning precludes the functioning of markets.
(*c*) Functioning of the economy depends mainly on administrative measures with little impetus from economic interests.

In foreign policy, it has maintained its own independent path, totally separate and often conflicting with the Soviet Union.

By 1976, there were 100 companies who had established trade relations with China, rising to 174 in 1980 and to 182 in 1981. 88 countries and regions concluded trade agreements or protocols with China in 1980. By the end of 1980, China had signed foreign credit agreements totalling $20 billion, and more than 360 joint venture projects were set up with foreign funds amounting to $1.5 billion. China's export trade in 1980 was composed of primary products for 54 per cent of the total (foodstuffs, farm and mineral raw materials 27 per cent, petroleum 24 per cent) and manufactured goods for 46 per cent of which textiles, light industrial products and handicrafts represented 34 per cent and heavy and chemical industrial goods only 12 per cent of which machinery accounted for 3.7 per cent. Much has to be done in the range, quality and design of these products, whilst in energy, China is beginning to experience shortages although petroleum exported was only 12 per cent of output and coal exported only 1 per cent of output, it does mean that there is little scope here for export expansion as things exist. Longer term, China's economic development will depend on export earnings from coal, steel, oil and petroleum-related commodities, but in the short term will have to focus on tourism and consumer goods. Meanwhile, transportation remains a problem and harbour facilities are not sufficiently developed to serve an expansion of foreign trade.

China is expected to become the 46th member of the Asian Development Bank, although the bank will retain the membership also of Taiwan. Presently China and Taiwan do not sit together on any intergovernmental bodies as both claim sovereignty over Taiwan. A compromise has therefore to be reached, but the indications from negotiations that have taken place are that this is likely to be achieved. Membership is likely to be effective as from 1986, and for China to be the third largest shareholder contributing more than India's subscription of $1.1 billion, but less than Japan and the United States which have equal shares of $2.36 billion.

Joint ventures

China wishes to attract both equity and contractual forms of joint venture. In 1979 the government established the Foreign Investment Control Commission to scrutinise and approve all joint-venture agreements. The law on joint ventures requires foreign investors to abide by Chinese laws and decrees; secondly, it protects the rights and interests of foreign investors; and thirdly, it stresses the need to accelerate the pace of China's 'Four Modernisations', which include the comprehensive modernisation of agriculture, national defence, and science and technology. Enterprises which are export orientated receive a special priority. The foreign investor is expected to provide the advance machinery and equipment while China contributes the necessary land and workforce. This means that ventures which are labour intensive are best suited to these conditions.

Arising from this law, the China International Trust and Investment Corporation was established. Known as CITIC, it operates under the control of the Chinese State Council, and on behalf of various ministries, provincial and local administrations.

Clothing, electronics, food and hotel projects are particularly suitable areas for joint venture. China's first three joint ventures were all in the tourism industry: one providing the catering service on all international flights out of Beijing, and the other two being hotel projects. All three involved a Chinese majority holding of 51 per cent, and Hong Kong companies. China has since received many more proposals but is trying also to steer the direction of these investments to special industrial zones such as that of Shenzhen, Zhuhai and Shantou in Guangdong Province and Xiamen in Fujian. Of these special zones, the most important is Shenzen, located near the Hong Kong border. Substantial sums have been invested to attract foreign partners to these areas such as by improving the availability of electricity, adequacy of ports, rail and road services.

Enterprises pay tax on a scale from 6 per cent to 34.5 per cent maximum. In September 1980 special legislation was passed to tax individuals and joint ventures. Repatriation bears a 10 per cent tax but ventures planned to operate over ten years or those in special industries receive preferential treatment, as do ventures which reinvest profits or which introduce high technology into China.

References

1. Fong, Nellie and Koontz, David, 'Joint Ventures with China', Arthur Andersen's Chronicle, 40(1), 1981, pp. 13–18.
2. Fureng, Dong, 'Some problems concerning China's strategy in foreign economic relations', International Social; *Science Journal*, (97), 1983, pp. 455–66.
3. Griffin, Keith and Kimberley, 'Institutional Change and Income Distribution in the Chinese Countryside', *Oxford Bulletin of Economics and Statistics*, vol. 45, August 1983, no. 3, pp. 223–48.
4. Harding, Harry, 'The Transformation of China', *Brookings Review*, Spring 1984, pp. 3–7.
5. Reeder, John A., 'Entrepreneurship in the People's Republic of China', *Columbia Journal of World Business*, Fall 1984, pp. 43–51.
6. Dennis, Robert D., 'The Countertrade Factor in China's Modernisation Plan', *Columbia Journal of World Business*, Spring 1982, pp. 67–75.

17. TRADE, AID AND DEVELOPMENT

The meaning of development aid and exporters' use of world aid agencies

In November 1974 at the World Food Conference in Rome, Henry Kissinger was heard to say,

within a decade no child will go to bed hungry, no family will fear for its next day's bread and no human being's future capacity will be thwarted by malnutrition.

More than a decade has passed and still 500 million are to be found hungry, with 40,000 children dying every year.

Trade whereby a nation pays for its imports by means of its exports does not really take place according to the normal rules as far as the developing countries are concerned. The less developed countries range from the newly industrialising, but still agricultural, to the raw-material supplying (and usually single commodity dependent), to those without tangible exports but with great import needs. The total financing needs of the less developed countries was estimated by the United Nations Committee on Trade and Development (UNCTAD) to be of the order of 11 billion dollars per annum throughout the 1980s, rising to 21 billion dollars per annum for the 1990s, but still at 1980 prices. Apart from the size of the capital injection required, the other problem which these countries face is that they lack qualified people in sufficient numbers to allocate and direct inward capital flows. This is the 'absorptive capacity' which is sometimes referred to, which is necessary for development and usually found to be lacking (Reference 1).

The discussion and debate which has taken place on the question of development aid from the richer countries of the Northern hemisphere to the poorer countries of the Southern hemisphere, has led to this question being referred to as the 'North-South debate'. However, the continued discussion over this question has also produced many reports such as the Brandt Commission Report which (Reference 2) we shall discuss later. Although piecemeal, an evolution has been taking place with regard to thinking on development aid. In the past, development aid was administered by the former colonial powers to their newly independent states more in the form of enlightened charity. The colonial master usually continued also to claim credit for the infrastructure that was left behind as the state became independent. Colonial charity or self-interested subsidy behind exports continues as an issue. So called 'mixed credits' which contain an aid element in the package, can in the longer term work out more expensive than international tendering. The mixing of aid with commercial export lending is an issue which has troubled the OECD for many years.

According to the rules which are not strictly observed, the aid element cannot be less than 20 per cent. If under 25 per cent other countries must be notified promptly to the OECD. The US has referred to this as predatory financing.

Table 17.1

OECD Development Assistance Committee Members' Aid Contributions

	As percentage of GNP			£m
	1981	*1982*	*1983*	*1983*
Australia	0.41	0.57	0.49	496
Austria	0.33	0.35	0.23	103
Belgium	0.59	0.59	0.59	314
Canada	0.43	0.41	0.45	942
Denmark	0.73	0.76	0.72	260
Finland	0.28	0.30	0.33	101
France	0.73	0.75	0.76	2581
Germany	0.47	0.48	0.49	2097
Italy	0.19	0.24	0.24	544
Japan	0.28	0.29	0.33	2479
Netherlands	1.08	1.08	0.91	788
New Zealand	0.29	0.28	0.29	40
Norway	0.82	0.99	1.06	385
Sweden	0.83	1.02	0.88	514
Switzerland	0.24	0.25	0.31	210
UK	0.43	0.37	0.35	1058
US	0.20	0.27	0.24	5241
DAC Total	0.35	0.38	0.36	18,153

Source British Overseas Aid 1983, ODA.

Table 17.2

Reasons for suspecting a consistent trade against the LDCs

1. The high cost of capital due to market imperfections and direct transfer costs.
2. The consistent underestimation of returns.
3. A growth threatened by the political situation.
4. The discount rate includes a higher rate factor for LDCs.
5. The longer gestation period for LDCs due to lower levels of motivation, skills, governmental efficiency and infrastructure.
6. A typical firm would cut off any projections within a LDC at five years.

In the past, to aid the newly independent state, financial help would have been offered but these 'soft' credits offered at preferential rates of interest were 'tied' in that they were available only for the purchase of certain items. In a shrinking world trade situation, rivalry amongst the leading industrialised nations has helped to curb this particular practice although other malpractices continue unabated, as we have seen. In addition, there has also been the development of external sources of financing, e.g. World Bank, and Eurodollar market. The Eurodollar market based in London created the opportunity for the less developed countries to borrow for any particular purpose that they considered to be necessary. Development has also progressed through the active agencies of the United Nations, e.g. UNCTAD and the International Labour Organisation ILO which has been responsible for establishing management development centres and pro-grammes in many parts of the developing world. However, to help shape perspective on this problem, it is worth remembering that world military expenditure greatly exceeds spending on development aid. The two new great colonial powers, the USA and USSR, account for half of annual global military expenditure of approximately 450 billion dollars, while annual spending on official development aid is only 20 billion dollars. To take another perspective on this, the World Health Organisation estimate that it would cost about 450 million dollars to eradicate malaria forever as a disease in the same way as they have done successfully with smallpox, which now no longer exists. Regrettably, the WHO is short of funds and is unable therefore to undertake this programme, which requires funding of the level of only one-thousandth of world annual military spending.

Aid may be channelled on a bi-lateral basis between the respective governments or through official world aid agencies such as the World Health Organisation, World Bank, etc. The World Bank will spend 80 billion dollars on aid between 1983–86. However, awareness of British exporters to the potential offered by this was very low according to a 1983 survey of 1,000 British exporters which revealed that 85 per cent were virtually ignorant of the world aid agencies as a source of overseas contracts. The provision of low technology for poorer countries earned British exporters 166 million dollars in 1982. A spokesman for the UK Department of Trade World Aid Sector, Mr Peter Morris, stated:

We are doing well in some areas and not so well in others, but for every pound Britain invests in the World Bank, we are winning work valued at £1.60.

As development advances though, there would be fewer contracts available for infrastructure development, e.g. highways, etc. and more for higher technology and manufacturing production knowhow – a product life cycle in action.

Debt and the newly industrialising countries

Mexico, Brazil and Poland are all examples of newly industrialising countries. They are also the countries most frequently spoken about with regard to the international debt crisis. Each of these countries invested heavily, in the 1970s. In some instances there was over-investment; in others an impossibly short time horizon scheduled either for production resulting from imported technology or for the repayment of these loans on a medium-term basis rather than a long-term basis. Elsewhere, the money was channelled into consumer imports and illegal capital flight which could do nothing to support the domestic economy. The crash of these, the largest of the newly industrialising countries, makes the more moderate industrialisation policies adopted by such countries as Malaysia or Thailand appear more prudent, but there still remains a massive bunching of debt maturities in the mid 1980s.

The appearance of these newly industrialised countries on the world product market has been evident for many years. Their industrialisation

Table 17.3

The newly industrialised countries: comparative estimates of total external debts

US$ billion	Best estimate from data sources	Current 'Market estimate'	Difference in US$ bn	in %
Algeria	14.78	15.4	−0.62	−4.0
Argentina	29.20	43.6	−14.40	−33.0
Brazil	85.45	93.0	−7.55	−8.1
Cameroon	2.30	2.5	−0.20	−8.0
Chile	17.26	17.9	−0.64	−3.6
Colombia	10.28	11.8	−1.52	−12.9
Costa Rica	2.99	4.1	−1.11	−27.1
Ecuador	5.99	6.8	−0.81	−11.9
Indonesia	23.83	25.0	−1.17	−4.7
Ivory Coast	5.25	7.0	−1.75	−25.0
Korea	31.86	40.1	−8.24	−20.5
Malaysia	12.43	12.0	+0.43	+3.6
Mexico	89.91	89.0	+0.91	+1.0
Morocco	9.86	13.0	−3.14	24.2
Nigeria	9.64	12.0	−2.36	−19.7
Peru	9.36	11.8	−2.44	−20.7
Philippines	23.49	24.6	−1.11	−4.5
Sudan	5.58	8.0	−2.42	−30.3
Thailand	9.29	11.0	−1.71	−15.5
Tunisia	3.95	4.5	−0.55	−12.2
Turkey	18.45	17.0	+1.45	+8.5
Uruguay	2.33	4.2	−1.87	−44.5
Venezuela	27.07	34.0	−6.93	−20.4
Yugoslavia	18.35	20.5	−2.15	−10.5
Totals	468.68	528.8	−62.69 +2.79	−15.1

Source: 'International Debt: Banks and the LDCs', *American Express Bank Review*, no. 10, March 1984.

policy, eagerness for exports, and generally low factor costs have enticed many multinationals to set up subsidiaries or engage in joint ventures and fully exploit the free ports where they exist. Sports goods, watches and electronic goods including domestic electrical equipment and home computers, are now all to be seen emanating from these centres. Average growth rates for these newly industrialised countries has been consistently higher than world averages at around 5 per cent. By this means, it is envisaged that Brazil's economy will equal that of West Germany by the year 2000.

Classification of developing countries

First, there are those countries which are high-volume, low-value raw material exporters but have an infrastructural base. Many of the countries in this group have sizeable populations and hence domestic markets; geographic size; agricultural bases, industrial nucleus; relatively sophisticated transportation and communications infrastructures; relatively large numbers of skilled labourers and competent technocratic and managerial elites. These countries have a fairly good chance of imposing self-restraint on growth after the oil or phosphates run out. Algeria, Iraq, Iran (all oil-producing) and Morocco (phosphates) are in this category.

Secondly, there are the high-volume, low-value raw material exporting countries with little infrastructure. These countries are characterised by small populations, small internal markets, little agriculture, and lack of industrial bases. They have little infrastructure where needed, no skilled workforce, only a smattering of technocrats and managers but possess the capital to attract the people they need from other countries. Libya, Kuwait, Qatar, UAR and Oman are examples of this group.

Thirdly, there are the low-volume, low-value traditional exporters with infrastructural bases. These countries are reasonably well endowed with roads, railways, ports, skilled labour, educational centres, and relatively extensive domestic markets. They do not have the creditworthiness of the earlier two groups or the duality to influence their growth. Here, the examples offered may include India and Egypt, both endowed with a university system and service and management elite superior to many of its neighbours. In the Middle East, many of the oil states have chosen to invest in universities when 10 years ago there was no proper schooling. Countries such as Egypt and India have long had this established infrastructure. Their economies remain poor though because of over-population and lack of arable land and their agricultural output and export earnings are therefore low in relation to import demands. Egypt benefits from its OPEC neighbours whilst India, although still enjoying good links with Britain, exhibits the characteristics of an independent country which seeks to remain non-aligned to any particular economic bloc.

The main point about this latter cluster of countries is that in the transfer of technology it is easier and much less costly to transfer know-how that is firm-specific rather than industry-specific. A certain level of knowledge may be assumed beyond which training is required. Transferring technology to countries other than these would require perhaps a greater grounding in the basic fundamentals of the technology before the specifics of the actual technology were due to be transferred.

Egyptian and Sudanese cotton, Tunisian olive oil, Turkish labour do not earn as much foreign exchange as oil and gas. Egypt uses approximately 40 per cent of its export earnings to service its public external debt. Egypt, Sudan, Syria, Tunisia and Turkey are countries which belong to this group.

UN Price Stabilisation Agreements to aid single-commodity exporters

There are still many countries today whose economy is dependent on a single commodity or crop. These include Nigeria (90 per cent oil), Zambia (94 per cent copper), Mauritius (90 per cent sugar), Cuba (84 per cent sugar) and The Gambia (85 per cent ground nuts and ground-nut oil). For these countries, sudden movement in the trading price of their particular commodity or harvest conditions can bring success or ruin. To mitigate this, UNCTAD has been instrumental in recent years in arranging price stabilisation agreements for sugar, tea, coffee, cocoa and rubber, while OPEC has sought to maintain control over the price and volume production of crude oil.

Meanwhile, certain of these supplier countries have been actively developing their infrastructure so as to diversify their economy more in future years. Saudi Arabia has moved into steel and is to use the gas presently flared from its oil wells for production in its own plants. Oil remains the leading commodity in world trade, accounting for one-eighth of it. There are great disparities, however, in its worldwide consumption. While this creates more business for the oil states and more revenue, their problem is in finding a way out of dependency on oil. Without an infrastructure of any kind, many of these states such as Oman, hire expatriates to work for them as consultants, advisors, university lecturers, language specialists, doctors, nurses, etc.

In the least developed nations the populations are rural and illiterate, and these countries have little exporting. Examples are South Yemen which is dependent upon the port of Aden, and Somalia which is dependent upon the export of animals. Others have no exports. Oil was discovered in the eastern part of North Yemen in 1984, close to the Saudi and South Yemen border. There has also been an oil strike in South Yemen but it appears likely that it is the same oil-bearing structure. It will now take about four years before this find bears any fruit.

There are many countries in this category with severe long-term constraints on development, and they have been identified by means of three criteria:

1. Per capita GDP of a hundred dollars or less at 1970 prices.
2. Share of manufacturing of 10 per cent or less of GDP.
3. 20 per cent or less of the population are literate.

A 1977 estimate put their combined population at 258 million or 13 per cent of the population of all developing countries. Average income per head in 1977 was 150 dollars or 80 dollars in 1970 prices, and their growth rate of income per head over the last two decades has been less than one per cent. If we choose to take a higher threshold of 250 dollars per capita income, then the combined population we have to consider amounts to 1,215 million in 1976 with more than half in absolute poverty. The United Nations has singled out 23 of these least developed countries for special attention. They are located in two main areas. The first extends across the middle of Africa from the Sahara in the north to Lake Nyasa in the south. The other begins with the two Yemens and Afghanistan, stretching eastwards across South Asia and some East Asian countries. These belts extend also into other areas, e.g. in Africa it extends into Kenya; in Asia, it extends into Burma, Cambodia, Vietnam and parts of India. The question then arises whether parts of countries which have the same characteristics and handicaps as the least developed countries should not be treated on a par with them, e.g. India.

The Food and Agriculture Organisation (FAO) published a report in 1974 which tried to work out how many could be fed by the soils of the Third World. Beginning with maps of soils and climates, it then superimposed to create cells with distinctive combinations of soil, slope, rainfall, etc. Each cell was then checked by a computer against 15 major food crops to select the crop that would produce the highest yield of calories. From there it was a simple step to calculate the potential caloric output, work out how many this would feed, and compare the results with actual populations. As the level of farming has a great impact on yields, the sums were done for a low level of inputs roughly equivalent to subsistence farming. On these projections the Third World would be able to feed just over one and a half times their expected population of 3,600 million in the year 2000. All major regions would be capable of self-sufficiency in food. However, assumptions included felling two-thirds of the world's tropical forests, cultivating all available land, and not feeding any grain to livestock. By making adjustments for other land use and land coming into cultivation, by the year 2025 only Asia should be self-supporting.

In 1975 there were already 54 countries that could not feed their existing populations from their entire land base using low inputs. The number will rise to 64 by the end of the century. Twenty-nine of the 57 such countries in Africa, with two-thirds of the continent's population, would be critical in the year 2000.

Recommendations for change

Brandt report

The Brandt report was an independent investigation into the urgent problems of inequality in the world and the failure of its economic systems, by a group of international statesmen and leaders from many spheres. *'North-South: A programme for survival'* (Reference 2) emphasises the belief that major international initiatives are needed if mankind is to survive. The tone, however, is not negative nor filled with projections of doom because although recognising present problems, it also pinpoints areas of mutual interest between North and South, and how in future years imaginative responses will be required to avert an imminent global economic crisis. The 'dialogue of the deaf' between the rich countries of the North and the poor countries of the South must end. Instead of a dialogue of Southern 'demands' and Northern 'concessions', there must be a symbolic relationship based upon mutual benefits.

The report makes a number of recommendations, such as seeking an action programme comprising emergency and longer-term measures to assist the poverty belts of Africa and Asia and particularly the least developed countries. Measures would include large regional projects of water and soil management; the provision of health care and the eradication of such diseases as river blindness, malaria, sleeping sickness and bilharzia: afforestation projects; solar energy development; mineral and petroleum exploration; and support for industrialisation, transport and other infrastructural investment. Such a programme would require additional financial assistance of at least 4 billion dollars per year for the next two decades, of grant or special concessional terms, assured over long periods and available in flexibly usable forms.

Other recommendations include:

1. Creation of an International Grains Agreement, larger international emergency reserves, and the establishment of a food-financing facility which would help assure food security internationally.

2. New trading rules recognising that the GSP Generalised System of Preferences (GSP) negotiated in UNCTAD in 1968 for the developing countries is in need of revision. It also recommends that GATT and UNCTAD should merge into one body.

3. A new international framework to allow developing countries and multinational corporations to benefit from direct investment.

4. Legislation to regularise the activities of multinational co-operators with regard to ethical behaviour, business practices, cartels, etc. An international code would be a useful step in that direction.

5. Co-operation by governments in their tax policies to monitor transfer pricing and to eliminate the resort to tax lowness.

6. Harmonisation of fiscal and other measures and policies towards foreign investment among host governments.

7. International discussion and consultation on measures affecting direct investment and the education of multinational corporations.

8. Greater information flow both between and within nations improving the speed, relevance, and current standing of existing systems.

9. Greater support for technical assistance and transmission of technology. More support to be given to provide the local basis for research and evaluation of needs.

10. Research into more efficient production, development, and marketing to defend and improve the market competitiveness of those raw materials mainly produced in developing countries.

11. A study of the implications of technological breakthroughs in the

North which may lead to automation, and deprive the South of its comparative advantage in low wage costs.

12. Research and development aid studies. Only 1 per cent of research and development in the North is concerned with the problems of the South; whereas 57 per cent is devoted to defence, atomic and space research.

13. Aid agencies should use more local skilled people to avoid perpetrating dependency on individual countries.

14. Freedom to choose within a 'tied' aid package.

15. Greater international co-ordination of research affecting the south.

16. A substantial increase in the transfer of resources to developing countries so as to finance:

(*a*) projects and programmes to alleviate poverty;
(*b*) exploration and development of energy and mineral resources; and
(*c*) stabilisation of the prices and earnings of commodity exports

17. Enlarging official development finance by:

(*a*) a sliding scale of contributions related to national income;
(*b*) an increase of official development assistance to 0.7 per cent of GNP by 1985, and to 1 per cent by end of the century;
(*c*) levies on international deals on arms production; and international levies on the global commons, especially sea-bed minerals.

18. Improved lending facilities through:

(*a*) Increased monetary capability of the World Bank.
(*b*) Doubling the borrowing to capital ratio of the World Bank from its present gearing of 1:1 to 2:1, and similar action by Regional Development Banks.
(*c*) Abstaining from the incorporation of political conditions and the operations of unilateral institutions.
(*d*) Channelling an increased share of development finance through regional institutions.
(*e*) A substantial increase in programme lending.
(*f*) The use of IMF gold reserved either for further sales – whose profits would subsidise interest on development lending – or as collateral to borrow for on-lending to developing countries.
(*g*) Giving borrowing countries a greater role in decision making and management.

19. A new approach to development finance:

(*a*) Funds for development must be recognised as a responsibility of the whole world community, and placed on a predictable and long-term basis. All countries – West and East and South, excepting the poorer countries – should contribute. Their contributions should be on a sliding scale relating to national income.
(*b*) More funds to be raised from levies related to international trade, military expenditures or arms exports.

(c) World Bank and Regional Development Banks should take new steps to increase their lendings.

(d) Borrowing for on-lending to developing countries should take place against the collateral of the retained portion of the gold reserves of the IMF.

(e) The serious gaps found in the present range of financing, particularly the lack or programmed lending, must be filled.

(f) Major additional multilateral finance is required to support mineral and energy exploration and development in developing countries.

(g) The commercial banking system should continue to lend to the developing world and on an adequate scale. The World Bank and other financial institutions should provide guarantees and play their part in ensuring a continued flow of commercial funds.

20. Finally, an Emergency Programme 1980–85 whose principal elements would include:

(a) a large scale transfer of resources to developing countries;
(b) an international energy strategy;
(c) a global food programme; and
(d) a start on some major reforms in the international economic system.

The UNCTAD code on Transfer of Technology

Originating as one of the aims of the New International Economic Order which was inaugurated by the General Assembly at its sixth special session in May 1974, this code has still to be ratified by all parties, as of 1984.

Taking as its base the fact that transfers of technology between developed and developing countries account for 10 per cent of transfers, but that technology is in effect a wasting asset, this was a bold attempt by three main groups to codify the position with regard to technology transfer.

The parties to the negotiations included *Group B*, a fairly homogeneous group consisting of the United States, Canada and the EEC as well as the rest of the OECD countries. This group presented on the whole a common front, the only real difference being in the degree of liberalism they wished to show towards the developing countries. *Group D* composed effectively the Soviet bloc countries. This was the smallest group with less technical expertise at its disposal but at the same time an open mind on a number of the controversial issues. They tended to back the 'Seventy-Seven' but at times were very conscious of their own interests either as the recipients or the suppliers of technology. Finally, the *Group of Seventy-Seven* which had the greatest numerical representation, some 60 consisting of three sub-groups: the Latin American countries; the Asian countries; and the African countries. Each sub-group was at pains to ensure that its specific views were given due weight and so the work of harmonising a Seventy-seven position was an arduous and time-consuming operation. They were short not only of experts in the field of technology, but also of trained negotiators. Very often the countries concerned were not able to send delegates from capitals, and had to rely on delegates from their missions in

Geneva. Either this was a diplomat with little knowledge of the subject, or the country's representative to GATT which practised a very different method of negotiation. The Chinese who were not formal members of any of the three groups chose to ally themselves with the Seventy-seven.

The principal issue was the question of the cost of technology embodied in licensing. Transfer terms were considered by recipients to be unduly severe and the restrictions placed on the use of this technology were seen to serve to perpetuate the technological dependence of developing countries on the industrial world and prevent the growth of indigenous industry.

What prevented the Code from being ratified in 1981 was the insistence of the Seventy-seven that it should be of a legal binding nature. It was clear, too, that there was to be no coercion of suppliers in order to compel them to enter into transfer of technology against their will. Nevertheless, guidelines have certain advantages in that they can be applied immediately on a universal basis without waiting for domestic legislation, and irrespective of whatever national court has jurisdiction. The preamble was subscribed to by all the participating countries and recognised that science and technology plays a fundamental role in the socio-economic development of all countries, particularly in accelerating the development of developing countries. Secondly, it was declared that technology is the 'key to the progress of mankind' and that all peoples have the right to benefit from its advances. It further urged developed countries to work with developing countries 'as a decisive step in the progress towards the establishment of a new international economic order'. It stressed the equal opportunity to be given to all countries to participate, irrespective of their social and economic system and emphasised the need for the special treatment to the developing countries, and the need to improve the flow of information so that countries could select the technology that was more appropriate to their needs.

Group B wished to establish that applicable international law be observed in the case of co-operation following nationalisation. Another matter of concern was that all developing countries should accede to the provisions of the Paris Convention for the protection of property and abide by them. This was not made explicit in the final form presented only as being 'consistent with their international objectives' which left much ambiguity.

As to restrictive practices, 20 were identified of which 14 were the subject of substantial agreement with six being proposed only by Group D and the Seventy-Seven. These dealt with limitations on volume or scope of production; the use of quality controls; the obligation to use trade marks; the requirement to provide equity capital or participation in management; unduly long duration of arrangements; and limitations on the use of technology already imported.

The second general issue outstanding concerns the multinational corporations in cases where the international transfer of technology takes place between the parent and its subsidiary or between two companies in common ownership. In such circumstances the members of the group forming the transactional corporation may already be subject to internal restraints, which may be considerable. A balance must therefore be found between the legitimate interest of the group as a whole and the effective transfer of technology.

The only provision not yet settled is one calling for preferential measures so that industrial property rights granted to a patent holder in supplying countries should not be used by the holder to restrict imports of products from developing countries. The participating governments recognise the need for appropriate international collaboration whether between governments, intergovernmental bodies, members of the UN system, or the institutional machinery of the present code, in order to strengthen the technological capacity of all countries.

There are two aspects which concern the law to be applied to the transfer of technology. The first relates to the substantive requirements either of the supplying country or the recipient country. This law will be applicable by virtue of the territorial jurisdiction of the country concerned over acts or omissions which are required by its general law, irrespective of the bargain existing between the parties. On the one hand, this will consist of the legislation dealing with the supplying of technology, the physical condition of the products supplied, requirements as to credit, restrictions on strategic materials, etc. On the other hand, there will be the legislation of the required country which will apply to the technology delivered. The latter will be the more likely incidence of national legislation and may refer to any of the matters permissible.

The Seventy-Seven observe that the courts of the acquiring country should have jurisdiction over disputes arising out of the contract concerning public policy or sovereignty. The difference between the Seventy-Seven and the other two groups is substantial and to date has not been bridged.

As to the future of negotiations, some Africans believe that it is better to have no code at all than to have a bad code. There is the question of US participation in the code should it find the final proposals unacceptable. In the final analysis, without the participation of the technology suppliers in Group B there is no hope of any kind of co-operation arrangement.

References

1. Behrmann, Jack N., *Industrial Policies: International Restructuring and Trans-nationals*, Lexington Books, 1984.
2. *North:South: A Programme for Survival*, The Report of the Independent Commission on International Development Issues under the Chairmanship of Willy Brandt, Pan Books, 1980.

18. THE UK IN WORLD TRADE

The difficulty of trying to describe an elephant depends upon where you are standing. Your perspective may be accurate as to its hind quarters but blind to its trunk. An all-round view is required but this is very difficult to achieve. Similarly, when coming to discuss the workings of the UK economy in world trade, there is this similar abundance of perspectives and lack of cohesion amongst the analyses of the day. Rather than subject the reader to one view, presented below are some of the more important findings of recent times upon the workings of the UK economy in world trade. The first thing to note then is that there are seeming contradictions throughout.

UK export performance

The first is the contradiction that since 1982 the UK has recorded a deficit on trade in manufactures and that this trend has both continued and increased since. While labour costs in the UK are broadly similar with West European levels, productivity is much lower. UK price competitiveness was thought to be 20 per cent less in 1982 than in 1975. According to CBI estimates – and with West Germany, our industrial model, experiencing inflation of approximately 8 per cent – it would require 10 years of zero inflation to claw back a 30 per cent gap in competitiveness.

An OECD comparison published in *The Observer* on 31 March 1982 used Gross Domestic Product (GDP) per head for 1980 expressed in dollars of constant purchasing power, as reproduced in Table 18.1. However, this reveals the UK to have not only a low average growth rate but also an inflation rate higher than all her Western industrialised trading partners with the exception of Italy.

Yet another survey of British industrial exports by Freight Information Services (Reference 1) over the three years 1979–81 shows the EEC share of Britain's total machinery exports to have fallen from 33 to 29 per cent (see Table 18.2). The list of markets selected included the key markets which account for over three-quarters of all British exports. The survey shows that the only market where there has been an increase in export volume is in the Middle East and North Africa. At the same time, it has to be acknowledged that the Civil Service strike of 1981 resulted in a six-month gap of accurate statistics. Yet the evidence which exists seems to point to the diversity of a high export volume in the face of a recession in the industrialised countries. British machinery exporters would appear then to be far from thinking of the EEC as their home markets.

Table 18.1
Growth of inflation: a comparison between European countries

	GDP per head (1980 US dollars)	Average annual growth rate % (1975–80)	Average annual inflation rate % (1976–81)
1. US	11,364	3.9	9.8
2. Luxemburg	9,822	2.4	5.7
3. Germany	9,428	3.6	4.4
4. Denmark	9,087	4.6	11.0
5. France	9,040	3.3	11.2
6. Belgium	8,724	2.9	6.1
7. Netherlands	8,614	2.6	5.6
8. Japan	8,467	5.1	5.7
9. Austria	8,372	3.5	5.2
10. UK	7,629	1.6	13.4
11. Italy	7,202	3.9	17.2
12. Spain	5,840	2.2	18.0
13. Ireland	5,066	4.0	14.5
14. Greece	4,683	4.4	18.5
15. Portugal	3,684	5.2	22.0

Source OECD Observer, March 1982.

The questions, Who are the British exporters? How many? What size? Which industry? are answered in a study by the Department of Trade, ironically, reported for the last time before they were discontinued completely as a statistical exercise. In 1981 then we are told that for the first time since 1976, the exports of larger companies grew at faster rates than total exports and the number of enterprises accounting for half of UK exports (excluding diamonds) fell to 72. This reduction was partly due to an increase in the importance of oil exports which rose by 50 per cent, and increased the proportion of UK exports accounted for by oil companies to 18 per cent. Two-thirds of UK exports (excluding oil and diamonds) were conducted by 415 enterprises. Around four-fifths of UK exports (excluding diamonds) are by enterprises with related concerns overseas and in 1981 these related concerns purchased 30 per cent of UK exports (Reference 2).

The EEC now accounts for the bulk of UK trade but relatively few British exporters are able to speak a foreign language and so are at a natural disadvantage. Britain's share of world trade is also down, falling by a fifth between the years 1975–80. Sales of machinery, vehicles and other manufactures declined sharply. Exports to the EEC have fallen and there has been a sudden decline also in trade with the US. The Soviet Union, Eastern Europe and the rest of Europe outside the EEC all reflected a static position. Non-achieving UK industries included motor vehicles, textiles, telecommunications and audio equipment. Responsible for a

Table 18.2
Key exports and markets

	Total trade (m. tonnes)	Percentage share of selected markets			
		EEC	Rest of W. Europe	Middle East, N. Africa	N. America
Machinery					
1979	2.437	33	12	15	13
1980	2.523	31	12	15	11
1981*	2.327	29	11	19	12
Road Vehicles					
1979	1.509	45	14	7	8
1980	1.359	43	14	9	7
1981*	1.211	39	14	14	7
Chemicals					
1979	7.117	55	13	5	5
1980	6.877	53	14	6	5
1981	7.090	55	14	6	4
Manufactured Materials					
1979	10.467	36	11	8.7	16
1980	8.261	41	12	8.8	9
1981*	8.515	40	11	9.2	11
Beverages					
1979	.777	27	8	6	31
1980	.709	27	8	5	30
1981*	.696	26	7	6	32

* Estimates
Source Freight Information Services.

slight trade surplus in 1978, they were responsible for more than two-thirds of a £6.8 billion deficit in 1983. Apart from petroleum, as we might expect, only three standard industrial categories – non-ferrous metals, organic chemicals and aerospace and other transport equipment – managed to improve their international competitiveness substantially in the same period. For manufacturing as a whole, the ratio of imports to exports worsened by 34 per cent over this period, which transformed a balance of £4 billion at 1983 prices to a £68 billion deficit. The manufacturing account has been deteriorating as fast as the oil account has been improving.

In addition, since the introduction of the 'floating' exchange rate for sterling in 1972 much damage has been done to the export trade by the signal failure to outline an exchange rate strategy for exports. North Sea oil has done much to reduce the oil deficit and make Britain self-sufficient in oil, but has also worked against the interests of exporters in making sterling stronger than it would otherwise have been. In this way, the benefit of oil did substitute for imports but also created a loss of cost competitiveness compounded also by a relatively high inflation rate and low productivity.

The *Sixth Annual Survey on International Competitiveness* (Reference

International Marketing

Table 18.3
Distribution of total UK exports by category of enterprise 1971 to 1981[1]
(including oil, excluding diamonds).

| | *Percentages of total exports, excluding diamonds, on an Overseas Trade Statistics basis* | | | | | | | | | | |
	1971	*1972*	*1973*	*1974*	*1975*	*1976*	*1977*	*1978*	*1979*	*1980*	*1981*
Accounted for by:											
United States-controlled UK enterprises	18	18	18	20	20	19	18	18	19	18	17
Other foreign-controlled UK enterprises	6	7	7	6	7	8	10	10	10	11	10
UK associates of foreign enterprises	5	5	5	4	4	4	4	4	4	4	4
UK enterprises with overseas affiliates	55	55	56	57	54	55	53	51	50	48	51
Other enterprises	16	15	14	13	15	14	15	17	17	19	18
Total	100	100	100	100	100	100	100	100	100	100	100

Note [1]Approximate estimate for all exports, excluding diamond exporters, including concerns not covered by Table 17.5.
Source British Business, 27 May 1983.

3), published in 1985 by the European Management Forum, had some harsh words for Britain. Britain had performed badly in 1984 and had a poor outlook for 1985. Its place in the survey had been dropping since 1981. Britain did not come out well in any category and very badly in others. The only bright spot was a high rating for financial dynamism. Elsewhere, natural endowments plus the will and ability to promote trade also earned Britain top ten placings. Britain scored low on taxation; dynamism of the economy; human resources; and the redeployment of resources from old to new technologies, and the training and promotion necessary for innovative research and development. Strong points were the expanding service sector and North Sea oil and gas, but the survey expressed grave doubts about whether these would be enough to offset very deep seated structural problems. Its forecast for Britain was that Britain's virtual specialisation in low-value products will put it more and more into competition with low-wage, but increasingly productive, Third World countries.

In any event, longer term projections are not good (Reference 4). It is envisaged that oil output in the North Sea will be 82 million tonnes in 1991 and 39 million by 1995. This will leave the UK again as an importer of oil. It is feared that the deficit on the machinery side could need £9.8 billion by 1988 which would eliminate any oil surplus. Additionally, there will be the major costs of the Trident sale from the US priced at £8.7 billion but costed at $1.53 to the pound sterling. This will need re-evaluation for both project cost and currency value fall.

The Connell Report

Between 1962 and 1975 the UK's share of the 11 main industrial countries' total exports of manufacturers declined by two-fifths. No other country came close to this rate of deterioration; the US was closest, losing its share about half as rapidly over this period. The first reason is slow productivity growth, combined with increases in factor costs, leading to cost and price disadvantages, and eventually to devaluation and further consequential inflationary pressures. Faster productivity growth is one condition of improved trade performance and faster growth. The second problem is the long-term fall of market share by value even when cost competitiveness is maintained – failure to compete in respect of failures of the product other than price. Improvements – product design, marketing, reliability, delivery, servicing, up-to-dateness, and reputation – are just as important a means of raising the value of saleable output per man employed as are increases in physical productivity.

Three factors (Reference 5) that have contributed to the deterioration of the UK export performance are:

1. Companies have treated exporting as a marginal activity rather than integrating it fully into their operations. A more serious and permanent commitment is required if they are to develop their overseas markets to the full.

2. Companies have devoted insufficient efforts to increasing competitiveness in non-price terms. Foreign firms seem to have paid rather more attention to other aspects of exporting. The resources devoted to design and the development of new products are probably of particular importance although after-sales service and other factors are also involved.

3. UK firms have spread their exporting effort too widely over different geographical markets. They need to concentrate more on key markets and try to match their competitors in the resources devoted to exploiting them.

Exports accounted for 29 per cent of GNP in 1976 compared with 26 per cent for West Germany; 20 per cent for Italy; 14 per cent for France; and only 8.5 per cent for the US. Goods represented 70 per cent of total UK exports in 1976.

The analysis reinforces the view that the deterioration in the UK's export performance is not the result of the broad product structure of its export trade, but is related rather to performance within industries. Average value-per-tonne comparisons, comparing the average value per weight of different countries' exports of a particular product group, have produced results showing substantially different values per tonne. This may indicate either the export of a different mix of products or across-the-board differences in non-price characteristics, or both. Most countries do not publish data on the whole range of products exported in both value and tonnage terms, but mechanical engineering is one exception.

West Germany was chosen as the country with which to compare UK exports, both because it is the world's largest exporter of manufactured

Table 18.4

Distribution of direct exports by category of enterprise and size of total exports 1981 (excluding oil and diamond companies)

Values in £m

Size of total exports	United States-controlled UK enterprises		Other foreign-controlled UK enterprises		UK associates of foreign enterprises		UK enterprises with overseas affiliates		UK enterprises with no overseas affiliates		Total	
	Total exports	Of which related exports	Total exports	Of which related exports	Total exports	Of which related exports	Total exports	Of which related exports	Total exports	Of which related exports	Total exports	Of which related exports
Over £50m	3,151.2	2,110.0	2,161.6	896.5	1,087.8	213.2	13,127.6	3,803.4	493.8		20,022.1	7,022.9
Number of enterprises	21		16		7		72		5		121	
Over £20m but not more than £50m	1,183.1	431.1	345.0	165.8	238.9	49.8	2,407.6	601.3	589.5		4,768.1	1,248.0
Number of enterprises	38		12		9		74		20		153	
Over £10m but not more than £20m	614.6	174.8	260.9	69.1	70.5	18.3	900.6	196.6	384.0		2,230.6	458.8
Number of enterprises	44		19		5		66		29		163	
Over £5m but not more than £10m	371.5	98.8	217.5	45.2	70.7	17.9	743.2	106.5	548.4		1,951.2	268.4
Number of enterprises	53		30		9		103		79		274	
Over £1m but not more than £5m	304.4	67.7	221.0	50.0	38.5	4.8	565.3	89.9	699.3		1,828.5	212.4
Number of enterprises	114		88		17		205		279		703	
Under £1m	18.9	2.4	53.3	6.6	2.3	0.1	43.2	9.0	83.8		201.5	18.2
Number of enterprises	50		168		9		82		197		506	
Total	5,643.7	2,884.9	3,263.2	1,233.1	1,508.7	304.0	17,787.5	4,806.7	2,798.8		31,001.9	9,228.7
Number of enterprises	320		333		56		602		609		1,920	

Source British Business, 27 May 1983, p. 367

Table 18.5

Distribution of direct exports by category of enterprise and by industry group, 1981 (excluding oil and diamond companies)

Values in £m

Industry group	United States-controlled UK enterprises		Other foreign-controlled UK enterprises		UK associates of foreign enterprises		UK enterprises with overseas affiliates		UK enterprises with no overseas affiliates	Total		
	Total exports	Of which related exports	Total exports	Of which related exports	Total exports	Of which related exports	Total exports	Of which related exports	Total exports	Total exports	Of which related exports	Number of enterprises
Food, drink and tobacco	241.0	102.5	361.0	70.7	8.2	—	1,673.3	459.2	220.1	2,503.6	632.4	116
Chemical and allied industries	1,056.7	410.5	368.0	201.7	212.2	290.0	2,541.5	1,223.3	82.1	4,260.5	1,864.6	159
Metal manufacture and engineering	2,417.2	1,282.5	1,386.6	628.7	749.4	125.4	5,981.5	1,285.6	510.4	11,045.1	3,322.2	510
Shipbuilding and vehicles (other than motor vehicles)	0.1	—	2.3	0.7	27.2	10.9	1,841.8	368.1	55.6	1,927.0	379.6	29
Motor vehicles	1,093.0	892.7	141.2	29.9	—	—	1,187.7	591.1	25.6	2,447.5	1,513.7	32
Other manufacturing industries	557.1	122.2	414.4	147.5	374.9	108.3	3,095.4	568.0	567.5	5,009.3	946.0	554
Other activities	278.6	74.4	589.7	153.9	136.7	30.4	1,466.4	311.5	1,337.4	3,808.8	570.3	520
All industries	5,643.7	2,884.9	3,263.2	1,233.1	1,508.7	304.0	17,787.5	4,806.7	2,798.8	31,001.9	9,228.7	1,920

Source: *British Business*, 27 May 1983, p. 367.

Table 18.6
The top 100 UK export markets in 1984

						(UK export value in £m)
1	USA	10,149.5		51	Mexico	150.1
2	West Germany	7,458.0		52	Thailand	149.7
3	France	7,082.4		53	Cyprus	146.8
4	Netherlands	6,128.0		54	Bahrain	138.6
5	Ireland, Republic of	3,393.5		55	Qatar	133.8
6	Belgium & Luxemburg	3,051.7		56	Brunei	122.7
7	Italy	2,902.7		57	Trinidad & Tobago	113.3
8	Sweden	2,888.6		58	Venezuela	102.4
9	Switzerland	1,549.5		59	Hungary	100.5
10	Saudi Arabia	1,387.2		60	Sudan	95.6
11	Spain	1,234.6		61	GDR	92.3
12	South Africa	1,205.1		62	Syria	91.9
13	Denmark	1,197.4		63	Philippines	91.8
14	Australia	1,186.5		64	Malta	89.5
15	Canada	1,183.2		65	Canary Islands	84.6
16	Norway	968.4		66	Ghana	82.9
17	Japan	925.3		67	Morocco	79.9
18	Hong Kong	897.4		68	Czechoslovakia	78.1
19	India	781.0		69	Lebanon	76.2
20	Nigeria	768.5		70	Chile	75.0
21	USSR	735.2		71	Panama	74.3
22	Iran	703.1		72	Puerto Rico	72.7
23	Finland	684.5		73	Romania	71.6
24	Singapore	556.4		74	Zimbabwe	68.6
25	Egypt, Arab Republic of	427.7		75	Zambia	66.7
26	Israel	393.0		76	Cuba	64.4
27	Oman	390.3		77	Iceland	64.2
28	Portugal	385.8		78	Ethiopia	63.4
29	New Zealand	367.5		79	Sri Lanka	61.2
30	Greece	354.3		80	Tanzania	60.4
31	Iraq	343.1		81	Yemen, North	58.8
32	Turkey	331.4		82	Bulgaria	55.9
33	Austria	320.9		83	Bangladesh	51.6
34	China	317.3		84	Jamaica	48.1
35	Kuwait	301.5		85	Tunisia	47.1
36	Dubai	298.9		86	Yemen, South	45.2
37	Malaysia (Malaya, Sabah			87	Colombia	43.5
	& Sarawak)	283.3		88	Zaire	36.3
38	Pakistan	282.5		89	Angola	35.6
39	Algeria	272.4		90	Ecuador	34.3
40	Libya	246.5		91	Peru	33.8
41	Brazil	238.7		92	Gibraltar	32.0
42	Bahamas	220.4		93	Liberia	31.0
43	Korea, Republic of	219.4		94	Barbados	30.7
44	Abu Dhabi	215.9		95	Uganda	29.3
45	Jordan	192.5		96	Sharjah, Ajman etc	27.0
46	Indonesia	186.7		97	Ivory Coast	25.3
47	Kenya	176.1		98	Mauritius	24.4
48	Poland	170.0		99	Bermuda (UK)	22.8
49	Yugoslavia	163.9		100	Antigua	22.7
50	Taiwan	150.6				

goods and because its similarities to the UK make it probably the most appropriate model of industrial success from which the UK might learn. An important question is whether the UK has lost share more quickly in fast-growing markets than in slower-growing ones. If this were the case, then it might suggest that a lack of flexibility has resulted in UK exporters missing new business opportunities. The evidence indicates that improvements in non-price competitiveness have played an important part in the West German approach to tackling this particular problem. It would be wrong to suggest that there are any correct industrial processes as every company faces a different situation. However, the West German lesson may now be a particularly appropriate one for the UK and thus for many of its industrial companies.

Barclays Bank report on export competitiveness in France, UK and West Germany

The Barclays Report (Reference 6) opens with the statement that probably the most important finding is the difference in the role of management, and particularly middle management in France and Germany in contrast to the UK. The more the study progressed, the more impressive appeared the all-important role played by middle management in Germany and France. Respondents repeatedly affirmed that it was the scope and encouragement given to middle management that translated concepts and possibilities into achievements during the past 25 years. It was middle management who actually organised the industrial machine and got the results.

This concept was stated repeatedly but also in a more negative form – that it would have been virtually impossible for French and German middle management to achieve what they have, had they been restrained by the fiscal, political, and industrial limitations imposed upon British managers. Thus in France and Germany it was still possible to recruit the most talented young men from high schools and universities, to entice the enterprising and imaginative people and fill them with enthusiasm.

The lack of continuity in the UK was due to the fundamental differences in the industrial philosophy of the two main political parties. The British 'stop-go' was claimed as another factor in the lack of continuity. Germany and France has suffered from it but not as widely. Many of the British companies had to change production programmes several times a year (in one example, 14 times within one year). They listed over 40 changes in the last 15 years alone in purchase taxes, hire-purchase regulations, VAT and related matters, compared with less than half that number in France and Germany.

In Germany, impressive industrial growth rates had been obtained and sustained, despite a very hard currency and an exceedingly high-cost economy. The economy proceeded with the minimum of intervention. A final general comment emerging from the report is the perception of Britain's potential: we were seen to be well placed to be one of the world's most successful exporters with identifiable advantages – geographical position, a stable political system, highly developed science and technology, a reputation for commercial fair dealing, and a sophisticated approach to retailing and merchandising.

How to avoid the 'British disease'

How to Avoid the British Disease was a report with recommendations by two UMIST researchers. Recognising the weakness to be in management, they called for a new approach that was manager-led and manager-inspired. A very high level of company profitability could be obtained while affording workers freedom, happiness, and human dignity. Their prime ingredients for industrial harmony were as follows:

1. Better leadership in a total sense. This enables people to identify clearly the problems facing both themselves and the company. This develops within people the ability to solve problems and to make genuine joint decisions. With this approach it is essential to understand people's needs, drives, aspirations and potentialities. In addition, the management must be seen to be acting in everyone's best interests, and towards the growth fulfilment of the individual, as well as the company.

2. To move from a vertical to a lateral communication structure, thus making the organisation flatter and more decentralised. This promotes the acceptance of responsibility and commitment at the lower levels of the company. Often it is only at these levels – the 'coal face' – that the problem is sufficiently understood to enable a working solution to be found.

3. The encouragement of 'temporary' representative project groups. These support the new management structure in solving specific problems by the use of the 'above average' ability of individuals in specialised activities.

4. To increase job satisfaction by effectively utilising both job enlargement and job enrichment programmes. The prime emphasis must be placed on the satisfaction which comes from human achievement.

5. To move quickly towards single status for all employees, thus making people aware that they are an integral and valued part of the whole enterprise. To achieve this, it is essential to pursue policies which discourage class distinction and antagonism.

6. To pursue policies which distribute rewards equitably. An essential element of this objective is the introduction of an integrated wage payment system. It is of crucial importance that this system reflects agreed differentials in job responsibility, skill and effort.

Queen's Award for Export winners: no prime example

A study (Reference 8) at Strathclyde University of Scottish Queen's Award winners in 1978 reported the conclusion in the title of a journal contribution *Scots Queen's Award Winners don't excel*. The study investigated 25 of 41 Scottish Queen's Award winners: three had had more than 10 years experience of exporting; twelve had more than 30 years' experience. Of the total 25, 19 had more than half their total sales accounted for by exports. Exporting therefore was not a marginal activity but over the whole sample, only a few had employed a market research specialist. 80 per cent said that the longer they were in exporting, the less need there was for research; 80 per cent that the nature of the market was important, but that companies already operating in oligopolies knew their companies, product, and market conditions. Eight of the 24 subscribed to an Export Intelligence Service.

The sample covered a wide spread of industrial activities but the findings indicated that these award-winners had an amateurish approach to research, with products only being adapted reluctantly; poor after-sales service; domination of cost-plus pricing; exports being more profitable than home sales; prices still being quoted in f.o.b. rather than c.i.f.; confusion over the role of the agent; insufficient attention to promotion; and a generally negative attitude overall to exports.

With regard to adaptation, companies which customised their products or offered modifications tended to regard their export sales as being at least as profitable as home sales. After-sales service was found to be 'appallingly bad'. The reason offered 'is apparently that companies are anxious to do the right thing but are unable to find a balance between the cost of after-sales service and profitability'.

As to strategy, the study found that the evidence pointed to firms basing their strategies mainly on negative attitudes. Export markets were treated as secondary to the domestic market and much delegation of responsibility was therefore passed to the export agent but with it too, control and often total interest. Relations between exporters and agents were found to be mishandled as was the gathering of market information and market research in general. There was little indication offered that any changes were likely either. As the author points out

It might have been expected that the marketing practices of the Scottish Queen's Award winners would be exemplary. That they were not gives rise to considerable worrying speculation about the attitudes, policies, and practices of non-winners.

Table 18.7
UK public expenditure on overseas aid

Bilateral and multinational aid								£ million
	Bilateral aid					Contributions to multinational agencies		
		Financial aid						
	Total gross expenditure	Gross total	Loans		Grants	Technical co-operation (grants)	Total	Financial aid	Technical co-operation
			Gross	Net					
1979	940	682	125	50	371	186	257	177	80
1980	967	703	106	−18	373	223	264	211	53
1981	1,152	805	144	45	444	216	347	297	50
1982	1,091	674	101	7	362	211	418	366	53
1983	1,033	660	84	6	344	232	373	320	53

Source Overseas Development Administration, 1984.

Table 18.8
Regional distribution of bilateral aid

£ million

	Total	Africa	America	Asia	Europe	Oceania	Unallocated
1979	682	230	42	293	8	28	80
1980	703	257	37	263	14	36	95
1981	805	267	49	317	37	33	101
1982	674	247	92	182	20	32	101
1983	660						

Source Overseas Development Administration, 1984.

UK contribution to aid and development

Total gross expenditure on overseas aid has fallen in actual as well as real terms. Approximately one-third of this aid is in the form of contributions to multilateral agencies. There are less loans, and fewer grants with more being channelled through the multilateral agencies. Of this declining total, South America has almost doubled its receipts of British aid whilst Asia has been cut back by almost half, with very slight movement amongst the others. It has also to be said that 63 per cent of gross British bilateral aid went to the 50 poorer developing countries in 1983. Overall, some 75 per cent of bilateral aid in 1983 was tied in some way to the purchase of British goods.

References

1. *Financial Times*, 'UK industrial export values continue decline in 1982', 4 May 1983.
2. *British Business*, 27 May 1983, 'Company analysis of direct exporters in 1981', pp. 366–67.
3. EMF, *Sixth Annual Report on International Competitiveness*, European Management Forum, Switzerland, 1985.
4. Andrew, Tessler, 'Invisibles buried future', *Management Today*, July 1984, pp. 74–8.
5. Connell, David, 'The UK's performance in export markets – some evidence from international trade data', NEDO, London 1979.
6. *Barclay's Bank Report on Export Development in France, Germany and the United Kingdom*, Barclay's Bank International, London, 1979.
7. Chatterton, Allen, and Leonard, Roy, *How to avoid the British Disease*, Northgate Publishing Co Ltd, London, 1979.
8. McFarlane, Gordon, 'Scots Queen's Award Winners don't excel', *Marketing*, April 1978, pp. 29–31.

Recommended further reading

John M. Stopford, Louis Turner, *Britain and the Multinationals*, Wiley, 1985.
John H. Dunning (ed.), *Multinational Enterprises, Economic Structure and International Competitiveness*, Wiley, 1985.

INDEX

Page numbers in *italics* indicate tables.